Abnormal Psychology

Human Behavioural Problems

Abnormal Psychology

Human Behavioural Problems

M. Rajamanickam

AUTHORSPRESS

Publishers of Creative & Scholarly Books

Worldwide Circulation through Authorspress Global Network
First Published in 2004
by
Authorspress
Q-2A Hauz Khas Enclave, New Delhi-110 016 (India)
Phone: (0) 9818049852
E-mail: authorspressgroup@gmail.com
Website: www.authorspressbooks.com

Abnormal Psychology: Human Behavioural Problems

ISBN 81-7273-166-3

Printed in India at Kensington Press

Preface

Human behaviour is studied from various angles and dimensions. It is because of the complicated nature of behaviour that the behavioural scientists have to look from different angles and different dimensions. Though the theory of holism is accepted in principle that the whole is greater than the sum of its parts, the information obtained in parts serve certain specific purpose in dealing with some problems, particularly in treating certain physical and mental illness or disorders. In this study of human behaviour, Psychologists of the present times are becoming very curious about the new inventions and discoveries made in various sciences like, anatamy, biology, physiology, neurology, zoology, biochemistry, endocrinology, geneties, immunology and medical sciences.

If we are really interested in getting reliable and panoramic understanding and communicatable information of the field psychology we must try to synthesis every new information available in these areas related to human behaviour and go above any one single discipline. A very recent doubt raised by the biological psychologists is, whether the capacity of the brain can be increased by experience of the person? Can any discipline experimentally determine whether the human sexual orientation is inherited or accidental or environmental? Therefore in order to gain some substantial information about human behaviour we must show interest in a variety of disciplines or backgrounds. A precise approach for this endeavour may be based upon the behavioural and bio-social foundations.

In the normal course, every system of the human body is functioning systematically. The behavioural functioning also is normal as it must be. But if any system of the human body is affected by some means, then the normal functioning of the behavioural system also is affected. Which of the systems is affected or damaged? It has to be explored by examining by various methods and techniques. In this attempt man makes use of his knowledge gained from various sources and applies to it to bring the affected system to the normal level. Of all the bodily systems, the brain and the nervous system are the most important and complex systems. The brain and the nervous system are subjected to a variety of impairments, malfunctions and breakdowns. Human beings, wherever they are, are subjected to the malfunctioning of the brain, which is generally stated as mental disorder or behaviour disorder. The current statistic is that atleast one person in five around the world is suffering from some type of neurological or psychotic disorders.

The nature of these disorders may vary in severity and intensity, from depression and withdrawal from society to complete incapacity and inability to do anything in life situation. In between these two levels of disorders there are different shades of psychotic disorders. Inspite of establishing quite number of hospitals and clinics for preventing and treating the disorders, the toll of these disorders is increasing enormously.

The aximatic term, "prevention is better than cure", is most often highlighted by certain organisations. But in the highly industrialized countries life has become very fast and hasty. However precautious measures were taken accidents occur enormously in all crowded cities and on highways. Brain injury is the common incidence which results in behaviour or mental disorders. The causes of the mental or psychotic disorders are many apart from the brain damage or injury.

Human beings are subjected for emotional disorders, which are caused due several reasons. Conflicts of ideas or opinions, frustration, quarrel in the family, constant failures in achieving the goal or in getting a job, constantly getting abused and ill treated by the master or mistress, severe anxiety or worry, deep sense of sadness due to loss of livelihood, strong feeling of destitute, a feeling that he/she became an orphan, socially disowned, all these are common causes of behaviour disorders at present in Indian communities. The causes of delinquency also produce more delinquents which ultimately result in criminal behaviour and sociopathic or psychopathic personality. Some persons who are impulsive in nature often meet with emotional disorders. They often become aggressive and hostile towards others and in case they cannot project on these, they direct them towards themselves and suffer. In the present society this tendency among the people is increasing.

Alcoholic and drug addiction and dependency now-a-days is increasing among the youth and young adults, resulting in various types of behaviour disorders. Many human beings spend most of their time in hallucinating and unwanted fears of persecutions and delusions and in imagined emotional reactions.

The branch of Psychological Science that studies systematically about these mental disorders, discussed in this book, is called Abnormal Psychology or Psychopathology. This book deals with all the major mental and emotional illnesses or disorders in a systematic manner with recent developments in the field. I earnestly hope that, it would certainly attract the Academic Population and also the general readers who are interested in human behaviour problems.

I am extremely thankful to Kcherry Sudershan of Authorspress for his interest in bringing out this book in an attractive manner. He deserves all appreciations for publishing scholarly works.

M. Rajamanickam

Contents

CHAPTER 1

Behavioural Disorder

Introduction

Psychology is the study of human behaviour right from the time of its birth through babyhood, childhood, pre-adolescent period, lateradolescent period, young adulthood, later adulthood or middle age, and old age. Human behaviour at every stage varies according to the developmental processes, that is, age, experience, company, education, occupation and the type of life one chooses to live. During the course of these stages man faces several types of situations or problems and people or social groups. In the course of all these stages the situations or the circumstances might have been with many ups and downs and man might have come out successfully by performing his task skilfully. He is successful, happy, healthy and prosperous in his every walk of life. But things do not go on like this forever in a man's life. There are instances which make him unhappy and unhealthy which may put him in some mental or physical disturbance and confusion. There are changes, often occurring in his behaviour. He does not look bright and happy as he was sometime ago. He lacks the capacity for adjustment. He does not smile at his wife, children and friends and exchange pleasant words and affection as he was doing previously. He looks differently, speaks differently and commits more mistakes in his work. All these indicate that there is something wrong in him.

The man is deviating from the normal system of behaviour. He is thrown away from the normal order of behaviour. This stage we may ordinarily call as behaviour disorder. Although the individual need not be considered as insane, he has lost his capacity for normal adjustment and everyday efficient functioning. We use the concept 'behavioural disorder' as a general term. It incorporates several mental ailments.

Behavioural disorders occur in a very wide variety of forms, which vary in severity. The very mild forms can be seen in the adjustment of an individual's behaviour. Sometimes, the mild forms of maladjustment go unnoticed, unless they are revealed in some problems.

The office manager fires the superintendent for not completing the chart. The man on returning home fires his wife for not keping good evening tiffin for him. His wife, in an angry mood, beats her child and throws the vessels, making horrible noises. The chairman of the board gets very much upset on knowing the heavy loss to the company that year. The driver is frustrated for the extra work his master often gives him by driving further for a distance of 50 kilometres and he drives rashly resulting in an accident. The mother scolds the girls for scoring poor marks in the examination and the girl is very much frustrated and runs away from home, causing anxieties to the parents. The child by throwing tantrums expresses her frustration for not getting the toy she wanted from her mother. Like these there are so many ways human beings reveal their maladjustment or frustration. All these may have different degrees of intensity from very mild – form of abnormality to a severe form of insanity.

What is Abnormality?

The simple meaning of abnormality is deviating from the normal or going away from the normal system of order. It is something which is in disorder, disarray. It may be also a state of confusion or an upset. Any correct definition of abnormal depends upon a suitable definition of normal.

The concept 'normal' is derived from the Latin word 'nor-mae' which means a carpenter's rule, square, or authoritative or standard, usual, common or typical. Therefore, normal means conforming to, not deviating or differing from a type of standard. Normal is an accepted standard by all means.

Normal is also defined from a statistical point of view. The best example is the normal probability curve. It is a symmetrical bell-shaped curve, representing the normal distribution and showing the probability associated with the value of each variable. In a distribution the mean or the median is at the centre having clustered most of the sample cases and having few cases falling on the slope extending to the end of either side. Thus few cases of the sample are scattered on either side. There may be moderate cases and extremes cases. The standard deviation of the distribution indicates the levels of dispersion. It is stated in terms of cases falling at the edge of plus one SD and minus one SD, plus 2 SD and minus 2 SD, and plus 3 SD and minus 3 SD. This is with regard to the sample distribution, a sample down from a population. In the same manner, in a culture we find normal and abnormal persons. Most of the people in a culture or society are normal just like the normal probability curve. But there may be few persons in the culture who are not falling on the mean or median of the normal curve, deviating from the general population and falling at the edge of +1 SD and -1 SD. These people are little maladjusted.

After one ± SD the curve slopes down deeply in the distribution which indicates that some cases are going away or deviating from the normal to some abnormal level. Statistically, they come under +2 SD and -2 SD cases. Just like the cases in the normal distribution, in every culture there are people suffering from mild abnormality like severe maladjustment, frustration, aggression, conflict, neurotic anxiety, phobia, regression, grand mal, hysteria, mania, and many other minor abnormalities. The normal curve at ± 3 SD level goes more and more away from the normal level. In every society there may be abnormal cases of extreme types as the cases falling on extreme levels in ± 3 SD.

Therefore, we may state that anything that is not normal is called abnormal. The word abnormal is originally derived from the Latin word 'abnorma' or 'a + 'nor-mae' and it was stated as anormis and anormous which means irregular or mis-shapen. Later on, it was called abnormal which was meant deviating from the type, contrary to the rule or system. In French, the word is called 'anormal' which is taken in English as abnormal.

Therefore, we may state that abnormality in human beings is a state of mental illness ranging from maladjustment to extreme cases of mental illness which needs rigorous treatment. The downward incline of the normal curve of ± 2 SD and ± 3 SD is a good example to explain the level and the nature of abnormality in every society.

It is observed that abnormal cases all over India are increasing considerably and in every state capital these are two or three mental hospitals to treat the mental patients. Even the district headquarter hospitals have a branch to treat mental patients.

Abnormality means the quality of being abnormal, monstrosity, depreciatory, and hideously evil. Thus the word abnormal carries many meanings. But when we apply it to humans it refers to mental illness, insanity, madness, mental disorder, psychosis, psychogenic disorder and others. Man is not born with abnormality or he is not born abnormal. Abnormality is caused. It is a causative state due to several factors. Since the abnormality is revealed in the behaviour of the individual we call it behaviour disorder.

Every culture or society has set up a standard with regard to the behaviour of the individual and he has to adapt the standard. We may call it cultural norm or social norm. Persons irrespective of age gender and status are expected to behave according to the norm. There is age norm, gender norm and status norm. A person of the age of four or five may behave like a child irrelevantly, not adhering to the norm. This may be excused or accepted by saying, 'after all he is a child.' Thus the culture or society does not expect much from the child or a little boy or girl in behaviour. But in the case of an adult person society does not tolerate the child-like behaviour or any type of behaviour that deviates from the cultural norm. It is not accepted and it is not normal behaviour. In every culture there are persons who at times do not adhere to the standard behavioural pattern. Such behaviour patterns we may term as abnormal behavioural pattern. Everything that they do may be very unusual and they may easily quarrel with everybody, beat themselves and cry, run against the moving train. They always behave against the age norm.

Just like age norm, there is also gender norm. Every man or woman is expected to adapt to the cultural norm decided for them. There is a limit for a man's sexual expression and behaviour. Any abnormal expression of sex is against the cultural norm. A man may be sex deviant extremely, may misbehave with women in the streets, which is an abnormal symption of expression of sex. Culture or society prohibits such behavioural pattern and brands the person as insane or abnormal. Similarly, in the case of women there may be abnormal patterns of behaviour, like when a woman throws away her dress and expresses all sorts of sexual symptoms.

Thus the behaviour of an individual is determined to some extent as to how one should be at various age levels and how one should behave with regard to sex. Unlike other behavioural patterns sex is given more importance in every culture. It is associated with morality, discipline and religion. When Kinsey (1948) published his work *Sexual Behaviours in the Human Male*, there were severe criticisms against it. The main criticisms were that he violated the moral and religious norms and principles. Though what he wrote in his book were right, in a sense he wanted to set up biologically correct and average norms for human sexual behaviour. He was not interested in evaluating the merits and demerits of the existing restrictions that society had levied on people. He only wanted to know the existing type of behaviour of the people. Kinsey, being a biologist, has suggested a biological norm for human sexual behaviour. But the critics have commented that the biological norm must be accepted as standard. They had failed to think that what is considered as normal at one time becomes abnormal another time, and what is normal in one sense, is abnormal in another sense. In a sense the social norms or the moral and religious norms are also considered as abnormal in the extreme level. What is moral for the culture is immoral for another culture, and what is standard norm in one religion which is normal is considered as abnormal in another religion. Animism has strong faith in sacrificing animals in the religious rites, while civilised religions totally prohibit such sacrifices. Therefore, the line of demarcation between normal and abnormal in many cultures or societies is not very strong.

Thus people do not act always according to their age or sex, or culture. An individual in a society has several relative things to do. He has to play some important roles in the society. He has many responsibilities to deal with and duties to perform. His status in society is an important factor that determines his role behaviour. Whether his role in this context is normal and accepted by society or abnormal and hence not accepted depends upon the outcome of his role. Sometimes he may find his role very difficult and his methods of approaching the problem ineffective and not successful. The behavioural role of the person is becoming less and less normal and his status in the society is diminishing. The role is getting dim and not clear. He finds that the progressive ways are blocked and he is getting frustrated. He is put in a stressful state. Day by day the stress is becoming unmanageable. His search for an alternative for escaping the stress is not successful. At this stage the man is more frustrated and maladjusted.

Therefore, when a man fails to act or behave according to his age and fails to perform aptly his gender role, or fails to perform successfully and maintain his status he is looked upon by the society as maladjusted or an abnormal person. Societies or cultures are not of the same type everywhere. Behavioural roles vary considerably from culture to culture. Some are highly civilised societies and some are of very ordinary types. Highly civilised societies or cultures expect too much from the individual. The ordinary or not very much evolved societies or cultures do not bother about individual's roles. The individual's role in a highly evolved society should be what the society expect from him.

A person may be performing everything that his culture demands. The demands may be simple or complicated, the person may be fulfilling the demands of the culture at the expense of his efforts and motives. He was normal all these years and he was able to maintain it. But when he finds that the demands of the culture are too much which are beyond his interest and motives he inwardly curses the cultural demands and feels unhappy within him. He feels that he has no freedom from the culture or society to act according to his whims and fancy. He is frustrated inwardly and becomes helpless. At times he may reveal his unhappiness by some means to his family people and also to his friends. It may be in the form of expressions of temperaments and moods. Thus the personal adjustment of the individual is in between severe strain and normal (coming back). His feelings are oscillating between adjustment and maladjustment. His personal pride is on one side for free action and his cultural demands are on the other side. But the individual cannot totally disregard or neglect the demands of his culture, because it is in his culture and society he performs his role. His ambitions are fulfilled only in his society. A man's feelings and thoughts are the parts of his total behaviour pattern.

A man can live a normal life in a culture only when he maintains an integrated life of his motives and emotions. Any conflict in his motives and emotions may throw him off the track of normal life. The inner harmony of his life suffers from disintegration and he loses all happiness of life. He is in a state of maladjustment or abnormality. Consequently, he is developing a behaviour disorder. Therefore, it is very necessary that one should learn to live within the limits assigned to the age, gender and to the demands of the culture if he is to be called as normal. Further, he must be able to live harmoniously with the family members, other neighbours, relatives and with the society. He should also maintain the status in the society. If his personal feelings, thoughts, ambitions, aspirations and goals come into conflict with that of the family, other realities and society or culture then he gets into problems and himself becomes a problem to others and to the society. At this stage we may state that he is an abnormal case. It is not that everyone at this stage is stated as abnormal. Some may manage to avoid getting into problems or abnormality.

Deviation from normal level may vary in degrees. All the deviants are not driven to abnormality. Some manage the situation with suitable defence mechanism and escape from abnormality. But persons constantly face severe conflicts between their own demands and the demands of the culture, often succumbing to abnormality or behaviour disorder. The rapid development of science and technology, the fast growth of industrialisation and frequent cases of terrorism in India and all over the world are becoming threatening forces to the normal happy life of human beings. They are put into constant anxieties and uncertainties and also constant fear of safety for life. All these have psychological consequences in the life of a man.

Any incident or event at the present time may cause his death. The present day generation has come to think that it is living in the midst of dangers. Thus man is in state of constant fear and worry – that he may lose his job (the livelihood), living abode and his life any time. In such situations an individuals personal feelings, emotions, thoughts and motives cannot be part of his total behaviour pattern and he cannot identify his goals, aspirations with that of the demands of the society or culture. Everything is driving him only to maladjustment or abnormality. The end result of the psychological consequence is the behavioural disorder.

According to Coleman (1974) normal behaviour conforms social expectations, but abnormal behaviour does not conform social norms or expectations. He states that behaviour is abnormal if it is maladaptive. Maladaptive behaviour is determental to the individual and also to society. Vllmann and Krasner (1965), (1969) were of the view that abnormal behavioural patterns fail to meet the social expectations. It is because such behaviour is disturbing to other people and the society. It is strongly viewed that it must be changed. Abnormality may be also stated as non-conformity to the existing social norms or demands.

In the proceeding pages we have discussed various paradigms. All may provide some guidelines about the natural or abnormal behaviour or behavioural disorder. The physiological paradigms state that physiological processes make people behave abnormally. But the learning paradigms state that it is the information experiences that make people behave abnormally. After discussing many models of abnormality, Davison and Neale (1990) define abnormality from the statistical point of view. The statistical approach is to measure the specific characteristics of the people, like the personality traits and the way in which persons are behaving, and the distribution of these characteristics in the population. As we discussed the statistical approach earlier, in a population distribution the normal curve would show that majority of the people fall in the middle of the curve as far as any particular characteristic is concerned and very few people fall at either extremes. If a person is stated as normal it implies that he is not deviating much from the average in the particular trait or behavioural pattern. Generally, the statistical approach is used sometimes for diagnosing mental retardations. Many psychologists have studied mental retardations by applying statistical methods.

If an individual's intelligence quotient is above 70, then his intellectual functioning is considerably subnormal and it is designated as mental retardation (Grossman, 1983, Fagan and Singer, 1983). Abnormality is defined involving the personal sufferings of the people. People are often abnormal if their behaviour is full of distress and torment, and harmful to themselves. It is generally observed that people suffer very much from anxiety disorder and depression. But some anxiety disorders do not cause much distress. In some cases it was observed that anxiety disorder is inherently subjective. People who suffer from this often complain that they are suffering from something of the unknown. It is also difficult to designate the nature of their disorders as their psychological states often vary very much. Disability was also found to be one of the causes of abnormality. There is also a base of substance which often makes people suffer from disability. They suffer from social and occupational disabilities. Such people have poor work performance, commit more errors, quarrel with their spouse. These definitions of abnormality or behavioural disorder are too broad or too narrow.

These definitions did not include the criminals of various types and the prostitutes who violate the law and order and social or cultural norms. There are notorious elements of anti-social type and abnormal sex deviants who often escape from the observation of the behavioural scientist.

Abnormal Psychology and its Subject Matter

Abnormal psychology is a branch of psychology which mainly deals with abnormal behaviour of human beings. It is the study of deranged behaviour of people in society. It is also stated as the study of behavioural disorder of human beings, who were once normal and behaviourally healthy. The shortest definition offered by Strange (1965) is that abnormal psychology is a branch of the science of psychology which was developed mostly in the last quarter of the nineteenth century. Though its development is approximately stated as the last quarter of the nineteenth century the subject matters for abnormal psychology were available long before the nineteenth century. It has a long history with the much bigger storehouse of information. The types of behaviour that brought under the heading of abnormal behaviour range from a minor maladujsted man in the street to the clinical psychology treatment level in the laboratory of mental hospitals. Strange states that the main contents of abnormal psychology in the scientific form has come only from the laboratories of the university psychology and physiology departments. The laboratories of psychopharmacology and medicine were also providing relevant information regarding behaviour disorders. Abnormality has been dealt with by various types of professional persons like the practising clinical psychologists, the psychiatrists and the psychoanalysts. Each one contributed his might to the development of abnormal psychology by way of diagnosing, testing and treating the mental patients. In identifying the various types of disorders abnormal psychology, like all other fields, had developed the concepts of its own. In the classification and description of various abnormalities, abnormal psychology uses quite a large number of words to indicate the different shades of abnormalities. They are the subject matters of abnormal psychology. Though we describe them in the later section, let us mention in brief the important abnormalities which are considered as the subject matter of abnormal psychology.

The specific disorders that are discussed here are not sudden or recent outcomes of the studies made by psychologists or psychiatrists, but the outcomes of years of hard work in various areas. These were indicated with terms and concepts which were not in the everyday usage in psychology. The popular usage fails to convey the correct meaning of the disorder. Therefore, it is imperative to explain them with the psychological concepts of the present times. The seriously maladjusted person is often stated as mentally ill and becomes an object of ridicule. The severe disorder is stated as insanity. A wise man is stated as sane and a man who is severely disordered is called insane. But these are not psychological terms. Sane or insane is a legal term. The court makes the judgment whether a man is sane or insane. But the term used in the psychological world is psychosis (psychotic).

There are terms referring to mildly maladjusted cases. Psychologically such persons are referred to as suffering from neurosis. It is also stated as mild personality disorder. Generally these persons may be said to be suffering from nervous breakdown or neurosis. Karen Horney (1937) states that generally the strivings and needs of such neurotic persons are always self-defecting operations.

The classification of the general behavioural disorders is so complex that it is very difficult to put them in universally acceptable categories. Though attempts have been made by the World Wealth Organisation (WHO) and the American Psychiatric Association (1952-1968) (1980-1987), the classification underwent several changes and modifications. For example, some of the mild forms of behavioural disorders like conflict, frustration, stress, anxiety vary in intensity to the extent of making the individual inactive and senseless. Therefore, we state here only those characteristics which are generally termed as behavioural disorder or abnormal behaviour as the subject matter of abnormal psychology.

Anxiety

Anxiety is defined in various ways. It is generally a state of fear and apprehension. But this definition does not reveal every-thing about anxiety and what we expected. Some state anxiety as anxiety state, which means a neurotic tendency characterised by free floating, that is, the physiological effects seen in fear as the prominent symptom.

Anxiety is also stated as the psychoneurosis marked by abnormal fear, tension and anxiety. Luzarus (1968) states that anxiety is a stress emotion. According to him emotions are of two types, one is positively toned emotions like love and joy and the other is negatively toned or stressed emotions like anger, fear and anxiety.

Since the negatively toned emotions are the results of stressful relationship with social environment and motivational factors they are considered to be important in various types of maladjustment and mental ill health. The various psychological processes involved in this type of maladjustment are conflict, frustration, aggression, restlessness, tension, apathy, fantasy, stereotype, and regression. Individuals, whose attempts to achieve their goals when blocked, are often thrown into these states of maladjustment. All these are rooted in emotional stress. Though normal, at times individuals succumb to even severe maladjustments leading to behavioural disorders.

Neuroses

This is one of the important behavioural disorders widely discussed in abnormal psychology. A group of disorders are involved in neuroses. This is one of the behavioural patterns an individual may develop in an unresolved conflicting situation. Generally, neurosis is a form of maladjustment and the individual is unable to cope up with his conflicts and anxieties. The state of affair is not very severe as to produce a deep personality disorder. There are quite a number of neurotic patterns included in neuoses. Some of the important neurotic patterns are the anxiety neurosis, phobic neurosis, obsessive, compulsive neurosis, hysteria and its various types like conversion hysteria and neurasthenia.

Psychoses

This is one of the severe forms of mental disorders which requires treatment. The patient is mostly hospitalised for treatment. The psychiatric patient often shows changes in personality. The change of personality is accompanied by agitation, delusions and hallucinations. The patient's normal social functions are often impaired. Though there are certain common characteristics between the neurotic and psychotic patients, in psychotic there are certain physiological changes which are genetically based. There are various types of psychoses, like manic depressive psychoses, functional psychoses and organic psychoses. All these are subject matters of abnormal psychology. A student of abnormal psychology cannot miss all these in his studies.

Schizophrenia

Schizophrenia is a very serious and the most common type of psychosis. It is one of the functional psychoses. It is characterised mainly by social withdrawal and apathy. It has been estimated that in United States 50 per cent of the psychoneurotic patients are suffering from schizophrenic problems. There is lack of harmony in the persons. There is often split personality traits, and the person is often involved in autism, delusions and hallucinations. Generally, it is defined as one of the psychotic disorders characterised by severe disturbance in thought, emotion and behaviour, illogial thinking, faulty perception, often withdrawing from the world of reality, and the person often lives in the world of fantasy. There are various types of schizophrenia, such as simple schizofrenia, hebephrenic schizophrenia, catatonic schizophrenia and paranoid schizophrenia. The schizophrenic patient does not take care of his health. He looks pale and unhealthy for want of nutrition, rest and sleep. Generally a schizophrenic patient has no knowledge about his illness and health condition. This is one of the important subject matters of abnormal psychology.

Functional Psychoses

Schizophrenia is one of the functional psychoses. There are also other two groups of functional psychoses. One is the affective psychoses which consists of manic depressive psychosis and involutional psychosis. These two psychotic relations are characterised mainly by moods and emotions of abnormal types. They often fluctuate between mild and extreme types. The other is a group of paranoid psychoses, it is stated as paranoia and paranoid states. The paranoid psychoses are mainly characterised by delusions. The person is involved in false beliefs. These two groups of paranoid psychotic cases are not as much as the schizophrenic cases. Manic depressive psychoses involve varieties of emotional disorders. These are mainly manic depression, and a wide fluctuation in moods. Regarding depression, there are various types of depressions, such as simple depression, acute depression, hyperacute depression, and agitated depression.

Involutional Psychoses

The involutional psychosis is mainly characterised by malancholia which involves both mental and physical decline. It is a time in life following climatic, that is, changes of life. It may take place in a person in the late middle age, and depression is the disorder. The involutional psychosis is generally stated as involutional melancholic characterised by depression, agitation and apprehension. It is different from other depressive reactions.

Paranoid Psychoses

Paranoid psychoses also belong to the group of affective psychoses. It is also stated as paranoia and paranoid state. Paranoid psychosis is a mental illness mainly characterised by delusions. Paranoid psychosis is a mental disorder in which the person has persistent delusions of persecutionary type, delusions of grandeur and delusions of jealousy.

Organic Psychoses

It is a type of mental disorder mainly caused by the damage of some tissues and brain injury, drugs and also by infectious diseases like general paresis and epidemic encephalitis. Abnormalities may be caused due to the organic factors. In a number of combinations the physical environmental stresses may build up in an individual body and cause behaviour disorders. It may be severe damage to the brain which may result in mental disorders. Therefore, organic psychoses are mainly caused due to physical and brain damage or injuries. Heredity is also considered to be one of the causes of organic psychoses. Injuries and chemicals may affect the brain and nervous system and may cause mental disorders. The brain tumour is a growth causing mental illness. The organic psychoses or mental disorders are the largest categories listing about 69 varied mental impairments. These result from organic or physical damage caused by drugs, diseases and degenerating effects of aging.

Psychosomatic Disorders

This is also called psychophysiological disorders. Psychosomatic illness is a physical illness that has psychological causes. It is a disorder with physical symptoms which involves damage of the tissues in one organ system. It is the result of continued emotional mobilisation under severe stress, usually involving single organ system, the autonomic nervous system. The autonomic nervous system is put into severe stress, and ulcers and hives are the common symptoms. If a person continues to have emotional disurbance for a longer period his autonomic nervous system becomes overactive and causes continued excess secrection of hydrochloric acid which causes physiological illness. Man has become very curious to know the relationship between the emotional stress and the changes in the bodily parts, for centuries. Later on, it has been assessed that the continued excess secretion of the acid causes several psychophysiological illnesses.

Some of the important psychosomatic or psychophysiologic disorders are skin disorders, musculoskeletal disorders, respiratory disorders, cardiovascular disorders, gastro-intestinal disorders, endocrine disorders and some special disorders. All these psychosomatic or psychophysiologic disorders seem to include a very wider range of disorders, and the emotional state plays an important role in all these disorders. This classification is made by the American Psychiatric Association (1968).

Somatogenic Disorders

The somatogenic disorders are the behaviour disorders caused by organic factors. It originates in bodily organs or tissues. It is similar to organic disorder. It is different from the psychological origin. If any of the factors disrupt the brain there is a change in the behaviour. When there is an injury to a small part of the brain, the result is localised in that part of the body over which the brain has control over. That part of the body becomes insensitive. In other words, it is stated as paralysis. The specific part of the body does not function. But if the large part of the cerebral cortex is injured the consequence is inactivity of the whole personality, the whole bodily parts, or the whole behaviour is affected. The somategenic disorders include chemogenic disorders, endocrine disorders, toxic disorders, genogenic disorders and histogenic disorders. Each one involves a group of disorders.

Mental Deficiency and Epilepsy

The subject matter of abnormal psychology includes also the mental deficiency and epilesy, since these are also considered to be somatogenic disorders. Mental deficiency refers to a mental state in which a person is not able to function like a normal person. His level of intelligence is very low. Mental deficiency is equated with feeble-mindedness, which is classified into three categories like idiot, imbecile and moron. Mental deficiency is of several types. It is synonymous with feeble-mindedness. The mentally deficit person is not able to do anything on his own. Mental deficiency, feebb-mindedness and mental retardation are used synonymously. But mental retardation is mainly an emotional problem whereas mental deficiency is a somatogenic problem.

Epilepsy is a disorder of the central nervous system characterised by loss of consciousness with or without convolutions. In some cases it is due to brain damage, but in some it is due to severe emotional shock and it is generally called fits. Epilepsy is of many types and marked by sudden and various recurring attacks.

Character Disorders

Character disorders, conduct disorders, moral feeble- mindedness, psychopathic personality, constitutional. psychopathic inferiority are the terms synonymously used. Character disorder is a recent term quite suitable to explain the behaviour disorders of various types that we come across in our everyday life in the society. The individual, out of conflict and frustration, acts out of the social norms. Character disorders include conduct disorders which include the persons who act out their hostile, violent and antisocial impulses. Specifically in conduct disorder individuals "behave out" their adjustment and personality problems. These may have a very wide range of disorders or irregularities, violations of physical, social and moral 'norms', and sexual deviations.

Thus the subject matters of abnormal psychology are so wide that we cannot put an end at any level as time to time new behavioural disorders are added to them. Further, the names of behavioural disorders are often changed or replaced with new names.

Modern science and technology are developing so fast that every day something new is discovered. It may be a machine or medicine or mental illness or therapeutic techniques for treating the mental patients. In this way people have learned to consume some substances for their illness. Our dietary codes resolved to protect people from consuming harmful substances. There is a long history of searching, testing and using different substances for nourishment and also for relief from pain, control of anxiety, and for the pursuit of pleasure or even to induce panic and psychotic states.

Methods of Study of Abnormal Behaviour

Abnormality is attributed to a state which is not normal. But, we find in our everyday life many things are not functioning in the normal state as we expect. To put it shortly, it is human nature. Everyone wants to have things to go in his own way, not conforming to the social norms. But there are extreme deviations in the behaviour of some negligible percentages of people in the society. These people are taken for granted as not normal and they must be observed and attended with some medical or quasi-medical cares. There were different ways of conceptualisation and treating of such abnormal behaviour. Its problems and its classifications and assessments were so varied that there were very little agreements with regard to its causes assessment and treatment.

The reason for the diversified views was that the studies were mainly based upon beliefs, observations, conceptualisation, opinions collected from others, past history, myths, witchcrafts, and so on. Many of the information about abnormal behaviour are based upon armchair speculations. Everyone speculated the matter in his own way, described and theorised. This type of study was going on for centuries till the scientific methods and approaches were thought about. This field of study is highly speculative, and facts come to our rescue very rarely and the speculative ratio of the data is very high. Therefore, a scientific method of study has to be devised for this field.

The study of abnormal behaviour for centuries was based upon observation, recording, comparing, theorising, classification and assessment. These methods of study can no longer be continued as the results are not subjected to test, retest and verification, and are not very much reliable. Therefore, in the study of abnormal behaviour we must make use of science and scientific methods. 'Close observation' is one of the methods of a study in psychology. It is true that scientific observation and scientist's investigations are through experiments and they were regarded as laws and theories and they formulated hypotheses and verified them by the results obtained in observation. Even observations of rare results were regarded as inventions and discoveries. On verification if they found any change in the results they also changed their hypotheses.

Any systematic observation and interpretation is a scientific study. Science is a systematic body of knowledge. Similarly, observations systematically performed become scientific study. Any systematic study or observation is a scientific study, and if the information is evaluated and found correct, laws and principles are formulated on verification of observed information. Testability and reliability are the characteristics of scientific methods. Testability means that an act or incidence is repeated to see whether the same results are obtained. Reliability refers to the extensity of the true level of the result.

Psychologists try to apply these methods in the study of abnormal behaviour in individuals. An event that has occurred under some specified circumstances should recur under the same circumstance in individuals. The symptoms may be the same. This should occur irrespective of individuals, places and countries. Everywhere the same event occurs and the same symptoms appear. In the study of abnormal psychology this method is generally applied for collecting information, and for interpretation of the results and for formulating laws and principles.

Research Methods

In every empirical study the data are collected by observation. Research studies often end with purely descriptive information. Researches sometimes find several events and they try to relate them. Particularly in the field of abnormal psychology there are quite a large amount of descriptive information and literature. Regarding the symptoms that appear in persons, were diagnosed and classified as having particular disorders. The symptoms appearing in some persons are also related to other types of persons, like other gender or other social classes. For example, hysterical symptoms are more common in women. But since it is rooted in emotion, sometimes the symptoms may also manifest in men.

Epidemiological Research

Epidemiology generally means a branch of medical science concerned with occurrence, transmission and control of epidemic diseases. This method is more commonly used in the study of abnormal behaviour. Epidemiological research means the study of all frequency distributions of illness in a population.

By epidemiological research information is collected about the rates of illness and the correlates of illness of a large sample or population. The important characteristics of epidemiological research method are prevalence, incidence, and risk factors. Prevalence refers to the size of the population in which the disorder is studied at a specific place and at a specific time.

The term incidence refers to the occurrence of new cases that take place at some time or period in a year. Risk factor refers to a variable or condition that is likely to develop the disorders that are studied.

In psychopathology, generally the health care facilities are provided, for which a knowledge of various diagnoses is very important. Epidemiological research method is also used to find out the causes of illness. There are instances quoted by authors that epidemic diseases are caused by drinking contaminated water. Davison and Neale (1998) cite an incidence of outbreak of cholera in London city and John Snow was able find out the cause of the outbreak of cholera. It was due to the drinking of the contaminated water in a particular area, where the cholera cases were higher in London city. Snow investigated in another area where there were upstream communities. The water was clear and the number of cases were few. Quite a number of instances can be quoted where the epidemiological research methods were used to find out the causes of illness.

In the field of psychopathology we do not find much evidence that epidemiological method was used for diagnosing cases or to find out the causes of illness. However, epidemiological methods were used in certain areas and interesting results were brought out. It was found that depression was more common among women than in men. By knowing this relationship we can get more information to find out the causes of the disorders. Similarly, the epidemiological research results show that more schizophrenia cases were found among the people of lower socio-economic status. This may provide certain information to the aetiology of the disorders.

Cases Study Method

The case study is a quite familiar method of data collection. It is by observation of one's behaviour and recording the information obtained from a person and also the information obtained from others about the person. A person is observed at a time and all personal information such as his family background, educational background, occupational status, medical history, marital status, adjustment problems, ambitions, and aspirations, personality traits, emotional problems, successes and failures in life and so on. These information are obtained and recorded systematically. Then the clinicians describe each category of information for treating the person. The clinicians may try to find out what type of role case history plays for the study of abnormal behaviour. Lazarus and Davison (1971) have made extensive studies and made clinical innovations. The case histories have been used four ways in their practices. In one of the case studies made by Thigpen and Clecklay (1954), the patient revealed wonderful symptoms. In the descriptive uses of case study the patient revealed multiple personality. The authors described the patient as "Eve White". The patient exhibited at various times three very different personalities. It seems that the description of the patient's case extended to a fallback, and it is called, "The three faces of Eve". The time at which new personalities appeared the other selves also come to know each other. This case has become a very remarkable one in literature. It provides a good account of a multiple personality.

Further, the case has an added importance as it is the original report of the authors. Thigpen and Cleckly provide such valuable information about the interview procedures they adopted. The interview information throws much light upon the behaviour of the woman patient and also how the treatment has developed to the extent of revealing the multiple personality of the woman.

But sometimes the data collected in a case study seem to be not so much reliable. Chrismore and Pittillo (1977) in their book, *I am Eve* have stated that Thigpen and Cleckley have not done the work of "Eve White" perfectly. According to them there are some discrepancies in their studies.

Clinicians use the case history method for gathering information from the psychiatric patients. The patient may be suffering from depression and also might have had many delusions and fantasies. Based on these, patients are given treatment, taking into account that the case history information is true. Patients may be providing information in the case study everything that they experienced and also remembered certain information of the depression states. Since the patients often had delusions and fantasies, it is more likely that they might have narrated the events of their delusions and fantasies. Clinical studies reveal that women patients often report of sexual assaults by their fathers, uncles and brothers. Since some of them cannot be repeated and verified such case study information are delusional or fantasies. Right from the time of Sigmund Freud (1938) these problems were prevalent. Therefore, the data collected by the method of case study may have several unreliable information which will not help seriously to treat the patients. It is important for the clinicians to observe the patient deeply, whether he is in communicable state sincerely or in a depressive or fantasy state. Otherwise, the study could be questionable at all stages. Therefore, in applying the case study method the patient should be brought to the normal state and should be in a position of having natural conversation with the clinician and also ready for providing correct information about him/her. Information obtained only in such a situation would be reliable for analysis and treatment.

The case study concentrates on a single individual. Information is obtained in great detail which may be useful in clinical setting. The essence of psychological studies rests on an individual behaviour and personality characteristics. The case study can provide such information. This is true in the case of normal human beings. But the results obtained in a single individual cannot be generalised. We cannot formulate any principles or hypotheses.

Correlation Method

This is a statistical treatment to the results obtained in a study. Two groups of data are required for correlational method. It is a systematic arrangement of data obtained from an experimental group in two separate variables. The scores of the two variables are systematically associated or related and the level of association is determined by the correlation coefficient. There may be a significant positive correlation (+1.0) or no correlation (0.00)) or negative correlation (-1.0).

The correlation method is mostly used for epidemiological researches. Though the correlation method requires greater sample, it is also used in studies of smaller samples. A question is raised and an answer is found in this method. For example, the intelligent (x) students perform better in language ability test (y). These two (xy) variables are related. The level of association is tested. Similarly in abnormal psychology a question may be raised – is psychosis highly prevalent in lower socio-economic status group? A high correlation coefficient indicates that both variables (x,y) have high scores. If one has high scores and the other low scores, then the correlation coefficient may be low. The association between the two variables is very poor. Then the correlation method establishes whether there is any relationship between two or among more variables.

In every field of psychology a large number of studies of this type are carried out everyday between variables. But in abnormal psychology the application of correction method is limited to certain variables only. In recent times it appears that more statistical methods like the correlation methods were applied and experiments also were designed, because it is interesting to see the relationships between two or among some of the abnormal behavioural patterns.

Instead of fully depending upon the interview and case study information it is more fascinating to apply the correlation method between two abnormal variables and to find out the result. If one is severe, the other also must be severe if the correlation is to be high. If one is low and the other is high then the correlation may be low and insignificant. Therefore, in the study of abnormal behaviour the correlation method is gaining more information. Any variable can be correlated with any other variable of which both may be abnormal type or one may be abnormal and the other normal type. The result may help the experimenter to know how the abnormal factor has influence upon the normal function or vice versa.

Experimental Method

The experimental method is the most reliable method in collecting data for the analysis and for the interpretation of the date. It is also found to be easily communicable. But the important aspect of the experimental method is the experimental design. This is considered to be the basic characteristic of the experimental method. First of all, the experimenter should find out a suitable problem for study and then he should formulate the hypothesis. In formulating an experimental hypothesis, he should find out an independent variable which could be manipulated in whatever manner he wants in the experiment. It is important that some of the factors of the independent variable should be under his control. Then he should carefully watch the changes or the results in the dependent variable and record them. The changes or results in the dependent variable are expected to depend upon the manipulation of the independent variable.

An experimenter wanted to study the severe reaction of emotional shock in a group of students, studying in the final year of a degree course. The hypothesis was, severe emotional shock is related to anxiety. Twenty students were invited to his laboratory. They were all 20-21 years old, came from different parts of the city. They were asked to write down the severe emotional shock or the most pleasant feeling experienced in life. They were asked to go deep into their memories and write down only the most felt experience. They were given 30 minutes' time. The answers were collected when they were ready. Then an anxiety scale was given to all of them and they were asked to answer all the questions as required at the top of the questionnaire. This was a 30-minutes test. On completing, the questionnaires were collected. First, the students who experienced severe emotional shock were separated from those who had written their very pleasant experiences. It was found that there were 12 students who experienced severe emotional shock and eight students who had pleasant experiences. The anxiety scores of these two groups were obtained by scoring the questionnaires. The mean scores of these two groups were worked out. It was found that the students who experienced severe emotional shock scored higher than those who had pleasant experience. The high score indicated high anxiety and the low score indicated low anxiety. The difference between the two groups was found to be highly significant at .01 level. Therefore the hypothesis is accepted.

In this area it is also possible to design a single subject experiment. In dealing with abnormal patients the only way of getting information is to conduct an interview and to make a case study. Reliable information for treating the patients can be obtained only by these methods. In case, these data are not sufficient a single subject experiment may be designed for getting further information. The single individual subject is exposed to more than one treatment. There is no specific time limit. It is believed that information obtained in this manner may be valid internally. But these results cannot be fully generalised. The validity is only to some extent. Therefore, in such cases it is better to combine methods.

It is generally possible to combine the experimental method with the correlation method. The experimental design itself should be a combined one and the hypothesis also may be formulated. This procedure is generally called the mixed experimental design. Patients of various types should be exposed to different treatments. In this type of treatment the independent variable is different kinds of patients and the treatmental outcome is the dependent variable. It is possible to correlate these two variables. For example, one patient may be suffering from obsessive neurosis, another patient may be suffering from compulsive neurosis. These two patients have two different types of disorders. The first one is dealing with thoughts of recurring type and images not invited to the mind, often uncontrollable and irrational, whereas the second one is an irresistible impulse to repeat same act over and over again. This is not connected with any purpose. It may be observed how often the recurring thoughts and images take place in the first patient and in the second patient how often he repeats the act over and over impulsively. These results may be related to the disorders.

The methods of study of abnormal behaviour that we have discussed in the preceding pages may throw a clear idea about ways and means of understanding various types of neurotic and psychoneurotic disorders. When a single method of study is found to be inadequate for understanding some specific disorder, it is suggested to combine more than one method, which is supposed to facilitate the study of the problem and where more information can be elicited.

General Causative Factors of Behavioural Disorders

Having discussed several forms of neuroses and psycho-neuroses and their diversity of functions briefly it is also important to understand the general causes of behavioural disorders of various types and uncover the importance of the factors in causing the behavioural disorders. There are several factors operating and interacting in the development of behavioural abnormalities in a very unclear manner. It is because in the case of human abnormalities it is very difficult to state everything in a clearcut manner as one factor may overlap into another in causing behavioural disorders. Authors like Page (1960) have enumerated the difficulties endured by the patients. It was observed that there were stages in behavioural disorders or neuroses. Similarly, there are several types and different levels of degrees of abnormalities or neurotic behaviour.

It was observed that each type of neurosis or subtle abnormality has its own specific origin and causes. Therefore, it is not possible or easy to indicate the general causes of the behavioural disorders. One main reason is that some of the symptoms in several types of neurotic disorders appear almost the same. Studies of recent times reveal a somewhat clear picture of these causes.

Human behaviour is generally associated by different types of forces and several factors act and interact upon the behaviour. Some of them may be facilitating human behaviour and some of them impede the behaviour. The factors may attack human behaviour in varied combinations and make the human behaviour similar everywhere. The forces that often play an important role in human behaviour are mental, physical and environmental. These factors and other psychological factors put pressure on humans constantly. Though many withstand the pressures and behave normally, some fail to face them and are subjected to various types of behavioural disorders. The forces that put heavy stress on individuals of unstable personality produce behavioural disorders, while persons of stable personality are not disturbed by the stress of those forces.

If an organic factor is associated with behavioural disorder, the brain damage is involved. In an unstable personality a very small amount of brain injury may cause behavioural disorder. But in a healthy personality a severe brain injury only may cause a behavioural disorder, the behavioural disorder equal to that of the behavioural disorder of an unstable personality. Another person shows the symptoms as these two persons. The third person had a normal personality before the brain damage. Further, he also had the family situation which was very painful. All these three persons exhibited the same behavioural symptoms.

In all these (patients) persons the affecting factors, we can see, brought forth the symptoms of their disorders. But in certain cases these causative factors become very severe that they unavoidably cause a breakdown in the normal behaviour. In such cases the brain tissues are comprehensively injured. But in some cases even factors that are very simple become the causes of severe breakdown in a person already inclined to it. These susceptible factors include all the conditions that have made individuals weak and irresistible to stress and reduce the individual's ability to withstand frustration.

Factors that cause disorders may be organic or functional. The organic factors are generally those factors that are related to some physical injury or damage in the brain or endocrine system. On the other hand, the functional factors are those associated with psychological and social influences that hinder the individual from learning to adjust himself to life situations. Therefore, there are always the two, organic and functional factors entangled in mental disorders of the individuals. However, a specific disorder may be called organic or functional when the causative factors appear at the time of development of the mental disorder.

It has been observed in several cases that a person who had severe brain injury in some situation has been diagnosed as suffering from organic psychosis. After giving treatment to his brain injury he recovered from the organic psychosis. But he revealed certain peculiar behavioural patterns. Even though the person regained his physical health and strength, he had revealed certain abnormalities. He was totally confused about his physical environment and mistaking men and matters. Strange (1965) quotes several instances. In this case the person's brain injury was caused in an automobile accident and his case was classified as organic psychosis. But after healing he exhibited the symptom of functional psychosis, the delusion of grandeur. This is not the result of his brain injury. Persons suffering from brain injury or organic psychosis will not exhibit delusions of grandeur. This means that severe brain damage reduces the capacity in the person to adjust himself to life. Clinicians who treat psychotic patients often find that there are relationships between organic and functional psychoses.

The consequences of organic disorders which are caused by brain damage and endocrine glands do not get terminated fully even after healing of the organic disorders. The patient may return to the normal level physically and recover his health and strength. But the patient has symptoms of functional disorders. The patient exhibited several psychological and social deficiencies. The functional disorders mainly were the incapacity to adjust himself to the social situation. The patient was not able to remember the old things correctly. His vision was as good as before his disorders, but he failed to perceive correctly men and matters. From the after effects of the organic disorders, it appears that there are probabilities for the development of functional disorders.

Functional disorders or psychoses are characterised by severe psychological stress. They find their origin in psychological stress and severe anxiety. They generally result from and individual's failure in social learning and other psychological causes. Functional psychoses are quite similar to psychogenic and psychosociogenic disorders. These are caused by the factors characterised by psychogenic and sociogenic disorders. Psychogenic factors stem from the personality or psychological composition of the individual.

Another causative factor is the sociogenic factor. This factor is one that stems from interpersonal relationships, particularly social groups such as family, peer groups, and fellow workers with whom the individual is often closely put together. The individual often fails to adjust himself with the members of these groups. The constrained maladjustment with the members of the groups put him in severe dissociation and stress.

Human being must deal effectively with a variety of demands in physical, psychological and social situations for survival and for flourishing in this world. These demands cannot be ignored. Failing to meet the demands may cause severe consequences. In psychological study of adjustment, we often speak of two kinds of demands. The first demand is internal in nature, arising from the biological composition of the individual. It is an essential one, and should be met for survival and comfort. Man must be protected from damages and illness, and should have food and water sufficiently to keep himself warm and healthy.

The other demand is external in nature, generally arising from the physical, and social environments. Of these, from the psychological point of view the social demands are the most important in the life of man since they deal with the emotional behaviour of human life. These demands are positively toned emotions like joy, love and affection and negatively toned emotions like anger, fear and guilt. This is because man lives interdependently in a society with other human beings. When the demands of the individual exceeds his capacity, then problems arise. Failing to fulfil the social demands and other personal demands may result in tension and stress. The environmental conditions and social pressures make him weak physically. Members of the same culture may fail to offer the social relationships which may be damaging the psychological demands. To what extent a man meets with the environmental and social demands is a matter of his capacity to adjust to the situation. Thus adjustment becomes essentially a matter of problem-solving factor. In problem solving, adjustment involves mainly learning, intellectual activity, perception, memory and acquisition of skills to get along successfully with environmental and social demands. In problem-solving activities when the adjustment fails severe stress is produced. There is also disturbed behavioural pattern, distress and bodily disease.

Therefore, to understood more about the failure and ineffective adjustment, more must be known about the stresses of human life and the conditions that can cause stress and reactions.

Stress may be defined as the occurrence in an individual causing certain physical and psychological symptoms when he meets the environmental and social demands and when adjustive mechanism is very much taxed beyond the level of the his resources. The causes of severe stress also become the causes of functional psychoses or disorders.

Generally functional psychosis is caused by poor social adjustment or learning, mostly by psycho-social causes. It is caused without any known pathological changes in the tissues or in the conditions of the brain, disurbing severely the emotions, thought and behaviour. Functional disorder is also treated synonymously with psychogenic and psychosociogenic disorders.

Different views are expressed with regard to the causes of functional disorders. Experimental evidences attribute the causes to the damage of tissues and part of the brain. Environmental and social demands cause maladjustments in the individual, and also severe stress, resulting in mental and physical illnesses and so on. It is also said that all the illnesses are stress related. But evidences for this are yet to be known. However, there is also relationship between bodily functions and the overall adjustment of the individual's behaviour.

CHAPTER 2

Relationship between Brain and Bodily Impairment

Introduction

Human physical behaviour involves the nerve impulses and the motor nerves which find their roots in the central nervous system, the brain and in the spinal cord. Behaviour is controlled and coordinated by the central nervous system. Every physical movement is controlled and directed by the brain and the spinal cord. Therefore, any disturbance in the brain and the spinal cord by any means directly or indirectly, affects human behaviour. In other words, a type of behaviour disorder takes place. This can be observed in some specific impairment in sensory areas. For example, a small injury in the auditory area of the brain may cause problems in the auditory sense. The person may fail to hear what we speak or any sound produced as the induction of some information. A severe damage may cause total deafness. This may cause other disabilities also. We may even find a complete overall change in the individual's behaviour. He may mistake one thing for another and may cause confusion in his everyday activities.

It is because of his inability to hear and know what is going on around him that his ego is hurt and he may develop other behavioural disorders. He may deny his disabilities and try to compensate the loss by some other means. He has to face psychological, social and environmental factors and react to them. His attempts to adjust to these situations may fail and may result in maladjustment and behavioural disorders. After some treatment the patient may feel that he is all right and may ignore his defects and carry out some activities successfully. But this will not take place all the time in all activities. When he finds that he cannot make any improvement in some activities he gets very much disturbed and becomes more distressed.

It is also expected that the defense mechanism and the change in the social and physical environments can make up the damaging effect of the brain in the long run, and adjustment may take place in the individual person. But if this is not taking place or has failed in the organism to the effect of adjustment, then abnormal behaviour patterns are developing in the individual which is the cause of the brain injury. Brain injury in a particular part causes damage to that sensory area. But sometimes two areas of the brain get injured and two sensory areas get damaged. For example, any injury in the motor neurons of the brain causes permanent (paralysis) damage. If the motor-cortex of the brain is injured there is temporary damage. It results in loss of movement or sensation. The speech area in the brain is identified as neocortex. Damages are likely to take place in the motor neurons or in the motor cortex causing permanent or temporary damage in motor activities. This is called paralytic attack. At the same time the neocortex area of the brain may also get damaged and it results in speech disorder. There is no clear vocal sound and words are not properly pronounced.

The paralytic attack may be in a part of the body, mostly in a leg or in a hand. There will be no more movement or sensation in the part of the body. The person also has speech disorder, and is not able to speak out words. Cases of this type are quite common in the contemporary society. When a small part of the brain which is having control over some activity or sensation gets damaged, man loses his sensation or activity in that specific part. The face, jaw and some parts of the body get paralysed when the specific part of the brain is damaged.

After Broca's (1865) study of brain disorders, quite a number of scientists like Changeux (1970) et al and a group of scientists studied the snake venom. They were able to isolate the toxin, the 'bungarotoxin' which caused the paralysis. They dealt with it in such a way that it cannot be retrieved with motor and plate. Further, Patrick and Lindstrom (1973) in the United States conducted experiments on rabbits which resulted in the formation of antibodies. When the antibodies formed, the rabbits became *myasthenic* with symptoms similar to those of human beings. *Myasthenia gravis* is a severe muscle weakness, characterised by muscular fatigue. This disease in humans is called auto-immune disease. This is one of the disorders of motor neurons and the spinal cord. Albuquerque (1976) et al have demonstrated that the receptor responsive to myasthenia disease is reduced by their treatments. Subsequently, Fambrough et al also have shown that there was a reduction in the number of receptors in the myasthenic muscles.

Poliomyelitis: This is another infectious disease, very acute, caused by a virus that has special affinity for the motor neurons of the spinal cord and also motor neurons of the cranial nerves. In extreme cases of infection it causes paralysis. If it attacks the motor neurons of the respiratory centres, death may occur. These authors have made extensive studies on the disorders of motor neurons and the spinal cord.

This disease was occurring sporadically and epidemically in North America. But when the vaccines were developed by Salk in 1950 and by Sabin in 1960 the disease was well controlled (Kolb and Whishaw, 1996). There were also cases reported of this disease in tropical countries. Many who were infected with the virus, on taking the vaccination against this disease have shown no sign of any symptoms. But some, even after taking the vaccination, have shown the symptons of fever, headache, and malaise. But only few persons have developed paralysis.

Chemical functions of the body and Behavioural disorders

The human body has to maintain the internal balance constantly which is generally called chemical equilibrium. This is a very complex process, biologically we call it homeostasis. It is a process of maintaining balance among the chemical mechanisms of the body. The functions maintained by this system are the growth of the bodily parts, regulating the reproductive system, setting right the tissues, regulating the digestive system, regulating the oxygen to the whole body and also the process of elimination of wastages. A number of substance agents are involved in the process of metabolism for regulating the chemical processes or relations. Sometimes the processes are speeded up and sometimes they slow down. Among the important substances a group of complex proteins, vitamins and hormones secreted by the endocrine glands are involved in the homeostatic mechanisms.

The important substances which are needed for growth and reproduction are the hormones. If these systems do not function properly due to the deficiency of vitamins and due to under or over secretions of hormones in the endocrine glands and due to the lack of digestive hormones or enzymes in the body, the resulting consequence is behavioural disorder. The individual at this stage fails to maintain the normal behaviour. Certain chemical substances from external environment also attack the glands and cause damage. For example, oxygen deficiency and high humidity may cause damage to various parts of the body, the brain, the heart and lungs, resulting in behavioural disorder. Certain poisonous chemical substances like carbon monoxide may hamper the functioning of the brain or the central nervous system thus causing behavioural disorder.

Psychological and Social Factors Causing Behavioural Disorders

Psychological studies on behavioural disorder throw much light upon casuative factors such as organic, frictional, hereditary, chemical, psychological, social and environmental factors and so on. Psychological, social and physical environmental stresses put individuals in a most distressed state, ultimately causing behavioural disorders of various types. Therefore, a correct understanding of behaviour disorders is to be made from several approaches like the psychobiosocial, which include psychological, heredity, physiological and social. We shall discuss here mainly the psychological factors which play an important role in behavioural disorders. Psychological problems generally arise in the developmental processes. The newborn child is helpless, but has to grow and become an adult human. He is under the care and control of his parents and other elders.

In the process of development, the infant faces several problems. The physical growth, his diet habits, contact and relationship with others, peer groups, social situation and contacts, reaction to various bodies all may be having an influence in the development of personality of the individual right from childhood, through adoleconce, adulthood and old age. During the course of development to a mature adult, the individual is ready to endure and accept many difficulties like the task of learning and problem solving. He is slowly changing from the world of seeking pleasure to the world of reality. The child in the developmental process learns to identify his parents, brothers, sisters and other relatives, and also learns to identify the outsiders. Then he slowly learns to speak and walk. He is fully dependent upon others for everything, like getting his needs.

As the child grows, he learns to adjust and cooperate with others. Piaget (1959), a Swiss child psychplogist states that the child slowly moves from a complete egocentric state to a state of complete relativistic, that is, seeing things as others see them. The child while trying to reach and grasp the world of reality the home conditions should be congenial. The parents must love and accept the child and must show affection and encouragement. The home must be a sweet place where the parents must love each other and also maintain a healthy atmosphere. They must be emotionally well adjusted. The child must feel secured and must be willing to accept the discipline the parents want. The child mainly needs love and affection, care, and constant attention. The personality development of the child will be healthy and sound if the parents and the home play a pleasant role.

But if the parents show an indifferent attitude towards the child and fail to show sincere love, affection and care and avoid when the child needs love, that will be the very infortuante time in the life of the child who may feel very much miserable causing very severe stress that results in neurotic and other abnormal reactions or disorders. According to Horney (1942) the world seems to be hostile and threatening to the child when he is isolated and left helpless. The child is put into severe stress and this becomes the cause of neurotic anxiety. When he is isolated he feels that he is neglected and rejected by parents. Then he feels destitute and thinks that he is lost in this world. He becomes mentally upset and runs away from home not knowing where he is going. Everyday there are announcements in in the media giving particulars about a boy or girl not found from a particular date. Such children develop behavioural disorder of some type as the home conditions are not happy. Quarrel among parents broken homes, sibling preference are also the causes for the children to run away from homes.

Children in some homes are over-protected and they are not allowed to do anything on their own. It is mainly maternal over-protection. This child has to depend upon the mother for everything. Even at the stage of going to school the child is fully tied down to the mother's apron and is not left free. The mother may be emotionally unstable and suffering from anxiety neurosis and other abnormal tendencies which may have an adverse effect upon the child. The child is in a severe anxiety state and becomes neurotic. This is how the behaviour disorders develop in children.

Problems of Adolescence

As the child grows older and reaches the adolescent stage the problems are different. Sometimes the child may carry the childhood problems with him to the adolescent stage also. The adolescent in every culture is put into severe training. He has to become very conscious of his education, school life, play and peer groups. Parents expect him to identify himself with the responsibilities of this period. The physical growth of the adolescent makes several changes in the body. It is the period of puberty and sex hormones are produced. There are changes in the physical characteristics, increased sex drive and development of secondary sex characteristics like change of voice, appearance of pubic hairs, development of breasts in girls. The adolescent is full of energy and so he is very active, does not care about anything. William James (1898) said that the adolescent period is full of storm and stress. The production of hormones are mainly responsible for the adolescent being over-emotional and he becomes rebellious. Margaret Mead (1928) stated that the physical changes in an adolescent are not directly responsible for the change of behaviour since in American culture heterosexual activity is permitted. The adolescent is quite carefree as his role in the society is well defined and he is expected to be independent and should accept the disciplines.

However, even though the adolescents accept what the society demands and what their parents expect from them, they often become rebellious, fall victims to negative emotional tones. These characteristics vary from culture to culture. In Indian culture adolescent demands are to high. This also varies on the basis of socio-economic status of the family. In high income groups the demands of the adolescent is generally met by the parents. But in middle and low income groups it is different. Parents very much expect their children to study well and get through the examinations and got good jobs. Adolescents who are below the average level do not fulfil their parents' desires, do not carry out their advices and refuse to accept disciplines. When they score low marks in an examination their parents become severely critical and get angry. The adolescents are afraid of facing such situations and get frustrated. They fail to carry out their parents' advices. Sometimes parents may punish them for not carrying out their duties properly. This results in some unstable adolescents running away from homes. They develop a sense of fear, fustration and aggression. Some are involved in delinquent activities, like stealing and misappropriation of things. If they are caught they are sentenced and put in prisons.

Adolescent problems are increasing day by day in India. The number of juvenile delinquents are mostly from the middle and low income groups. Newspapers carry instances of their breaking the doors of the prison and running away. The media presents every day several cases of runaway adolescents from homes. Some emotionally very unstable adolescents commit suicide either by hanging or by self-immolation on knowing that they failed in the examinations. These pathological conditions are rapidly increasing in India mostly among girls. The main reasons seem to be that their home is not pleasant and happy and their parents are always nagging that they must come up well in life.

Problems of Young Adults

Adulthood is the stage when the individual attains full maturity to become an independent individual. It is very difficult to state at what age this stage begins. It also depends upon one's culture. An adult is one who is able to live independently without the help of his parents or other adults. This definition of an adult may be applicable to almost to all cultures. But at what age adulthood begins and at what age it ceases is not clearly defined. Some classify adulthood into three categories as young adulthood, middle adulthood, and later adulthood. The old age is treated as a separate stage.

The young adult must prepare himself for serval stages of his life. He must get into a vocation first and prove that he can lead a life independently. Having succeeded in getting a job for his livelihood, he develops confidence that he can get along in this world. Then comes his marital state. His married life involves important emotional adjustment problems. Having, lived freely alone all these years, now he has to adjust and accommodate his feelings and emotions to that of a lady whom he has married.

There may be often differences of opinion, misunder-standings and qurrels. Both of them must come to a state of give and take policy in every aspect of the family life. Otherwise there may be emotional outbursts, frustations, aggressions and even separation. Instances are occurring every day where the young husband and wife go to the extent of divorce within a few months or years of their marriage. The wife is unable to withstand the cruel treatment of her husband, and in laws, commits suicide and dies. Newspapers publish very sad instances of marital discords. There are also extreme cases reported in newspapers that a young husband kills his wife as she is not faithful to him or a young wife forced to kill her husband as he is ill treating her. Problems of these types are increasing in these days in middle and low socio-economic status groups. These are mainly due to emotional maladjustment on both sides.

Another problem the young adult faces is parenthood. Naturally there may be children after three or four years. In dealing with them the young husband and wife sometimes get disgusted and often develop negative emotional reactions. In giving birth to female children the wife is very much blamed by her husband and in-laws even though it is not her fault. The husband is mainly responsible for this. He contributes the chromosome which results in giving birth to female children. In the middle and lower socio-economic status families the young wife is sent back to her parents' home for not giving birth to a male child. It is also happening in some cases that the husband disowns his wife and gets married to another. There are quite a number of reports in the local dailies about these instances. The young wife with her female children become helpless and destitute and in certain cases she commits suicide after killing her female children. The psychological consequences behind such instances are fustration, aggression, hatred in life and emotional disorders.

Problems of Middle Adulthood

The period of middle adulthood varies from culture to culture. During this period the individual is in his forties. His responsibilities in the family and occupation may vary and increase. His social contacts and commitments also go on increasing. His children reach adolescent period and he has to readjust himself to the emotional development of his children. The family expenditure also may be increasing because of his children's education. The requirements of his children may be increasing and becoming costlier. At times he has to face some financial strains. If both husband and wife are earning members they may not face financial strains. His children may make demands without understanding their parents' financial position. At this stage he may be even driven to the necessity of borrowing money for his children's education. This puts further strain on him and he may get frustrated. He may face severe stressful situation and may develop anxiety. These is an internal threat and his ego becomes weak and he develops the an ego anxiety, a fear of the ego, a fear of taking any decision. He gets severe emotional breakdown to the level of developing a psychotic condition. This is how the behaviour disorder takes place in middle adulthood.

Problems of Later Adulthood

The problems of later adulthood are varied in all aspects. The person himself is at the peak of his occupation, many may be working under him and he may be exercising control over others. His responsibilities are very much increased, involving more decision making. He could command better respect in his position then he was getting on the earlier occasions. His family responsibilities also increase, getting his children married or employed elsewhere. If he is in business he trains his sons to take up the business lines. The individual is between fifty-six and sixty-five years of age. When his sons get occupation elsewhere and leave with their families and when his daughters get married, he and his elderly wife are left at home. There is nobody by the side of them to take care of them. He is going to retire soon. When he thinks about his retirement and the type of life he has to find out becomes a big problem and he gets depressed. His attempt to find out a vocation to keep himself engaged for the rest of the life becomes a serious matter that may develop into depression and anxiety. He may often regress into his past life which he has lived in a very pleasant manner. He may even at times invite a peaceful death. But those who cannot cope up peacefully with the rest of their life may develop anxiety neurosis or a psychotic state.

Old Age

The old age period tentatively falls between sixty-six and above. The person at this stage is completely free from all responsibilities and fully dependent on others. But there are people even at this stage living happily, choosing a vocation in which they are interested. If he lives with his wife he has no feeling of loneliness. Since both are old, they cannot do certain things without the help of others. Their children are away and they come home once in a while. Nowadays children do not keep their old parents with them. But there are families who keep their old parents with them and take care of them. It depends upon the culture. Generally in India, the Hindu families are joint families and kept their old parents with them, taking care of them. But now things are changing. The children of the present generation wish to live away from their old parents. As result of this, old people are left alone. If the husband and wife live together they may find some solace. But if the spouse is dead, the life of the living old person becomes very precarious. Such people are alone, they develop feelings of loneliness and when this stage continues for a long time they develop a sense of fear in being alone. They are prone to abnormal tendencies like anxiety neurosis or psychosis, or old age abnormalities like senile psychosis. In senile psychosis there are a number of different reaction syndromes. These differences become clear as and when the illness develops into severity. There is general degeneration of the brain and in the ability of the personality traits. The progress of the disease is slow and gradual. The mental symptom includes loss of memory. The person is always in a depressed state, never bothers about his dress and often withdraws from others. In a severe psychotic state the person even runs into the street without a shred of cloth on him.

The illness of the most psychotic persons is classified as simple psychosis. The senile psychotic person once goes out never returns home, because of his memory defects. Nowadays many retired old people prefer to go to 'Old Age Homes 'and wish to take shelter there for the rest of their life. They are taken care of by providing everything like food, dress and medicine, and when they die Old Age Homes take care of their cremation.

Genetic Factors and Behavioural Disorders

Genetics is a branch of biological science dealing with heredity and variations in organisms. Heredity is the transmission of characteristics from parents to offsprings by means of genes. Heredity also is meant the transmission from one generation to another of genetic factors that determine individual characteristics responsible for the resemblances between parents and offsprings. It is the sum total of the inherited factors or their characteristics in an organisation. Gene is a unit of heredity capable of reproduction and mutation occupying a fixed position in a chromosome and transmitted from parents to offsprings during reproduction.

Generally it is stated that "the genes are the carriers of heredity". We all have inherited certain traits from our parents, grandparents and ancestors. Here we are not dealing with the mechanisms of heredity, but the genetic abnormalities. The sperm cell (male) and the egg cell (female) have 23 pairs of chromosomes. During the process of fertilisation the 23 pairs of sperm cells join with the 23 pairs egg cells. The females have two 'X' chromosomes (XX) and the males have one 'X' and one 'Y' chromosome (XY). If both parents contributed 'X' chromosomes, then the child will be a female child. But if the male member contributed 'Y' chromosome and the female member contributed only the 'X' chromosome, then the child will be a male child. Thus the male child inherits an 'X' chromosome from his mother and the 'Y' chromosome from the father. Therefore, the 'Y' chromosome of the father has the fundamental biological characteristics for determining the sex.

When a cell is fertilised, first it divides into two divisions and then these two again divide and go on multiplying in numbers. During the process of multiplication sometimes a part of the chromosome may be lost or the female member may possess only 45 chromosomes, a deficit of one. This may result in the death of the organism. This shows that the fertilisation is not complete or perfect. But if the organism survives, a female child may be born with one 'X' chromosome (XO) and not with two 'X' chromosomes (XX). This kind of genetic abnormality is called 'Turner's syndrome'. When the females in this condition grow, they lack verbal and spatial abilities. They have webbed neck and fail to develop the characteristics of puberty. In the case of males the abnormality is due to sex chromosomes. It results in breast development in males. The males fail to produce sperms.

In males there is another type of chromosome abnormality. They may have few extra 'Y' chromosomes (XYY). These males grow taller than the normal height and in some cases they grow more than seven feet. They are extremely aggressive. The extra 'Y' chromosome causes the adrenal glands to secrete a huge amount of male hormones. These males reach sexual maturity earlier and have abnormal sex drives. They may be violent and have high criminal tendencies. The cause of their aggressive behaviour is genetical and not social. This type of men are extremely sex deviants. Since they are violent, aggressive, criminals and sex deviants they easily get involved in any type of behavioural disorders.

According to behavioural genetics the individual differences in behaviour are attributed in part to genetic make-up. It is also found that in most of the studies based upon genetics there is a high correlation with sociopathic behaviour. The results are found to be mostly criminal and antisocial behaviour. But it is also not possible to conclude that all sociopathics are criminals and all criminals are sociopaths. Lange (1929) studied and compared the identical and fraternal twins in criminal behaviour. He found that criminal behaviour was found to be higher in identical twins than in fraternal twins. He found that genetic factors are behind this. In another study by Krang (1936) with better sampling procedure there was not much difference between identical twins and fraternal twins of the same sex. According to his conclusion, both the pairs of twins were genetically almost equal.

It is also observed in most recent studies that heredity plays an important role in criminal and sociopathic behaviour. Hutchings and Mednick (1974), Mednick, Gabrielli and Hutchings (1984) have studied the rates of criminality and biological relations. There was high biological relation in criminality. In United States, Cadoyet and others (1989) found that adopted children by the parents of antisocial personalities were genetically disposed to antisocial behaviour. Therefore, we may conclude that genetic factors have an important role in the behavioural disorders of human beings.

CHAPTER 3

Forms of Human Abnormalities

Frustration

Of all the organisms living in this world man is the most complex organism. Unlike other organisms man has many demands and needs for survival. He has varieties of motives to fulfil his demands of various types.

Human behaviour is motivated behaviour. Every behaviour pattern is with some purpose directed to achieve something required by the individual. In this way human beings have very wide varieties of motives. Every motive is to fulfil his demand or need. The motives to fulfil the bodily needs are called physiological motives or drives. They are hunger, thirst and comfort. For survival man has to fulfil these needs.

Man is a social animal. He lives in a society. He has to fulfil the demands of society and also make himself a socially acceptable and respectable person. Thus he has several social motives like achieving better status in society, getting a lucrative position, achieving laurels and so on.

In addition to all these motives man has psychological motives such as the feeling of security, love and affection, a desire to have mastery over others and achieving self-esteem. Thus human beings have innumerable number of motives in fulfilling the demands or needs. All human activities are goal-seeking activities. Unless man arranges his motives in some order they may come to clash and cause confusion. In the this task of striving to achieve the goals, he may be meeting with some problems. Sometimes goals are not easily achieved.

In the goal seeking activity, in dealing with the problems, there are circumstances in life which inevitably interfere and prevent him from achieving his goals. Further attempts might have also failed. This puts much stress on him. All his attempts to achieve the goals are blocked as the environmental situation is beyond his capacity to handle. The reaction to all these is frustration. Such a frustrating situation determines to a great extent the level of adjustment of the individual to life. The individual's coping mechanism, if inadequate or weak, results in a threat to his mental health. In the problem-solving situation he meets with several types of frustrations and stresses. The frustrations may be due to the personal limitations, or conflict or environmental obstacles. According to Hilgard et al (1975) there are several reactions to frustration. Some of them are tension, aggression, apathy, fantasy and stereotypy. All these are rooted in emotional maladjustments. Frustration and conflict are often stated together. Man gets frustrated when his goal-seeking behaviour is blocked. But when he cannot decide between two similar goals or ideas he faces conflict. Hilgard et al (1975) state that a major source of frustration is conflict between two opposing motives. Even in the case of a single motive frustration may occur. The single motive may have several ways to reach the goal. Conflict arises as to which way to accept to achieve the goals.

Frustration may be seen in restless behaviour or extreme movement. It is also seen in unhappiness and unhappy activities and also in the increasing level of excitement. Tensions or restless movements may lead to severe feelings of anger or aggression, hostile attacks and destructiveness. Aggression may be direct aggression or displaced aggression. Direct aggression shows against the object of frustration, but when direct aggression or attack against the object of frustration is not possible aggression is displaced against an innocent person or object instead of the real cause of frustration.

Apathy

Apathy is one of the consequences of frustration. It is utter indifference to the situation. The person withdraws from the situation out of frustration. Fantasy is imagination or day dreaming. This takes place sometimes as a consequence of frustration. Stereotypy is the continued behaviour of the same type without any real purpose which may be punished if it is not flexible. This is one of the reactions to frustration. Regression is going back to the earlier life when frustrated. It is childish mode of behaviour to cope with the frustration situation. The individual, out of a feeling of insecurity, goes back to the period of the past when he was happy and had security. It is also returning to the childhood behaviour which is primitive type of behaviour as a result of frustration.

Stress

Modern psychologists use the theory of stress in place of frustration and conflict. This is a very recent development in the field of psychology. It was Selya in 1936 who introduced this concept in connection with his model, the 'general adaptation syndrome' (GAS), stating that it is a severe physical stress. According to Selya (1952) stress has three stages. In the first stage the autonomic nervous system is stimulated to resist the stress. In the second stage the organism tries to adapt the stress by its coping system and resists it. In the third stage the organism fails to respond to the stress and it is driven to the stage of exhaustion, and the organism suffers severe damage or dies. This stress is adapted in the psychological field with some changes. Researchers like Apply and Trumball (1967) observed some psychological changes like the increase in certain hormones. For them stress is a stimulus associated with environmental conditions. It may produce changes in behaviour like cognition, emotion and physiology. In this context only, frustration and conflict are equated with stress. Lazarus (1968) is considered to be one of the exponents who made extensive study on psychological stress. According to him, the presence of stress is felt in the way in which we perceive and appraise the environment. Individuals differ in perceiving and appraising the environment. Some may cope with the stressful situation and some fail and suffer from damage. Therefore, stress may be defined as the environmental stimulus that exercises strain on the physiological and psychological capacities of the organism and causes damage to the welfare of the organism. Stress is the cause of several illnesses, such as psychopysiological disorders, ulcer, hypertension and all emotional disorders.

Behavioural Disorders

Human behavioural disorders are so numerous that we cannot enumerate them so easily. Modern diagnostic techniques and treatments are so well advanced as to reveal some new result every day with some new type of abnormalities or disorders. As result of it behavioural disorders take innumerable forms. Therefore, a classification system has been devised to make more meaningful categories out of the many kinds of behavioural disorders. The classification is made mostly on the basis of the behavioural symptoms the people display. Individual persons who behave almost in the same manner are placed under the same category. The most important and main diagnostic categories brought under a very wide classification systems are mainly the neuroses, psychoses, psychophysiological or psychosomatic disorders, and personality disorders. These main categories are further classified into several branches.

It is also better for us to see the classification made by the American Psychiatric Association (APA). This is called *Diagonistic and Statistical Manual, DSM-1*, published in 1952. The *DSM-II* was published in 1968. The *DSM-III* was published in 1980. The American Psychiatric Association published a thoroughly revised version of the *DSM-III-R* in 1987. The list of disorders given in all these are almost the same, except the additions of few cases in *DSM-II, DSM-III* and *DSM-III-R*. According to these classifications the following major behavioural disorders are discussed here.

1. Anxiety Disorders

These disorders have been included in the list of major disorders only recently. They are phobic disorders, panic disorders, generalised anxiety disorders, obsessive-compulsive disorders and post-traumatic stress disorders.

2. Mental Retardations

The major abnormal behavioural patterns also include borderline mental restardation, mild mental retardation, moderate mental retardation, severe mental retardation, and profound mental retardation.

3. Organic Brain Syndromes

Senile and presenile dementia, alcoholic psychoses, psychoses associated with intracranial infection, psychoses associated with other cerebral conditions, psychoses associated with other physiological conditions – this category of disorders includes acute and chronic brain sydromes and psychotic and non-psychotic brain syndromes.

4. Psychoses (not related to physical conditions)

These include schizophrenia, simple type, hebephrenic type, catatonic type, paranoid type, acute schizophrenic episode (this category includes also latent type, residual type), schizo-affective type, childhood type, and chronic type. The major affective disorders are involutional melancholia, manic depressive illness, circular type paranoid state, paranoia and involutional paranoid state.

5. Neuroses

These include anxiety neurosis, hysterical neurosis, conversion type, dissociation type, phobic neurosis, obsessive-compulsive neurosis, depressive neurosis, neurosthenic neurosis, depersonalisation neurosis, hypochannical neurosis.

6. Personality Disorders

These include paranoid personality, cyclothemic personality, schizoid personality, explosive personality, obsessive-compulsive personality, hysterical personality, asthenic personality, antisocial personality and passive-aggressive personality, Sexual deviations, homosexuality, fetishism, transvestism, enlitinism, voyeurism, sadism, masochism, alcoholism, alcohol addiction, drug dependence, opium, carbiturates, cocaine, hashish, marijuana psycho-stimulants, hallucinogens, and other drug dependence.

7. Psychophysiologically Disorders

These include psychophysiological skin disorder, psychophysiological musculoskeletal disorder, psycho-physiological respiratory disorder, psychophysiological cardiovascular disorder, psychophysiolocical homic and lymphatic disorder, psychophysiological genitourinary disorder, psychophysiological endocrine disorder, psychophysiological disorder of the organ of special sense. All these disorders are psychogenic origin.

8. Special Syndromes

This category includes speech disorder, special learning disturbance and other psychomotor disorders like sleep disorder, feeding disturbance and neurosis.

9. Transient Situational Disorders

This category mainly includes emotional disturbance of a transient nature. This is generally stated as adjustment reaction of infancy, childhood, adolescence and adult life.

10.. Behaviour Disorders of Childhood and Adolescence

This include hyperkinetic reaction, withdrawing reaction, overanxious reaction, runaway reaction, unsocialised aggressive reaction and group delinquent reaction.

11. Psychotic Disorders without Manifestation

This category includes mental, social and occupational maladjustment, dyssocial behaviour and other social maladjustments.

These classifications have undergone several revisions. At present the revisions made in *DSM-III-R* is considered to be the latest. But further addition or deletion from this is not ruled out. The development of neuropsychology and bio-psychology brings out every day some new results out of the researches carried out in these fields. Therefore, let us discuss the major behavioural disorders that have a strong footing in the field of abnormal psychology.

Anxiety Disorders

We have stated above several reactions to frustration. The reaction to frustration sometimes may be mild and sometimes very severe. Whether it is a mild form or a severe form it has its own reaction to cope with it. Anxiety is the concept that can be used to explain all these forms suitably. It was Sigmund Freud who had formulated this theory of anxiety when he was treating the neurotic patients in his clinic. This was very widely used in the last quarter of the nineteenth century and in the first half of the twentieth century, by the Neo-Freudians. According to Freud, in normal persons the demands of the id and superego are met by the ego, since the ego is strong. But a rude id and a dominating superego may threaten the ego. This is a threat to the integrity of the ego and the ego develops anxiety which Freud called as ego-anxiety. This causes internal threat. It is a fear, different from normal fear. The anxiety that the ego develops is called neurotic anxiety. When some external situation threatens and does harm to the person, in order to keep himself going with the normality, the ego tries to defend against the threat. Then the ego builds up a defence mechanism and the first basic defence mechanism is the repression which according to Freud is a dynamic process. The materials repressed do not appear on the unconscious level.

Anxiety can be found in normal persons as well as in psychopathics. This is an emotional state often occurring in psychopathics. Modern psychologists have redefined anxiety. According to them anxiety raised much controversies and at last it was decided as an important aspect of behavioural disorder. Anxiety is the emotion of fear, Freud said. Anxiety is the chief causative factor of neuroses. Repressed anxiety, according to the psychoanalytic theory of neurosis, reveals the underlying problems. The behaviour associated with the forms of neuroses varies very much. For example, fear, avoidance due to fear, irresistible act, repeating an act over and over again, paralysis and conversion-hystenia, all these are grouped under neurotic anxiety. Further diagnose of anxiety disorders were made subjectively. It was clearly experienced that there was the feeling of anxiety. The important forms of anxiety disorders are five as given by the *DSM-III-R* classification (1987). They are phobic disorders, panic disorders, anxiety disorders obsessive-compulsive disorders, and post-traumatic stress disorders. These disorders are not absolutely new. They were described in different contexts in various behavioural disorders.

Phobic Disorder

Generally it is called phobia. It is of various types. Formerly it was classified one among the psychoneuroses. But now according to APA classification, *DSM-III-R,* it is discussed under anxiety disorders. Phobia is a morbid irrational fear of something held by an individual as a neurotic condition. The concept phobia is derived from the Greek word 'phobos', the meaning of which is fear or dread. In abnormal psychology it is named as phobia to explain a person's irrational fear of some object or situation which is not there. The person himself admits that there is nothing, but fears imagining about the object or situation. The recent definition to phobia is that it is anxiety disorder in which there is intense fear and avoidance of some specific object or situation which was perceived irrationally by the individual and the same experience he carries afterwards repeatedly.

It is true that some persons are extremely fearful of high places or deep landslides, closed areas or rooms, snakes, rats and so on. There are several types of phobias. One is simple phobias. The common sources of simple phobias are mainly animals like cats, dogs, rats, snakes, places and situations like, steep heights, closed rooms and places. Some anxiety neurotic persons are very much fearful of open rooms and places and they rush to close the doors of the windows and rooms. The phobias are labelled with the Greek words. For example, *acrophobia* is the fear of high places. *Agorophobia* is the fear of open places and *claustrophobia* is the fear of closed places or rooms. There is no objective damage to the persons who suffer from these phobias, but the distresses they experience are sufficient to disrupt their normal life. They seriously avoid the objects of their fears. In the studies made by Mark and Gelder (1966) phobias are common.

Mostly simple phobias occur among women and they occur in the early years of life.

Some people are very much fearful of blood and the phobia is called *hematophobia.* In a population certain percentage of people are very much fearful of being alone which is called *monophobia*, contrast to this, some are fearful of seeing the crowds which is called *ocholophobia.* There are also some people more fearful of fire which is called *pyrophobia.* There might have been some dangers occurred either to the individual or he might have seen the horrors of danger caused by fire in his early years. Such instances may contribute to the development of phobias. Phobia is a pathological or neurotic fear. It is different from the normal fears.

Phobias are viewed differently by various theories. According to the behaviouristic theory phobias are learned reactions. The founder of behaviourism, Watson (1920), has demonstrated this. A person may be conditioned to fear. A harmless stimulus may become the basis of an avoidance response. It need not be the real object of fear. Anything similar to one which caused harm may form the basis of fear. For example, a piece of rope in dim light may appear like a snake and cause fear to a person who passes that way with a sense of fear of snakes.

A person may develop phobia for an object which has caused him severe painful experience. The fearful experience is such that anything that is similar to that object in some form also makes him react in an alarming manner. Some say that some people are allergic to some insects or objects. It is an aversion and they avoid to face or see such insects or things. Therefore, what is involved in phobia is mainly avoidance, avoiding seriously an object which is similar to the object which is the cause of the phobia.

Panic Disorder

This is an anxiety disorder which puts the individual in an unusual position. The person is inspired with sudden fear. Panic is always sudden, overwhelming and often spreading quickly. It is a sudden overwhelming feeling of terror or anxiety. It may sometime put the whole group of people into extreme terror or anxiety. Panic is considered as an irrational fear.

In the panic state an individual makes a harsh sound and exhibits several symptoms like hard breathing, high heart palpitations, feelings of giddiness, trembling and the feeling of disaster. It is similar to the reaction to agorophobia. There may also be chest pain, and the feelings of choking and sweating. Panic disorder is an attack that occurs frequently. The person who is subjected to panic attacks often feels that he is outside of his body and the world. For him the world is not real. The person connects himself with an event that has caused him severe painful feelings to the level of panic disorder. To quote an incident, for example, a person went to some place with his friends for sightseeing where there were beautiful towers, bridges and buildings. Suddenly he and others were in a bomb blast causing serious damages to the towers and buildings. Some of the persons whom he accompanied were torned to pieces and died before his eyes and he somehow escaped narrowly. He received a severe shock and raised reverberating sounds and fled away from that place panicking. From that him onwards he received attacks of panic disorder periodically. Similar incidents are occurring every day. Somewhere an anxiety disorder of this type is quite common. Panic disorder is stated as agorophobia.

A group of people may develop panic anxiety disorder if they happened to witness an incident of sudden occurrence of great blaze around them. Each one of them may carry this experience and exhibit the panic disorder whenever happens to see a huge fire incidence. Studies were made by Ayers et al (1974) and found that panic disorder was found to be more among women than among men. In the diagnosis of panic disorder it was found that the persons had four attacks in a month at the rate of one in a week. In *DSM-III-R* revision it was stated that panic attacks are sometimes with agorophobia and sometimes without it. According to the study made by Barlow et al (1985) it was observed in the diagnosis that more than 80 per cent of the patients were found to be suffering from one of the anxiety disorders and also had panic attacks. Breier et al (1985) had observed that there was panic disorder existing with major depression and the occurrence of these two were quite common. Crowe at al (1987) studied the anxiety disorders of twins and they found that panic disorders are occurring in families. According to them the panic disorder was found to occur more often in identical twins than in fraternal twins.

In one of the recent studies made by Ley (1987) the mechanism of the acid effect had received greater attention. One approach brought about the result that over-ventilation or overbreathing let to panic attacks. If the breathing air contains more than the normal amount of chemical (sobalt) a metallic element (CO_2), it is likely to cause panic attacks. Gorman et al (1988) have observed that anything that is over-sensitive (CO_2) could stimulate the mechanism of over-breathing which may generate panic attacks. Persons who were attacked by panic disorders reveal serious mental and physical illnesses. Hibbert (1984) states that these patients develop more physical sensation which is a sign of the development of some serious illness leading to full-fledged panic attack. According to a multinational study carried out by Ballenger et al (1988) it was presumed that over-ventilation was the important cause for the panic disorders. The treatment for panic disorder as suggested by Clark, Salkovskis and Chalkley (1985) is the respiratory control. Their patients were taught to breathe and all their patients have shown great improvement.

Generalised Anxiety Disorder

This is one of the anxiety disorders, classified by the American Psychiatric Association. This is generalised in the sense that it is pervading in all kinds of anxiety disorders. Generally the person is persistently anxious. He is found to be often anxious and worried in all life situations. He is in the state of continuous fear of getting into accidents. He often feels that he is in very bad difficulties of money. The persons's sufferings are such that he is often put into worry and anxiety which is stated as 'free-floating anxiety'.

The person may be having several physiological sufferings. They are mainly stomach upset, rapid heart beat, diarrhoea, dry mouth, frequently urinating, sweating all over the body, rapid pulse rate, high respiration rate, hyperfunction in autonomic nervous system, muscular tension, pains in the neck, and shoulders and eyelids. The person may be reporting many things. He often says that he is getting tired and unable to relax his body. Sometimes he feels shy and ashamed of being like that. He often imagines that he is going to get into some trouble and die.

In the generalised anxiety disorder, according to Freud, there is always a conflict between the id and the ego in the unconscious level. Since the id impulse is sexual and aggressive in nature the id is always aggressive to manifest its nature. But the ego does not permit it and it lies dormant at the unconscious level. Generalised anxiety disorders are mostly physiological in nature (Natarajan, 2001). It is more active and harmful as and when human beings become old. Constipation is the most troublesome of disorders, affecting elderly persons. They are always with the movement of bowels. It is their anxiety about irregular motions that cause headaches, exhaustion and loss of appetite.

The other bodily ailments, according to Natarajan, are intestinal cancer, hernia, piles and fissure in the anus, under-secretions of thyroid glands, excess calcium in the body, lack of potassium and mental depression. For fear of frequent urination elderly persons, especially women, avoid drinking adequate water. They suffer from arthritis and hence restrict mobility which may involve strokes in hips and knees. Chronic constipation may affect the overall health of the person. Avoidance of immediate attention may even endanger the life of the person. Elderly people with constipation may strain during defecation which may trigger off an attack of chest pain. There is also a likelihood of *syncopal attack* due to transient reduction of blood supply to the brain. Generally irregular movement of bowel may cause severe anxiety and needless worries. It was observed that excess potassium losses cause severe ill health, apathy and weakness.

The treatment for the generalised anxiety disorder is almost the same as given to phobic disorder. The psychoanalysts help the person to confront the true cause of their conflict. By this means they believe that the person can resolve it. The behavioural treatment is to help the person to reduce the overall tension which was the main cause of his anxiety disorder. From the community psychological point of view, the generalised anxiety disorder is caused by the community. According to this, human sufferings are the results of unhealthy living conditions. They are helped to adjust to the environmental conditions by the community workers by making changes in the social environments. They adapt to the intervention and preventive approaches.

Obsessive – Compulsive Disorder

This is one of the anxiety disorders often discussed jointly in recent times. But formerly they were discussed separately. Obsession is the persistence of an unwanted idea. It is a persistent thought or idea of irrational type. But the person cannot get rid of it. He has no control over such a thought or idea or emotion and urge. The thoughts, ideas and images are often recurring. Sometimes this may occur even in a normal function. Obsession may also go to the extreme form of suspecting everything. The person in the extreme form may state that he has seen God and can even describe the situation.

Compulsion is an anxiety state in which there is persistence of an act. Though it is irrational and the individual knows it, he cannot avoid repeating the act. The persistence is of irresistible impulse performing seriously the irrational act over and over again. In Shakespeare's *Macbeth*, Lady Macbeth had been suffering from compulsive neurosis. She washed hands several times every day to clean her blood-stained hands. She murdered King Duncan when he was resting in her house after dinner. She said in her anxiety once that "even the waters of seven oceans cannot wash my hands." Some walk on the road touching every lamp post. If they miss one of them they go back and touch it. Compulsion is an impulse to perform some task which one cannot resist even though he does not like it.

An obsessive-compulsive disorder is an anxiety disorder in which the person is having persistent thoughts, ideas and images which are very impulsive in nature. Though the person knows well that his thoughts and images are irrational he cannot control them and is compelled to repeat certain acts again and again, resulting in notable distress and interference with everyday activities. Thus in the person who is suffering from obsessive-compulsive anxiety disorder there is persistence of thoughts and images and also some compulsive act to be performed repeatedly and often. In both the functioning the common characteristic is irrational persistence. The person may know it. But he cannot control it, therefore, the functions in both are irrational and uncontrollable and must be performed. The impulses involved in it are forceful and the person is fearful of stopping it.

Obsessive-compulsive disorder in some has its root in the childhood period, but mostly in the early adulthood period.

Psychoanalytic treatment reveals that the childhood compulsory toilet practices of the person have the fixation of the anal stage. Psychoanalysts find it difficult to deal with the obsessive-compulsive disorders. In the extreme cases all normal activities are cut off. The person is in high tension and psychoanalysis cannot deal with the patients alone. Therefore, the treatment is combined with medicine and psychology.

In obsersive-compulsive patients, even if the attack is in a less severe form, they try to escape from the psychoanalysts, whereas the method of treatment is very much successful in the case of hysteria. From the behaviouristic point of view, Meyer and Chesser (1970) state that obsessive-compulsive disorder is learned behaviour pattern, reinforced in the consequence. The repetitive act is one way of reducing the fear. The patient feels relieved by this act.

Obsesive-compulsive disorder, according to Lazurus (1968) seems to be forced upon the person against his will to think about something which he did not want and also to make him forcibly engaged in some unwanted actions. Though what the person thinks and does are irrational he cannot help himself. Like phobia, transforming certain unacceptable impulses into another form is not easy. Instead, more terrible thoughts have to be faced. These thoughts involve dangerous hostile sexual impulses. But these threatening impulses are in a disguised form.

Treatments to obsessive-compulsive disorders according to Coleman (1974) fall under three basic strategies. The first strategy emphasises helping the patient to differeniate between the thoughts and images and actions. He is made to accept his prohibited desires that are common to all people and therefore he should assimilate them into his feelings. Secondly, the patient is helped to differentiate between the objective and imagined troubles. Thirdly, he is helped to prevent the obsessive-compulsive activities or rituals by means of presenting opposed stimuli or by causing a painful experience. Treatment to obsessive-compulsive disorder is a very difficult psychological problem as these two should be dealt with as an overall problem.

Post-traumatic Stress Disorders

The post-traumatic stress disorders are classified as one among the anxiety disorders in *DSM-III-R*. But earlier, it was considered as the disorder with head injury and considered to be chronic. It is an anxiety disorder, particularly a stressful event such as seeing a murder, a rape, combat or a natural disaster like floods, sudden fires, earthquake etc. It is an intensive after effect experiencing the trauma, a bodily injury or emotional shock often having a lasting psychic effect. The person may be having nightmares and dreams, often occurring and often having sleep disturbances. Though he may recover from this there may be various residual symptoms even after that.

The post-traumatic stress disorder caused by moderate brain injury may reveal several symptoms in the patients. The common after effects in such patients are chronic headaches, irritability, fatigue epilepsy, dizziness and loss of memory, inability to relax, impulsiveness, anxiety, depression, and severe psychotic symptoms. The person finds it greatly difficult in keeping the experiences out of his mind, however he tried, to do it in several ways. It is observed that the post-traumatic stress disorder is very acute and chronic. This disorder is very severe and long lasting if the trauma was caused by human beings, like murder or killing, torture, rape and natural disasters.

Studies reveal that children suffer from post-traumatic stress disorders, but the symptoms are differently exposed from the adults. Children, those who were very sociable previously, become quite withdrawn, lost interest in normal activities and school works. But at the same time children who were quite, became very aggressive and violent.

Minor localised brain injuries may cause various specific neurological and psychological defects. Any damage in the occipital lobe may damage the vision. Any damage in parietal lobe causes sensory problems. Very few persons develop post-traumatic epilepsy due to head injury (Gibson 1959). Personality changes also occur in some cases due to brain injury. Weinstrein (1961) in his studies found some changes in his patients.

The treatments for post-traumatic stress disorder vary depending upon the type of patients. Formely it was stated as war neurosis, but now it is named as post-traumatic anxiety disorder. Lifton (1978) is one who is specialised in post traumatic patients. He specially applied his three principles to Vietnam veterans. The three principles he formulated are immediacy, proximity and expertancy. The soldiers who were exhausted during World war II were treated by Grinker and Spiegal (1945). They used the procedure norcosynthesis for treating the soldiers who were suffering from the post-traumatic stress anxiety disorders.

The post-traumatic stress anxiety disorder was formerly considered as post-traumatic disorder fixing its cause in moderate or severe brain injury. Therefore, the treatment was mainly medical as it was considered as neurological and psychological defect. But if the post-traumatic disorder is due to brain damage the immediate attention is mainly medical treatment. O'Connel (1961) has studied the outcome of the treatment to a large number of patients who had moderate brain injuries. Some of them, according to his study, recovered in a short period. But many of them revealed symptoms of headaches and chronic symptoms of incapacity. In some cases there may be improvement when time passes on. Different factors may also have direct influence on the consequences of the brain damages. Isacson (1970) has observed that the age of the patients also may have varied results in brain injuries. In the stage of childhood period the results of brain damage differ from that of the adulthood. According to him, in the case of brain damage the consequences may vary from different types of neurological disorders to death. Some of the important neuroses are epilepsy and mental retardation.

Dissociative Reaction and Conversion Reaction (Somato form Reaction)

Dissociative reaction or state is a neurotic symptom of dissociation. This signifies that some psychological activities of an individual function independently of his whole personality. It is observed in dual and multiple personality cases. Dissociative reactions refer to a group of neurotic disturbances. In other words, they are also known as a type of neurotic anxiety disorders in which the individual's normal functions like the memory and identity suddenly and temporarily may be altered. According to the earlier definition dissociative reaction or disorder is a psychoneurotic reaction characterised by amnesia, fugue, somnambulism, and multiple personality.

In the earlier studies dissociative reaction was classified as a hysteria or hysterical neurosis. It is a way of avoiding stress. The person generally develops unacceptable behaviour. As result of it he denies his personal responsibilities. But according to the American Psychiatric Association classification, *DSM-III-R* (1987), dissociative reactions (disorders) are put into three major categories of disorders as psychogenic amnesia, psychogenic fugue and multiple personality. The important consequences of these disorders are losing the identity temporarily. There is also depersonalisation disorder in which the person's perception of the self is also altered.

The common characteristics are disturbing memories, thoughts, dissociating himself from the rest of the personality. The person is unable to integrate himself with the rest of the personality.

Amnesia or Psychogenic Amnesia

This is one of the dissociative disorders of the anxiety neuroses. The early and later classifications state the same characteristics in this case. The person at this state is not able to recall any of the past experiences. It is said that some annesia patients have brain damages. The materials lost to the conscious memory can be restored after passing sometimes. It can be also restored in the treatment. According to *DSM-III-R* classification (1987) amnesias are of four types such as localised, selective, continuous and generalised.

But according to the localised psychogenic amnesia the loss of memory is for only a limited period of time. Secondly, the amnesia is only for some selected events of distress. Thirdly, it is continuous from the time of a sudden shocking event to the present time. Or sometimes it may be a total traumatic event extending to the patient's rest of life. The person's behaviour during this time of amensia is not remarkable. Only his memory loss may cause some maladjustment. The person may be wandering aimlessly, and may not be knowing where he/she is going. He/she even forgeting his name, age, unable to recognise his close relatives and friends. But he is able to talk and read. He has with him the talent and the ability to function and also the knowledge he has acquired earlier. The psychogenic amnesia may continue in a person for few days or even for a few years. There upon the amnesia as suddenly disappears as it attacked the person suddenly. The person finds full recovery from it and rarely it reoccurs. In organic brain disorder memory loss is quite common. In organic disorder memory loss takes place slowly and it is not related to stress, and full recovery is very difficult. Further, the symptoms like the emotional disorder prevails in the patient.

Fugue or Psychogenic Fugue

In amnesia state the person goes away from the problem world. He further goes away in order to defend himself. This state is called fugue. Fugue is a defence mechanism by which the person is actually flying from the problem world. The patient leaves the home without the knowledge of others and wanders away for days, weeks and even for years not knowing anything to do. Suddently he finds himself in a strange place. This is the complete function of the amnesia for the period of fugue. Strange (1968) states that fugue literally means 'flight'. It is a neurotic symptom in which the patient with amnesia flees from home and starts a new life elsewhere. Fugue is a dissociative reaction in which the person quits the present life situation and starts a somewhat different way of life in another place. Though he is a patient of amnesia in the past life, his other abilities are not impaired and he appears normal to those who are around him. He may establish a complex social life.

The psychogenic fugue specifically takes place after the person has experienced some severe stress in the family which may be marital quarrels, personal rejection, war neurosis, or some severe natural disasters like famine, epidemic diseases, earthquake, tempest and so on.

Multiple Personality

Multiple personality is one of the dissociative disorders diagnosed by the American Psychiatric Association, *DSM-III-R* (1987). According to Lazarus (1961), multiple personalities are very rare. But this has been brought to light by Thigpen and Cleaklay (1987) through their famous book, *The Three Faces of Eve*. This has aroused public interest, and it was also introduced in motion picture. It is a case of a young woman who plays the role of several personalities. The important characteristic of multiple personality is that one personality is not aware of the other personalities. It is as if several types of personalities have been dissociated from one another and the person is sweetly moving from one personality to another. Each personality has a separate emotional and thought process. Each type is different from another in all respects.

According to *DSM-III-R* diagnosis of multiple personality, each person should have at least two ego states separately and two types of feelings, and emotions and thoughts should function separately independent of each other. One ego state does not have any contact with the other ego state, the first ego state does not have any knowledge of the second ego state or the other ego states. Every personality is wholly integrated in its own type and functions separately. Whatever the number of personalities functioning in an individual, only one personality functions and dominates at a time. Therefore, multiple personality may be defined as a dissociative disorder in which two or more separate personalities are present in the same individual, each one of them with a separate emotion, thought, memories and relationship of its own and behaviour patterns and only one of them may dominate at a given time.

Multiple personality is a most complete type of disorder. It has become a source of inspiration for the classical writers to produce their stories and novels. It has provided rich information for their creative imaginations. Several writers have introduced multiple personality characters in their stories and novels. The multiple personality disorder according to Davison and Neale (1987) begins during the early childhood period and later on. But it is very difficult to diagnose in the childhood period. When the child becomes an adolescent it is diagnosed. It was observed in several studies that multiple personality is chronic and very severe compared to other dissociative disorders. Complete recovery is very rare. It is left incomplete in many of the cases.

Somnambulism

This is another type of dissociative reaction. It is a type of neurotic reaction found in hysterical patients. This may be considered as an alternative or secondary personality. The person not only walks in sleep, but also performs a number of activities which are required for intelligence and adjustments. It is one of the developmental disorders and some children experience periodic or regular sleepwalking. The child, during the second or third hour of his sleep wakes up, goes out and performs some tasks and returns to his bed and in the morning when he gets up from his bed does not remember anything about what he has performed. In sleepwalking, he avoids obstacles, hears spoken words and also reacts to orders.

Conversion Disorder and Somato Form Disorder

Originally conversion disorder or reaction is considered as hysterical neurosis. Coleman (1974) deals with the hysterical neuroses under two categories. The first is conversion hysterical neurosis and the second is the dissociative hysterical neurosis. All those disorders discussed above are dissociative disorders. Conversion disorder formerly was called conversion hysteria with bodily reactions such as loss of sensitivity or paralysis as a symptom neurosis. Hysteria is an older term ordinarily used to indicate conversion and dissociative neurotic illnesses, involving the symptoms of organic illness without any related organic pathology. But hysterical neurosis is a disorder, characterised by involutionary psychogenic loss of motor or sensory functions. Hysteria is a Greek word which means uterus. It is used to indicate the disturbance of the uterus. It is a psychiatric condition characterised by excitability, anxiety and stimulation of organic disorder. It may also result in the outbreak of wild and uncontrolled feeling. It is restricted to women and thus it is caused by sexual difficulties. Hysteria thus is the result of intense emotional breakdown or fustration of strong sexual desire. When the strong sex motive is not achieved at the expected time, the person is subjected to an attack of hysteria.

Sigmund Freud was treating mainly the hysterical patients. On finding the different types of functioning in hysteria he reinterpreted the term hysteria as conversion hysteria. The hysterical symptoms were the expressions of repressed strong sexual energies, which are psychosexual conflict in nature, turned to or converted into bodily illnesses. Fomerly, conversion hysteria was said to be women's disorder. But Freud demonstrated this also in men. Therefore, both men and women may be subjected to attacks of hysteria. When the extreme sexual desire which is anxiously expected for a long period fails to satisfy due to sudden unexpected circumstances the person receives a strong emotional shock which results in nervous breakdown that is characterised by convolutional disorder. This may become chronic and the person gets the attacks whenever he faces similar instances, which may be stated as 'hysterical fits'. The hysterical fits may be caused in both men and women.

Conversion hysteria is a symbolic expression of a prevented sexual desire. It may manifest in paralysis as a punishment which is a disguised aggressive impulse. Conversion hysteria generally develops in adolescent period or in early adulthood. Conversion hysteria or disorder and somato form disorders are called Briquet's Syndrome. Somato form disorders, according to *DSM-III-R* (1987) diagnoses are in *three forms*. In the *somato form pain disorder*, the person may be having the pain which may not be having any organic symptom, however it is investigated. The person's pain has temporal contact with conflict or stress. The person may avoid activity which he dislikes to get the sympathy of others. Another somato form disorder is body *dysmorphic disorder.* In this, the individual is very much engaged in imagined defeats in experience. The third somato form disorder is the *hypochondriasis* in which the individual is in the state of fears of having incurable diseases. The person exaggerates everything related to him, mainly physical ailments and some abnormalities.

The psychoanalytic theory studied the conversion hysteria or disorder and the somato-form disorders. Studies of this theory have been towards hysteria and assume that conversion disorder, somatisation disorder were found to be similar in origin. Breuer and Freud (1895) have stated in their studies that conversion disorder is caused by severe emotional shock. But the effect is not expressed as the memory function is cut off and the conscious memory has no knowledge about it. Experimental studies have been made by some contemporary psycho analysts like Sackeim, Nordlie, and Gur (1978). They tried to give psychodynamic interpretation to one conversion disorder, specifically hysterical blindness. The hysterically blind persons were given visual tests. They said that they were influenced by some stimuli. But the persons totally denied of seeing anything. In the studies made by Grosz and Zimmerman (1970) among the hysterically blind persons different type of results were obtained. There was almost perfect visual performance by an adolescent girl patient.

Treatment to conversion disorder or somato form disorder has a long history right from the time of Freud. Psychoanalytic approach has been made by several psycho analysts like Ochitel (1982) who was able to reduce the hysterical disabling problems in patients though it was not very much successful to deal with conversion disorder. Behaviour therapists observed that several anxiety disorders are associated with somatisation disorder and connected to some incident or to the patient's life situation. Arkonic and Guze (1963) treated a woman who was extremely anxious about her uncertain and unhappy marriage and about the situations in which she was subjected to the talk of the people. Therapies like systematic desensitisation and other therapies were administered to the patient which the therapists believed that would reduce the patient's fears and help the patient to reduce the somatic complaints. As the results were not to the expected level, they resorted to the assertion training and social skill training, and coaching the patient in more effective ways, and made the patient to approach and talk to the people, make compliments and accept criticisms. In these ways behaviour therapists made use of extensive techniques to deal with somatisation disorders.

CHAPTER 4

Neurasthenia and Hypochondriasis

What is Neurasthenia?

Neurasthenia is a neurotic disorder characterised by complaints of chronic weakness, frequent cases of fatigue and lack of interest in life. It is also stated that neurasthenia is marked by constant mental and physical fatigue, and the patient suffers from various types of aches and pains. Neurasthenia means weak nerves. This is a derived meaning. Generally the term neurasthenia indicates abnormal weakness and fatigue, numerous pains and aches. This has been viewed by many psychologists as anxiety neurosis. According to Lazarus (1965) all the neuroses or psychoneuroses are caused by severe physical and mental strains or stresses. Beard (1905), an early American psychiatrist, was the first to use this neurasthenia to the general weakness of the nervous system, and stated that the condition was the result of prolonged conflict and overwork. This state exhausted the nerve cells of the essential biochemical parts and it resulted in applying the 'Weir Nitchell method' of treatment for the nervous exhaustion. This treatment involved complete rest and relaxation for a long period.

Neurasthenic patients seldom reveal their condition of over-work and also never corrected their condition by prolonged rest. Therefore, we may state that neurasthenia is a neurotic disorder caused by prolonged conflict and mental and physical overwork without any break or sufficient rest which result in the exhaustion of the nerve cells of essential biochemical substances. This state causes to the person severe chronic mental and physical fatigue, abnormal weakness, numerous pains and aches and various other illnesses.

Dynamics

But nowadays neurasthenia is viewed from a different angle. It is viewed that neurasthenia is mostly a psychological disorder and not so much physical in nature. It is stated that physical fatigue reaction does not cause so much of fatigue syndromes. It is rooted in prolonged conflict, frustration, deprivation of confidence and hopelessness. This state leads to loss of motivation, listlessness and fatigue. These are the results obtained by Cattell and Scheler (1961) and Guilford (1959) in their studies. They have further observed in their studies that there were continued motivational conflicts, hostility against his mate and development of guilt feelings for giving up totally the nurtured goals. It is also true that human beings are tired and listless when they are continuously discouraged and forced to do the work which is not liked by them.

Man generally feels and experiences listlessness and fatigue when he is involved in a job or work which is dull and dejected. In the neureasthenic state these reactions are very much elaborated as chronic fatigue reactions are in the same manner found in emotional adjustments. Generally chronic anxiety may disturb sleep and over-activity of the neurasthenic patient and, finally, it may lead to the damage of bodily resources.

Modern psychologists and psychiatrists made a classification of all behaviour disorders (mental illness) under two categories as anxiety disorders and psychological disorders. According to this, all neuroses are caused by different levels of anxiety disorders and all other mental illnesses including psychoses are caused by psychological disorders. The emotional disorders and the mental and physical stresses are the causes of mental illnesses. The recent classification *DSM-II* at one stage, has dropped the neuroses or neurotic disorders from the classification. But it is restored in *DSM-III-R* classification. Though neurasthenic is considered to be one of the important neurotic disorders it was dropped out, and finally it was restored. The symptoms are such that it cannot be avoided from understanding the causes and functions of the neurotic disorders.

Neurasthenia is a term used very earlier by Beard (1905) to explain its symptoms, nature and consequences. This was described by him from practical point of view. Though it is considered as an old term the symptoms, functions and the consequences cannot be attributed to any other term. Neurasthenia means 'weak nerves'. Therefore, anything related to weak nerves and its consequences may be stated only in terms as neurasthenia. This appears to be the most suitable term to explain all these aspects discussed above.

Symptoms

Neurasthenia a neurotic disorder characterised by chronic weakness, fatigue and lack of interest. Neurasthenia patients often complain of headaches, insomania, irritability, tiredness and pain in the back and so on. They often suffer from indigestion and constipation. The persons in addition to the physical ailments suffer from anxiety attacks. They may also suffer from some kind of stomach troubles. The neurasthenic patients like the hypochondriac patients take strong precautions for preserving their health. They often worry much about their health problems. Some psychologists are of the view that neurasthenia is a general psychoneutic symptoms. Freud later on began to revise his theory and introduced a new concept, psychodynamics. According to this new idea neurasthenia and hypochondriasis are said to be the real neuroses or psychoneuroses. It is because neurasthenia has direct contact with bodily ailments which is more sexual in nature.

Therefore, these two disorders, neurasthenia and hypochondriasis are often discussed and dealt with together to explain the patients' sufferings and the physical symptoms.

Just like other neurotic disorders, neurasthenic symptoms may have some important second gains. Coleman (1974) states that these patients create situations by their sufferings, to arouse the feelings of pity and sympathy in others and make them take care of these patients. They may even go to the extent of controlling the behaviour of others so as to make them pay attention to them aggressively. Just like any sick person in the family who commands more attention from the family members, the neurasthenic patient also gets the psychological benefits from these symptoms. Coleman (1975) calls this as the neurasthenic sincerity. This means that the patient makes use of these symptoms for his benefit without knowing the real functions of the illnesses.

The neurasthenic patient cannot get the benefits for a very long period. Finally, the relatives and friends reduce their attention and interest. The patient's listlessness, morbid outlook, self-centred attitude, continued complaints do not elicit the same happy relationships. All the symptoms which elicited sympathy and service do not hold the same level of function. This state results in the deterioration in the interpersonal relationships and causes damage to them.

In all the behaviour disorders culture plays an important role. In primitive culture or underdeveloped society behavioural disorders are not so much troublesome. But in a civilised society it is important that we must understand the origin and development of neurasthenic disorder patterns, because the culture puts a heavy pressure on the individuals with more responsibilities. Mentally healthy persons are able to cope with the conditions to make proper adjustments with society. But persons of weak nerves with their chronic feeling of fatigue are unable to cope with the situation and suffer severely.

Generally, the neurasthenic person lacks confidence in himself and is always more dependent on others for every thing. He feels unfit to face the situation, loses all hopes and feels severely frustrated. He feels so tired that he cannot face the problems which are very essential for him. Thus, he tries to escape from the world of responsibilities. If the person is stimulated he can exert his normal physical strength, but he does not exert habitually. He can concentrate his attention on persuasion, but he does not do it normally. His work motives are weak, he is listless, indifferent to directions. There is loss of power of concentration, loss of sleep, lack of refreshment and he never feels fresh after sleep. Apart from the chronic fatigue and tiredness, the neurasthenic patient suffers from constant headaches, backaches hip pains and complaints of several bodily ailments, stiffness, or heaviness of the neck, indigestion, lack of appetite, dizziness and hypersensitisation to irritations. These symptoms and complaints make him avoid the task which he does not want to do.

Neurasthenia and Asthenia

Neurasthenia has the same reactions as asthenic reactions. It is a neurotic disorder indicated by the feelings of general fatigue and weakness. Strange (1965) states that the term asthenic reaction is more commonly used in place of neurasthenia. Asthenic reaction is the symptom which indicates the disorder of neurasthenia. According to Kretsachmer (1925) asthenia may be defined as a type of personality disorder characterised by low energy level, quick fatigue and lack of enthusiasm. The symptoms attributed to asthenic type of personality are carried out to asthenic reaction and treated as a term equivalent to neurasthenia by Strange and some psychologists. Formerly, neurasthenia was associated with strong sexual abuses. But now it is differently stated. Some psychologists call neurasthenia symptoms as the general indication of psychoneurotic personality.

The neo-Freudians like Sullivan (1953) dropped this term neurasthenia in his writings. In place of it some present-day psychologists use the term asthenic reactions. Asthenic reaction is a personality disorder characterised by low energy level in the body, early fatigue and lack of enthusiasm. In the patient there is physical and emotional strain and notable incapacity to enjoy life. He often feels self-pity. The symptoms are also marked by mental and physical fatigue and various kinds of aches and pains. According to Coleman (1974), though there is some disagreement with regard to the occurrence of this disorder, approximately about 10 per cent of the patients are all neurotics. The neurasthenic form of neuroses are also found to be common among the young adults, specifically among the frustrated women in family life, whose husbands have neglected them.

The individual who is suffering from asthenic disorder sleeps for a very little time. Though the patient feels fatigued, he looks more energetic and also face could endurance. But in the family situation, occupation and in other routine works he is found to be listless, feels tired and shows less interest in life. Asthenia is considered more as a psychological fatigue rather than physical fatigue.

The asthenic patient often complaints of being tired all the time and extremely fatigued. From morning till he goes to bed he states that he has headaches and backaches. But at the same time the hypochondriac patient does not take any medicines and does not want any medical treatment. His complaint of fatigue becomes an excuse to get rid of any responsibility and tasks that are assigned to him. These symptoms in a person do not always appear. The manifestation of the symptoms in him depend upon time and situation.

The causative factors for neurasthenia, asthenia, and for hypochondria are rooted in the childhood period of the individual. These factors are common to both the disorders. The parents of these children often worry over them – that they are having a severe cold or something else, and they must be given some treatment. The parents mostly worry over their health. All these health factors that the parents observe and complain become the causative factors for the development of neurasthenia, asthenia and hypochondriasis in the later life of the children. Strange (1965) states that this state of affair becomes the basic neurotic anxiety and the symptoms are the same as in other types of neuroses.

All those symptoms that we have discussed above for neurasthenia are also attributed to asthenia by some psychologists. But actually asthenia reactions are not stated in the latest American

Psychiatric Association classifications (1968-1987). Strange (1965) and others state that these two terms are old and they should be dropped from usage. In the *DSM-III-R* classifications the terms neurasthenia and hypochondriasis are given place and not asthenia. Therefore, it is not fair to omit these two important anxiety disorders in our discussion. Asthenia is a term used by Kretschemer (1925, 1926) in his personality types. According to him, thin and angular types of persons are stated to be the asthenic type. Angular means thin, sharp, cornered. In Shakespeare's play *Julius Caesar*, Cassius was one of the Generals of Caesar, whom Caesar described as : "lean and hungry look, he thinks too much; such men are dangerous" (Act-1, Scene-II). Kretschemer derived the idea from this passage that physique has an influencing effect on personality and mental illness. He has elaborated this theory and evolved the types of personality on the basis of body built. Accordingly, a round and fat person is called pyknic type, the muscular person is called athletic type and the thin and angular person is called asthenic type. Kretschemer has stated that pyknic type persons are good natured and relaxed. The athletic types are forceful and energetic, while the asthenics are more interested in their own feelings. The pyknic is more likely to become manic depressive, while the asthenic has more chances of becoming a schizophrenic patient. Kretschemer not only describes normality in his types, but also says about the likelihood of abnormalities in his types. Among the types only 'asthenia' is more discussed by some psychologists as one of the psychoneurotic or anxiety disorders. Kretschemer has associated the abnormal characteristics of asthenia with schizophrenia and not with any type of neurotic disorder or with psychoneuroses. But some psychologists like Strange (1965) associate the asthenia abnormal characteristics with psychoneurotic disorders or anxiety disorders.

Earlier psychologists like Coleman (1974) mentioned about asthenia in their writings while discussing about antisocial or psychopathic personality characteristics. According to him, in the asthenia personality pattern, the individual reveals a mild version of neurasthenia with low energy level, quick fatigue, lack of enthusiasm, oversensitivity to physical and environmental strain and a marked incapacity to enjoy life. He often feels self-pity and gets the sympathy of others. Brazek and Grande (1960) have observed the change of behaviour under natural starvation. These scientists observed the prisoners of war in semi-starvation in concentration camps during the

Second World War. These prisoners were also suffering from nutritional deficiencies. As a result of these there were cases of physical neurological and physical changes. This means that asthenic syndrome was developed due to semi-starvation and nutritional deficiencies and not due to the type of body built.

Treatment

The treatment for neurasthenia is somewhat difficult as there are patients who suffer from psychoneurotic disorders having the same symptoms as those of neurasthnic and hypochondriac patients. It was also observed that in many neurasthenic patients these symptoms appeared along with other symptoms. The symptoms that manifest in neurasthenic patients sometimes conceal the real symptoms of neurasthenic disorder. These symptoms of neurasthenics appear with other neurotic symptoms and also with other forms of psychoses, like schizophrenia and paranoid. The schizophrenic symptoms appear like the symptoms of hypochondriasis. This was the reason that Kretschmer (1925-1926) while, discussing about the body types and mental illness, said that the asthenic type of person is more likely to develop schizophrenic disorder.

Since the symptoms of psychoneuroses are overlapping and the symptoms of psychoses also appear, in some neuroses like neurasthenia or hypochondriasis, a neurotic disorder may look like a psychosis and a psychosis may look like a neurosis. Therefore, the treatment must be made on the basis of causes and effects of the disorders and not on the basis of symptoms alone. Due to these reasons the treatment that can be successfully performed is the psychotherapy supplemented by drug administration. Tranquilizers are found to be more effective with psychotherapy.

The psychotherapist, while administering the tranquillisers is expected to be more careful. The patient should not get an impression that the treatment with the tranquilliser is going to do wonders. The patient must understand and accept that it is only a first treatment. Every anxiety neurosis or neurasthenic disorder is mainly based upon emotional adjustment. The patient is expected to relearn emotionally. He must have the willingness to make improvement in his emotional maladjustment and life problems. Further, there must be a change in his interpersonal relationship in the family and with other people. The therapist, in treating the neurasthenic patient, makes him capable of seeing and understanding clearly the inner nature of things or problems. The nature of personality of the individual is very much helpful in curing the disease. Therefore, it is important to predict the course or outcome of the disorder and also the healthy nature of the personality. If the personality is strong, then the outcome would be good and the patient may get rid of the disorder, but if the nature of personality is weak, then it would be very difficult to rescue the patient from the disorder.

Finally, we may state that neurasthenia is a psychoneurotic disorder mainly characterised by abnormal weakness, fatigue and an extreme amount of energy drainage and loss of vigour. Any amount of rest will not cause refreshment. The prolonged conflict and overwork causes nervous exhaustion which may require a long period of complete rest, a strong tonic and nutritious food, a change to some pleasant environmental condition. Some are of the view that it is due to some unresolved sexual problems.

Hypochondriasis

What is hypochondriasis?

Hypochondriasis is a psychoneurosis. Formerly it was considered as pure neurosis. Later on, when Freud introduced the term psycho dynamics, hypochondriasis and neurasthenia were interpreted as psychoneuroses. In the preceding section we have discussed about neurasthenia. The neurasthenia patients generally suffer from physical complaints. Patients with the symptoms of fatigue and other related symptoms are classified as neurasthenics. They often complain of headaches, insomnia, irritability and numerous pains and aches in the back and other parts of the body. They also suffer from indigestion and constipation, which are attributed to severe fatigue. These patients in addition to the above-stated sufferings also suffer from 'anxiety attacks'. These patients are called hypochondriacs.

The hypochandriac patients constantly worry over their health and take most elaborate precautions for maintaining their health. Since the patient mostly suffers from anxiety attacks, hypochondriasis is stated as a neurotic anxiety disorder with physical problems. Neurasthenic is believed to have a direct bad effect on body, having hatred for sexual energy. The person develops a guilt feeling because of his indulgence in masturbation which results in the development of neurosthenic reaction. Similarly, hypochondriasis is believed to be the result of over-masturbation and extreme hatred for sexual contact. Therefore, these two anxiety neurotic disorders have several similarities. Based upon these similarities of symptoms, some of the modern psychologists like Strange (1965) and others are inclined to amalgamate both these anxiety disorders into one category, which may be called a hypochondriacal reaction or hypochondriacal anxiety disorder. Therefore, it is neurasthenia that leads to the development of hypochondriasis. Hypochondriacal anxiety disorder may be defined as a chronic abnormal anxiety state concerning the state of one's health, even in the absence of any evidence of disease on medical examination.

Dynamics

Human beings are generally interested in maintaining their bodily functions. For any individual health is wealth. Therefore, everyone is interested in the state of his health. The hypochondriac shows extreme interest in his health. He exaggerates his illness state. By this means, he tries to escape from certain responsibilities or difficult stresses and gains various types of interpersonal relations. Hypochondriacal disorders have their origin in the early years of life of an individual. The childhood experiences of an individual have predisposing effect in an individual for the development of hypochondriasis in his later life.

To some extent the parents are responsible for the development of hypochondriacal disorders in their children when they become adults. Over-protection, too much of pampering or overindulgence of the parents on their children make the children to pay more attention and care on their health, all these predispose the children for becoming hypochondriacs later on. These types of children are likely to succumb to hypochondriac attacks in the early adult stage.

Another factor that contributes to children's hypochondriac disorders is the parents' extreme concern over their health. The parents worry over the child's small symptoms like crying sneezing, eating habits, indigestion and other minor symptoms and the child also sets too much of attachments to all these manifestations.

The individual who was in his parent's care all through the childhood period and early adolescent period is likely to be predisposed to the hypochondriacal disorders in his later years, mostly in his forties or fifties. He is very much concerned about his marital life, which is not happy, his occupational status is not very bright, his cherished goals are not achieved and he feels that he has failed in his life in fulfilling all his needs. He has reached a stage of severe development of hypochondriacal disorder and other neurotic disorders.

The hypochondriac is able to draw by his sufferings the attention of other persons and also arouse their sympathy and escape from the demands assigned to him. He is able to get rid of the unhappy life situation and enjoys the help and support from the persons from whom it is expected. Thereby he is able to exercise some amount of control over them and gains their goodwill and service. In this way he feels that his demands and grievances are protected. He feels that he does not require to strive towards the difficult and painful goals or achievements. He no longer requires to accept any difficult and unachievable demands. The stressful life situation puts him in the anxiety disorder state. This includes his breakdown to achieve his important goals.

The hypochondriac pays increased attention to himself and his pains and gets some help from others. Since he suffers from severe illness others help him in various forms more and more. He often skilfully manipulates his symptoms in a planned manner, controls the behaviour of other people around him for his purpose. If some programme is planned in which he is also included and some activity is assigned to him he tries to escape from it. But, when he is not interested to take part in it, there are some severe symptoms very much intensified which appear in him. This state of affair puts some pressure on others to suspend the programme. But this does not help him solve his problems. Actually all his symptoms do not help him to escape from responsibilities. Instead, they aggravate his problem. This type of neurotic behaviour becomes a self-defeating device for him.

Symptoms

Hypochondriasis is a neurotic anxiety disorder with physical problems. It involves a person's body functioning and also several presumed bodily diseases. The major physical ailments are foot pains, back pain, poor digestion and constipation. There may also be some hard breathing and severe cold attacks often. The individual in a hypochondriacal disorder state is always thinking about his health and the ways and means of preserving his body and organs from disorders. According to Coleman (1974) the hypochondriacal neurotic disorders are rare in a population. The occurrence may be only about five per cent.

The other major symptoms of hypochondriacal disorders are fatigue, tiredness and stomach problems. These patients often complain of very uncomfortable sensations, mainly in the stomach, chest, head and in the genital areas. Further, they also complain often that they are in poor health and sometimes feel miserable in their state of sickness. They are often concerned about their hypertension. When their neurotic anxiety disorder is intensified they become panic-striken and develop a fear of death. When they are taken to a famous physician for treatment they get only temporary relief. Hypochondriacal disorders are common mostly among the elderly persons of over sixty years. Kenyon (1966) in his study has observed that hypochondriac anxiety disorders commonly occur only during the period of adulthood and especially occur more among the women than men.

The hypochondriacs have excessive concern over their health. This is one of the aspects of general abnormality in them. Their very general complaints are weakness of lungs, weakness of heart, muscles, disorders in stomach, pain in the head, and trouble in the throat, and they have no clear idea about their sensations. In describing their ailments they often confuse the sensations of pain, pressure, heat and cold. These patients often look out for some new ailments and symptoms, so that they can escape from the pressures of situations of society. They also read medical magazines and find out some new diseases described in rhyme. On reading them these patients claim that they are sufficing from all these diseases. They are always in a state of anxiety to recover from the disease they are suffering from, and out of this anxiety they take all types of medicines and diets for rebuilding their physical health.

Recent Studies

Busse and Blazer (1979) have observed in their studies that there were about 20 per cent of elderly persons suffering from this disorder in communities. This is a recent study which varies from the results of Coleman's and Kenyon's studies. According to Busse and Blazer this disorder is very much prevalent among the people who are between sixty and sixty-five years of age. In a very recent study made by Siegler and Costa (1985) it was observed that the probation of cases were not greater among the elderly persons as it was stated earlier. Actually the health problems increase with the increase of age. It is because of this that the hypochondriacal disorder cases appeared to be greater. All the health problems in elderly persons need not be attributed to hypochondriasis.

In another study Costa et al (1987) have confirmed the results of the earlier study that people do not become more hypochondriacal as they become older. Siegler and Costa (1985) state that older people who have already several physical complaints might have developed long-standing personality traits which resulted in predicting that they have the hypochondriacal disorders. They are also of the view that excessive physical complaints seem to be related to maladjustment or neurotic disorders. This has nothing to do with age.

In a recent study by Rapier et al (1988) it was observed that there was only one per cent of older persons who had somatisation disorder or hypochondriasis. This percentage rate is the same rate as it is in the younger age groups. This study supports the results of the earlier study made by Meyer et al (1984). Hypochodriasis is an advanced state of neurasthenia. Except for a few symptoms most of the symptoms are common to both the disorders of neurasthenia and hypochandriasis.

Hypochondriasis and Somatisation Disorders

Hypochondriasis is stated as somatisation disorder by the presents day psychologists, following the *DSM-III-R* classification. The *DSM-III-R* has brought out a distinction between hypochondriacs and somatisation disorder. The hypochandriac's thoughts are fully occupied with the fear of having a serious specific physical disease. In the case of somatisation disorder the patient is concerned with many symptoms with himself. But this distinction appears to be not clear. A long range of symptoms were reported by the people who were examined by Banquet, Parley and Guze (1962). They have observed and listed the symptoms which Banquet has collected from a group of patients. Banquet was a French physician. In 1859 he had noticed the syndromes and described them and they were named after him as Banquet Syndromes. This is stated in the APA classification, *DSM-III-R* as somatisation disorder. The term somatisation is derived from the Greek word 'somatic' which means body or physical. The disorder occurs in bodily parts. According to the somatisation theory there are repeated multiple physical complaints from the patients. On medial examination it is found that there is no observable physical cause.

The patients', common complaints are fatigue, headaches, allergies, abdominal disorder, back pain and chest pain, genitourinary symptoms, palpitation and quite a number of symptoms. The person also feels the conversion symptoms. Several physicians often visited the patients as in the cases of treating the patients with medicine. Guze (1967) states that admitting the patients in the hospitals and surgical operations are also common. Among these somatisation patients there were some who often show sexual indifferences. Swartz et al (1986) in their studies have observed all these phenomena. The patients give dramatic and exaggerated version about their ailments which creates an impression that they have been suffering from these ailments throughout their lives without proper treatments. Robin et al (1984) state that one per cent of the somatisation disorders were prevailing in the US all the time.

Somatisation disorders as referred by the *DMS-III-R* classification may be stated as the disorders in which the physical symptoms imply physical problems, but there are no known physiological causes in them and hence it is believed that the disorders have connection with psychological anxieties and conflicts. It cannot be taken on one's own choice as the consequences are Briquet's syndromes (somatisation), conversion disorder pain disorder and hypochondriasis. Somatization disorders according to the studies by Kroll, Chamberlain and Halpern (1979), Coloninger et al (1986) start in late the adolescent period and it is more common in women than in men. Further, somatisation disorders are heriditary and according to Arconac and Guze (1963) the estimated cases are twenty per cent of the first-line relatives.

The person in the hypochondriacal disorder is preoccupied with anxieties and from that he suffers from serious disorders. The person overestimates all the ordinary physical feelings and sensations. All the minor abnormalities are mistaken for serious ailments. Some of the minor symptoms he experiences are stomachache, irregular heart beat, sweating and coughing. But these reported complaints cannot be medically diagnosed and treated, though somatisation disorder is similar to hypochondriasis disorder. On observing the similar symptoms in both, a clearcut difference between these two is not yet made.

Some psychologists use the term somatisation disorder in place of hypochondriacal disorder stating that it is an old term. Just like the term asthenia is used in place of the term neurasthenia the term somatisation is used in place of the term hypochondriasis. Though the terms are changed, the symptoms and dynamics of these disorders are the same. Recent psychologists use the term somatisation disorders in a broader sense involving into it quite a number of disorders. The intention is that hypochondriacal disorders are one of the disorders included in somatisation disorders. We are discussing here hypochondriacal disorder as an independent process of disorder relating it to the somatisation disorder.

Treatment

The treatment for hypochondriasis clinically is not very much satisfactory. Assuring the patient that he is healthy mentally and physically does not work very well. These patients are not convinced by the assurances. The negative laboratory tests and authoritative pronouncements are not accepted by the patients. It was observed that ignoring the physical complaints and paying more attention to positive aspects of the prevailing incidents may be helpful.

Goldstein and Birasbom (1976) state that making the person to involve himself in some activity like walking and playing may yield some positive results. The person must be made to forget or ignore his ailments. He must be made to move and act without giving any chance for his preconceived ideas, that he is tired, weak and so on. He must be motivated in such a way that he must show interest in accepting the idea and act accordingly. "Let us go and watch and enjoy the wonderful and exciting World Football Match. There is a spectacular circus where wild animals do wonders." In these ways the person may be motivated to move and he must be kept in sustained activities every day for a few hours. This type of therapeutic techniques were found to be somewhat successful in treating the hypochondriacal patients.

But Strange (1965) has stated that psychotherapy combined with tranquillisers is found to be more effective for treating the hypochondriacal cases. Psychotherapy is the main treatment and the patient must believe in it and accept it. The tranquilliser is the best curing pill which is not an easily available medicine. Therefore, the treatment is in the process of emotional relearning, which involves the patient's insight into his problems, a desire to improve his health and adjustment problems.

While neurasthenic is mainly characterised by extreme weakness, fatigue and tired and symptoms centred on 'weak nerves, hypochondriac concentrates on his health conditions. The patient is extremely worried about his bodily parts. The symptoms are more common among the patients who are above forty or fifty years of age and the symptoms are more common among women than in men. Hypochondrics are not easily amenable for treatments of any type. These patients exaggerate their problems and do not cooperate with the psychiatrists. They go on according to the symptoms they find in them and what they understand about their illness by reading about them in books and medical magazines, and want the physicians to act according to their demands. They want to take more medicines which they believe alone can cure their illness. It is only by suitable psychotherapeutic techniques that the patient can be convinced and guided for treatment. Tranquillizers and therapeutic technique alone bring them to normal.

CHAPTER 5

Psychosis

What is Psychosis?

Psychosis refers to any form of severe mental disorder in which the individual's contact with the world of reality becomes highly distorted. It is an abnormal state deviating from the normal state. The branch of psychology that studies this behaviour patterns that diverse widely from the generally accepted norms of behaviour, especially those of a pathological nature, their dynamic nature, symptoms, their classification, their treatment, and their theories that explain them with special reference to the experimental results is called abnormal psychology. There are several terms used in abnormal psychology to indicate the abnormal or highly disordered state of behaviour. They are mainly mental illness, mental disease, mental disorder, madness, insanity, mentally deviant behaviour disorder, behaviourally deviant and so on.

The studies and discussions on mental disorders were going on for a very long period in different names and the treatments for the disorders also were debated, and different views were expressed. But the correct classification on the basis of diagnoses of the various types of nervous and mental disorders were made only in the second quarter of the twentieth century. Psychoses were classified as one of the severe forms of mental disorders and they were differentiated from other forms of disorders like neuroses or psychoneuroses.

Therefore, we may state that psychosis (plural form psychoses) is a major or severe mental illness or disorder characterised by loss of touch with the world of reality with the symptoms of depression, delusions and hallucinations. These psychoses are either functional psychoses (learned) or organic (brain damage) psychoses.

There are different views expressed by psychologists with regard to the nature and functions of psychosis. One of the strong views is that it is organic in nature. It is rooted in the brain and the brain is damaged. Psychosis is often characterised by loss of contact with the world of reality and the psychotic patient often finds symptoms of delusions and hallucinations. Psychoses are either functional (learned) or organic or brain damage. It may also be emotional in origin in the psychotic state for the person's ability to think, remember, communicate, interpret reality, respond emotionally and behave appropriately are all impaired, and he fails to meet the ordinary demands of life. Applicable conditions have a wide range of severity and the duration may be very long. This state may be severe depression and schizophrenia.

Psychosis may be also defined as the major mental illness in which the person reveals severe damage or disorganisation of personality often characterised by depression, agitation, delusions, hallucinations, and the normal social function is very much impaired and the person generally requires hospitalisation. Psychoses are mainly classified as functional psychoses and organic psychoses. The psychotic patient is more severally disturbed than the neurotic patient. Some experts are of the view that it is from normality that continuity takes place through neurosis to a severe form of psychosis. The difference among the stages is a matter of severity in the nature of disturbance. Hilgard et al (1975) state that psychoses are different from neuroses physiologically, having physiological changes in the nervous system and are having genetic background.

The functional psychoses are made into two main groups. The first group of the functional psychoses are affective psychoses which are also known as manic depressive psychoses and involutional psychoses. These psychoses are described as having abnormality of fluctutations of mood and emotion. The manic depressive psychosis is called affective psychosis, because the symptoms of normal emotional responses are aggravated. The second group of functional psychoses consists of paranoid psychoses and also stated as paranoia and paranoid state. The term paranoia is a Greek word which means mental disorder characterised by delusions. These two groups of functional psychoses are other than schizophrenia and usually these are dealt with separately, even though schizophrenia is also a functional psychosis. The incidents of these functional psychoses are not so much as schizophrenia. The schizophrenic incidents are always higher.

Manic Depressive Psychosis

The manic depressive psychosis has a long history. It is a behaviour disorder and the ancient Greek physician, Hippocrates (460-657 B.

C.), with a view to understanding the abnormal behaviour, had set up a medical practice. This practice went through several steps of progress and finally Kraepelin (1855-1926) (1962), a German, was able to throw much light upon it. It was he who described this behaviour disorder and named it as manic depressive psychosis. It is a functional psychosis as it is rooted in emotional maladjustment. The manic depressive psychotic patient is found to be abnormally elated and almost always an emotionally active respondent. But the depressive patient is very much in deep sadness, often revealing significant retardation of activity and movements. The patients in both cases are extremely carried away by their symptoms of abnormal functions and the level of normal functioning becomes impossible.

The manic depressive psychosis may be exhibited in individuals differently. In some, the manic reaction is revealed, in some the depressive reaction is revealed. But in some patients both types of reactions are alternatively exhibited. In some there may also be the combination of both the reactions. The manic depressive psychosis on the basis of these functions is differentiated in the various types. They are the manic reaction type, depressive reaction type, and circular or mixed type of reaction. This distinction into three types is according to Coleman (1974). But Strange (1965) makes both the manic reaction and depressive reaction into four types. They are simple or subacute depression, acute depression, stuporous or hyperacute depression and agitated depression. Coleman makes each into three types as simple depression, acute depression and depressive stupor.

Manic Depressions

1. Simple Depression

In this state a mild feeling of melancholia is observed. There may also be a certain amount of retardation. These states may also show certain neurotic symptoms. This causes some confusion that it may be a neurotic depression. In this state the symptoms that are common in manic depressive repressive reaction such as delusions and hallucinations are not observed. The person with simple depression suffers most part of his time with painful thoughts as to how things have gone so wrong. Thus he develops terrible feelings.

2. Acute Depression

This is the severe form develops from simple depression. In this state the patient exhibits intense hatred and aggression. These are turned towards himself. He blames himself. He may be having delusions and hallucinations for a short period. He becomes irritable and restless and talks very loudly. His motor activities are very rapid. His facial expressions are often changing. His abilities for judgement and thinking are impaired. The delusions in him sometimes may form in such as way that they are based upon the moods which may be similar to paranoid depression.

3. Hyperacute Depression

The symptoms of hyperacute depression are mainly melancholia and retardation. These states are overacted and the patient becomes inactive. The patient is very much excited and also violent. He is very much confused about his states and he has no understanding about the environment in which he lives. He speaks everything inconsistently. He is so restless that he will not be having sound sleep or rest. His bodily functions are so heavy that he may have all kinds of diseases. His loss of sensibility may be such that he may attempt to commit suicide.

4. Agitated Type of Depression

In this state of depression the patient may have almost the same type of symptoms as hyperacute depression. The severity in both types does not vary much. There is a severe feeling of sadness and mood of perversion like melancholia. The patient may be expressing his feelings in an undesirable manner. His thoughts are on his death. His impulses are very violent that he may even commit suicide.

Manic Reactions

Let us discuss the manic reaction which is considered to be the other side of depressive reaction. These reactions are characterised by a mood of abnormal type with a reaction of elation. The manic patient is forced by his impulses to move constantly and vigorously protest anything that makes him follow some instructions. His speech is centred only on happiness. He lives in a world of 'a happy flight of ideas'. This means, that one idea follows another rapidly, making strong connections. The continuity and the connections of his speech depend upon the type of attack into which he has fallen.

A patient with a mild attack of hypomanic is not very much disturbed by the manic reaction. He may perform a good amount of useful things. But the delirious manic patient is very inconsistent in his speech and action. Sometimes, the patient may become irritable and outrageous. He very often gets into a happy mood and makes foolish jokes madly in words and deeds. He is very much sensitive to his environment, but he cannot act effectively. He will not carry out his activities of eating and sleeping unless he is forced. He utterly lacks the personal care as a result of which he is likely to run down physically and subjected to some infectious discuses.

The manic reaction phases are of four types: hypomania or sub-acute mania, acute mania, hyperacute or delirious mania, and manic stupor.

1. Sub-acute Mania (or Hypomania)

The sub-acute mania has so normal-like symptoms that it is not easily identified as abnormal. This means that almost all normal people have fluctuations in moods and temperament, from a feeling of sadness to a feeling of happiness and elation. But these states of feelings of sadness and happiness are not to the degree of manic state. Sometimes it is very difficult to identify the manic patient as he is only one step different from the normal. Only by careful observation of the patient can the hypomanic be identified. The pathological characteristics of the hypomanic patient are understood only from his movements and acts. He mostly neglects his duties and responsibilities. He may be having a touch with reality, but his moods and emotions are more important for him than his duties. The demands of reality are only secondary for him. He speaks rapidly and loudly to express his manic state. But he is a poor judge of his insight and things.

2. Acute Mania

Acute mania is an exaggerated state of hypomania state. All the symptoms found in hypomania are also found in acute manic state but in an acute manner. The person may talk very loudly and violently to express himself. He is very much boastful. The acute mania state develops from hypomania or may develop all of a sudden. The motor reactions are very rapid and there may be changes in his bodily parts. There may be severe change in his facial expressions, his eyes bulge and his movements are violent. He also becomes very irritable and destructive if there is any interference. He may speak to himself, sing and dance, move around vigorously expressing his gay attitude. There is a considerable amount of impairment in his insight and judgement. He often finds delusions and hallucinations for a short period. In his acute manic state he may amuse people around him by way of expressing his joy and also express his regret for having behaved indifferently. In the depressed state he often finds delusions of persecution. In contrast, in the manic state, he often finds delusions of grandeur.

3. Hyperacute or Delirious Mania

This is the most severe type of manic reaction in which the patent is in a very confused state. He is very much excited and violent. The hyperacute mania develops from acute manic state or form the hypomanic state. It develops frequently and suddenly. Any small sign of warning may result in hyper-acute manic state. The patient speaks everything in an incoherent manner. He is in a fully disorganised state. He has no understanding of his social environment. His activities are mostly violent, as he shouts and screams and moves here and there restlessly. He has wild delusions and hallucinations. He should be taken care of and restricted from certain activities. Otherwise he gets exhausted. If he is left alone, he easily faces death. He may be often having visual and auditory hallucinations. Since he has a burden on himself, he is physically very much affected and loses weight rapidly. This state makes him susceptible to some infections diseases.

4. Manic Stupor

This is a mixed type of manic reaction. The patient in this state feels happy and elated. But he expresses all his psychomotor reactions. The manic stupor is the opposite of agitated depression. The patient also feels depressed in this state. Since it is a mixed type of psychosis, he reveals both agitated depression and extreme happiness. He is lethargic and unresponsive and at another time he is overactive and elated.

Circular Manic depressive Reaction

This is a mixed type of psychosis. Having discussed the depressive reaction and the manic reaction which have quite opposite reactions, now we find both the reactions in the same person, alternatively at different times. Generally, the depressive reactions are observed in some patients who do not have the symptoms of manic reactions. Similarly, patients who reveal symptoms of manic reactions do not reveal the symptoms of depressive reactions but few patients have the attacks of both the reactions alternatively. This type of psychosis we call circular manic depressive reaction. The manic stupor type of psychosis is also a mixed type. But this type varies from the circular manic-depressive psychosis in certain ways. According to Kraepelin, the manic stupor patient reveals the symptoms of manic reaction first and slowly goes into depressive reaction.

The manic stupor patient expresses the feeling of elation and happiness, but is soon satisfied by sitting in a very insensitive posture revealing all the signs of extreme psychomotor retardation. In the mixed manic depressive state these symptoms may appear simultaneously.

A large number of studies on manic depressive reactions have been carried out during the course of 75 years right from 1925 and it has been found that there was a gradual decline in the number of cases of patients revealing the symptoms of manic depressive psychoses. It was also observed that in some period there was rapid decline in the number of cases reported. In the public hospitals in the United State the number of mental patients reported were reduced to two per cent. Bellak (1952) and Avieti (1959) have formulated hypothesis on the basis of the rapid dropout in the number of cases of manic depressive reactions. According to their observations, there was a real decrease in the number of cases, secondly, people learned to endure mild manic depressive reactions, thirdly, there was a change in the treatment and the manic depressive patients were classified and treated as patients of involutional category. Arieti has stated another reason for the reduced cases of manic depressive reactions. According to him the modern treatment of electric shock cures the manic depressive cases and reduces the cases for hospitalisation.

Some of the studies carried out recently have concluded that the manic depressive psychosis has a hereditary background but few studies made on this problem do not accept the genetic make-up as one of the causes of manic depressive psychosis. But, however, we cannot rule out the genetic make-up in this disorder. Certain families are easily affected by some diseases. Such families are inclined to manic depressive psychosis. But Arieti (1959) asserts that cultural factors cause this disorder. The culture that puts more weight on children by way of assigning greater responsibilities and duties becomes the cause of manic depressive psychosis.

One of the causes of manic depressive reaction is the factors that precipitate the unhappy event that took place in the early life of an individual. It may be a life event that disrupts the adjustment of the person. The individual might have learned to adjust by being in a state of unhappiness or in a mild manic depressive state or by being a mild hypomanic. The disrupted event might have occurred in the family. It may be the marital problem, death of a most loved one, loss of love, break-up of the family. The precipitating factor may be the loss of job, demotion, a junior being promoted and placed above him, failures of attempts to get into an occupation. Any of these events might be the cause of manic depressive reaction.

Therapy

Manic depressive psychosis has been treated with psychotherapeutic techniques. Sigmund Freud, according to Ostow (1955) did not like to use psychotherapy on psychotic patients, yet many patients with mixed depressions were benefited by psychotherapy. The therapists begin the treatment with the event which disrupted the patient in the early years of life. Where the patient was able to gain entry into the symbolic nature of his incident, he can understand and associate himself with the precipitating childhood incident. When it is not possible for the therapist to deal with the patient who is very rude, then hospitalisation is recommended. In the hospitals or in the outpatient ward or private clinics the best medical treatment is shock therapy. The patient is given several shock treatments to get him under control and when the therapies continue for a longer period, the attack of manic depressive psychosis is controlled. Shock therapy deals with symptoms only and when the symptoms disappear, the manic depressive psychosis is successfully dealt with.

Involutional psychoses (Functional Psychoses)

The involutional psychosis is another affective psychosis. The manic depressive psychoses and the involutional psychoses are of the same group. Two reactions (psychoses) are mainly characterised by mood and emotional maladjustments. The involutional psychosis is mainly marked by mental and physical deterioration. Involutional psychosis or psychotic reaction may be stated as a depressive psychotic reaction characterised by a psychotic period with change in life. It is called climatic period. In males this period may be in puberty in which the person acquires the function of procreation, the ability to give birth to children. In females it may be the time of puberty or maturity which qualifies a female to give birth to children and the other change of life is the menopause. The old age also is a change of life in which the person fails to adjust himself with others and to the situations. The last change of life is old age and death.

Individuals at each stage of their life find different difficult situations to adjust themselves to. There might have been disruptive incidents in the early years of life which may precipitate when he becomes an adult and develops schizophrenia. It was believed at one stage that all psychoses of melancholia occurred during the involutional period, that is, when the main changes in life take place. This takes place after the age of 40 years and it may continue till 55 years in women, but in men after 60 years changes may take place. These psychoses are not schizophrenia or paranoid reactions.

Involutional Melancholia

It is a type of psychosis followed by the climacteric period which is considered to be the critical period of life during which period there is decline of mental and physical conditions, characterised by depression. Kraepelin (1962), while classifying his system, has observed that the manic depressive psychotic cases were associated with climatric, the critical change in life of an individual. He was able to differentiate the involutional melancholia only from this. He was of the view that involutional psychosis or melancholia is something complicated, or some intricacy is involved in it. The complication or intricacy according to Kraepelin is climatric, a critical change in the life of a person.

In a severely developed melancholic state the symptoms are the development of strong feeling of anxiety, sin, agitation, strong depression and a feeling of unworthiness. There is a strong feeling of self-contamination in these patients. The person blames himself that he has committed an unpardonable sin and it is not worth living in this world, and feels that it is better to die. The patient wants to commit suicide and die which is an ever present danger in the patient. But the well developed modern method of treatment saved such patients from danger.

Mixed Involutional (Psychoses) Reactions

The involutional psychotic reactions, according to Orme (1997), are found to be mixed in some patients. There are mixed symptoms in patients very often. Though the other psychotic cases are reported, still there are mixed types of involutional melancholia. In the mixed types generally there are delusions of persecution and symptoms of depression. In the involutional cases the mixed symptoms can be delusions and depressions and also psychoneurotic reactions.

Treatment

The treatment generally given to involutional reactions is electric shock treatment. This treatment is found to be very effective for involutional reactions. Even very severe cases are treated successfully. The shock treatment mainly deals with the symptoms and not the reaction directly. When the symptoms disappear the patient gets insight into the past disruptive results and makes suitable adjustment to his life. The shock therapy is found to be successful not only in the cases of involutional melancholia, but also in the cases of mixed type of involutional psychoses and paranoid reactions.

Paranoid psychoses (Functional Psychoses)

Paranoia is a mental disorder mainly characterised by delusions of persecution and delusion of greatness or grandeur. It may be also stated as any condition characterised by delusions, as paranoid schizophrenic or paranoid state. Paranoia is a mental disorder characterised by any of these several types of delusions. But in this state the personality remains relatively intact. In the state of paranoia there is informal intense fear or suspicision. Paranoia is a form of schizophrenia characterised by a slowly progressive deterioration of personality, involving delusions and often hallucinations.

Generally, in the paranoid disorder the individual has persecutory delusions or delusional jealousy persistently, which is an unfound conviction that his mate is unfaithful. It is very often contentious, but not thought to be disorder. The paranoid person (personality) is highly suspicious, secretive, jealous and also argumentative, will not accept blames, and appears cold and unemotional.

Instead, a paranoid schizophrenic is a psychotic patient who has several systematised delusions and also hallucinations and ideas of reference. The patient may be agitated, angry, argumentative and also violent sometimes.

The term 'paranoia' is a very old term, used by the ancient Greeks and Romans to indicate any mental disorder indiscriminately. But the studies made by Kraepelin (1856-1926) used of this to some limited mental disorders. He used this term to explain the cases of exhibiting delusions and impaired contacts with the world of reality. In these days paranoid cases in hospitals are becoming rare. But Coleman (1974) states that there are quite a few cases registered under this category. According to him the exploited inventors, persecuted businessmen, fancied persons, persons claiming as prophets, persons who accuse that their mates are unfaithful, eccentric writers all fall under this category. They become a nuisance while effected, otherwise they usually maintain a normal life in the community. But at the same time they may cause serious troubles any time. The paranoid person is suspicious and feels that he is being isolated, mistreated, plotted against, spied upon and ignored. His delusional state mainly centres round one matter, that is, financial position. Paranoid psychosis is generally observed in elderly persons. A person faces many life problems when he becomes old. Since in old age he does not have sufficient strength mentally and physically, problems creep in and he is often agitated and involved in delusional system, mainly the delusions of persecution, delusions of grandeur and jealousy.

In studying paranoid psychosis in the process of classification, problems arise in differentiating paranoid schizophrenia, manic depressive reaction and involutional reactions. The symptoms of paranoia and paranoid state reveal almost the same type of symptoms as in paranoid schizophrenia. A person is classified as paranoid only when the symptoms are mainly of delusions and if other symptoms are not found. Generally, while diagnosing the psychotic patients if there are hallucinations the psychosis is classified as paranoid schizophrenia and not as paranoid.

Studies of recent times state that the cases of paranoid psychic patients in hospitals are becoming less and less. It is also observed that patients without other psychotic symptoms are considered as not psychotic by his relatives and friends. Delusions of various types are the most important symptoms in paranoid patients. Generally delusions are irrational false beliefs. They are systematised false beliefs. Delusion is a strong false belief opposed to reality. In spite of logical evidences the false belief persists in the person contrary to reality. These are delusions of persecution, grandeur and of jealousy.

Delusions of Persecution

This type of delusion persistently takes place in most of the paranoid patients and this is the most important symptom. The patient strongly believes that someone is plotting against him and is going to injure him as also inducing others to harm him. The patient strongly believes that some secrete conspiracy is going on against him and also some false propaganda is made against him among his friends. The patient in such despair may even try to commit suicide or even attack those whom he suspects of doing all thee. He also tries to convince people what he believes is correct.

Delusions of Grandeur

The paranoid patient strongly believes that he is the most important and powerful person. In the state of delusion of grandeur he speaks of his own eminence and claims that some eminent person is in love with him. The delusion of grander is a compensation for the patient's failure to achieve something he wanted. The disappointment is compensated by this means. He sometimes claims that he is born in a very noble family, born with special features of a great leader. According to Bleuler (1923) the delusions of persecution and the delusions of grandeur go together. He states that there is no delusion of persecution without the delusion of grandeur. The delusion of grandeur is intended to compensate for all the disappointments the patient has experienced.

Delusions of Jealousy

The paranoid patient reveals the symptoms of jealousy often against his mate. He feels that his mate is very unfaithful. He may collect some small evidences and justify his suspicision or delusion. Jealousy may be also projected against his colleagues or employer, that his honest service in the firm is not recognised while others, dishonest services are recognised.

Causative Factors in Paranoid and Paranoia State

We have discussed in the preceding section that manic depressive psychoses and involutional psychosis are mainly functional psychoses. Neither physogenic nor hereditary factors can be attributed to them. But it is observed that the paranoid state does not have any cultural and social backgrounds for the origin. Home and childhood experiences are found to be the common factors in the development of paranoid psychosis. Especially in the advancing years this type of psychosis occurs. The breakdown of paranoia has been noted in childhood period. The poor relationship between mother and child during the first five years and the attitude of the child towards his parents of the opposite sex were found to be the causes of attack of paranoia. In the developmental process it was observed that most of the paranoid patients were found to be morose and sad, alone and suspicious, stubborn and against discipline. Peer group relationship and social adjustment and participation in cooperative and play activities were absent in their early days. Loss of parents in the early childhood period, too much of pampering by the parents all resulted in the development of the paranoid psychosis in the later days. The patient in the early years has a great deal of difficulty with other people. He has no understanding of his own and the motives of other people. He has grown without the social skills and never been friendly with other people. He feels insecure and tense and has developed intense fear. He becomes, finally, the victim of comments for other people. At this stage of the childhood period the individual developa a defence mechanism of denial and projection. In the adolescent period there is the development of the feeling of self-condemnation and unworthiness due to the development of sexual maladjustment.

Therapy

A successful treatment for paranoid psychosis can be given by some highly technical methods that were developed in recent times. The paranoid state is generally very short lived and the chances of eliminating the disorder are more these days. But the difficulty rests with the therapist, who sometimes fails to maintain proper communication with the patient. But the ideal psychotherapist in the case of paranoid patient must be free from the feelings of insecurity as the patient sometimes becomes hostile, aggressive and threatening. The therapist who tries to become close with the patient may force the patient to intensify his paranoid defences. By this means the therapist crates a sense of confidence in the patient, that he is very much interested in understanding what the patient is feeling and revealing. The therapist listens silently to what the patient is narrating about his past experiences without interrupting him. A skilful therapist is careful and slow in forming an opinion about the patient and making a judgement of the cases. This is because it is very difficult for the therapist to know how much information of what the patient said is true and factual and how much is based on his delusions.

If everything goes on very well, then the patient will be in a position of going into his past experiences and speak out everything which may allow him to know the repressed anxiety that is producing materials. He may also join with the therapist in all these threatening past experiences.

When the therapy becomes successful the patient is in a position to reduce his anxiety and tension. By these means the patient is able to slowly establish the contact with the world of reality. The patient does this gradually. He does not go into his delusional system. He cannot fully disown his delusional system as it has been with him for a long time. The delusion becomes an internal nature and often guides its purposes. The patient can be fully free from the delusional system only when the anxiety state is fully removed. But the paranoid psychosis is a complicated disorder, very difficult to cure in patients.

The problem with the paranoid patient is that the therapist does not have easy access for having communication with the patient. The patient first of all does not trust the therapist. Sometimes the therapist may face the patient's hostility and aggression. Therefore, the therapist has to find out slowly the way of dealing with the paranoid patients. In his approach there should not be any chance for the patient's suspicion. The patient must be left alone and the therapist should watch whether the patient gets free from the delusional persecution.

CHAPTER 6

Schizophrenia (Functional Psychosis)

What is Schizophrenia?

Schizophrenia is one of the affective or functional psychosis. The other functional psychosis are manic depressive psychoses, involitional psychosis and paranoid psychosis. We have discussed these in the preceding sections. But though schizophrenia is one of the functional psychosis it has always been given special treatment by psychologists in discussing the patterns of abnormal behaviour. Scholars in the field of abnormal psychology have been treating schizophrenia copiously as it has certain special significance. One of the reasons they find is that it is the severest and very widely prevalent type of psychosis.

The United States Department of Health, Education and Welfare (1961) has stated that in the United States one in every 50 persons is admitted in the hospital with schizophrenic complaint. The incidences of occurrence of this psychosis are so numerous that among the patients admitted in hospitals, one in four was found to be a schizophrenic patient of some type. It was also observed that most of these patients were below 35 years of age and were having prolonged treatment for more than 10 years in hospitals.

Researches on schizophrenia are so large that varied results were brought out now and then and different views on them were expressed. Kantor et al (1953) were of the view that schizophrenia has two polar types of extreme ends, such as a process syndrome and a reactive syndrome. According to them the process type refers to a gradual development of schizophrenia in a person whose personality was unstable before the onset of schizophrenia. The reactive type of schizophrenia is sudden in a person whose personality has been normal before the attack, but the person had some signs of schizophrenia. The credit goes to Kraepelin (1856-1926), a German psychiatrist and the Swiss psychiatrist, Bleuler (1857-1939) who formulated this concept and described the functions of schizophrenia. Kraepelin first named this mental disorder as 'Dementia Praecox' in 1898. But Bleuler later on coined the term schizophrenia. It is a Greek word. 'Schizo ' means diverge, split, division. The Greek word 'skhizein' means split. Phrenic means diaphragm, pertaining to the affecting part, the diaphragm, or the frame. Thus both the words schizo and phrenia are Greek words, the meaning of which is something affecting the mind, dividing or splitting. This is applied to explain the mental disorder or disease by Kraepelin and Bleuler.

Therefore, schizophrenia may be defined as a form of mental disease in which the personality is disintegrated and detached from its environment. It may be also defined as a group of psychotic disorders characterised by progressive deterioration of personality, withdrawing from reality, hallucinations, delusions, social apathy emotional instability and so on. Schizophrenia is considered as an extraordinary disorder which has raised continuous contrasting views among the psychologists and biologists during the last century with regard to the nature and causes of the disorder. It has been drawing the attention of psychologists, psychiatrists, biologists, medical men, religious men, poets, dramatists and writers of various types. Poets and novelists made use of madness to draw the curiosity and anxiety of the people. From this point of view schizophrenia may be defined as a type of psychosis characterised by disordered negative functioning and poor social adjustment, literally splitting of thoughts and emotive processes probably due to brain malfunction. The findings of recent studies show that certain forms of mental or psychotic disorder have biochemical, anatomical and genetic backgrounds. Koll and Whishaw (1983) were of the view that the universally accepted criterion for diagnosing schizophrenia was the elimination of the functioning of other neurological disturbances of affective disorder. But some authors emphasise the presence of bizzare hallucinations and the disturbance of thought. It is known that the symptoms of schizophrenia are heterogeneous.

Schizophrenia for a long time has been treated as a functional disorder and it is not of the organic type. Numerous studies were made at the gross morphology of the brains of schizophrenics, both in autopsied tissue and in MRL (magnetic resonance imaging) and CT (computerised temography) scans. But, though the results vary, most of the researchers agree that schizophrenics have brains that weigh less than the normal persons and in which the ventricles are found to be enlarged. This is according to Gershon and Rieder (1992). Further, it is also observed that schizophrenics have smaller frontal lobe and thinner parahipocaopul gyri. One of the most interesting findings made by Kovelman and Scheibal (1984) was that the schizophrenics have a more haphazard organisation. From these studies it is clear that there are acceptable evidences that the schizophrenics have some disorganisation in the brains. But schizophrenia is a very serious and the most prevalent type of psychosis. Bellak (1958) made a detail study of schizophrenia and covered all aspects of schizophrenia and updated his earlier works in his hook *Schizophrenia.* What was generally called psychobiosocial approach to the study of psychotic disorders was called by Bellak as multifactor psychosomatic theory. According to him schizophrenia is a 'psychiatric syndrome' which means that it is not a single disease. Schizophrenics may reveal a group of symptoms and not one. Bellak states that in the diagnostic label it is understood that a number of conditions may manifest themselves disturbing the ego severely. These conditions are mainly psychogenic weakness of the ego which are caused by many factors. The symptoms of schizophrenia are also seen in these conditions such as the long psychobiosocial processes, causing of defective ego and the individual's inability to maintain proper contact with reality during this period.

The American Psychiatric Association (APA) (1980, 1987) has made an elaborate classification of the mental disorders. In the publication of DSM-III-R the American concept of schizophrenia has been defined precisely and new concepts also have been coined. Schizophrenia, now listed, as *schizoaffective disorder* in a separate section. In DSM-II schizophrenic episode is diagnosed as schizophrenia form of disorder or brief reactive psychosis which is listed in a separate new section. In schizophrenic form disorder, the psychotic symptoms like the emotional disturbance, fear, confusion, vivid hallucinations should not persist for more than six months. But the brief reactive psychosis should not exist for more than a month, specifically the extreme stress. What is stated in mild forms of schizophrenia in DSM-II is now diagnosed as personality disorders. Therefore, in the light of recent studies and diagnosis of schizophrenia, it may be defined as a group of psychotic disorders characterised by major disturbances in thought, emotion and behaviour, disordered thinking in which ideas are not related logically, faulty perception and attention, irregular motor activity, flat emotion, reduced tolerance for stress in interpersonal relations. It makes the patient withdraw from people and reality, often going into fantasy and a life of delusions and hallucinations.

Types of Schizophrenia

In the latest classification DSM-III-R, three types of schizophenic disorders are listed. They are hebephrenic, catatonic and paranoid. These three types were proposed by Kraepelin in the beginning. These types provide further information on what schizophrenia is like and the different types of behaviour in diagnosing it. But the earlier classification of schizophrenia falls into four types as simple, catatonic, paranoid and hebephrenic. Later on, the American Psychiatric Association (APA) in its classification of DSM-II made it into five types as childhood, schizoaffactive, acute undifferentiated, chronic undifferentiated, and residual type. All the patients may be placed into any one of the above nine types. But in the factor analysis made by Guertin and Zilaitis (1954) four types of schizophrenia were isolated. They are simple schizophrenia, hebephrenic schizophrenia, catatonic schizophrenia and paranoid schizophrenia. These four types are stated as clinically diagnosed type of schizophrenia.

Simple Schizophrenia

This type of schizophrenic patient is disturbed in what is going on around him and what others are doing, but he is very much dependent on his family. The patient is isolated and his personal habits are disintegrated. But he is able to converse and answer the questions which means that he has some contact with outside world, but is unable to adjust to life. In simple schizophrenic there is awareness of time and place and the mental functions are not seriously impaired. The attack of simple schizophrenia is gradual, but sometimes it is sudden. Some regress into earlier thoughts. The simple schizophrenics cannot be hospitalised unless they become very aggressive or commit crimes. The person's disorder cannot be observed if he is sentenced to prison when he has committed a crime. In Kant's study, it was observed that nearly two-thirds of the cases were having a family history of functional psychosis. There were also patients from poor homes, broken homes, foster homes and maladjusted homes of the same number.

The onset of this disorder is gradual for a long period and it begins between puberty and early middle age, approximately from the age of 12 to 40 years of age. Though it is said that these patients are free from delusions and hallucinations, Kant has observed some evidence of the presence of delusions and hallucinations. Most of the simple schizophrenic patients are kept at home and they are engaged in simple mechanical or manual works, but they will not make any progress in the work. Sometimes the patients go into regression and live in their childhood days, when they were happy and free from any responsibilities or problems. A majority of the patients feel shy and become hypersensitive in their dealings with others. They also become antisocial in activities, mainly destructive. At this stage they are hospitalised. There may also be symptoms of threats and attempts to attack other persons. It was also observed that the simple schizophrenics are sex deviants, involved in acts like voyeurism, rape and watching other people's sex activities.

Hebephrenic Schizophrenia

The patients of this type are differentiated from other types in various ways. This is one of the severe types of psychoses. The patient often reveals a childish behaviour. Kraepelin called it as hebephrenic type, but the APA in its classification, DSM-III-R called as disorganised schizophrenia. The disorganised schizophrenia is characterised by a number of diffused and regressive symptoms. For example, delusions and hallucinations, sexual hypochondriacal, religious and persecution symptoms are abundant and less organised than these symptoms are found in paranoid schizophrenia. The patient often develops unexpected ideas and involves in unhealthy bodily activities. The patient often shows meaningless smiles on his face, speaks incoherently. He completely disregards his personal interests like keeping himself neat and clean. He never cares for his personal appearance. Among these there is a silly type of behaviour like childish arguments and they are emotionally maladjusted. The depressed type of patient is found to be very odd and irritable, often complaining of hypochondria. The apathetic and autistic type of patients are often impulsive and driven to a state of excitement. The hebephrenic schizophrenia develops gradually and also grows out of simple and paranoid schizophrenia which were observed in earlier diagnoses. The patient is often given to delusions and hallucinations.

He complains of hearing voices calling him by filthy names. The delusions are mainly persecutory.

Catatonic Schizophrenia

This type of schizophrenia is not very serious. The person often behaves strangely and withdraws from others. He present himself in a very strange appearance and the same creates an impression that his psychosis is incurable. This type of schizophrenia always develops suddenly. The patient may be having the symptom of indifference, apathy and withdrawal tendencies. His behaviour alternates between excitement and depression. The symptoms of this type of schizophrenia are headache, sleeplessness, loss of appetite. He often has delusions of persecution, ideas of reference, and emotional indifference. The patient is highly suspicious of everybody, also very sensitive with little self-control. The catatonic schizophrenia patients have more clear symptoms of motor disturbances. They adopt a peculiar type of facial expressions. They make repeated gestures in a peculiar manner using fingers, hands and arm movements. In some patients there may be an overall level of activity. The patient is involved in such an excitement that there may be great expenditure of energy. At the other extreme the motor symptom is catatonic immobility, adopting unusual postures, maintaining it for a very long period. The patient stands on one leg, having the other leg bent at his back. He may remain in this position for a whole day. There may also be motor symptoms of waxy flexibility in catatonic patients.

Paranoid Schizophrenia

Paranoid schizophrenia is identified mainly by the symptoms of delusions of persecution and false beliefs. But this patient is unable to have well integrated delusions as his thought disturbance is not able to do consistent logical thinking since the symptoms are characterised by schizophrenia. The paranoid schizophrenic patient is found to be very calculative, aggressive and also ego-centred. He claims himself to have superiority over others. The inherent feeling of inferiority complex in the patient develops a defence mechanism which is revealed in various ways. In an agreement with others the patient refuses to hear and accept the words of others. Though the delusions of the patients are persecutions, there may be also delusions of grandeur sometimes. The patients may be having some over-estimated sense about their own position, importance, power, knowledge and identity. They may also have delusions of jealousy, suspecting their mates as unfaithful. For these patients, delusions are followed by vivid auditory and visual hallucinations. Paranoid schizophrenic patients often have the ideas of reference. By this means they often connect important events within their delusions. These patients, while walking on the street, if they happen to see some persons who are going about their routine work everyday, suspect them, stating that they being are watched for doing some harm to them. They even suspect the media of making reference to them. These patients are highly excited, agitated, aggressive, argumentative. They are more vigilant and verbal than other types of patients.

Causative Factors of Schizophrenia

Schizophrenia is classified as one of the functional psychoses. It has its root cause in various affective, cultural, social, physiological factors and in the role of learning. Recent researches find its root cause also in organic factors like the brain and tissues. The term affective refers to one's feeling, state or mood. Affective disorders are those in which there are disturbances of mood. There are types of affective disorders and these disorders are of two major types that represent the extreme in mood. One is depressive and the other is manic. The depressive refers to severe dysfunction and the manic signifies an extreme elated feeling. Most of the people might have had the experience of some form of mild depression and they can understand what the feeling must be in the extreme form. The manic psychosis is more difficult to understand. Strange (1965) states that the ego functioning is found to be playing an important role in causing the disorders of schizophrenia. The severe ego disturbance is the primary characteristic of schizophrenia. Therefore, it is important to know what are the psychobiosocial factors appear to be present in the defective ego development of the patients.

Social Factors

Enormous amount of studies were made on schizophrenia in recent times and found that this disorder occurs in all cultural and social groups throughout the world. This is what Penedict and Jacks (1954) concluded from their studies. But the occurrence of schizophrenia varies from group to group as some groups put more stress on individuals and they find it difficult in maintaining the normal mental health. It is because of this that this type of psychotic cases are very high in civilised society compared to the primitive one. One important factor that causes schizophrenia in civilised society is that individuals develop guilty feelings because of the ethical and moral codes and they develop hostility which turns inwards. This damages the ego and it becomes one of the causes of schizophrenia. This is not taking place in primitive society. In a complex culture generally there is more promotion of personal guilty feelings which make the psychotic individuals difficult to adjust themselves in society.

Biological Factors

These factors have been stressed by several scholars as the basic factors underlying the mental disorders. They are of the view that heredity, endocrine system and physical constitution play an important role in causing these disorders. Recent studies also emphasize heredity, as there are increased schizophrenic cases in families. The family history provides adjustment information for the prevalence of schizophrenia. Kallmann's (1958) studies of family history of 1,000 schizophrenic cases revealed that genetic factors contribute to an average level of chances for becoming a schizophrenic patient. It is estimated that an individual on the average has a chance of one per cent of becoming a schizophrenic patient. But it was observed that if one of his parents had this mental disorder, then the chance of getting this disorder is increased to 16 per cent. In case, if both the parents had suffered from schizophrenia, then the chance for their children to develop schizophrenia is 68 per cent. Studies were made among twins and found that if one twin suffered from schizophrenia, then the chances of the other twin becoming schizophrenic was 68 per cent. Based upon these findings Kallmann asserted that heredity is a highly influencing factor in predisposing an individual for the development of shizophrenia. Some scholars believe that heredity alone is not the sole cause of this disorder as there are cases among the twins that one of the twins is free from this mental disorder. Therefore, the environment also is predisposing individuals to schizophrenia.

Physical Factors

Scholars have observed that physical constitution is associated with mental disorders. Kretschmer (1926) ascertained that physical constitution has a predisposing effect in an individual for the development of mental disorders.

According to Kretschmer schizophrenic patients are mostly asthenic or slenderly built persons. Sheldon (1944) accepted Kretschmer's classification and conclusions with regard to the body type associated with mental disorders. But later studies state that mental disorders are found among all types of body built. Children who are timid, lonely, sensitive become schizophrenics when they grow into adulthood.

Psychological Factors

Schizophrenia is a severe mental disorder greatly nurtured by psychobiosocial settings. Scholars often stress that the severe ego disturbance is the primary characteristic of schizophrenia. Here we are to examine how these factors such as psychological, bio-physiological and social factors play the role in predisposing of the individual to the disorder of schizophrenia. Though importance is given to bio-psychological factors to the development of schizophrenia, the role of psychological factors are in no way less significant. These psychological factors, like conflict and frustration, were found to be powerful factors in the development of schizophrenia. Most of the present psychological explanations of schizophrenia are based upon the works of Freud (1856-1939) and Meyar (1866-1950). The important characteristics of dissociation and disorganisation were first suggested by Meyer, who observed that the schizophrenic was not capable of learning to adjust to the stressful situation. They were emotionally imbalanced and sometimes over-excited. Their emotions are strong, painful and violent, and ultimately result in repression. The repression is so severe that it affects all his emotional reactions. He sees that the world is very hostile to him and therefore he withdraws from the world of contact. He develops fear to show any affection or love for his relatives and friends. There is often repeated failure of adjustment in his life. Jung (1875-1961) is of the view that schizophrenia is the cause of expressed complex. The causes are more of psychological than the other factors as it is mainly rooted in feelings and emotions and in the failure of adjustment of the individual to the environment.

Therapy

The causes of schizophrenia rest in these factors discussed in the preceding sections. Though one of the main causes is considered to be the severe disturbance of the ego, patients have different sets of causes. Therefore patients have some difference in the treatment. When the specific cause is not known, attempt is made to remove the symptoms. If the psychotic patients are in the state of not being able to communicate, then some kind of shock therapy is given. It is observed that sometimes the electric shock therapy and insulin shock treatment are found to be effective and the schizophrenic patients get relieved of their problems. Strange (1965) is of the view that shock treatments themselves are not sure of giving complete cure or provide long standing result for schizophrenia. But what is more important in these treatments is that the patient is communicative and reactive to the psychotherapist. There are also other forms of treatment such as occupational, recreational, artistic type, fine arts like music, dance and instrumentation. If the patient is engaged deeply in any one of these forms, there is a likelihood of getting better result from the patients.

The psychobiosocial factors may have different combinations in causing schizophrenia. But in the treatment it is every difficult to identify the specific cause of this disorder and remove the cause. One easy way of treating the patient for schizophrenia is to get him admitted in the hospital as it is not possible to deal with him at home by the relatives. It may also lead to infectious diseases, diseases like pneumonia, tuberculosis which are possible as the patient is getting physically weak day by day. At the hospital the patient gets the care of the doctors periodically and treatment is given medically. There are trained persons to provide good nursing, the type of food necessary time to time and other professionally needed helps which are available so that the patient may feel comfortable which may reduce his problems.

Generally, schizophrenic patients are treated with very wide types of medical, drug and psychological therapies. The treatments sometimes vary from person to person. For some schizophrenic patients the shock therapy was found to be effective. It makes the patients accessible for psychotherapy. But the prediction of the cause of schizophrenia is in no way better than most of the other functional disorders. Therapists find that the other functional psychoses are not so complicated as schizophrenia is, because in the aetiology all factors are involved. The incidence of occurrence is lightly complex, particularly in the modern industrial and technological society. Recent researchers Kovelman and Scheibal (1984) have confirmed the earlier findings that the structure and function of the pre-frontal cortex of the schizophrenic patients is abnormal and the brain is involved in the abnormal behaviour of the schizophrenic patients. This also confirms the view that schizophrenia is a developmental disorder.

Somato and Drug Therapies

These are some of the therapies most widely administered in hospitals for treating the schizophrenic patients in United States. In the second quarter of the twentieth century the insulin coma therapy was said to be the most successful in treating the schizophrenic patients. Sakel (1938) has claimed that about 70 per cent of patients have shown significant improvement for this treatment. But later on it was observed from some results that this type of treatment was risky and may result even in death.

During the same period a Portuguese psychiatrist Moniz (1935) discovered a surgical method of treating schizophrenic patients. It was a surgery performed in the frontal lobes of the brain (motor area). The procedure is called the prefrontal lobotomy. According to this procedure the tracts connecting the frontal lobes to the lower centres of the brain were destroyed and there was no connection between these two parts. Since the origin of the problem areas was destroyed the patients appeared to be free from the trouble. Meniz claimed that his treatment was very much successful. But after some years the behaviour of the patients who had this treatment varied. Some became violent and aggressive and others lost their cognitive abilities. It was because the part of the brain (prefrontal lobes) that was responsible for the cognitive activities was destroyed. The persons became very dull and inactive and some finally died. This technique was given up.

The electroconvulsive therapy was also in use during the same period. Cerletti and Bini introduced this therapy around 1938. Though this therapy had some advantages, it was found to be ineffective in the case of patients who suffered from severe depression and delusions.

Around the middle of the twentieth century the drug therapies were widely practised. This was stated as the antipsychotic medications. The drug therapies were generally called neuroleptics. Though these therapies had some benefits in the beginning, they caused some neurological problems. The most recommended neuroleptic drugs were phenothiazines. Though these drugs were discovered earlier, they were not put to use on humans till the 1940s.

The French Surgeon, Labourite, had succeeded in using the antihistamines for common cold and asthma as they contained phenothiazines. Labourite had also used this drug for reducing surgical shocks. The phenothiazines almost reduced the positive symptoms of schizophrenia. The patients were discharged from the hospitals, but were asked to take maintenance doses of the drug. They therefore kept going to the hospital for ascertaining the dosage levels now and then. The drug phenothiazines reduced the long standing symptoms and hospitalisation, but the patients were keeping continuous contacts with hospitals and sometimes got readmitted for further treatments.

It was observed that the drug phenothiazines had some side effects which caused more uncomfortable feelings to the patients as the drugs consisted of a group of tranquillisers including chlorpromazine and rasarpine (rauwalfia). The drugs of rauwalfia (rasarpine) made the patient quiet by depressing certain areas of the hypothalamus. The phenothiazines blocked the reticular activating system in the brain. This made the patient less emotional, calm and more uncomfortable. He felt dryness of the mouth, unclear vision, and he developed constipation.

Further, the patients often had low blood pressure and jaundice. Therefore in place of this drug therapy the patients were treated with neuroleptics which were durable and were injected periodically. Though phenothiazines had certain disadvantages, it was considered to be the best easily available treatment for schizophrenia.

In treating the mental patients the use of surgery for psychiatric disorders is a continuous problem. The surgical treatment is stated as 'psychosurgery'. Schizophrenic is treated by the use of psychosurgery. Psychosurgery, according to Valenstein (1980), is the destruction of some area in the brain to relieve severe intractable psychiatric disorders. The current techniques were differentiated from the earlier techniques. The earlier techniques were crude and named lobotomy operations. The term psychosurgery is suggested in place of it, although both are following the same procedures. Thus the 'prefrontal lobotomy' is named as 'psychosurgery".

Deinstituionlisation

A most recent development for diagnosis and treatment for schizophrenia is deinstitutionalisation. This was originally planned for treating persons who were mentally retarded. It was for providing educational and community service that the organisation was started in the 1960s rather than treating them in hospitals. What was designed and organised for the mentally retarded was also extended to all mental health patients.

In the United States the civil court has taken the matter of reading the patients in the mental hospital very seriously and has issued notice to the mental health professionals that they must treat the patients more carefully. They should not be kept in mental hospitals against their will and the professionals must attend to the specific treatment only in the cases of the committed patients. The quality of care should be upgraded in mental institutions. Many states have accepted the policy of deinstitutionalisations. Many states have accepted the policy of deinstitionlisation and got discharged the patients from mental hospitals and discouraged their admission in mental hospitals. The concise rule of conduct is the trust the mental patients have in the community. It also mean that anything is preferred other than the institution, the *mental hospitals.*

Then, if it is accepted, what is this community which can be more helpful than the hospitals? Some programmes in place of mental hospitals were formulated. But many wondered whether the community services could reduce the chronic mental illnesses. Gralnick (1986) is of the view that the seriously ill are largely neglected. But unless they are found to be a danger to themselves and to others they cannot be committed. That stage may take place after some years. By this time the problem becomes chronic and very difficult to deal with these patients. According to Gralnick deinstitutionalisation which was designed to reduce the mental illness, may aggravate the problem. According to the policy of deinstitutionalisation a mental patient may be taken care of only when he is a danger to himself and to others.

Deinstitutionalisation is an outcome of the services of community psychology. Community psychology is an approach to alleviate community mental health problems by intervention programmes. Community psychology emphasizes prevention and finding out the potential difficulties of the individuals instead of waiting for the troubled persons to start consultation. The place of the professional mental persons to meet patients is the natural environment and not the therapists' clinics or hospitals. These services of community mental health persons should be available all the 24 hours at the patients' places. The dictum of community psychology is that "prevention is better than cure". The community service personnel should see that incidents are not occurring.

Therefore, Caplan (1964) has formulated three levels of prevention: primary prevention, secondary prevention and tertiary prevention. The primary prevention tries to reduce the occurrence of new cases of social and emotional problems in a population or community. This is by altering the stressful and depriving situations in the environment and helping the individuals to the extent of resisting the stress and adjust themselves to the adverse conditions.

The secondary prevention refers to the efforts to detect the problems prior to their becoming troublesome and to prevent the development of the problems. The community service personnel like the physicians, social workers, teachers, police, and the court officials should make quick and correct assessment and take remedial measures to deal with the problems.

The tertiary prevention is to find out ways and means to reduce the consequences already taken place. It may be a mental disorder of some type. Mental health workers also keep themselves busy helping the persons who have recovered from mental health problems and help them to participate in community activities and also help them to put in some occupations. Thus the deinstitutionalisation is mainly an intervention programme. The causative factors of mental illness in the community should be removed to keep people mentally healthy.

Deinstritutionalisation is the name assigned to non-mental hospitalisation and non-mental health clinic for the mental patents who are in need of treatment. It is not referring to a specific place where the mental patients can have treatment. Deinstitutionalisation finds its root in the dissatisfaction expressed, about the ways in which the mental patients were treated, by the American mental health professionals and the psychologists who were dealing with the mental health of the people. Community psychology has emerged from the community mental health movement in 1960s. Hobbs (1964) strongly stressed not only prevention of diseases but also the creation of a healthy environment. He viewed that the mental health professionals should be concerned not only about the mental illness, but also the human well-being in general. Mental illness is not the private organic distress of an individual persons, but it is a social, ethical and moral problem.

The whole community is responsible for the unfortunate of incidence the mental disorder. Rappaport (1977) states that the community is the child of Community Mental Health Movement and therefore it should take care of the community's well-being. The environment is mainly implicated in the case of mental illness. Community psychology is an action-oriented profession which attempts to bring about revolutionary changes in the community by eliminating the factors that are causing behavioural disorders and social problems in the physical and social environments.

The tendency is to provide mentally retarded individuals with educational and community services and not to provide institutional care. The retarded individuals have a right to have treatment in the least restricted residential area where the retarded people live, whether it is a small or medium-sized home, because it is integrated into the community areas which is supposed to be the natural atmosphere. The deinstitutionlisation process, that is transferring the patients from the institutions to a non-institutional or natural area, should not take place all of a sudden. It should take place gradually and a transition period is invariably needed. This prepares the individual patient for moving from the mental hospital or the institution to the community home where the patient may feel at home. The individual is provided with medical care. The residents, trained persons or nurses and other concerned people and aides attend to the special requirements of the person all the time.

Deinstitutionalisation has certain disadvantages. The mental patients outside the institution are not provided with all required facilities. It is also doubtful whether deinstitutionalisation can reduce the rate of chronic mental disorders. Gralnick (1988) states that the problem may become more chronic and it would be more difficult to deal with the patients. Many patients may not have a home to live in. If they were discharged from the mental hospitals where do they go? Or where do they be taken? The deinstitutionlisation instead of altering the problems, creates more problems. Therefore this programme should not be applied to all mental patients or retarded persons.

CHAPTER 7

Organic or Somatogenic Psychoses (Disorders)

What is organic psychosis?

Psychosis is a severe and major disorder or mental illness characterised by the loss of contact with the world of reality, which is revealed in the symptoms of delusions and hallucinations. Psychoses are of two major types. They are functional (learned) psychoses and organic psychoses. We have discussed the functional psychoses in the preceding sections.

We shall now discuss the other type of psychoses, the organic psychoses. Organic psychoses in also stated as psychiatric disorder caused by diseases, injury, drugs and other structural changes. Abnormal behaviour may occur due to several factors which damage some parts of the brain or nervous system. When some part of the body is seriously damaged, the behaviour of the individual is hampered and various types of symptoms may manifest. Organic disorder is one such which causes behavioural disorders. Scholars discuss the organic psychoses also under somatogenic disorders. The term somatogenic is derived form the Greek word, 'Soma' or 'Somat' which means body. Generally 'Soma' refers to cell body including the cell membrane, nucleus and cytoplasm.

Somatology is a branch of biology which is concerned with the structure and functions of the body. Another meaning derived from the Greek word is that it is a branch of anthropology which deales with physical characteristics of human beings. Therefore, we may state that 'Soma refers to the totality of an organism's physical make-up.

Biological psychologists (1996) state three approaches in relation to the brain and behaviour disorders. They are somatic interventions, behavioural intervention and correlation.

The somatic intervention is most commonly employed by experimenters who alter a structure of function of the brain to see how this change alters the behaviour of an individual. In this approach or experiment the somatic intervention is the independent variable and the change or behaviour is the dependent variable. The behavioural effect is observed. For example, a part of the brain is stimulated electrically and the behavioural effects are observed.

The behavioural intervention is the experimenter's intervention in the behaviour of the organisms and they watch for the consequent changes in the bodily functions. In this case the behaviour is independent variable and the change in the body is the dependent variable. For example, putting together two persons of opposite sex is supposed to lead to increase in the secretion of certain hormones. The bodily change is the increase of certain hormones. This is dependent variable and the behaviour is independent variable.

The third approach examines the brain-behaviour relationship, a given bodily measure varies with given behavioural measure. For example, the size of the brain is correlated with the level of intelligence. Or the individual differences in sexual behaviour correlate with the levels of certain hormones in the individuals.

Thus, the relation between the brain or bodily parts with the behavioural changes is established. Any somatic intervention causes behavioural change. It may be behavioural disorder. This means that when some part of the brain is damaged, it results in somatogenic or organic disorder. Therefore, the concept somatogenic is invariably used in the discussion of mental disorders.

On the basis of this, somatogenic disorder may be defined as the behavioural disorder emerging from organic factors. The somatogenic factor is one that originates in the bodily organic or tissues. The disorder is bodily in origin, distinguished from the psychological origins.

If any of the bodily factors disrupt the normal functioning of the brain, then there may be some change taking place in the behaviour of the individual. This change of the behaviour is not normal, but abnormal which we call behaviour disorder. In other words, we may call it somatogenic disorder or organic disorder or organic psychosis. If the injury takes place in a small part of the brain, it is called paralysis. Organic disorders or organic psychoses are causes by any organic condition of injury which disrupts the central nervous system and disturbs the behaviour of the individual person. But if the cerebral cortex which is supposed to be the larger part of the brain is affected, then the consequence is the psychological disorder which makes the whole personality disorganised. The personality might have been very healthy and strong before the injury of the brain.

But the injury now caused an important disruption in the individual revealing severe abnormal symptoms. However, the severe mental disorder depends upon the level of maturity of the mental development and emotional adjustment. Mental disorders occur due to brain infections as the bacteria or viruses enter into the brain and damage the nerve tissues. There are several types of psychoses associated with the damage of the brain tissues.

Organic psychoses are mostly associated with the brain dysfunction or impairment. When this takes place the whole of the sensory and motor functions, emotional and psychological functions are impaired. The disorders are considered as psychological and behaviour abnormalities. Therefore, it is important for a therapist to know that a psychological problem has a clear physiological or organic cause. The American Psychiatric Association has made an extensive classification of the mental disorders and mentioned in DIM-III-R, two major categories as *organic mental syndromes* and *organic mental disorders*. The organic mental syndromes are delirium (a state of mental confusion), dementia (damage of mental faculties), amnesia syndrome (total loss of memory), organic mood syndrome (affective disturbance) and so on. These have groups of psychological and behavioural symptoms which are caused by several factors. The other one is organic mental disorders in which the symptoms are associated with specific organic or somatogenic cause.

Somatogenic or organic disorders are discussed in different manners by different authors on the basis of the type of information available for them at that time. Since enormous amount of researches are going on everyday on mental disorders, different types of results are released on mental disorders and on the types of treatments. A specific type of treatment of the subject matter of abnormal behaviour cannot be claimed as the sole authoritative information. Therefore, whatever type of treatment is available we are to assimilate it for our purpose. It is better to discuss organic disorders or somatogenic psychoses with the most familiar and recent information available for us.

We shall discuss some types of organic psychoses which are associated with some bodily parts. These we may stated as : (1) Disorders caused by infectious diseases (2) Disorders caused by brain tumours (3) Disorders caused by head injuries (4) Disorders associated with toxic substances (5) Psychoses of the aged persons. In the following section we will discuss all these types of organic or somatogenic disorders.

The organic mental syndrome is a general term for indicating the behavioural disorders that result from certain malfunctions attributable to the known and unknown causes. The mental syndromes manifest in various forms which are not easily identifiable and any mental disorder of organic type is the result of some damage to some part of the brain, which is revealed in some type of behavioural disorder.

Organic Psychoses Caused by Infections Diseases

Human environmental conditions are not always congenial for happy living. They may change due to natural conditions or man himself may be changing it for his purpose. These changes of conditions may spoil the healthy atmosphere which may cause various kinds of diseases to human beings. Their living environment is getting more and more highly polluted which produces poinsonous substances. These poinsonous substances cause all sorts of epidemic and other infectious diseases. People suffer and die due to these diseases. The sufferings caused by these diseases are so painful that some people prefer death rather than suffer for days, months and years. Some even go the extent of committing suicide. On one side the deadliest physical diseases are caused by the environmental pollutions, on the other side mental diseases like organic disorders are caused by infectious diseases.

Man's attempt to conquer these calamities have not brought a permanent solution for all these. When his physical and mental health becomes weak by some means he falls prey to may diseases which cause impairment in his behaviour. Human mental make-up is such that it sometimes gets impaired and behavioural abnormalities appear and the person gradually loses contact with the world of reality. What type of mental impairment has taken place? There are several types, mainly psycho-neuroses, and psychoses which may cause him to suffer.

The psychotic impairments are more severe than the psychoneurotic disorders. The main psychotic disorders are functional psychoses and organic psychoses. The organic psychosis or disorders are caused by several factors. Some types of organic disorders are caused by infectious diseases. When the infection becomes severe the disease damages the brain and also may cause death. Therefore it is ascertained that organic disorders are caused by some diseases and infections.

Infection may be defined as the invasion of the body by some pathogenic microorganisms and the resulting condition in the tissues is an infectious disease. Any organism such as a bacterium, protozoan, is a virus of microscopic size which may become pathogenic and freely invade an organism. The central nervous system (the brain) is invaded by a wide variety of infectious agents such as viruses, bacteria, fungi and metazoan parasites. The diagnosis and the treatment for the infection are important aspects of clinical observation. Therefore, the infections are important aspects of clinical observation. The infections to the central nervous system normally spread out from the infection of the various parts of the body, namely, ears, nose, throat (ENT) into other parts of the body. The pathogenic microorganisms may also enter directly into the brain where there is head injury and skull fractures. Infection of the nervous system is very serious as the affected nerves and cells are destroyed. There are a number of ways by which infection destroys the neural cells.

The important symptoms of the infections are lowered blood pressure and other symptoms in blood circulation, fever, general malaise, beaches and delirium. The cerebral infections include the generalised symptoms of increased intracranial pressure such as vertigo, nausea, convolutions, mental confusion and localised symptoms of disturbance of the brain functions.

Types of Infections

Man's living atmosphere is full of poisonous and toxic substances. These substances spread out disease-causing germs which are of macro types and pathogenic, capable of causing infectious diseases. There are several types of infections that affect the central nervous systems, and the brain. These are (1) Viral infections (2) Bacterial infections (3) Mycotic infections and (4) Parasitic infections.

1. Viral Infections

The infections caused by the viruses mainly affect the brain. Viruses refer to any group of submicroscopic entities consisting of a single nucleic acid surrounded by a protein coat, and capable of replication within the cells of animals and plants. Most of them are pathogenic and cause diseases. A virus may also stated as an aggregate of nucleic acids that is made up of DNA (Deoxyribonucleic acid). Some viruses like rabies are called neurotropic viruses. These viruses have special affinity for the central nervous system, the brain, and cause injury (lesions) in the whole region of the brain. As a result of it the brain gets damaged.

2. Bacterial Infections

These infections are caused by a large group of cellular microorganisms called bacteria. Most of the bacteria are parasites. The important characteristics of these are producing diseases. The bacterial infections of the central nervous system result from an infection of these microorganisms via the blood streams. The most common disorders resulting from the bacterial infections are meningitis and brain abscesses. The brain abscesses (inflamed area in the body tissues) may also produce a variety of bacteria. Abscesses are produced by bacteria that cause death to cells in the affected area.

3. Mycotic Infections

These infections are caused by fungus entering into the brain. A fungus is composed of a large group of lower plants that exist on living or dead organic materials. The central nervous system strongly resists this infection, but the fungi invade the brain whose resistance is reduced by other diseases such as tuberculosis, pneumonia or brain injuries.

4. Parasitic Infections

A parasite is an organism that lives on another living organism. The most important diseases the paresite may produce are amoebiasis and malaria. These parasitic infections invade the brain and cause severe diseases. Amoebiasis is caused by infection of the protozoan amoeba which results in encephalitis and brain abscesses. Malaria is caused by *protozoa* of the *genus plasmodium* which are transmitted by infected mosquitoes. The cerebral malaria is caused by the bite of these mosquitoes.

Diseases caused by Infections

The various types of infections cause diseases in the organisms and impair the functions. Inspite of the human being very careful, the infections get into the bodily parts and cause disorders. This mainly takes place in the central nervous system, mostly in the brain. The infections get into the brain through ears, nose and threat. The microorganisms like the viruses, bacteria and fungi get into the body and infect the brain. They enter the brain and damage the brain and nervous tissues. There are mainly two types of diseases caused in the brain by the infections. They are (1) Cerebral syphilis and (2) Epidemic encephalitis.

I. Cerebral Syphilis

Most of the mental disorders are connected with the brain. It is because the brain cells are damaged or destroyed by infections. The microorganisms get into the brain and destroy the nerve and brain cells and cause cerebral dementia. Syphilis is an infectious disease caused by the microorganisms called *Treponema pallidum.* This is an animal microorganism named *spirochete* which also causes syphilis.

Cerebral syphilis has a long history right from the fifteenth century onwards. There are also references in the medieval literature. Girolamo Fracstore (1483-1553) an Italian physician, astronomer and a poet in the city of Verona wrote a poem in which he used the name of the disease, the poem itself, named as *syphilis.* It is based on the analogy of *Aeneas, Thebais,* etc., the Trojan princes whose adventures are described in this poem in which a person Shepherd Syphilus was the first person who suffered from this disease. The Trojans were the inhabitants of ancient Troy.

Syphilis was studied in detail by quite a number of scholars for a long time and provided with interesting information. According to Kemble (1936) it was the sailors of Columbus who were mainly responsible for spreading this disease all over Europe. Columbus, an Italian navigator and am explorer who had lent his services for Spain for exploring new lands in the end of fifteenth century first landed in West Indies in 1492. Here his sailors had contacts with the West Indies women and got infected with this disease. They carried the same to Europe. Kemble had stated that Columbus, himself had contacted this disease and it had become severe when he made the second voyage to West Indies is 1494, and the symptoms of syphilis appeared. During the third voyage in 1498 the syphilis attack became very serious in Columbus and he died of it in 1504.

Thus, the cerebral syphilis had played a disastrous role in the lives of human beings in the past. The present century is witnessing still severe consequences through syphilis and related diseased due to our present of acceptance of premarital permissive promiscuous bahavioural pattern.

Pusey (1933) states that syphilis is an infectious disease that has played a very disastrous role in the lives and happiness of human beings and was the cause of innumerable number of lives all over the world in the last centuries. The reason is that it is an infectious disease which can easily and rapidly spread out. But the most important reason is that syphilis is an infectious disease which is rooted in human sex life. It is a sexually transmitted disease.

There are also other infectious diseases which find their roots in human sexual life. Some of them are AIDS, syphilis and gonorrhoea. In any discussion of human sexuality it must be remembered that many serious diseases including syphilis, and gonorrhoea can be communicated through sexual intercourses. The *human immunodeficiency virus* (HIV) can be passed through genital, anal or oral sex, which may cause the *acquired immunodeficiency syndrome* (AIDS), an insidious fatal disease which has no cure. Syphilis may be defined as a general disease caused by infection or contact with the micro-organism *threponeme pallidum* which is characterised by an ulcerating cancer, usually on the external genital organs and progressing through the lymphatic system to nearly all tissues of the bodily parts, producing serious psychotic symptoms.

The other similar disease is *gonorreoea* which is also sexually transmitted. Gonorrhoea may be defined as an infectious venereal disease caused by a *gonococeus* which is characterised by a burning sensation during urination is the case of men and a mucopurdent discharge from the urethra or vagina in the case of women. The third deadliest infectious disease sexually transmitted is the AIDS. We have discussed this disease in detail elsewhere in this book. Human sexual life is an important part of life, that we must take it for granted some of its most basic elements, for example, the two sexes, are required mainly for reproduction, one male and the other female.

The male tends to be somewhat stronger and more aggressive than the female and that an adult human in some important sense is a man or woman. Whether a man and a woman are required to produce young ones or not, when they meet with sexual motive the resulting consequence is sexual intercourse. This sexual intercourse might have been planned or accidental. If a person is infected with any of the diseases, the other also gets infected. This infected disease may be syphilis or gonorrhoea or even AIDS. Thus syphilis is an infectious disease sexually transmitted to an uninfected person (male or female) by an infected person (male or female). Syphilis, or the specific disease, is caused by *Treponema pallidum* by sexual cognition or accidental contacts (acquired from) or by infection.

There are three stages of this disease, distinguished as primary, secondary and tertiary. The first is characterised by *chancre* (ulcer) in the part affected. The second is characterised by diseases of the skin and mucous membrane, and the third involves the bones muscles and the brain in the disease.

Types of Syphilitic Syndromes

There are three different syndromes associated with syphilitic brain infections. These are (1) General paresis (2) Juvenile paresis and (3) Meningovascular paresis.

1) General paresis

General paresis refers to the loss of physical and mental ability due to brain disease, which is caused specifically by syphilis. It is also stated as an incomplete paresis. Generally, paresis is stated as the mental disease caused by the progressive brain injury due to syphilitic infections of the brain. This disease or disorder is also known as *general paralysis*. Sometimes this may take 10 to 20 years to appear after the infections. At the this stage it needs immediate treatment, otherwise it may result in death. The syphilis bacteria is called *spirochate* which enters into the brain step by step and destroys the brain tissues.

According to clinical observation and analysis, paresis is a paralysis of motor functions. It is a disease of the central nervous system. It is also called dementia paralytica. General paresis develops in a person when he is not given treatment for syphilis for two or three years. If the person fails to take treatment at this stage the result is death. Paresis approximately occurs at the age of 50 for both men and women. Ford (1970) and Strange (1971) state that syphilis cases increased rapidly in United States and in 1970 alone there wears one million persons suffering from syphilis and not treated. There are wide variety behavioural symptoms. There is lack of judgement. The person neglects important things. He is not taking part in joys and sorrows, affections and anxieties. He may be interested in promiscuous sexual activities against moral principles.

General paresis is identified with a wide range of psychological symptoms. Individuals who contract general paresis in the early stage neglect it and they are very careless. In the beginning the individual may see these symptoms but think they may due to work and tiredness. There may be some changes in their personal habits.

The person may fail to understand and judge things and he may avoid important problems showing utter indifference to everything. He fails to take part in the events of joy and sorrows, love and anxieties. When the disease advances several physical symptoms appear, the eyesight becomes dim and unclear. Speech disorder takes place with a stuttering voice.

The patient of general paresis becomes very much aware of his appearance and his mannerism, and he also becomes unethical in his behaviour. His memory impairment makes several confusions. He faces money problems often and involves in various anti-social activities. All sorts of negative emotional reactions take place in him and thus his personality gets impaired considerably. There are three types of general paresis, according to clinical investigations. They are (a) expansive type, (b) depressive type, and (c) demanding type.

a) Expansive type

The expansive type of patient generally makes an overestimation about himself. He considers himself to be extremely well.

He claims that he is the richest man in the world and possesses millions of worth things with him. The person mostly lives on delusional ideas.

b) Depressive type

The depressive type of the patients react in a depressed manner and also become discouraged. But the patients to some extent realise that their failure to react in the live situations. These patients often develop unexpected and fantastic delusions. They accept that they have disorder of their brains. There is a tendency among them to commit suicide. They develop anxiety and extreme depression.

c) Demanding type

The demanding type of patients face gradual deterioration of personality and intellectual functions. The other symptoms are memory loss and apathy, personality disorders, and withdrawal from the environment. There are often delusions and halluciations.

2) Juvenile paresis

This type of paresis occurs in childhood and adolescent periods. This is a common disorder in many countries. The symptoms of juvenile paresis are the same as that of general paresis. But it is accompanied by mental and physical disorders. There is often loss of memory, failure to understand things and to make judgements. The patients usually have speech disorder and motor irregularities. According to Parran (1937) more than half of the children were found blind from birth due to symphilis in the family. Many children die in the first week of their life. If the child continues to live observable symptoms are not seen till the child attains the stage of maturity.

3) Meningovascular paresis

This type of syphilis is little different from the general paresis. Meninges is a membrane enveloping the brain and spinal cord. The syphilitic viruses damage the blood vessels and the meninges of the brains. The symptoms of this syphilis vary from that of general paresis. There are continued headaches, giddiness, vomiting sensation, blurred vision, but speech and writing abilities are not affected. The brain damage also is not to the marked level.

Treatment

All types of syphilistic diseases should be attended only by medical specialists. It should be attended immediately after the infection. Any delay in the treatment may cause danger later on, because once the infection has reached the brains and started destroying the brain tissues treatment of any type may have little result. But the invention of pencillin had dramatic effect in treating the syphilis in the 1950's and now the problem relating to syphilis have eased enormously.

The American Medical Association (1969) provided statistics with regard to the rapid increase of syphilis all over the world. Fleming et al (1970) stated that there was an increase of more than 20 lakhs of new cases of syphilis every year in the United States during the 1960s and 1970s. But the case a medical treatment received dependend upon the amount of damage caused in the cerebral area of the brain. In many cases treatments were not taken until the disease caused extension of damage to the brain.

In the case of juvenile paresis the treatment is almost the same as that given to the general paresis. Juvenile paresis should be controlled as early as possible. Pregnant women who suffer from syphilis are likely to infect the developing child in the stomach and the child will be born with the infection. Such a child is said to have congenital syphilis.

The meningovascular syphilis is also called cerebral syphilis. But all the syphilitic diseases discussed are all cerebral syphilis in the sense that they all attack the brain or the central nervous system. This syphilis spreads out more rapidly than the other forms. Early treatment is urgently needed. If the treatment is delayed it may result in death.

All these diseases are associated with virus or bacterial infections and the infections are of different types. Therefore, treatment varies with types of infection. Virus infection is extremely difficult to treat. It has no antidotes, the only way is to allow the diseases to run their courses. Sedatives are administered to keep the patient more comfortable. But the important exception to this disease is the treatment is rabbis. According to Kolb and Wishaw (1990) the number of case of cerebral infections by bacteria or virus have decreased with the treatment of antibiotic drugs. This is the usual treatment for these infections. It is necessary in some cases to drain the inflamed areas of the tissues (abscesses) for relieving the intracranial pressure or to reduce pressure where there is oedema or pus formation. Antibiotics are often used to treat the associated disorders but the mycotic or the parasitic infections treated are not so successful.

II. Epidemic Encephalitis

This is an inflammation of the brain tissues as a result of infection caused by virus. The epidemic encephalitics is the disease of the central nervous system caused by a filterable virus. This was identified only after the First World War in Europe and America. It is mostly found among children and young adults. It is now widely prevalent in developing countries in Asia and Africa. It is an infectious disease commonly found with the symptoms of bad cold or flu. When the disease advances the symptoms are fever, drowsiness and stupor. The patient is found to be very lethargic and sleeping all the time.

One of the symptoms sometimes found in the patient is the paralysis of the eye muscles and there may be some difficulty for the patient in having correct vision. Due to this the patient becomes lethargic most of the time. The disease is called *sleeping sickness*. The patient sometimes reaches a serious stage resulting in excitement, agitation and irritation. Coleman (1975) states that in children and young adults the after-effects of this disease may be very serious. The children who are well behaved and cheerful become ruthless, impulsive, destructive, homicidal, and sexually deviant. These children should be hospitalised, otherwise serious consequences may ensue.

The after-effects of the acute state of this disease is Parkinson's syndromes in adults. It may result also in paralysis of the bodily parts. The handshaking or headshaking is mostly found as after-effects of this illness. But the most serious after-effect of epidemic encephalitis is the stiffness of the muscles, jerking of the head rhythmically. Patients may have respiratory problems based upon emotional excitement. Some of the mental symptoms of Parkinson's disease are the loss of interest in life activities and the inability to concentrate on work. The patient becomes very pessimistic, depressive, develops utter disregard for his life and tries to commit suicide. The patient mostly lives in systematised delusions. Though this state mostly prevails in men above 60 years it is also found in some women.

Treatment

Epidemic encephalitis is an infectious disease caused by the invading virus and bacteria. It is cured mostly by medical treatments. However, the immediate attention is to administer antibiotics which would destroy the invading virus and bacteria. There are some new techniques of drug therapies, which may control the infections of the brain tissues. It is also possible to control this disease by psychological and educational methods in children.

CHAPTER 8

Organic Psychosis caused by Brain Tumours

What are tumours?

The general meaning of the term 'tumour' is any abnormal swelling or a mass of tissue formed by a new growth of cells, normally independent of the surrounding structure. It may also be stated as a mass of new tissues that persist and group independently which may be called neoplasm. It surrounds the tissue and has no physiological use. The psychosis associated with brain tumour is also stated as cerebral neoplasm. Strange (1965) states this as histogenic disorder. Histogenic is derived from the Greek Word 'histo', 'dzo' 'nessis', which means the production or development of organic tissues. 'Histogenetic' is an adjective term having the quality of producing tissues, relating to the formation of tissues. Therefore, we may define brain tumour as a mass of tissues formed by a new growth of cells, normally independent of the surrounding structure in the brain, interfering directly with its specific functions and behaviour.

Development of Brain Tumours

The brain tumour may develop in adult persons mostly in the middle age after 40 years. The tumour may cause a variety of disturbances in behaviour.

Tumours account for a relatively high percentage of neurological diseases. The brain is the most common place for tumours. According to the earlier classification, these tumours are of *two types*. One is the *benign tumours*. These tumours and not likely to occur after removing them. The other tumours are *malignant tumours* which are likely to recur after removing them. This may often develop to the extent of causing death. Although a distinction is made between benign tumours and malignant tumours, it is found that benign tumours may become malignant. Many benign tumours in the brain are untraceable to the surgeons. Any serious attempt to trace it may cause risk of life. The tumour or neoplasm of some muscles leads to speech disorder. It may also cause sensory and motor disturbances if the specific area of the brain is affected.

A tumour mostly appears in the central nervous system, but there is likelihood of its appearing in the intestinal area or prostate (a gland in males) in males and in females it occurs mostly is the breasts and the uterus. Since the brain is safely placed in the skull, only a small tumour may develop in the brain which may give strong pressure, causing very serious trouble, and affect the normal behaviour of the person. But the cases of brain tumour are very few and many cases are not identified for psychotherapeutic treatments. Clinical observations mainly state the place of occurrence of brain tumour, the size of the tumour and the fast growth of the tumour, the change of personality and the individual's capacity to tolerate the stress of the tumour.

But generally tumour means a swelling, and an abnormal growth of new tissue. It is independent of its surrounding structures. The growth may take place in any part of the body. Though in the beginning the individual does not feel any disturbance, later on the tumour may become malignant. If it is visible in any part of the body, it may easily be operated by surgical means. But, since it mostly occurs in the brain, it causes problems of abnormally and the person may be put into severe condition, resulting in behaviour disorders. The person may reveal many symptoms.

The brain is affected by several types of tumours. When a tumour is formed in some part of the brain it would immediately cause change in the behaviour of the organism in many ways. A tumour may grow as a separate entity in the brain which is called *encapsulated tumour*. These encapsulated tumours sometimes may have a form and may produce a cavity in the brain in which fluid may be collected and normally put up with the tumour cells. Since the skull is not an expanding part, any additional or increasing contents pressurise the brain which results in impairment. The other tumours are called *infiltrating tumours*. These tumours are not clearly identified. It is believed that these tumours mostly destroy the normal cells and occupy their places.

Symptoms

Brain tumours reveal the general symptoms and also certain specific symptoms, when the general symptoms appear then the tumour is developed into a bigger size. The symptoms are mainly headache which is in a continuous process, loss of memory, vomiting, depression, suffocation and also swelling of the optic nerve. As and when the tumour advances the patient is not able to understand the time and place. The patient neglects his personal habits, develops irritability and the feeling of vomiting, disorganisation in sensorimotor activities, hallucinations, apathy and a general confusion in the intellectual activities.

The final stage of this disease is the same as the other types of brain damages and the patient is driven to a dull and inactive life finally leading death. Levin (1949) made an extensive study of the symptoms of brain tumours in several patients who were between 22 the 65 years of age. He observed about 18 symptoms before the patients were admitted in the hospital. He found more number of patients revealed symptoms like memory impairment, depression, headaches, visual sensory impairment, drowsiness, irritability, restlessnes and so on. He also found that these patients showed different levels of emotional reaction to the organic images. According to the studies made by Mctaggart et al (1951) patients who had serious brain tumour in the brain areas of frontal, temporal and parietal lobes, experienced psychological complications. Patients who had problems in frontal lobe were found to be absent-minded and had memory defects. Tumour in certain specific parts of the brain like the sensory areas causes sensory hallucination like visual hallucinations, auditory, gestures and olfactory hallucinations.

Certain symptoms of the brain tumours are generalised. These symptoms are revealed in an individual as a result of increased intracranial pressure. These symptoms include swelling of the optic disc, headache, vomiting, reduced heart rate, mental dullness, double vision and a violent involuntary spasm in the muscles. But the patient may not be exhibiting all these symptoms at a time. A tumour in the speech area of the brain may damage the speech activities of an individual more than a tumour damage in the visual area of the brain.

How brain tumours are diagnosed and recognised

This process of diagnosis and recognition of the brain tumours falls under three stages or hypotheses. According to the first stage or hypothesis, a tumour may be existing. The second hypothesis is that there is a tumour which is confirmed, and the third stage is that the location of the tumour is within the nervous system of the organism. On the basis of this diagnosis the types of brain tumours are evolved.

Types of Brain Tumours

Brain tumours are of several types. But all of them are not correctly pronounced and recognised. Four of the brain tumours are clearly distinguished and identified. The criteria applied in this process are where they originate. These are, (1) Gliomas, (2) Meningiomas, (3) Metastatic tumours and (4) Pituitary Adenomas.

1. Gliomas Tumours

Glioma has its origin in glial cells. Glimo is a general term to indicate all the brain tumours that originate in the glial cells. These tumours pass gradually through the brain material. Kolb and Whishaew (1996) state that about 45 per cent of the brain tumours are gliomas type. The shades of gliomas tumour range from benign tumour to highly malignant type. The most often occurring gliomas tumours are (a) astrocytomas, (b) glioblastomas tumours and (c) medulloblastomas tumours. These tumours are very essential for the professionals who are dealing with brain pathology.

a) Astrocytomas

Astrocytomas is a type of brain tumour caused by the growth of the glial cells called *astrocytes*. These cells grow slowly in the brain. Astrocytomas are most common among the adult persons who are above 40 years of age. These are not very malignant because of the slow growth. Once they are treated they stop further growth and cause no harm. The prediction of the course of this tumour is possible, because of the survival of the patient after the operation. It was observed that for about 20 years there was no complaint from the patients. About 40 per cent of gliomas accounted for it.

b) Glioblastomas

This type of tumours are most common among the adult persons and these grow very rapidly. As a result of its rapid growth they become very malignant. These tumours attack persons over 35 years of age. The type of gliomas accounts in it for 30 per cent. The tumours make sudden growth of the cells, a type of immature cells ordinarily formed during the brain development. These tumours are formed by different types cells and grow rapidly and the patient will not survive for long time after the surgical operation.

c) Medulloblastomas

This type of tumours emerge from the growth of germinal cells, mostly in children. The germinal cells pass gradually through the cerebellum or brainstem. It is observed that the patient will not survive for more than two years. It is estimated that about 11 per cent of gliomas is accountable for this type of tumour.

2) Meningiomas Tumours

These are the growths connected to the protective outer layer of the brain or the cerebral cortex. These tumours grow outside of the brain. They are fully enclosed and the most harmless of all the brain tumours. Meningiomas tumours do not forcibly enter the brain, but they often multiply and put pressure on the brain and disturb the brain functions. Most of the meningiomas are finding place over cerebral hemisphere. But some fall in the cavity. This makes it very complicated to remove them in the surgical operations. The tumours also degenerate the overlying bone of the skull. This may be prevented only by removing the meningiomas completely.

3. Metastatic Tumours

Metastasis refers to the functions of shifting or transferring the disease from one part of the body to another. This is the common characteristics of malignant tumours. This transfer does not take place directly. The metastatic tumour in the brain is an established brain tumour which transfers the tumour cells from some other part of the body. They mostly transfer disease cells to lungs and breasts. It is commonly indicated that lung cancer is the cause of the transfer of the diseased tumour cells from the brain. Metastatic tumours are multiple and the treatment becomes very complicated. The prediction of the course of this diseases is also not appreciable.

4. Pituitary Adenomas

Apart from the major types of brain tumours discussed above there are also other tumours caused in the brain. One of them is the pituitary adenoma. This generally appears in the pituitary glands area. The pituitary is located in the hypothalamus area and not a part of the brain. But still tumours in that area cause pressures on the brain. The adenoma tumour is usually benign, a mild type occurring in glandular tissues. It has a gland-like structure. It may cause functional abnormalities in the hypothalamus area.

Brain Tumours and Personality disorders

Brain tumours also cause personality change. Individuals in society face heavy stress from biological, psychological, social and cultural areas. Persons well matured and balanced may withstand the stresses, others suffer from severe stresses which result in brain disorders or pathology. We may state that any small new growth of tumour in any part of the brain causing behavioural disorder seriously is concluded as organic psychosis caused by brain tumour. Some tumours are so malignant that they destroy the brain and body tissues. Mild type of tumours exert pressure on some parts of the body structure. Tumours, however small, may exert great pressure on the brain and cause disorder in behaviour. Brain tumours cause extraordinary changes in the personality make-up of the individual.

Treatment of Brain Tumours

For brain tumours since located inside the skull mostly any type of treatment other than surgery is beyond the scope of the treatment or cure. The medical surgery may relieve the patient from the sufferings and can cure the brain tumour. The success of surgical treatment depends upon the nature of the tumour. The size and location of the tumour in the brain area needed may define the type of surgery. There may be complete recovery from the brain tumour in some cases, but in some serious cases like enlarged and widespread tumour some symptoms may appear which are indications of paralysis, causing deterioration in intellectual activities. This type of brain tumours require an individual's major surgery, probably more than one operation. Such surgical treatments may result in death of the patient.

In one of the studies made by German (1959) it was found that about 40 per cent of brain tumours were curable, 20 per cent were partially curable and the rest of them met with death. Cole (1970) states that the success of the surgical treatment for brain tumour depends upon early diagnosis of the disease and early treatment. It is also important to diagnose the disease correctly. Sometimes psychogenic disorder is mistaken for organic disorder. There are some improved techniques for determining correctly the brain tumours which are developed very recently.

Surgery is the only way to make a definite histological diagnosis. If it is possible tumours may be removed in the same manner as in other parts of the body. An early diagnosis of the tumour may be successful for treatment. Radiation therapy is good for certain types of tumours. Mostly, the glioblastomas, medulloblastomas and metastatic tumours may be successfully treated. Chemotherapy is found to be not very much successful in treating brain tumours. The problem is in making the drugs pass through the blood-brain-barrier (BBB) and to distribute it in the tumour areas.

The various types of techniques applied for the treatment of brain tumours are becoming only temporary solutions. Treatment with medicines, however powerful, may only reduce the severity of the disease. The patient may feel comfortable only for sometime. Even in the case of surgical operations, the removal of the tumours is not the end of the disease. Whether it is a benign type or a malignant type recurrence is not ruled out. The reason seems to be that most of the brain tumours do not end within the region of the specific area of the brain.

Recent observations state that most of the brain tumours are malignant in character and they transfer the diseases from one part of the body to another part indirectly. Therefore, by removing the brain tumour by surgical operation, the tumour retains its malignant characteristics and passes on the disease through blood to another area. The metastatic tumours transfer the disease cells to mostly to lungs and intestine in the case of men, and to breasts and uterus in the case of women.

The clinical observations generally indicate that the cancer in lungs or intestine are the caused by transfer of the diseased tumour cells from the brain. When the diseased tumour cells make their appearance in any part of the body, other than brain, physicians commonly call it cancer. Any infection in lungs or intestine is tested for cancer by physicians. In women the breast cancer causes large swellings around the breast and in uterus, causing bleeding. For all these the treatment with medicine may reduce the severity temporarily, surgical operation is inevitable. Some physicians treat the patients with medicines, Most physicians advice the patients to get it operated immediately.

Generally cancer, tuberculosis and pneumonia are synonymously treated by physicians. These three diseases are caused by infections. It is established that cancer is caused by diseased brain tumour cells. Further deep diagnosis may bring out the real causes of pneumonia and tuberculosis though at present they are said to be caused by infections. It may be hypothesised that the diseased brain tumour cells cause these diseases by the process of transferring the diseased cells from the malignant brain tumours.

At present the infectious diseases like the cancer, tuberculosis and pneumonia are treated mostly by medicines. The radiation treatment, though successful in some cases, does not fully cure the cancer. Nowadays more people suffer from cancer of lungs, intestine, nose, throat, mouth and in eyes in the case of men and in breast and uterus in the case of women.

In the case of lungs cancer the patient may sometimes suffer from suffocation or hard breathing. It is because the lungs become weak and is not able to supply oxygenated blood to the heart and brain. The mass tissue formed in the lung is surgically removed, similarly in the intestinal cancer. Cancerous growth in the breasts and uterus are removed by operation. Similar in the cases of cancer in the nose, throat, mouth and eyes. But the specific brain tumours that transfer the diseased tumour cells to other parts of the body are not yet identified. As in the case of lung and intestinal cancer the cause of the other cancers also may be underlying in some of the malignant brain tumours. Therefore we may assume that a cancer in any part of the body is caused by transferring the diseased brain tumour cells to that part. It is also hypothetical that cancer, tuberculosis and pneumonia are the offshoots of malignant brain tumours.

CHAPTER 9

Organic Psychosis caused by Head Injuries

Introduction

The development of science and technology and the rapid industrial growth has made human life very busy, active, tensional and more stressful. Neck-breaking competitions in trade and commerce result in rivalry, aggression, violence and terrorism. People are involved in innumerable number of accidents and die and getting injured every day. Many die, some escape and few recover from injuries. Head injury in various forms is one of the major accidents human beings face these days. Generally, all head injuries lead to brain damage. The ancient Greeks and Romans right from the time of Hippocrates and Galan considered injuries to the head and brain as the causes of major mental disorders.

Nowadays we find that head injuries are very common and numerous accidents are caused on the roads, there are train accidents, aeroplanes crashing, accidents in metal industries and in mines. Even though hundreds of people get head injuries every day the number of persons seeking treatment in mental hospitals are very few.

Head Injury

Injuries to the head do not end with the head alone. The injuries might have been caused outside or inside the head. But any injury caused by a severe below on the head causes cerebral trauma. Traumatic head injuries generally cause cerebral trauma (brain injury). A trauma is a bodily injury having a lasting psychic effect. Cerebral trauma refers to the injury to the brain usually resulting from a severe blow to the head. It is the most common type of brain damage in people. But what amount of injury can cause damage to the brain to such an effect that there is behavioural disorder of organic psychosis? There is no correct agreement among the scientists on this issue.

Therefore it becomes very difficult to provide reliable information with regard to the nature of closed head injuries and the type of disorders caused by them.

But with the recent developments in the area of surgery and treatment, highly sophisticated procedures of neuroradiology, it becomes possible to state reliably that the brain damage from head injuries has become an important mental health problem in the present day. The most important procedures recently developed to deal with the head injuries are the *Magnetic Resonance Imaging (MRI)* and the *Positron Emission Tomography* (PET).

The magnetic resonance imaging (MRI) is an imaging in which a computer draws a map from the changes measured in the magnetic resonance of the atoms in the brain. It is also known as nuclear magnetic resonance (NMR). The functional magnetic resonance imaging functions in such a manner that changes in brain elements such as iron and oxygen are measured during the performance of a specific behaviour. The functional MRI is also used to measure the brain activity at the time of behaviour or rest.

The Positron Emission Tomography (PET) is an imaging technique in which a patient is given a radioactivity labelled compound like glucose which is metabolised by the brain and the radioactivity is later on recorded by a detector. Studies, according to Kolb and Whishow (1996), reveal that a blow to the head produces cerebral concussion, a state of unconsciousness for a short period. These persons who had this experience have been confused about the events that occurred during the blow to the head. The incidences of closed head injuries are quite common in highly industrialised countries. There are two important factors in the occurrence of closed head injuries such as age and sex. Children and aged persons are more likely to get into closed head injuries and persons, particularly males, above 15 years are likely to have brain injuries.

Studies indicate that cerebral trauma affects the brain and causes damage to functions in several ways. But what is head injury and what is brain injury? We have discussed this matter in connection with the organic disorders of psychoses. These disorders damage the brain functions. Therefore it is implicit that a head injury should be such that it must damage or injure the brain and impair the brain functions. The head injuries should be traumatic and cause cerebral trauma. A strong blow to the head may cause some mild injury or bruises which may cause a concussion or unconsciousness for a short period. This may not cause severe injury to the brain. Therefore we may state that an accident may be called head injury only if it causes damage to the brain and impairs the functions and which can lead to behavioural disorders or organic psychosis of some type. Thus in our discussion head injury involves brain injury with all the consequences.

A head injury that has caused cerebral trauma affects the brain function and causes behavioural disorders. A trauma caused by a bullet injury may result in damaging the nerve and the brain cells. A cerebral trauma may impair the blood supply to the brain parts. It causes bleeding within the skull which results in intracranial pressure causing increased damage to the brain. Further, there may be swelling in the brain due to the increased intracranial pressure, which results in further damage to the brain. If the head injury causes compound fracture of the skull, it opens the brain and may lead to infections. Head injury may cause scarring in the brain tissues and the seared brain tissues become the cause of epileptic attacks. Later, the sudden appearance of the epileptic attacks may be traced to head injury.

Types of Head Injuries

Head injuries are caused by various factors. According to Kolb (1996) there are mainly two types of head injuries. One is open head injuries and the other is closed head injuries.

Open Head Injuries

Open head injuries are caused by a severe head blow by some hard material. An iron rod may penetrate into the head and cause wounds. A big stone may damage and break the outer frame of the head. A bullet may be fired on the head and it may penetrate through the brain materials. A dash against a hard surface may cause wounds, injuries and bruises. This type of open head injuries may also cause bleeding. Many persons who have open head injuries may remain unconscious for sometime. Such people produce symptoms that may require some urgent treatment for the wounds and may recover very rapidly. The effects of these injuries may resemble a surgical cutting of a small area of the cerebral cortex or some part of the head.

Closed Head Injuries

The open head injuries are significantly different from the closed head injuries. Closed head injuries are caused by a strong blow to the head. This causes the brain to severe types of physical forces. We observe first of all there is damage at the place of the blow or hit, and is called *coup*. This means, where the sudden traumatic incident has occurred. The brain is closely and firmally packed by the bones inside. In the next stage, the brain is given strong pressure at the time of the coup in the opposite direction of the skull. This causes an additional bruise to the brain which is known as *counter coup*. In the third stage, there is twisting of the nerve fibres as the brain movement takes place. This causes microscopic lesions. This occurs throughout the brain, but it occurs mostly in the frontal and temporal lobes.

The movement of the brain occurs because of the pressure caused by the twisting, and this twisting causes damage to the fibre tracts of the brain. This causes disruption between the two sides of the brain. Thereby, there is a disconnection syndrome. The wounds and the strains caused by the incident cause bleeding within the skull which also puts pressure on the surrounding area of the brain. Further, the blow to the brain as in other parts of the body produces *oedema*. This is a collection of fluid around the areas of the damaged tissues. This oedema is also a source of pressure to the brain.

Closed head injuries are generally followed by a loss of consciousness and too much of strain of the nerve fibres in the brainstem and reticular formation. Lezak (1983) states that the duration of loss of consciousness or length of coma can indicate the severity of damage caused by the injury. This stage is highly associated with intellectual impairment, deficit of social skills and mortality. The longer the coma the greater the chances for serious impairment and death.

Symptoms

Though the brain is protected inside the bony skull which has a rare chance of getting damaged, a strong blow or hit on the head with a hard material may cause damage to the head and to the brain and to the blood vessels. When the head is injured by a severe blow or hit, the person may have injuries in some parts of his head, face, and in other parts. Apart from these physical injuries, the person is in a confused state, feels headache, memory is disturbed, and he is emotionally very much frustrated. In severe injury the individual undergoes a great deal of personality change Temperamentally he is thoroughly maladjusted and there are increasing mental disturbances. The general intellectual functions of the person is very much lowered. There may be injuries or damages in different parts of the brain which may be the areas of sensory and motor functions. When these parts are injured there may be disorders in the senses like seeing, hearing, smelling and tasting, and the arms or legs may not be functioning properly. Damage of the frontal lobe results in personality disorder.

One of the important symptoms of head injury is the development of chronic disorders. The force of the blow may be even without any fracture, but the brain may suffer the rupture. Head injuries generally cause the person to be unconscious and it may take hours, days for the person to regain his consciousness. There are certain specific symptoms caused by the nature of injuries. One is cerebral impairment which is also known as cerebral conscussion. This is a mild head injury. This interferes with circulation of blood and other brain functions. In this state, there may be momentary loss of consciousness. He may be in a confused state regarding his consciousness. There is also loss of memory and the person may not be remembering the accident in which he was involved. The person may regain his consciousness in a few hours or days. But the common symptoms are headaches, excessive fatigue and dizziness.

The other symptom is cerebral bruise or cerebral contusion which may be caused in severe injury to the brain. In this state the surface of the brain is bruised severally. This may cause unconsciousness for a long period, that is, for several hours or for several days. There may also be other symptoms like delirium. In the state of delirium there is mental confusion, disorientation, restlessness, excitement and the patient may experience hallucinations. The patient on regaining his consciousness makes several complaints. He has severe headaches. He is very sensitive to sounds and light. He often feels nausea and weakness. Some of the symptoms indicate that the sensory areas of the brain are disturbed. He is seen to be irritative. The intellectual and motor functions are also damaged.

The third important symptom is *cerebral mangle* (tearing). It is also stated as *cerebral laceration* or tearing of the brain tissues. The head injury is such that the brain cerebral tissues are impaired and cause damage to the brain and behaviour disorder. The penetration of some metal rod or a bullet piercing through the skull may cause this injury. The resulting symptoms are also the same as cerebral contusion. The immediate symptom is the state of unconsciousness.

There is mental confusion, headaches, intellectual and motor functional disorders. There may be high temperature, increased pulse rate and blood pressure. The person may be feeling very weak and a coma state is quite common; it may result even in death. On recovery from the unconscious state, the patient may be in a very excited state, restless and the hallucination is a common occurrence.

There are chances for the severely head injured patient to recover from it. However, the patient reveals certain residual symptoms like headaches, anxiety, fatigue, and irritability. There may also be loss of memory and impairment in intellectual and motor activities. Damages in sensory areas to the brain may result in loss of certain sensations. Injuries are possible in the partial lobe and in the occipital lobe, which may result in loss of sensations like touch, pain, temperature and vision. Some psychological and neurological defects also may follow the brain injury.

Closed head Injuries and behavioural change

Head injuries often cause change in the behaviour of the organism. Head injured victims show behavioural change in two ways. In the case of closed had injuries, caused by an accident, injuries are very severe. It is because, when the blow takes place the head is made to move and thereby the motion increases the effect and multiplies the nature of severity of the injuries in the whole brain area. The CT scanning of accident victims, the suffering from prolonged coma spreads out the brain injury and enlarges the lower chambers of the heart. This is traced by the computerised tomography scanning (CT), a highly sophisticated technique.

The unrelated or discrete impairment is more associated with the damage of the frontal and temporal lobes which are more susceptible to closed head injuries. The specific injuries cause more general impairment. It is spread out throughout the brain. The impairments are characterised by loss of complex cognitive functions and reduction in mental speed. These problems are revealed from the patient's complaints that he is not able to concentrate and also not able to do things as well as he was doing before the accident.

The accident victims who have the brain damage in the frontal and temporal lobes due to closed head injuries have severe effects in their personality traits and social and adjustment skills. In Lezak's studies it was observed that the accident victims who had severe head injuries resumed their duties at sometime, but were unable to carry out the work as before. The head injured persons often had chronic effects, but they were associated with neurological symptoms. However, they may be referred to psychiatric examinations. But it is assumed that psychological assessment may be useful in the case of persons who are seriously handicapped with cognitive defects.

The closed head injuries, according to Levin, Benton and Grossman (1982), are of two types such as primary and secondary brain injuries. The effects of *primary brain injury* are laceration (hurt) of the brain from depressed skull fracture and immediate impact on behaviour.

The effects of *secondary brain injury* are intracranial haemorrhage, oedema in white matter, diffused brain swelling, ischemic brain damage, raised intracranial pressure and brain shift. In addition there are numerous secondary effects of which the most important are ischemia, oedema, damage to the white matter and the corpus collosum.

Whatever type neuroradiological measures can produce objectively after closed head injury, the behaviour is the most important measure of the wholeness of the nervous system. There are two common measures of behaviour immediately after the head injury period. These two are *coma* and *amnesia.* The most useful indicators of brain injury are the depth and the duration of coma, prior to the development of the procedures of CT and MRI. But after the development of the CT and MRI procedures and the Glasgow Coma Scale, the degree of unconsciousness was subjectively indicated. In the Glasgow scale, there are three indications of wakefulness, indicated by the Scale, eye opening of the patient, motor response and verbal response. This Scale is able to provide reliable information about the recovery state of unconsciousness of the patient objectively. The Glasgow Scale is a Coma Scale which can identify the various levels of coma or unconscious state, and also the state of recovery of the patient by administering it serially.

The alternative measure of severity of the closed head injury is the post-tranumatic amnesia (PTA). This was first stated by Russull around 1930. It is ascertained that post-trauma amnesia (PTA) duration associates with the memory disturbance of the patient.

Brain Injuries and Speech disorders and related symptoms

The relationship between brain mechanism and language was ascertained by the observation of language impairments which occurred due to brain injury in a person, resulting from accidents, infectious diseases in the brain and strokes of the head. Evidences are available with regard to injuries and behavioural disorders right from the ancient times onwards. The early Egyptian medical records, known as Edwin Smith Surgical Papyrus were written 3,000 years ago. Finger (1994) quotes in his writings from the ancient medical reports that the injury to the temporal bone by a severe blow to the head caused people to become dumb.

The information available for us with regard to brain injury and cognitive impairments is from nineteenth century onwards. It was Paul Broca who first observed it in a person who had lost his ability to speak. The person's brain was injured in the inferior frontal region, a region which controlled the speech of human beings. This region is known as Broca's area. Studies in the following years found that there was some common syndrome of language impairments related to the distinct brain injury. It was also stated that about 90 to 95 per cent of the cases of language impairments were due to brain injuries. This is called *aphasia.* The damaged region of the brain in these cases were on the *right hemisphere.*

Studies were made by neurologists and researchers who had prime concern about language disorder and the specific region of the brain destruction. The main brain region according to them was the left hemisphere that was related to language abilities. Studies on brain injured people indicate that language abilities depend on the left hemisphere of the brain in all the right-handed persons and in most of the left-handed persons. Carl Wenneche (1848-1905), was a neurologist, studied in detail about brain injury and aphasia. He observed several syndromes of aphasia resulting from the brain injuries. Therefore, brain injury in a specific region causes speech impairments and behavioural disorders.

Closed Head Injuries and Recovery

Recovery from the closed head injury is said to take place in two to three years. But it was observed that the bulk of cognitive recovery takes place during the course of the first year. The memory recovery of the patient is little slower than the other faculties like general intelligence, and the final recovery level of the memory is slower than the other cognitive functions. The results of many studies on the quality of life, specifically, the social life, stress levels, and leisure activities were poor in the case of those who had closed head injuries, and also the conditions were becoming chronic. In the studies by

Klonoff, Snow and Costs (1986) it was observed that after four years more than 50 per cent of the cases had reported physical problems like limb weakness and pain and also stiffness which indicated that persons who had closed head injuries often had multiple problems in addition to the problems of brain injuries. Relatives of these patients felt greater strain in attending on them. From the studies of Brooks, Campsie, Symington, Beattie and McKinlay (1986) we understand that of the relatives of the patients who were spouses and parents 74 per cent complained that there was personality change after five years of the head injury and more than 50 per cent complained that the patients had mood changes, temperament, irritability and signs of violence.

Treatment

The treatment to brain injury is mainly medical attention. Immediate medical care should be given and the patent should be treated. There is no other treatment which can do better. The fractured bones, should be set right first and the blood clots should be cleared. Many patients with minor injuries or mild attacks may get relieved from sufferings. Many suffer from headaches, excitement, loss of memory for a long period of time in the cases of severe injuries.

The patients even after recovery face adjustment problems. Some patients learn to adjust at lower levels like domestic and social functions. But others find it difficult to adjust to the situations. They are found to be intellectually impaired. There are certain factors of situations favourable for quick recovery from the sufferings of the brain injuries. The one important factor is an unconscious state for a short period, which may help the patient to recover easily and quickly. The patient's personality development, if well balanced, may withstand the damage. There should be motivation for the patient to get rid of the sufferings quickly. The atmospheric conditions should be favourable for the treatment. There are also other factors, which have direct contact with the brain injuries. The nature of brain injury and the type of patients also have some influence in the successful treatment of the brain injuries. The results of the treatment vary in the case of children from those of adolescents and adults. It is also found that emotional states seem to be one of the predisposing factors in brain injuries.

In the case of brain damage and disorder, the two important causes are brain tumour and head injury. The head injury results in damaging the brain. But with regard to the treatment, since the brain is a very subtle and delicate part of the body it should be handled very carefully. Any injury to the head by any mean needs immediate and urgent attention. He should be first given a first aid of whatever type of aid is immediately available. The hospital may be far away or a physician may not be available immediately at the place where the incident has occurred. Therefore persons who happened to be beside should give first aid if the injury has caused severe bruises or wounds. What type of aids could make the injured person comfortable? This is the urgent need and any person who witnessed this can lend his services. Victims of alcoholism, drug addiction, and those who suffer from organic disorders are subjected to head injuries on roads and they need urgent first aid before they are taken to a hospital.

CHAPTER 10

Organic Psychoses associated with Toxins and Metabolism

How Toxins Impair Human Behaviour?

We have been discussing various types of organic psychoses in the preceding sections. Generally organic psychoses refer to the damage of the brain and brain tissues. Organic psychoses also are caused by other factors like toxins, metabolism and glandular systems. The development of science and technology has provided people with innumerable good things and also harmful things which pollute the environment with toxic elements. These toxic elements are poisonous materials greatly affecting the health of human beings and causing all sorts of curable and incurable diseases. The industrial smokes, the garbage burning smokes, the smells of poisonous chemical substances and gases, the smokes released by all sorts of transport vehicles, trains and planes, and other poisonous gases produced by waste materials spoil the health of the people and cause diseases.

Man inhales certain amount of poisonous air and gas every day. He cannot escape from this and he does not know what sort of disease he is acquiring from these. What part of his body is affected? Medical and psychological scientists have to detect the nature of the diseases and how they attack and damage various parts of the body. The poisonous material, anthrax, developed recently, is used by the terrorists for killing people. The anthrax gets into the blood of humans and animals, damages the blood vessels and death results.

The brain and its related parts are very much damaged by these toxic elements. Man is exposed the influence of these materials. He may then contact diseases like skin eruptions, gastric and intestinal disorders, acute and chronic bronchial asthma, severe brain disorders, loss of sensations, and impairment of motor and intellectual functions. Let us discuss here the toxic materials that damage the brain and cause behavioural disorders.

People are very much interested in eating tasty and nutritious food. But at the same time such food materials, specially the mushroom species, produce poison as they are fungus formed and cause death. Even a small amount of this plant, when ingested, produce severe psychotic symptoms. Poisonous substance, damage the blood vessels and cause mental disturbance and behavioural disorders. There are certain common psychoses caused by toxic elements. The disease followed by the mental disturbances are pneumonia and diphthenia which are acute infectious diseases marked by high fever and hard breathing. Toxic mental disturbance may also be caused by severe exhaustion and by ingestion of metal substances of various types and gases.

The mental disturbances caused by toxic materials reveal the symptoms to sound and light. The affected person gets nightmares and his sleep is very much disturbed. As the mental disturbance or delirium advances the person's consciousness becomes obscure and he is in a confused state. There is also loss of memory and he is not able to identify places, persons and senses. He gets often visual and auditory illusions and hallucinations. He is emotionally excited and the significant emotional reaction is frightening. He becomes highly suspicious due to the fear and he often complaints that somebody is planning to kill him, on hearing the footsteps of someone. Levin (1960) states that if the toxic psychosis is not very severe, there is no danger to the brain and the patient can get rid of the disease very soon.

Persons who work in difficult areas like desert, forest, high seas often get exhausted and may suffer from delirium. The reasons might be the severe physical exhaustion, unavailability of food or starvation for several days. Sailors who go on expeditions on high seas continuously for many days, even for months, extremely fatigued and may go into severe delirium states. The behaviour, thoughts, perceptions and expectations of these sailors are vacillating between survival and death since they are in the extreme desperate state.

Toxic Substances

In the human environmental situations, there are several metal and gases that man cause severe toxic delirium or psychosis. The most important metal poisoning is lead. Persons working in metal industries are subjected to chronic lead poisoning which will lead to *encephalopathy*. Encephalopathy is a pathological condition of the brain. It is an occupational psychosis. Mostly employees working in paint manufacturing industries, printing, typewriting letter manufacturing industries, and plumbers are subjected to chronic lead poisoning and suffer from toxic psychoses.

In toys and cosmetics manufacturing industries lead is enormously used and the lead materials are copiously handled by the workers. These result in chronic lead poisoning. Serious lead poisoning causes psychotic symptoms, which include headaches, fatigue, irritability, restlessness, confusion, insomina, anxiety, tremors and hallucinations.

Mental disturbance is associated with carbon monoxide. Inhaling carbon monoxide leads to impairment of the blood capacity in oxygen-fulfiling functions. The nerve cells in the brain are damaged and they do not function properly. If this state is very severe, the patient is in a coma state or suffers from delirium. Though it is possible to get rid of the delirious state, the poisoning of carbon monoxide sometimes causes death of the patient. Cole (1970) states that in the brain there is a protective mechanism which usually prevents the toxic or poinsonous substances to enter into the brain. This mechanism is known as *blood-brain-barrier*. Though the mechanism prevents most of the harmful substances it also shows certain substances needed for healthy functioning of the brain. The protective mechanism however is vigilant, there may be instances of ingestons, inhalation of certain toxic elements and oxygen deficiency or depravation may occur which damages the heathy functioning of the protective mechanism of the brain (the blood-brain-barrier) and impair the brain functioning.

Apart from lead and carbon monoxide, the other metals which are poisonous and impair the brain functioning are mercury and manganese, a metallic chemical element. These poisonous substances cause emotional disturbances, irritability, social shyness and the person is easily discouraged. The manganese poisoning is very severe. It damages the functioning of some aspects of the motor systems in the brain and spinal cord. It also causes muscular shaking and speech disorders.

Post-operative Disorders

Following the major operation, certain psychological and physical disturbances are observed in toxin psychotic patients. This has been a baffling problem for the physicians. The main post-toxic psychosis operation is the reaction of toxic delirious. In some cases the reaction involves anxiety, delusions, hallucinations, depression, confusion and fear. If the delirious state causes a severe reaction then there is high fever. But not all post-operational psychotic patients have the toxic nature reactions. Generally these cases occur in persons who have the characteristics of schizophrenia or manic depressive psychosis.

Malnutritions and Disorders

The human food habits are not highly nutritious. There are nutritional and vitamin deficiencies in human food. Certain disorders like psycho-neuroses are caused by the nutritional deficiencies. Particularly 'B' complex vitamin' deficiency causes weakening of muscles, depression and intestinal disorders. People who use highly polished rice and fully live on it suffer from vitamin B complex deficiency. Most people in India, Myanmar, Malaysia, Siam and in other polished rice-eating countries suffer from this deficiency, and to compersate this deficiency they directly use vitamin B complex pills.

There are many reactions to malnutrition. Most of the people, due to nutritional deficiencies, have physical changes, loss of weight, as time goes on people become more irritable, less sociable and lose their sense of humour. On putting them in restoration programme they rapidly turn to a normal state. For normal functioning of brain metabolism, minerals like calcium, vitamin 'C' sodium chloride and copper should be added.

Natural calamities often put people into nutritional deficiencies and cause behavioural disorders of various types. Famines, floods, cyclones, tempests and earthquakes may make people suffer from partial or severe starvation for a period of time. There are historical evidences that apart from death by severe starvation, there are instances of psychoneurotic disorders among the people and they resort to all sorts of antisocial activities in search of food.

In India there were instances of famines. There were 31 famines, occurred between 1769 and 1878 and 17 famines in Mediterranean areas. Rajamanickam (1999) and Morison (1918) have stated that there was a very severe famine is Bengal from 1769 to 1778 and this famine was said to have killed one-third of the total population of about 10 million people in Bengal, and put others in various types of sufferings. During the femine period people became mad without food and started looting government granaries. Infectious and epidemic diseases spread out and killed millions of people. Periodic hunger, vitamin and nutrition deficiencies killed millions. People became irritative, aggressive and violent. In the prolonged state the severe psychological reactions of the mental syndromes were disorder in thought process, inability to concentrate, lack of interest, and day dreaming. Wars also were causing several psychotic disorders. According to Broze and Grande (1960) the Second World War caused neurological, physical and mental changes. One of the important mental syndromes is asthenia, causing thought impairment. People all over the world suffered from malnutrition which includes several psychotic symptoms such as severe depression, apathy, disinterestness in life, decline of intelligence, loss of self-respect and fear.

Organic Psychoses and Endocrine Disorders

The endocrine system consists of several glands which secrete hormones for the efficient functioning of the body, physiologically and psychologically. Any under-secretion or over-secretion of these glands may severely affect the psychological functioning of the body. Any disturbance in the endocrine glands may cause physical abnormalities. An endocrine disorder is caused due to under-or oversecretion of the hormones. Men growing into abnormal heights and abnormally short growth of the midgets are caused by hormone secretions.

Thyroid Glands

The thyroid gland secretes the hormone thyroxin which plays an important role in the metabolism of the body. Intensive studies were made on the thyroxin irregularities. Whybrow et al (1969) studied quite a number of persons who had thyroid dysfunction. They observed severe psychological disorders.

There were pathological symptoms in most of the persons with pathological symptoms in most of the persons such as over-secretion or hyperthyroidism activities and higher metabolison. This state causes loss of weight, tension, tremor, emotional excitement and damming of cognitive activities. Some of the psychotic symptoms that usually appear are severe anxiety, agitation, delusions and hallucinations. Whybrow et al (1969) stated that there were visual hallucinations in some patients. In the case of hypothyroidism (under-secretion) there was iodine deficiency. The metabolic process was much reduced, but there was increase of weight in individuals. There was loss of memory of the recent incidents and impairment in cognitive activities. The most common psychotic symptom was severe depression in under-secretion of thyroxin. According to Whybrow's (1969) study the depression in a female subject was so severe that the she was often thinking of committing suicide. Richter (1970) states that prolonged hypothyroidism causes residual effect in congnitive activities.

Adrenal Disorders

The adrenal consists of two glands, located above the kidneys. The outer part is called cortex and the inner part is called medulla. The cortex extracts hormones called cortin. The adrenal cortex secrets the hormone called steroids that function in secondary sex characteristics. The adrenal cortex may cause Addison's disease when there is under-secretion or cortin deficiency. This causes several metabolic disturbance. The blood pressure drops as also the body temperature. The skin colour changes into dark. There is also severe giddiness and tiredness in the mornings. Some of the other mental symptoms are reduced vigour, sexual functions are depressed there are headaches, loss of hope and lack of will power for achievement. The main psychotic symptom is that the brain metabolism is very much disturbed in the patient and it may lead to schizophrenic personality characteristics. In some cases there may be imbalance in adrenal hormone; an excess of cortin may be produced and a female gets the appearance of male physical characteristics due to over-secretion of the hormones from the adrenal cortex. The female takes the male physical appearance. The person gets a beard face gets a male's voice and the body becomes stiff. This occurs naturally.

The medulla secretes the hormones adrenaline (epinephrine) and norepinephrine. These hormones activate the organism to meet any emergency situation like running quickly to escape from any dangerous situations and also to help in the process of metabolism. In this process more sugar is supplied to the cells and they function to release and spread out more red corpuscles into the blood. According to Strange (1965) an organism can survive without the adrenal medulla and its hormones, but it cannot live without the adrenal cortex and its hormones.

The B complex vitamin is found in fresh green vegetables, when it is deficient in food for a long period it results in the deficiency of nicotinic acid. This causes disorders like extreme physiological and behavioural deviations. The common disease *pellagra* occurs in which the patient shows violent psychotic behaviour. This disease reveals the symptoms like digestive disturbances, skin eruptions, anxiety and disinterestedness in life. If the patient suffers from extreme deficiency, real psychotic disorders appear. These symptoms are mental confusion, loss of memory, hallucinations and inconsistency in behaviour. In extreme case death is also possible.

Treatment

The clinical observation of this disorder varies significantly from one patient to another. But during the course of the disease it varies in some patients. Since this treatment is for the adrenal disorders, it becomes primarily a medical matter. The medicines cortisone and the drugs try to stop the seretions of corticold which may help for recovery. But there may be cases of tumour and other conditions. In such cases surgical operation is the best treatment. Early diagnosis and treatment for adrenal disorders may result in relieving the patient from these sufferings. The psychiatric approach may not settle the adrenal disorders. It was also observed that there are progressive treatments which may save the patients by administering strong vitamin therapies and adapting other recent techniques.

CHAPTER 11

Organic Psychosis of the Aged People

Psychosis in later life

Man since birth goes through the process of growth, development and maturation in several stages from helpless baby stage though infancy, boyhood, adolescence, young adulthood, later adulthood, middle age and old age. At all these stages the most important changes that take place are full physical growth, mental, social and moral development. Man puts himself into action with all acquired and learned capacities and makes achievements for making his life more comfortable and happy. In his ambition for achieving a better status in society he has to struggle hard. As he advances in age to the middle years, the decline in all his capacities are slowly taking place. But, since he has developed a good physical stamina, he never realises about his declining phases that are taking place in him. His physical energy gradually declines, sensory processes slowly diminish and his mental functions slowdown. Unless a drastic change takes place in him he does not bother about anything since he is in a continuous process of making progress for fulfilling his life goals.

During the course of his life he reaches the final stage of this life in fifties or sixties. At this stage the effects of all his accumulated efforts make him aware of his physical and mental faculties declining. He has to accept that he is physically and mentally diminishing in strength. If the personality development is strong he can withstand the strain and stress he is experiencing in the aged state or after 50 years. Otherwise he gets depressed and loses hopes in life. At this stage he may develop defensive mechanisms and deny everything that is happening in his life. As he further advances in his age he faces problems of adjustment with other people. The severe problems, the elderly person faces is the fast declining functions of the brain and the central nervous system. Symptoms indicate abnormally psychotic symptoms.

Types of senile Psychosis

On the basis of the symptoms the psychoses are classified under two types. One is senile psychosis and the other is psychosis with cerebral arteriosclerosis. These two types of psychoses cause organic brain damage. Some of the functional psychoses may also develop among the older persons. The most common mental illness is the psychotic depressive state. But the two important psychotic disorders of the older people are *sensible psychosis* and *cerebral arteriosclerosis*. Shekhmator (1968) states that 80 per cent of the psychotic patients are older persons.

1. Senile Psychosis

Senile psychosis is also called senile dementia. Senile psychosis or dementia may be defined as a form of psychosis caused by the deterioration of the brain or damage of the brain due to old age causing behavioural disorders. Dementia is an old term which means a mental deterioration following actual degeneration of brain tissues. Schizophrenia formerly was associated with dementia. Kraepelin (1962) named it as Dementia Praecox. It is also defined as a disorder that can be brought on by progressive deterioration of the gain caused partially by old age and characterised by memory impairment, inability of abstract thinking, loss of standard and control of impulses, lack of personal hygiene and greater amount of disorientation. Senile psychosis varies in severity from mild organic brain syndrome to severe and aggressive mental decline and death. Senile psychosis develops in a person gradually and as and when his age increased his physical and mental functioning capabilities are reduced.

The individual suffers from the psychotic state without knowing the consequences. As result of this, it becomes difficult to determine when the disorders have taken place. The consequences vary from person to person. Further it also depends upon the nature of the brain and the level of its degeneration and the time the person has experienced as a severe stress in his life.

The individual responds to persons and situations incorrectly as he fails to recognise men and matters rightly. Due to this he slowly withdraws from the situations. His social contacts become rare and mentally he is not alert. He becomes intolerant to changes and is depressed. He does not recognise any new idea. The person also suffers from the loss of memory to some extent. These types of symptoms are mostly found in the patients who are classified as simple type.

The memory defects in the person makes him to forget events that took place very recently. He cannot remember even the road or street where he lives in. When there is a change in the residence the patient often misses his road or street and often gets lost. As the person further advances in his age, things may become more severe. In such cases the person must be admitted in a hospital, or some person must be with him at all times. Most of the simple type of senile psychotic patients have the symptoms of delusions and hallucinations. The person who has certain complications of the senile brain damage may resort to defence mechanisms for the purpose of adjustment. He may overrate everything to protect his ego. This psychological process is called *projection.* The patient often is subjected to delusions of various types. The delusion of persecution is to justify his false ideas by saying that people are hostile towards him and planning to kill him. He may be suspicious of other people and accuse them of trying to rob his properties and harm him.

In the delusion of grandeur he exaggerates about his achievements. He claims that he was above everybody in all respects. He also claims that he is very handsome and everybody loved him very much. This type of patients are said to be suffering from a paranoid type of senile psychosis. The common symptom observed in most of the patients is depression, which is also associated with the delusion of persecution. The patient is also highly agitated and declares that he is of no use to his family or society. These patients of senile psychosis should be kept always under watch. Otherwise they may commit suicide and die.

Persons in the advanced stage, that is, after 65 years, become physically and mentally weak. The sense organs and other parts of the body lose their strength and the persons may not be in a position of carrying out their activities as desired. Sensory apparatuses do not provide correct communication. As a result they become weak and deteriorated in their sensitivities. In old age there may also be malnutrition. Due to these reasons he is hard of hearing, has poor eyesight, taste, smell and touch. Due to these defects in the sensory apparatuses infectious diseases attack them. Germs of various types, viruses, bacteria and fungus invade the brain through nose, ears and eyes and he is subjected to severe illness; he loses all hopes in life and cuts off contacts with the world of reality and stops taking care of anything. What is to be predicted about the consequence of this disease is death. The patients are easily accessible to any complicated disease like pneumonia, tuberculosis and cancer, leading death.

There may be also senile psychotic patients who are young. They may fall between 45/50 years. Preschizophrenia is a senile brain deterioration occuring in the early old age and accompanied by mental disorders. It is a branch of senile psychoses. These patients understand what is going on around them, but they do not understand the part they have to play. These patients are understanding about what is going on around them, but they do not understand the past they wanted to play. These patients when young, actively performed their duties. Now they pretend to be normal. They are very much interested in speaking about what they were in the past. Though they try to speak, they cannot have any meaningful dialogue with others because of their loss of memory. These early senile psychotic patients have a motivation to be busy, but what they do are without any purpose and unacceptable.

2. Psychosis Associated with Cerebral Arterioscelerosis

Cerebral arteriosclerosis is a type of psychosis similar to senile psychosis. It may be defined as organic senile psychosis in which the walls of the cerebral arteries get thickening. Cerebral arteriosclerosis is also defined as the condition that is marked by loss of elasticity and by thickening and hardening of the arteries, eventually, resulting in dementia. It is a vascular disorder. There are several vascular disorders that affect the central nervous system. The most common disorders are cerebral ischomia, migraine strokes, cerebral haemorrhages, angiomas and aeteriovenous aneurysms. Cerebral ischomia includes a group of disorders. The symptoms of these disorders are caused by insufficient blood supply to the brain. This ischomia either occurs suddenly which is called as stroke, or this may occur gradually. The blood supply decrease can have any of these causes as thrombosis, embolism and cerebral anterioscelerosis. The reduction of blood supply results in insufficient oxygen and glucose and also from a variety of factors which cause mainly narrowing down of the blood vessels. Another cause of narrowing down of the vessels is inflamation of the vessels or spasm of the vessels. The fatty substances and certain mineral substances get collected in the arteries going to the brain. These substances are deposited in the arteries, choking them. The brain area suffers without proper blood supply and nourishment and the brain tissues get degenerated. This may take place both in large and small arteries. Either there may be blockage of blood in the vessels or haemorrhage leading blood clots. Large vessels may cause more damage than the smaller vessels. But the blockage is gradual in the small vessels. The brain areas are softened when there is degeneration in the brain tissues. According to Yalom's (1960) study softening occurs in 90 per cent of the patients of arteriosclerosis senile psychosis.

It is also possible for a sudden blockage in small vessels and may cause several temporary psychological and physiological symptoms. This is the indication of small stroke. The important symptoms are mental confusion, emotional instability and trembling hands resulting in change in handwriting. It is also observed that small strokes may take place successively causing increasing deterioration and change in personality. In the case of blockage of blood in large arteries the person is subjected to severe strokes. This stroke is generally called cerebrovascular accidents. It causes damage to the brain function. At this stage the patient may be in a coma and may result even in death. By proper treatment the patient may recover with a certain degree of brain damage.

Cerebral arterioscelerosis is generally diagnosed as senile psychosis. This disease may prevail at the middle ages and at early old age of 50/55. Coleman (1974) states that the average age of the cerebral arteriosclerosis patients who were first admitted was 77 years. More male patients than female patients were found to have this disease.

According to a clinical observation made by Yalom (1960) it was found that the symptoms in the patients of cerebral arteriosclerosis of psychosis appear suddenly in almost half of the cases. The patients were in acute confusional state. This state occurred because of the cerebral vascular accident. These persons were not able to identify or recognise places, persons and time. They got paralyses attacks on one side of the body. Rothas Child (1956) found that about half of the patients admitted for treatment had paralytic attacks and most of the cases were severe. In severe cases the symptoms of the confusional state were not cleared by treatment, and the patients succumbed to death. But in some cases there were mental deficiencies which developed gradually. The accompanying psychological symptoms were emotional instability and irritability.

In senile psychotic state the memory defect may increase. This incidence occurs in the patient if he is tired and has emotional stress. The patient generally suffers from emotional instability and he often weeps with any provocation. He becomes highly irritable and suspicious, and develops delusions of persecution. Due to these states there is a general impairment in his intellectual activities. The person's interests in the outside world is reduced considerably. There is loss of moral judgement in the person and there is a tendency for sexual offences. He never differentiates his sexual approaches, whether it is an adult person or a child. The patient is often driven to a depressive state and does not understand the impairment of his physical and mental faculties. If the onset of the disease is very acute, then there is progressive damage in all the faculties and ultimately the patient meets with death. The cerebral arteriosclerosis of the senile psychosis does not vary very much from other senile psychoses. As a result of this sometimes diagnosis becomes very difficult. Sometimes there are mistaken identify of the cerebral arteriosclerosis from senile psychosis. The senile psychosis develops gradually and continues for a longer period. But sometimes the cerebral arteriosclerosis is caused by cerebrovascular accident and the patient is made to suffer for a short period resulting in death.

Treatment

Any aged person who is suffering from senile psychosis of any type is himself a problem. The person is kept at home or hospitalised. He is mentally disordered and it is very difficult to get him relieved of it. Persons who suffers from senile psychosis require hospitalisation when they manifest symptoms such as depression, mental confusion, violence, noisy and antisocial behaviour. Authors like Lipscomb (1971) and others state that hospitalisation should be the last resort. The reason is that when there is sudden change in the environment and the type of life causes stress for the patient, treatment should be based upon the needs of the patients. This normally should be wider approach involving medical and psychological procedures. The medical approach is mainly surgery and improvement of the physical health of the patient by providing nutritious dieting system. It is found that psychotic symptoms of senile psychoses are controlled by administering mild drugs with tranquillising effect. This will have an effect on emotional disturbance also.

But this type of treatment to the patients who suffer from senile psychosis of cerebral arterioscelerosis at the advanced stage will not have any effect. This is the view expressed by Jabcobs et al (1969). According to them, this approach is effective specifically in the case of memory loss. The memory loss for the immediate incidents can be reduced in aged patients.

Studies in this area indicate that the group psychotherapeutic approach to the aged patients suffering from senile psychosis of cerebral arterioscelerosis is used successfully.

With regard to the treatment or therapy Kolb and Whishaw (1996) state that there are three experimental approaches to brain damage. They are the rehabilitation procedure which has a variety of behavioural and psychological therapies. The second is pharmacological therapies which can be applied to get recovery immediately after the surgery period. The third procedure is transplatation techniques which can be applied to regain the normal brain functioning.

Rehabilitation

Rehabilitation procedures are widely applied which yield mixed results. The aims of rehabilitation is to bring back the patient to the functioning stage that should approximate the previous function of these patients. From the rehabilitation point of view to know what is going on in the brain is not important. It is important to know what procedure may be applied to restore the patient to the normal level. There should be stimulation of the bodily parts in the early stage of post-operation. There should be some kind of interaction like speaking to the patient. The impaired part of the body may be made to move forcibly. The practice may be continued till what is required for the impaired parts. Some tasks may be assigned and the patient should continue till he gets much familiar with them. These assigned tasks should be relevant to his real-life situation.

In some therapeutic centres or hospitals nurses are engaged to feed the patients and they are moved in wheel chairs. Physiotherapies, if any, may be given where the patient is put up, mostly at the bedside. Patient's relatives or family members may be permitted to be present at the time of physiotherapy. Putting the patient into long work period may have little gain as there is likelihood of strain and frustration on the part of the patient. The excess task given to him need not be of complex type. It may be cut into small or short components.

Pharmacological Therapies

In reducing the effects of brain damage the pharmacological therapies have been receiving importance and much interest was shown to them. Studies on the this therapy were carried out extensively by Feeny and Sutton (1987) and their results revealed that certain functions can be restored in brain damages. According to the researchers the rate of recovery in the functions of brain damage can be increased by pharmacological treatments. The mechanisms underlying the effects of the therapy are transmitter systems. These systems are function in the recovery processes.

Transplantation Techniques

By therapeutic techniques the brain tissues are transplanted. In this technique the fetal tissue is cut apart from the fetal brain. The fetal tissue contain undeveloped embryonic cells. The tissue is transferred to a saline solution which is treated to separate the fetal brain cells from glia (supportive cells) blood vessels and other tissues. Then it is injected into the respective or appropriate place in the brain of the organism. This aspect of the procedure may be carried out in several ways. Brain tissues may be used from different parts of the brain, different persons and persons of different ages. The injection or planting procedure in future may involve the injection of other substances such as nerve parts which can be combined by grafting into the brain. Since it is a very complicated issue, progress in this area is slow and also a successful transplantation or grafting seems to be a risky task.

In brain damage there is degeneration of tissues. The degenerating part is replaced by brain grafting. Mostly in Parkinson's disease the technique should be immediately applied, because it causes the loss of specific groups of cells. A safety device for the disease is to make brain grafting of embryonic cells with the brain. But grafting techniques in human beings are still in the experimental stage. Complete success is not yet achieved. The grafted part in human beings does not grow sufficiently in the large human brain. The grafted part may not be properly adapted into the brain ciculartorly system and some times the same disease reappears and causes the same trouble. Winder et al (1992) made positive reports of the transplantation cases. But these patients developed Parkinson's symptoms later on. Therefore the transplantation was not a cure of the disease. Continued active therapeutic approaches may prevent regression and also help to recover the patient from what is expected. There are also several inherent useful ways to restore the brain tissue damages. But only few clinical techniques were sufficiently developed. In view of these it is believed that behavioural therapy is found to be the most useful treatment which yields expected results in treating the patients.

In the therapeutic techniques discussed above, the important process is grafting or transplanting the tissues, in which surgery is involved. An organ or a tissue from one part of the body or from another body is transferred to a location in the brain where it is needed due to damage or destruction of the tissue in the brain. Grafting means joining or incorporating the damaged brain tissues of a patient with tissues from another body or person. This is expected to grow with the tissues of the brain and help blood circulation in the brain.

CHAPTER 12

Brain Syndromes associated with Presenile Dementia

Introduction

The mental disorders at one stage were not properly classified as some of the syndromes among them had the same characteristics. A group of diseases of the central nervous system (brain) revealed the characteristics of progressive mental disturbances and deterioration. All these diseases were classified in the beginning as simple presenile dementia (psychosis). These diseases appeared also in young persons. They were named as Pick's disease and Alzheimer's disease. There are also other two diseases associated with the names of the persons who have first described them. They are Parkinson's diseases and Huntington's disease.

Pick's Disease

Pick's disease was announced by Arnold Pick in 1892 in a research paper. Pick was a Czechoslovakian physician who was able to identify this disease as a degenerative disorder of the central nervous system. It is a presenile psychosis generally caused by progressive brain deterioration. This disease diffuses the tissues (atrophy) of frontal and temporal lobes of the brain, and impairs memory, concentration and the ability to think abstractly, finally resulting in severe psychosis and death. This disease becomes more and more pervasive. It mainly affects the brain and reduces its weight. It sets on people, aged 45/50 years. The symptoms that appear are absent-mindedness, irritation, blaming others for personal failures and delusions of persecution. The person is highly agitated and disoriented.

The changes in behaviour cause some confusion in diagnosing Pick's diseases. The changes are quite similar to the general paresis or one of the functional psychoses. The diseases can be diagnosed only after some years. This diseases may continue for more than 10 years causing gradual impairment of memory along with intellectual activities. There is also some amount of speech disorder. The person often forgets the task he is performing and goes for another task without completing the first one. There is emotional sluggishness and loss of interest in everything. The patient should be left in a rehabilitation centre or in a hospital for proper care.

Alzheimer's Disease

The onset of Alzheimer's disease is in the early and middle forties and the disease ends in death of the patients after two or three years of suffering. It is one of the presenile and senile dementia. The disease was first discovered and described by Alosis Alzheimer, a German neurologist, in the year 1860. The genesis of this disease is unknown. Alzheimer's diseases may be defined as presenile progressive brain disease accompanied by severe behavioural disorder. It is also stated as dementia involving progressively deteriorating the cortical tissues of the brain and marked by memory impairment, involuntary movements of limbs, deterioration of intellectual functions, and psychotic behaviour. This disease prevails more in women than in men.

Persons who suffer from this disease appear more absent-minded and lack of concentration and often are irritable. The patient often blames and finds fault with others for his failures and has delusions of persecution. Memory deterioration is a continuous process and the person becomes unceasingly agitated. Changes in the brain may be going on. According to Kowell and Ceal (1988) the axons and dendrites of the neurons in the cerebral cortex are damaged. Due to this there is general deterioration of tissues in the brain.

Parkinson's Disease

Parkinson's disease is a presenile psychosis characterised by severe muscle and uncontrollable tremors, a rigid foot movement, a masklike face without any expression and withdrawal. It is also defined as the disease of the motor system that is associated with *loss of dopamine* in the brain and is characterised by tremors, rightly and reduction in voluntary actions. It was James Parkinson, a British physician at London, who first discovered and described this disease in 1817, and it was named after him. Apart from discovering this disease, Parkinson was able to see this disease in persons in the streets of London. Persons suffering from this disease were watched by Parkinson himself. The movement of the victims were the same as those he observed in his patients in his clinic. Parkinson's disease was called '*shaking palsy*' or paralysis agitans'. But, Jean Chacot has suggested that the name of the disease should be in the name of James Parkinson to honour him and to recognise his service. Pakinson's disease usually had its onset in old age people. The symptoms of this disease vary enormously among the people which is the sign of the complexity of this disease.

Causes

The origin of this disease is said to be common in the family. It is also due to old age. Another cause attributed to this disease is viral. It is caused by virus infection. Generally persons over 50 years are susceptible to this disease. There are three types of Parkinson's disease. They are *idiopathic*, *postencephalitic* and *drug induced.* Parkinson's disease also may develop from arteriosclerosis type of senile psychosis. One type of this disease, the postencephalitic, originates as sleeping sickness. One of the major causes of Parkinson's diseases is associated with ingestion of drugs. The major tranquillisers are *reserpine*, *phenothiazine* and *butyrophenone derivatives.*

A recent discovery was made by Langston and Cowortken (1983) that Parkinson's disease may be also caused by taking *synthetic hereoin* which is a strong toxic substance for destroying the dopamine cells of the brain. It was also observed that quite a number of young drug users developed Parkinsons's disease and displayed complete symptoms of this disease after using contaminated drugs. Similar drug substances also may cause the same effect in persons. The history of the patients who were admitted in the hospitals of Vancouver in Canada and in the city of Helsinki of Finland revealed that there was an increase of patients below 40 years who were inflected with this disease. This evidence indicated the view that even water and air contains environmental toxins that may cause the effect similar to other virus substances. The environmental pollution may be the cause of various types of viruses and bacteria to emerge and these invade the brain of the human beings through ear, nose and throat and damage the brain in some areas, causing psychotic disorders.

Symptoms

The symptoms of Parkinson's disease are somewhat similar to other psychotic disorders. But they can be identified as they have certain specific characteristics. It was identified that there are four major symptoms such as tremour, rigidity, akinesia and postural disturbances. All these symptoms may appear in different bodily parts and each one may appear in combination with other symptoms. Some of the symptoms reveal abnormal behaviour and some appear with the absence of normal behaviour. Because of these reasons Parkinson described the symptoms under two major categories as positive symptoms and negative symptoms.

The Positive Symptoms in Parkinson's Disease

These symptoms are common, but they do not manifest as they are kept in check. The normal persons do not allow the symptoms to appear and they inhibit them. But the disease makes the persons to manifest the symptoms. The positive symptoms are tremors, muscular rigidity and involuntary movements. When the body is at rest the limbs of the persons make alternative movements and these movements stop during sleep in the person. The muscular rigidity involves the increase of muscle movements in both types of muscles at the same time. The extensor and the flexor muscles are involved in the movement. The rigidity may be severe to make the movements more. The involuntary movements are involved in the changes in posture continuously. This results in freeing the tremor and sometimes the rigidity.

The Negative Symptoms in Parkinson's Disease

The negative symptoms of Parkinson's disease were analysed in detail by Martin (1967) and they were put into five categories. They are postural disorders, disorders of righting, disorders of locomotion, disorders of speech and akinesia.

The postural disorders involve are inability to maintain a part of the body, for example, head and hand, in the normal position. A standing person may bend forword or his head may lean forward until he sits on his knees. In the postural disorders, there is difficulty in standing and sitting and the person is unable to stand on one leg. If he is pushed lightly he will not be in a position of taking a step forward to adjust his standing. The disorder of righting involves difficulty in getting to a position of standing from a lying position with the face upward. In the *disorder of locomotion* the body loses the gravitational level, when the weight of the body is put on one limb. The *speech disturbance* involves difficulties in producing sound and in the tone of voice. The *disorder of akinesia* consists of slow movements which may appear in facial expression, that is, in blinking, swinging of the arms while walking, and sitting motionless for several houses.

Treatment to Parkinson's Disease

The treatment of Parkinson's disease is to provide support and comfort for the patient. The major symptoms are influenced by psychological factors. The result of the treatment involves how far the person can get rid of his disability. It is better that the patient should have counselling as early as possible after the onset of this disease. The nature of the disease and its potential consequences are considered in relation to the length of the patient's life. Physical therapy is a must for Parkinson's disease. It involves heat massages to reduce the painful feelings in the muscles. Constant training and exercise are given to make the muscles and parts of the body adjust to the changes in movements.

Parkinson's disease is also treated with drug administration. The structure and function of synopses of the nerve cells have been understood and treatments are advanced. The pharmacological treatment increased the activity in the patient first. Secondly, reducing the activity in the structure highly increases the activity. Parkinson's disease is treated by administering anticolinergic drugs for reducing the heightened action of the cholinergic neurons. Movements must be encouraged as much as possible. Speech therapy is very helpful to the patient.

Recent Developments in the Treatment of Parkinson's Disease

An explosive research into the etiology and pathogenisis of Parkinson's disease (PD) was made by Stanley Farhn (2002), professor of neurology. The results of this search have brought new drugs that could slow down the progress of the disease and in the long run it may even cure it.

Farhn states that it is one of the major milestones, crossed recently in the neuro-medical history. He pointed out that it is the usage of genetic technology to locate the genes that cause Parkinsons's disease. Although the genetic causes are not thought to be the most common, they provide clues leading to the understanding of the pathogenesis of the disease and therapy clues to find treatment.

In some rare families in the US, it has been detected that heredity was the cause of Parkinson's disease and it was caused by mutation in the 'genes-a-synuclean', a protein found in nerve terminals. Several other gene defects have been subsequently located, but were yet to be identified. Regarding the treatment, cure never seemed so bright. At the best surgical and medical therapy for Parkinson's disease indicated the symptoms of the condition only and the cause of the disease is yet unknown.

A major principle in treating the symptoms of Parkinsons's disease is to base the therapy according to the type and severity of the symptoms. Even then, adverse effects from drugs are common and the complications have been impediments to satisfactory therapy. Continued researches are going on in the pharmaceutical organisations to develop medications to treat the symptoms of Parkinson's disease that would have fewer adverse effects on patients. The discovery of new symptomatic drugs to slow down the progress of the disease is immanent. The management of neurological problems is becoming a challenge for both researchers and health specialists as the problems are manifesting even among the younger people. The cause of the problems of Parkinson's disease is becoming a mystery. Research in therapy is on reduction of the cost of managing the disease and the new forms of the existing drugs.

Parkinson's disease is the effect of progressive degeneration of the brain neurons and dopamine. Medical therapy located the area of symptomatic relief. Though the existing drugs have some side effects, medical therapy remained the mainstay, though in some selected patients surgery is used for stimulating. But the planting of electrodes is getting to be expensive in India. Burn, the neurologist, and Ban Schlome (2002) an epidemiologist, who are working on neuro-disorders, said that people simply think that the disorders are due to old age or weakness, but a careful analysis of the patient's movements could reveal the symptoms such as alternating stiffness and movement disorders. There are many theories on the cause of Parkinson's disease including studies that could be due to genetic factors or even due to the use of pesticides.

Huntington's disease

Huntington's disease is originally called Huntington's chorea. Goerge Huntington an American neurologist, discovered and described this disorder in 1872. . Chorea is derived from the Greek word 'Khoreia' which means dance, also chorus. The Latin word is 'chorea'. Chorea is defined as a convulsive disorder characterised by irregular, involuntary contractions of the muscles. It may be also stated as a disorder of the brain marked by uncontrollable, irregular brief jerky movements. Huntington's chorea is a genetic disorder which causes deterioration in the intellectual function and abnormal behaviour when an individual reaches a certain age.

Huntington was born and brought up in a traditional physician's family in the city of New York and had the opportunity to observe people who had some kind of disorders. He was inspired by his father's and grandfather's professional practices. He also started studying medicine and became a qualified physician at the age of 22. He also wrote and published a treatise on diseases. *The history of the disease and its origin.* Huntington's disease is relatively very rare. The death ratio also is very negligible. Huntington's disease (chorea) is, therefore, declared as a hereditary one. It is a progressive deteriorative disease.

The symptoms of the disease are generally reduction of the normal activities and the individual's interests in life are limited very much. There is restlessness in the patient and also involuntary movements. These symptoms are attributed to hysteria or some other neurotic disorder. The involuntary movements in the beginning are very slight but may increase gradually. The whole limb or part of the body is involved in the movements and not in single muscle. Ultimately there may be movements of uncontrollable type and they affect mainly the head, face, trunk, limbs, thus affecting speech, walking, writing and other voluntary movements. There may be emotional and personality changes. The individual also experiences loss of memory, and inability to carry out the desired activity. Certain cortical diseases also may develop. The emotional disturbances are mainly anxiety, depression, mania, and psychosis of schizophrenic type. The younger patients may even try to commit suicide and die at the advanced stage of this disease.

The onset of this disease may take place in early years. Generally, persons suffers from this disease at the age of 30 to 50 years. Huntington's disease causes shrinking and thinning of the cerebral cortex. Studies on Huntington's patients were conducted very extensively and it was found that there was impairment in a sensory areas. They scored poorly in memory test, visual, auditory, touch and perceptual areas.

CHAPTER 13

AIDS Dementia Complex and Other Serious Diseases

Development of Serious Diseases and behaviour Disorders

Human beings are periodically becoming victims to various kinds of epidemic and infectious diseases. It is because the human body is not an anti-infectious organism. The history of human kind has seen several such incidents. Apart from the epidemic diseases such as plague and cholera, infectious diseases such as tuberculosis, cancer and yellow fever had caused disastrous consequences in the past. Tuberculosis is a severe communicable disease, caused by infectious tubercle bacillus which most frequently affect the lungs. Cancer is a type of malignant growth or tumour caused by abnormal and uncontrolled cell division which may spread out through the lymphatic system or bloodstream to other parts of the body. Yellow fever is an acute infectious disease of tropical and subtropical climatic conditions characterised by fever, haemorrhages, vomiting of blood and jaundice caused by a virus transmitted by the bite of a female mosquito of the species. All these infectious diseases have their share of killing millions of people all over the world.

But the development of science and technology produced effective medicines and the treatment of the people with the medicine saved them from disastrous consequences and death. Chemical and medical scientists were able to meet the challenges of these diseases by producing suitable medicines and methods of treatment, and saved humankind from dire consequences by the last quarter of twentieth century, that is, after 1975. Another dreadful disease is AIDS. It is acquired immune deficiency syndrome. Information about this disease is available only from 1980. AIDS is a highly infectious disease, fastly spreading out all over the world in a very short time. Unlike other infectious diseases like tuberculosis and cancer, this disease has perplexed the chemical and medical scientists.

They are hard trying to find a suitable medicine and method of treatment for AIDS.

AIDS Dementia

AIDs is a new disease and the correct root cause of it is yet to be known. AIDS may be defined as a disease characterised by the loss of immune function that is spread by the human immuno-deficiency virus (HIV).

Cause

Information to find out the root cause of this disease was traced in America in the year 1979. Blood samples were collected to trace the root of it from various sources and also the blood sample drawn from the people of Uganda on east coast of Africa. Research scientists are of the view that this disease has its origin in human sexual activities, since it is a sexually transmitted disease. Research results are available on this, which are not able to provide any correct information as to the origin of this disease in human sexual activities.

The available and reliable information is that AIDS is caused by an infectious virus called human- immuno-deficiency virus (HIV). The HIV was first isolated and identified by HO (1985) and his coworkers from the cerebrospinal fluid and neural tissues. HO observed certain neurotolgical symptoms. Almost at the same time Nurnberg found out in his patients the symptoms known as AIDS dementia virus. This virus is capable of invading the brain-blood-barrier (BBB). The brain-blood-barrier is a defence mechanism which does not permit anything other than oxygen, nutrients and waste products to pass through between blood vessels and the cerebra spinal fluid. The HIV somehow gets access to the brain and causes damage to it which results in AIDS dementia complex (ADC).

In causing AIDS, the HIV virus is mainly responsible, which destroys the immunity system of the body. This HIV enter the body through some source. It is stated as 'Acquired'. Though the human body has the capacity to resist anything that is harmful or disagreeable or any germ that may cause some disease the HIV somehow gets entry into the body. The human body is protected by some kind of energy from some diseases. This process is called immunity. This protective system, the immunity, may become weak or *deficit* due to several reasons. When this deficiency takes place in the body to a notable extent, then, certain symptoms begin to occur.

The concept *syndrome* refers to a group of symptoms which occur together in a disease and indicate the characteristics of the disease. But in the case of AIDS the group of symptoms refers to a group of diseases which are stated as AIDS and its related complex (ARC). But once the HIV of the AIDS gets into the body, it begins to attack the helping cell, the lymphocyte (J-4) of the immune system and destroys it. This is how the HIV begins to function and how a person gets contact with AIDS. A person becomes the victim of AIDS when the immune system of the body is fully destroyed. The human immuno deficiency-virus (HIV) is a highly infectious one, which mostly differs from other viruses and bacteria in various ways.

The HIV virus passes through genital, anal, or oral sex activities and causes acquired immuno deficiency syndrome (AIDS). This is a highly infectious virus. The virus is so minute that it even passes through the filter paper and cannot be traced. The important characteristic of this virus is that it attacks the helper cell (T–4) and severally damages it. Though the helper cell resists the virus with all its might, it weaken and dies down at last. At this stage the body is fully infected with the virus and the person becomes a full-fledged AIDS patient. The duration between the time of the virus attack and the time when the person becomes an AIDS patient varies from person to person and also depends upon the level of resistance of the helper cell. This period may vary from four to eight years.

Originally AIDS was prevalent in Africa long ago. One information according Khurana (1989) is that AIDS widely existed in Africa among the green monkeys. It might have been transmitted to human beings. Either it is by way of eating the flesh of the green monkeys, or the green monkeys might have bitten the Africans and the AIDS might have been transmitted through blood. Later on when the Africans migrated to America they carried the AIDS with them; there was an intermixture of races and AIDS spread among the Africans first and later on among other races who migrated to America. Several studies were made almost at the same time on AIDS.

The studies made by Nurnberg et al (1984) confirm that the HIV attacks the central nervous system. Navie and others (1986) while examining the dead bodies of the persons who died of AIDS, observed that the HIV had destroyed the brain tissues and the persons suffered from AIDS Dementia Complex. Utmann and others (1985) have observed the AIDS Dementia Complex in children aged two to six years. The root cause of the AIDS from the research results available mainly seem to be human sexual activities, the drugs human beings consume, and the intravenous injections by unhygienic ways.

The main root cause of AIDS is the abnormal sexual deviation and drug abuses. Since it is a sexually transmitted disease (STD) it is rooted in the promiscuous sex activities of the hetrosexual or homosexual. There are greater chances for this disease with greater number of sexual partners indiscriminately. Psychologists are of the view that one important cause of AIDS is the attitudinal change in different age groups towards the premarital, permissive and promiscuous sexual relations. The level of education at schools and colleges is positively associated with permissive attitudes towards premarital sex relations. According to the survey made by Glenn and Weaver (1979) the premarital sexual activities increased as the educational level increased. Phillips and Gromyko (1985) observed a remarkable change in the sexual behaviour of males and females.

The premarital sexual behaviour among the males and females was almost the same. Davison and Neale (1990) made several studies and concluded that there are generational changes in the premarital promiscuous sexual activities and other sexual activities which contribute to two sexually transmitted diseases. The first is the genital herpes which causes painful blister in the area of sexual contacts which is characterised by fever, headches and itching. In other words, it may also be stated as syphilis. The second is the dreaded, AIDS which has become a great public health problem today apart from the individuals problem. Since it is said to be spreading, it has created an alarming picture. This disease has also made people panic and has also become the cause of phobic neurosis.

AIDS has created a sense of fear. Further, it is also causing a sense of shame and social boycott which people consider as worse than death. The physiological consequences may be severe type of painful feelings. But the psychological consequences of AIDS are many, such as severe anxiety, depression, nervous tension obsessive-compulsive neurosis, a sense of guilt and shame, resorting to excessive alcoholic habits and drug additions, feelings of insecurity in life and phobic neurosis. There are all types of psychosomatic disorders in most of the patients. In one of the studies, it was observed that the patient's race, colour, religion, creed, environmental conditions, male-female proximity, eating and living habits, social life, sexual life and other contacts are involved.

One striking characteristic of AIDs is the infectious virus transmission which is taking place in the sexual contact through semen or blood. The transmission is greater in the case of multiple sex partners. Man's emotional reaction to sexuality is determined much more by psychological factors than physiological needs. Since the cause of AIDS is based upon sexual activities, any kind of restriction will not work successfully.

The transmission of HIV into the blood of another person is also made through injection by using the needle and syringe not properly cleaned and sterilised. This is another possibility of contacting AIDs. Another possibility of transmission of the HIV is through blood donation. The infected blood transfusion may be given to any person who is in need of blood. There may be also incidents involving bleeding cuts and wounds, bites, including incidents involving saliva in kissing of a person who is infected with HIV. As the prostitutes have sexual activities with multiple partners, they become the storehouse of HIV. AIDS was first prevalent in America and Africa. But now it has spread out to Myanmar, Thailand, Siam, and India. In India Maharashtra, Tamil Nadu and Manipur are identified as AIDS-infected states.

AIDS and Children

Adults have every reason to justify their contact with the dreadful disease. But to speak of the child having is unimaginable. Children die of AIDS. These children may have genetic deformities, likemindness, deafness, numness and feeble-mindlessness. *The Science Express* (1991) stated that according to the observations made by the World Health Organisation (WHO) AIDS became a major cause of death of infants and children during the 1990s. There is every possibility for the child to contact the AIDS virus from the mother through exchange of body fluids. Infection may also occur during pregnancy, delivery times and after the birth of the child through breast-feeding if the mother is HIV positive. Symptoms of AIDS in children appear within six months of its birth. The presence of AIDS was diagnosed in 1983 in United States. There were 321 cases of AIDS-infected children under the age of 13 years. These children had the infection during the time of pregnancy and 60 per cent of them died of AIDS. The most important symptoms appearing in children were dry cough and fever for a long time. There were also white spots in the mouth, mass swelling in the neck and in the armpits.

Symptoms

Generally the symptoms of AIDS are almost the same as the symptoms of psychosomatic disorders. But there are also other symptoms which appear in AIDS patients. There is loss of memory and lack of concentration in them. There is retardation in language and motor skills in children. Other symptoms observed are anxiety, depression, nervous tension, obsessive-compulsive neurosis, sense of guilt and shame, excessive alcoholic intake, feeling of insecurity in life and phobic neurosis.

Treatment: Preventive Measures

There is a fear that AIDS is incurable and it has no treatment or medicine but it can be protected from infection by avoiding multiple partners in sexual activities and in injection of any medicine making use of dispensing needle and syringe. In blood transusion, the blood should be tested properly. The 'Elise Test' should be taken and proper medicine should be administered. It is very difficult to get AIDS cured. Medicines and methods of treatment of AIDS are not in proper utility anywhere in the world. Some European-based pharmaceutical firm has developed an AIDS vaccine which is still under experimental observation. But it is not known how the AIDS virus gets into the white cells of the human blood. This has helped the scientists to develop new medicines to prevent the HI virus that would cause AIDS. Continued researches on AIDS now and then provide some new information and reveal that the AIDS virus makes its appearance in different forms causing some other new diseases.

One recent information is that a gene product called 'tat' of the AIDS virus (HIV) promotes the growth of tumour cells. This results in some kind of skin cancer. Therefore, it is found that there is direct connection between HIV and cancer. Due to these it becomes difficult to conclude with the available type of medicine and methods. It is always better to keep ourselves safe from infections of this deadliest disease rather than allowing ourselves to get infected and go in search of medicines and treatment. There are two approaches to avoid it. One is the psychological approach which is at present practised in United States and in most of the European countries. The second one is the cultural approach which is specific to India.

The Psychological Approach

Psychologically discussing the approach, there are two interrelated characteristics. The first is that at present AIDS is neither curable nor can be prevented by medical methods. The second is that it is preventable only by psychological methods. In a population there are high-risk people towards the premarital permissive and promiscuous sexual behaviour. The low-risk people towards the premarital sexual behaviour may be few and they may abstain from it on knowing the severe consequence it. Most of the medical scientists look at AIDS as a consequence of biological needs. But they do not realise that there is something deep in it. It is man's strong desire to fulfil his biological needs. This desire is strongly influenced by motives, beliefs, and attitudes that man has developed at a given time, in a given place. One of the most dramatic aspects of sexual behaviour is that it changes strikingly across the cultures, races, religions, castes, communities and generations. Kelley (1986) is of the view that the most powerful factors influencing human sexual behaviour are psychological and not physiological. He states that human beings respond more to erotic fantasies than to hormone levels. Most of the human sexual behaviour is influenced by both external and internal sexual images in the forms of pictures and words. The external fantasies to which human beings are exposed to are books, magazines, motion pictures and television programmes. These external images become the cause of the internal images of sexual thoughts and desires and lead human beings to sexual arousal and sexual dreams. Byrne and Lomberth (1971) state that the effects of erotic fantasies are always susceptible to overt behaviour such as sexual coercion, forceful sexual advances and rape. These sexual activities may take place irrespective of age, culture, place and time. The motion picture and the television themes are becoming very powerful stimulating forces with all sorts of sexual ideas, and instigate the youth to indiscriminate sex activities. The high risk youths are easily falling victims to these temptations and indulge themselves in all sorts of unapproved sexual behaviour indiscriminately, whereby they contact the sexual diseases of various types and create severe social problems. Thus AIDS is psychological in nature and can be prevented only by the psychological approach. The erotic fantasies should be curbed and social norms on sexual behaviour should be strongly enforced.

Cultural Approach

In India the high-risk population is rapidly increasing day by day. But the preventive measures are lacking. The medicines and methods of treating AIDS do not make any appreciable progress. As we have stated above, in the medical treatment AIDS may make its appearance in some other diseases. Therefore, the health authorities in India are of the view that AIDS could be controlled by the ancient yogic practices. Suresh (1991) states that there are certain sophisticated yogic practices which may save the men of the high risk groups from AIDS by these practices. But a vary favourable and congenical atmosphere towards the ancient cultural heritage and wisdom should be created.

The Indian cultural heritage with special reference to the yogic practice should be associated with AIDS and should be made a part of the national programme right from school to the college level. Venkoba Rao (1990) has stated that AIDS can be controlled by proper health education. The programme should be a part of physical education. The preventive measures, according to Rajamanekam (1992), should include all the precautionary measures like learning and acquiring correct knowledge about the diseases and avoiding the situations which are causing the disease, educating people who are not aware of the diseases and their consequences. The programme should also include explaining the type of suffering humankind is facing as the result of negligence of hygienic way life. People all know that prevention is better than cure. Therefore, if the horrors of the dreaded disease AIDS are explained through suitable media and authoritative channels, then it is possible to convince the people and make them aware of the problems related to AIDS.

But, having all these preventive measures on one side and having the destructive force on the other side will not cause any beneficial results. The destructive forces are the obscene media, such as the books of vulgar sex matters, magazines with obscene pictures, motion pictures and television programmes. The media nowadays have become highly offensive and outrageous to the accepted standard of decency and modesty. The offensive indecent themes destroy the modesty of the culture by instigating the adolescents and the youths of the country to premarital promiscuous and indiscriminate sexual behaviour. Anything that is obscene should be prohibited and in extreme cases there should be severe punishment if the preventive measures are to be successful.

Syphilis and AIDS

These two diseases find their orgin in human sex. Studies confirm that syphilis and AIDS are sexually transmitted diseases. Syphilis according to experts is as old as humankind and it has been dealt with in various ways. It existed by different names. The common name given to this is venereal disease which is transmitted by sexual intercourse. Syphilis is defined as an infectious disease caused by the microorganism 'Treponema pallidum'. The *Treponema pallidum* invade the human body through mucous membranes after being contracted either during sexual intercourse or oral genital relations. This disorder may also be transmitted from an infected mother to the baby in her foetus. The first indication of the disorder is a small sore in the area of the infected lips, genitals or anus and it may appear after 20 days. This is also called *general paresis* or *brain syphilis*. When this disease spread in Europe in last quarter of the fifteenth century it was called *Great Pox*. It was Columbus and his sailors who brought it from West Indies. Columbus himself suffered from this disease and died. In the first quarter of the nineteenth century it was called *general paresis* and it was described.

The *Treponema pallidum* is the animal microorganism, a 'spirochete' that causes syphilis by forcibly entering the human body. It was observed that some people are more prone to paresis than others. It was also found that men were more quickly developing this disease than women, and men suffer more severely than women. Syphilis attacks the brain, destroys the brain cells and causes behavioural disorder. Most of the symptoms of the syphilis are similar to the symptoms of the AIDS. Syphilis reaches a stage which is almost like Parkinson's or Huntington's disease. The invention of penicillin has made the method of treatment very much successful. Both syphilis and AIDS are infectious diseases, sexually transmitted and both damage the brain tissues. Both have almost the same type of characteristics.

Though syphilis was prevailing for generations people did not give importance to it. Since it is a sexually transmitted disease people did not wish to expose it. But however this disease received importance after the death of Columbus. Columbus developed mental disorder because of this. It is a contagious disease and also infectious. Within a very short period syphilis spread to the whole of Europe. There was no proper treatment and medicine to control it. A large number of people died of this disease in most of the European countries and in England. This continued till medical scientists discovered the penicillin and some other antibiotics in the 1950s to kill the syphilitic virus, *Treponema pallidum.*

Syphilis spread from West Indies to the European countries by Columbus whereas AIDS spread from Africa to America by the Uganda African Negroes when they were taken to America during the period of colonisation. When there was an intermixture of races the White Americans had contacted the AIDS and it spread throughout the country. In the beginning the Americans did not take cognizance of this disease since it is sexually transmitted disease they thought that it must be syphilis. When there were large number of deaths, researchers found that it was a sexually transmitted disease but not syphilis, and they gave the name, 'Acquired Immuno Deficiency Syndrome (AIDS)'. The specific virus that caused this disease was identified as the HIV.

Classification

In classifying AIDS, in the beginning there were some differences of opinion. The reason might have been that most of the symptoms were similar to psychological stress. Therefore AIDS was considered as functional psychosis. But Snider (1983) challenged this view. It was viewed that an organic mental syndrome had the characteristics of the HIV. It was also observed that there were neurological complications in AIDS patients. The organic mental syndrome was first described by Nurnberg (1984) when he observed it in his patients. He felt that it was attributable to HIV of the AIDS and not to psychological stresses. The AIDS patient was infected with 'cytomegalovirus'. But he states that the HIV directly attacks the brain.

Since the HIV of the AIDS attacks the central nervous system, the brain, and damages the brain tissues and causes behaviour disorders it may be traced as one of the organic psychoses. Similarly, syphilis (General paresis) may be treated as an organic psychosis since it is an infectious disease caused by the microorganism *Treponema pallidum* which is a malignant virus.

Recent development in the study of AIDS

Researches and experiments on AIDS are going continuously, and now and then and hopeful results are brought out. One valuable result revealed by the National AIDS Control Society Project is that there is hope for the children of HIV-infected women. According to this project, it is important to save their child from HIV infection. In preventing the mother-to-child transmission there is some hope yet for the already born children and to-be-born children of HIV-infected women. The superintendent of Kasturba-Gandhi Government hospital, Chennai (2002) said that in the year 2000 January there were about 19,000 persons who attended counselling, 14,500 were screened, 47 were treated with HIV positive and 21 persons were treated with AZI medicine and the compliances were good in cases.

Of the 25 babies born, 14 did not show any symptoms of HIV infection, but it was detected in three babies. However, after two months treatment the number of HIV infection was found to be one. All the screened patients were subjected to periodic check-ups from five to 50 years. The counselling on AIDS is an important aspect in dealing with AIDS. Three hospitals in Chennai – Kasturba-Gandhi Hospital, Ramaswamy Mudaliar Hospital, Royapuram, and the Institute of Obstetrics and Gynaecology, Egmore, are vigorously working on it.

It is reported by Bhattacharya (2002) that the increasing number of AIDS patients are going to the Government Hospital of Thoracic Medicine, Tambaram. This is causing great concern to the authorities and the state and it is becoming a tough time for organisations working on AIDS control and prevention to provide the patients adequate care. It is estimated that at least 50 fresh cases on an average are reported to the hospital everyday. The number is twice the size reported in the previous year (2001). This incident forces the authorities to construct additional wards to accommodate them. Out of 31 wards in the hospital (which include tuberculosis and cancer wards) there are four male wards, two female wards and one children's ward. These wards are exclusively dedicated to the AIDS patients.

Since the AIDS cases are increasing every day in Tambaram hospital the authorities are not able to provide beds for them. The AIDS patients are put on the floor and between beds. On March

2002 alone there were 234 AIDS patients undergoing treatment in various wards. The disease has reached an alarming stage in Tamil Nadu. The increase in the number of patients is the result of the intensive awareness drive. There are also an equal number of tuberculosis patients getting admission in this hospital. The AIDS and tuberculosis patients are put up mixed together in the hospital side by side and given treatment. It is believed that tuberculosis is an offshoot of AIDS. The treatment is also somewhat similar to both the diseases in the beginning for reducing the intensity of infection as both are infectious diseases. In Maharashtra also almost the same condition is prevailing.

Anthrax

Anthrax is a highly infectious disease of animals, especially of the cattle and the sheep, characterised by fever, enlarged spleen and swelling of throat. The plural form of this disease is *anthraces*. It is caused by the bacterium: *Bacillus anthracies* (Collins, 1979). This can be transmitted to human beings and it may cause *pustal* which is a pus-filled pimple or blister or both. The anthrax is a poisonous substance and it can be made a more powerful poisonous material. The anthrax is produced in powder form. It is also mixed in food and water.

On knowing the danger that the anthrax bacterium can cause to human beings, some of the terrorist organisations started manufacturing the anthrax. Afghanistan, Iraq and some of the West Asian countries manufacture anthrax in such a way that it should kill human beings instantly on smelling it even at a very small level. The anthrax first gets into the human body through the nose, ear and throat, reaches the lungs and damages the blood purification process. The blood oxygention process of the lungs is impaired. There are pulmonary arteries and the pulmonary veins which function between the heart and the lungs. There are two arteries which are tubular, thick-walled muscular vessels. The pulmonary veins are tubular vessels that convey oxygen-rich blood from the lungs to the heart. The oxygen depleted blood channelised from various parts of the body to the lungs through the pulmonary artery for purification. The lungs purify or oxygenate the blood and convey it to the heart through the pulmonary veins. From the heart this oxygenated blood is sent through arteries to various parts of the body including the brain.

The anthrax gets into the bloodstream from the lungs and goes to the heart and from there to the brain where it destroys the brain tissues, causing behavioural disorders and finally death. This is how the powerful anthrax bacterium, the 'Bacillus Anthracies' is functioning.

Some of the symptoms that appear are quite similar to other organic diseases. But certain specific symptoms are not yet correctly diagnosed. It kills man within a short period. Therefore, anthrax may be classified as one of the organic disorders. It damages bodily parts and causes behaviour disorders.

CHAPTER 14

Epilepsy

What is epilepsy?

Epilepsy is a disorder of the central nervous system characterized by periodic loss of consciousness with convulsion (sudden involuntary muscular contraction) or without convulsion.

In some cases it is due to brain damage but in other cases the cause is not known. It refers to a group of disorders of varying from momentary lapses of consciousness to generalized convulsions. Generally epilepsy is a disorder of the nervous system caused by brain to lesions or other pathology, and characterized by the disturbances of the rhythms of *electrical discharge from the brain.* Epilepsy has provoked wonders and worry on anxiety since the dawn of civilization (Rosenzweig 1996).

Epilepsy is a somatogenic disorder (Strange, 1965) and the term epilepsy indicates a group of different nature and quality of patients, and each group has a medical history of seizures and conversions. The symptoms of epilepsy are convulsive seizures. It is commonly called fits in Indian culture.

Of all the medical disorders, epilepsy is considered to be foremost an ancient one, which had been discussed in varied ways in different cultures. It is a most feared and also most revered disease. In the medieval period it was considered as divine expression or divine inspiration in a person. It was also called 'visit of evil spirit'. Therefore, the treatment varied from culture to culture. Epilepsy was mostly mentioned in ancient and medieval history and literature. Many of the historical personalities were said to have epileptic seizures. For example, Julius Ceasar in Shakespeare's play was described as an epileptic patient which was indicated by the words as 'falling sickness'. Similarly, Alexander the Great, Nepoleon, poet Byron, Van Gogh (1853-1890), the Dutch Painter, were all considered as epileptics. There was a time when the veteran administrators refused to admit persons who had one or two epileptic seizures in certain occupations. In Indian culture there is a custom to put an iron instrument, mostly keys, in the hands of the person who has epileptic attack or fits. Therefore, epilepsy is a disease which may attack any person who has brain injury or damage.

It is found that it is common to all epileptic patients to have the dysuhythmia which is a characteristic of brain wave pattern. The epileptic is a neurotic and introverted person. Some of the symptoms found in him are anxiety, depression and convulsive behaviour. It was Berger (1978,1989) who had discovered this electrical activity of the brain. According to Strange (1965), the development of the study of the *electroencephalography* which is most commonly referred to as EEG could distinctly trace the brain waves of the normal people and also of the epileptic patients. For each type of person the brain waves have special patterns. It has been estimated that about one per cent of people in every culture can be stated as an epileptic. But at the same time ten per cent of the people in a population have dyshymia type of epilepsy. It is very difficult to study the characteristics of epilepsy by studying the records of the EEG. Unless the person is an expert in reading the characteristics of the records it may result in wrong diagnoses. This instrument electroencephalography was originally discovered for diagnosing the electric activity of the brain or the central nervous system. But now it is used by physicians in their testing of the patients in their clinics.

The EEG is used mostly by cardiologists for testing their patients these days. Since this instrument records the electrical activity of the central nervous system, it has become a very essential in all the medical examinations and treatments.

Epilepsy is of many types and marked by a variety of sudden and recurring attacks of cerebral part of the brain causing partial or complete loss of consciousness. It may be mainly with psychomotor disturbance or even without it. The attacks are accompanied by loss of consciousness and convulsive (violent) movements of the bodily parts. The epileptic attacks may vary in intensity ranging from mild disturbance of consciousness for a few minutes to violent or wild anger.

Why and How epilepsy occurs?

Behind all human behaviour, based upon cognitive, conative and emotional activities lies the process of communication. The sources of information include sensory receptors, ongoing neural activity and other internal physiological events. The combined and organized behaviour of an individual depends upon the neural activities or signals that carry information within the nervous system and from the nervous system to the rest of the bodily parts. As we see something outside and read, the eyes are stimulated by the light and starts saturating signals that pass through the nerve cells to the brain. In the specific regions of the brain circuits of nervous process the incoming information. What are the signals of the nerve cells? They are the electrical signalling. The electrical signalling of the neurons are in the most important and powerful innovations in the biological or in the animal evolution. The electrical signalling that appears in animals is as diverse as human beings. These neural signals underlie the whole range of thought and action, from solving problems to the feeling of depression. In the activity of single neuron there are three kinds of electrical events.

These electrical events of the neurons become the cause of many nervous disorders. The electrical character of the nervous system signals offer the special biological advantages of rapid communication and the ability to generate receive and integrate a wide range of messages. However this fundamental property also is at stake. There is high metabolic demands of nerve cells. Inspite of it there is a potential cost of seizures. There are extensive connections among the nerve cells. Because of it the brain can generate massive waves of intensive nerve cells activity that involves the whole brain. A systematic excitation in the large groups of nerve cells causes the seizure. This is unusual electrical event in the brain and also causes injury to the brain. Following this there are also chemical changes exposing to toxins. Thus the seizure occurs which is generally called as epilepsy or epileptic disorder. These several types of seizures are identified by both behaviourally and neurophysiologically.

It is customary that people sometimes have suspicion of having some kind of nervous disorders when examined by a neurologist or by a physician specialized in the treatment of such disorders. Any neurological examination starts with a principle that every function is abnormal unless it is declared as normal. The neurologist first prepares a medical history of the patients and takes a general assessment of the patients' personality, facial expressions, and the structure membranes, and the sensory systems, tests of motor functions, listens to the heart beats, abdomen, head and the blood vessels and every organ system. The neurologist may demand some additional information like the EEG., brain scene. The neurologist mainly concentrates on the neurological disorders. But the normal functioning of the central nervous system may be affected by a number of disorders. The more common diseases included are the headaches, tumours, vascular problems, infections, trauma from head injury, metabolic and nutritional diseases and epilepsy.

Epilepsy is an electrographic seizure. It may occurs often if once the persons is subjected to it. It is always associated with altered state of consciousness. It is a common disorder, one in twenty in any population suffered from epilepsy. It is mostly an excited state of emotion and mostly in the extreme anxiety state which may result in seizures or attacks or fits. A man in his life time might have experienced atleast one mild seizure or even more.

The epileptic seizure is taking place with a warning sign in the individuals. The person, therefore, may know before hand that he is getting the attack and prepares himself for it. Bhatia (1969) states that the increasing signs are found in several forms in different individuals. The warning signs may be in pain, chocking sensation and the feelings, strangeness. On knowing the warning signs some people get frightened, some people exhibit emotional reactions and some people feel happy. The warning signs are mostly of visual and affective experiences and visual hallucinations are widely prevalent in the patients. If the warnings sign or the aura is an indication of epileptic seizure, the person can be trained to protect himself or even to prevent the seizure. But it was also observed that all patients do not get the warning signals for taking any precautionary measures.

In many cases epileptic seizures take place suddenly and the persons becomes totally unconscious. The person feels that he was stuck suddenly and he becomes in act and falls down as if he has received a strong fatal blow. There is stopping of breathing in the person who had the sudden seizure. His muscles become very stiff, mouth clinched, arms extended and legs stretched. In the general attack the patients' chest and abdomen are involved and he bites his tongue. The patient cries of painful feelings, the face becomes dark and pale. When the patient begins to breath normally the movements become jerky and the rigid stage turning to relaxed stage. The fast movements reduced gradually. During the attack period, if it is severe, the patient may urinate and also passes stools out. The stiff muscles relaxed and the patient turns to normal state. Some patients may return to normal within few minutes, while some may take longer time to recover the normalcy.

Symptoms of Epilepsy and the Diagnosis

Clinically it is to observed that the most significant characteristic of epileptic disorders is the varying intervals between seizures. The varying intervals may be in minutes hours, days, months and even years. Therefore it is absolutely impossible to state and describe the basic symptoms that are expected in all or in most people who are suffering from this disorder. But, however there are three important symptoms found in many types of epilepsy.

The first one is an aura or warning about what is going to happen the seizure. This may be in the form of some sensations like some odours, noises, or it may be a feeling that some thing is going to occur. *The second* symptom is the loss of consciousness which may occur in the form of complete collapse or sudden break down or looking steadily at a place. Generally there is often amnesia, total forgetting the seizure itself and the duration of consciousness the patient has lost. *The third* symptom is the movements. The seizure will have commonly the motor element in one of the parts of movement. The characteristics of movement may vary considerably. In the case of some patients, there are shaking movements. In some cases thee are automatic movements like rubbing the hands.

The diagnosis of epilepsy is made by using the EEG instruments. But it is very difficult to demonstrate and identify epileptic seizures. It is possible only under some special situations the recording of the EEG may reveal the seizure. It was observed that during the time of sleep the EEG record may show the position. The problem is that an abnormal recording of EEG does not meant that seizure existed. Even normal people who are not epileptic also may have abnormal recording. It was estimated that four persons in every twenty have abnormal EEG recording. In one of the recent studies it was observed that the Position Emission Tomography (PET) has revealed more reliable measures of functional abnormalities in epileptic patients.

Types of Seizures (Epilepsy)

There are several types of epileptic seizures. Sometimes they are classified as symptomatic seizures and idiopathic seizures. The *symptomatic seizures* can be identified by a specific cause such as mainly infection, trauma, tumour, vascular malformation, toxic chemicals, very high fever and other neurological disorders. The other seizure disorders are the *idiopathic seizures*. These disorders arise spontaneously in the absence of the other diseases in the central nervous system. The cause behind these disorders is the abnormal electrical discharge by the nerve cells. Epilepsy is found to be running in the families and it is long known. But it is not known whether there is a single gene responsible for the seizures. It is also assumed that certain environmental circumstances behind the cause of the epileptic seizures.

Recent developments in the study of epilepsy resulted in different types of classification. These types of epileptic seizure disorders identified as behavioural epileptic disorders and neuro physiological epileptic disorders. There are also several sub classifications of epilepsy. According to Kolb and whishaw (1996), the recent classification provides three major types such as partial or Focal seizures, which include simple partial seizures, motor or Jacksonian seizures, sensory (Jacksonian) seizures and Autonomic Seizures. The partial seizures include also complex partial seizures which are minor seizures like the absences, complex hallucinations, affective symptoms and automatism.

The second major seizures are the generalized seizures which include major seizures like the bilaterally symmatical without focal onset, absence attacks, tonic-clonic (Grandmal) bilateral myoclonic and drop attacks.

The third major seizures are the unclassified seizures, which include the minor seizures of the apparently generalized seizures.

The Focal Seizures

The focal seizures are those that occur locally and spread out. It is also called as Jacksonian seizures in which the attack occurs with jerks of a single part of the body, like in a finger, a toe., or the mouth and then it spreads out. If the attack begins with a finger in the form of jerks, the jerks spread out to other fingers, then the hand, the arm and to other parts of the body. This process is called Jacksonian march. Jackson first predicted this in the year 1870 that the seizures originate from the point of neocortex and the seizures represented that part.

The Complex Partial Seizures

The complex partial seizure is also a major seizure, originates most commonly in the temporal lobe of the brain which is not much frequently occurring seizures. The complex partial seizures are marked by three common occurrences such as subjective feelings such as forced, repetitive thoughts, alterations in mood, feelings of hallucinations. The *second* occurrences are automatism, which include repetitive stereotyped movements, like the lips cleaning and acts such as removing the shirt or coat buttons. The *third* occurrences are the postural changes in which the afflicted persons assume frozen postures.

The Generalised Seizures

The General seizures involve loss of consciousness and symmetrical involvement of body musculature. *Grand mal* and *petit mal* are the two common types of generalized seizures and account for the largest number of patients. Grand mal seizures involve in EEG pattern evident at many places in the brain. According to Rosenzweig et al (1996) the seizures are behavioural connected and this state is dramatic. The person loses consciousness and the muscles of the whole body suddenly contract causing stiff limbs and body. This is tonic phase of the seizures which is followed by a clonic phase after one or two minutes later. This consists of sudden alternative jerks and relaxation of the body. There will be confusion for hours and sleep follows. Generally the non-professionals when refer to epilepsy they refer to only the grand mal seizures.

The Petit Mal Epilepsy Seizures

The petit mal epilepsy seizures are more subtle variant generalized seizures. It is shown by electrical pattern in EEG recording, called the *spike-and-wave pattern* that exists for five to ten seconds. Since the period is very short, unusual electrical activity may occur many times in a day. During these periods the person is unaware of the environment and forgets what has taken place during the periods of the petit mal seizures. The person does not show any unusual muscle activity behavioural except the cessation of the on going activity. The grand mal and the petit mal seizures are called the generalized seizures because both are arising from pathology of brain areas that project to wider area of the brain. But some petit mal seizures involve no impairment of consciousness. For example, the focal motor seizures involve repetitive sudden violent activities. These frequently start in the boundary area of the limb and spread to other muscle parts. The partial seizures originate in the temporal lobe which causes unusual sensory responses, specifically some small sensations followed by sudden feelings of anxiety and there may be elaborate complicated gestures.

The EEG record of a petit mal seizures has a typical pattern of seizures called *"a three second spike and wave"*. One of the minor seizures of epileptic attack is the kinetic seizures which is ordinarily observed in children. In this seizures the child suddenly collapses without any warning. These attacks are of very short duration and the child may get up after few seconds. The falls of children out of a kinetic seizures may cause danger. Myoclonic attacks are also minor seizures of the petit mal seizures which are massive attacks that consist sudden flexion and extension of the body, which often start with a cry.

Epilepsy and Hysteria

Epilepsy and Hysteria have some common characteristics. Therefore it is better to discuss these two disorders. Epilepsy is a brain disorder marked by sudden changes in the electrophysiological state of the brain that are referred to a seizures. It may be also stated as the condition characterized by recurrent seizures of various types associated with a disturbance of consciousness. Epilepsy also may be stated as disorder of the central nervous system characterized by periodic loss of consciousness with violent attack or without it. In some cases it is due to brain damage but in others the cause is not known.

Hysteria is a mental disorder characterized by emotional outbreak susceptibility to autosuggestion and often physical symptoms such as paralysis. According to Strange (1965) hysteria is a type of psychoneurosis characterized by dissociation or conversion reaction. It may be also stated as a form of psychoneurosis in which bodily ailments result from psychological troubles. Hysteria or historical state is a disorder, which is a physical incapacity, a paralysis (pretrial or complete voluntary loss of motion), an anesthesis which is a partial or total loss of sensation and an analgesia, a state not having the feeling of pain. Anesthesia is older term for conversion disorder. In the late nineteenth century it was called dissociative disorder.

The term conversion disorder (hysteria) has a long history, goes back to the earliest writings on abnormal behaviour. Hippocrates, (460-370, B.C.) the Greek physician considered it as an association limited to women and related to the wandering of the uterus through the body. The Greek word hysteria means womb. It is assumed that the wandering uterus is desiring of the body for the reproduction of a child. Freud (1856-1939) an Austrian psychiatrist, the founder of psychoanalysis, considered the specific nature of the hysterical symptoms as the repressed instinctual urge. Hysteria was considered as the most important neurotic disorder in the development of abnormal psychology.

Hysteria was of great concern to all those who were interested in dealing with nervous and mental disorders. It has attracted all the physicians, medical scientists and neurologists all over the world. Charcot, Janet and Freud were very much interested in the study of hysteria. Janet in his study of neurosis used the concept dissociation to explain the neurotic reaction. He observed the psycholgentic implications of hysteria. He accepted the opinion of Charcot that there is a hereditary factor which predisposes the hysteria cases. Sigmund Freud formulated the theory of psychoanalysis for treating the hysterical patients. The symptoms of hysteria in most of the cases reflected the symptoms of other illnesses and diseases. Because of this the physicians found it very difficult to diagnose and identify the specific disease. It was also observed that the weak part of the body becomes focal part for the hysterial attacks. The hysterial patient often becomes blind, deaf, paralysed in parts of the body not able to feel or suffer great pains even when there is no damage to the nerve tissues. The hysterical attack may be conversion hysteria or dissociative hysteria or conclusive hysteria.

Paralysis is the most common symptom in hysterial attack. Paralysis is an impairment of or loss of voluntary muscle function or sensation. There are sensory defects, which may be called sensory paralysis in a part or area of the body usually caused by leison or disorder of the muscles or the nerves supplying blood to the parts. Generally disorder it is a disorder characterized by such impairment or loss of palsy or cerebral paralysis. It is also cessation or impairment of activity.

Epilepsy has most of the characteristics of hysteria and paralysis. Epilepsy and hysteria have fits and may cause confusion. Both are indicated by the characteristics of seizures, attacks, fits, loss of consciousness, impairment of activity loss of voluntary movements and so on. Sometime the hysterial attacks are taken for granted for epilepsy as the symptoms. The acute form of hysteria revealed the mass hysterical symptoms. It was also observed that severe attacks resembled the attacks of epilepsy and the same type of symptoms noticed. In the hysterical attacks the patient generally kicks, rolls on the ground, violently moves his arms, pulls his her hair, beats his/her breast, bits mouth, strikes persons standing around him/her and also the patient cries. While revealing all these symptoms the patient is not hurting himself/herself. Generally the symptoms of crying and laughing are abnormal in characteristics but at the same time the patients quite conscious of himself/herself and his/her activities.

Observers of hysterical patients view that there is a purpose in the fits and insanic behaviour patterns. Mostly these hysterical attacks help the patient in certain situations of stress and strain. The patient escapes from certain situations which he/she cannot cope with. There were instances that when the hysterical person comes to know that he is going to face a very difficult task, the patient is subjected to hysterical fits.

Unlike hysterical attacks, epileptic seizures are not serving any purposes for the patient. Epileptic seizures may take place any time either in day time of at night time. The seizures may occur even during the time of sleep. There are instances reported that when the person went to bed at night time, he was alright, but when he got up in the morning he was not able to make movements of his arms. Thus epilepsy may attack at any time without even any warning.

Hysterical attacks do not take place during sleep at nights. During the time of epileptic seizures, the patients eyes are not having any sensation of sight. The patient does not see the light, the bodily reflex activities are also not taking place. But during the time of hysteria the eyes are tightly closed and the pupils make movements and there may be normal eye sight. In the epileptic stage the patient get confused hopelessly and goes into a state of stupor. The face of the epileptic patient goes pale during the seizures. After the hysterical attacks the patient feels fresh and relaxed. But the hysterical patient generally gets the attacks due to severe emotional disturbance. A severe emotional shock may make him to get involuntary movements and may fall down and role in the ground. Hysterical attacks may continue for hours.

Epileptic seizures occurs all of a sudden whether any body looked at the person or not. But epileptic seizures lost only for few minutes whereas the hysterial attacks may continue even for hours. Hysterical attacks are most psychological in nature as they are caused by emotional shocks. But epileptic seizures are biological in nature and sometimes due to chemical or toxic substances.

The consequences of Epileptic Seizures and Behaviour

Early Research results state that the nerve cells changes are the cause of epileptic seizures. But recent research results suggest that the excessive neural discharges to other regions and the nerve cells changes are responsible for the epileptic seizures. It is said that seizures-induce death of neurons seems to arise as the consequence of the excessive activation of some types glutamate receptors (Choi, 1992). It is observed that the frequent storms of electrical activity that invade the brains of epileptics leave many signs, including some psychological and behavioural changes. Clinical neurologists have been suggesting for years that there is a connection between one the type of seizures disorder-temporal lobe epilepsy and certain personality traits (Trimble, 1991). It was observed by some researchers that there are emotional changes in these disorders and these are the direct results of frequent activation by the attacks of emotional circuits in the temporal lobe. The other researchers believe that emotional changes arise as the result of psychological (function) responses to the social trauma.

Experimental studies have been conducted on animals which revealed changes in emotionality. These emotional changes occur as the result of brain damage in temporal lobe structures. These are involved in some forms of seizure disorder. This process is called temporal lobe epilepsy which is associated with various psychological states in children and in adults (Trimble 1961). All these indicate that epilepsy is highly associated with emotional states like the hysterical attacks.

Researchers have observed that in the case of some patients with temporal lobe seizures cause aggressive behaviour. Hindler (1989) has observed strong aggression in a laughing infant, which was the result of strong olfactory sensation and other characteristics of temporal lobe seizures activity. In one of the studies made by Tonkonogy (1991) it was observed in a patient violent behaviour which was accompanied by tissue loss in anterior temporal lobe structures. Thus the epileptic seizures also stimulate emotional responses, aggressive and violent behaviour patterns.

There are some difference of opinions with regard to the behaviour of the epileptics. Strange (1965) states that except the psychomotor type of behaviour, the epileptics do not reveal much of abnormal behaviour. But for an a ordinary person epileptic means something abnormal and it is associated with negative behaviour patterns. An epileptic is considered to be an eccentric and potentially a violent person. Organizations hesitate to employ epileptics in their organizations for fear of their aggressive and violent behaviour. They are of the view that epileptics are unreliable and dangerous in their works.

Treatment of Epilepsy

Epileptic patients are treated with medicines. With help of drugs the epileptic seizures are controlled and many epileptics with convulsive disorders turn to sound normal personality. The general treatment for epilepsy is an anticonvulsant drug, mostly diphanyhanion, (DPH Dilantin), pehnobarbital and some other medicines. Though the reaction of these medicines is uncertain, it is presumed that they inhibit the discharge of abnormal neurons. These medicines stabilize nerourone membrane. If the administration of medicines fail to alleviate the seizures problems, surgery is the next alternative. Surgery is performed for removing the focus of abnormal functioning with focal seizures. The surgical treatment for epilepsy was first performed by Horsley in the late nineteenth century around 1800s. In the operation the Cortex was removed to alleviate the seizures. The modern technique of surgery for epilepsy was found by Otfrid Forerster in 1920, in Germany (Kolb and Whishaw, 1986). Later on Whilder Penfield stimulated by the works of Foerster, started a prolonged study of the surgical treatment for epilepsy and founded a Neurological Institute for this purpose. Along with Forerster and Penfield a group of researchers developed a technique for removing the Cortical epiloptogenic tissues from the patients of focal epilepsy.

This attempt has been very much successful treatment for the this type of epilepsy. The attempts of this team of researchers had provided a model for the basic applied medical sciences for developing successful and effective treatment for epileptic seizures.

Recent development in the Treatment of Epilepsy

While attempting to find out suitable methods of treatment for epilepsy, the biomedical scientists have tried by using a mild electric field to control seizures like activity in brain cells. The task hints at the possibility of controlling epilepsy in a similar way. In one of the recent issues of the Journal of 'Neuro-science' a group of researchers have described a feedback system that monitors the brain cells for seizures like firing. It was observed that when the firing begins, the system responded by applying a mild electric field, fewer than 50 millivolts per millimeter. When the electric firing stopped the electric field shuts off. The applied field whose strength is determined by the feed back loop alters the electrical charge of the operative nerve cells making them less responsive to the firing of neighbouring cells. But how this works exactly is still not clear. It is being investigated. Bruce Gluckman, professor of physics and Astronomy and Steven Schiff and Krasnow, professors of Neurobiology of George Meson University led a group of researchers towards this work (2001).

They applied the feedback system which made it possible to control the seizures like the activity automatically and over long periods. This procedure is combined with the low electrical field requirement, which had made the group to think about the long term possibility of medical applications. In their original experiments the brain tissues of rates were used. These experiments now started on live animals and human clinical trials are under consideration. A big question is raised now, whether brain cells in the living organism will respond to the electrical field in the same manner that the cells act in a laboratory situation.

In the experiments the normal firing of the brain cells is not clearly understood, but the chaotic firing characteristics of seizures can be described as a nonlinear system. The dynamism that generates the burst is found to be much simpler than all other functions. The nolinear dynamics have been found as useful in other medical applications as well, such as defibrillators which could correct irregular heart beats. Medical Scientists do not understand how a jolt in an electric instrument exactly restores a normal heart beat. But the defibrillator does it. In the treatment of epilepsy the group of researchers were able to observe and report the characteristics of the control techniques and also how the instrument could correct the irregular heart beat (2001).

CHAPTER 15

Antisocial (Sociopathic) Behaviour

What is Antisocial Behaviour?

Human behaviour is normally agreeable and pleasant provided if it is socially and personally adjustable and not harmful either to the individual or to the society. But if it becomes disagreeable, unpleasant, harmful to the individual himself and to others in the society, it is something different and should be taken care of. Though a deviant behaviour is an abnormal one, persons who are normal apparently get involved in some harmful and antisocial activities. Their activities may result in socially and morally not acceptable. Such behaviour we cell as antisocial behaviour, Antisocial means avoiding the company of other people which may be also called unsocial, Antisocial is a type of behaviour contrary or injurious to the interests of society in general. A person who is involved in antisocial activities and committing crimes may be stated as antisocial person.

Therefore we may state that any antisocial behaviour which is harmful to the society can be called sociopathic. Sociopathic behaviour is treated synonymously with psychopathic (personality) behaviour. Psychopath or psychopathic personality is referred to an individual who acts out his anit-social impulses and who appears devoid of conscience or remorse. Thus antisocial person is one who is afflicted with a personality disorder characterized by tendency to commit antisocial and sometimes violent acts and a failure to feel guilt for such acts. A persons of this type is a psychopathic personality. Psychiatrically an antisocial personality is characterized by the failure to develop any sense of moral or ethical responsibility and the capability of performing violent or antisocial acts. Therefore it may be stated that a sociopathic or psychopathic personality is not fully characterised as an abnormal personality. But he behaves in a deviant manner to some extent in some situations by not giving importance to social norms or moral principles. In every community such people are quite common.

An antisocial or psychopathic personality is referred to the personality characteristics and behaviour patterns that result in serious difficulties in the interpersonal relationships and generally make the individual into repeated conflict with society (Coleman, 1965). According to Bhatia (1969) the psychopathic personality has drawn the attention in recent years on account of its legal implications. Clinically it is a constitutional type of disorder. Therefore it may be defined as a constitutional disorder revealed itself in an antisocial behaviour. But this has not been experimentally established. Persons of this type are genetically lack of moral principles. These antisocial individuals are not mentally abnormal or insane and therefore they cannot be classified as mentally retarded or deficient. The most important characteristics observed in them are that they are morally and socially defective persons. They might have been brought up very well. But it is due to some innate tendencies which make these persons not adhering to the demands of the society.

The antisocial behaviour patterns are found more among the male members of a community than the females and also among the younger persons, mostly among the later adolescents and young adults. This category of antisocial personality consists of mostly mixed type of people. There may be business men not following any principle in their trade, quack medical practitioners, perverted religious preachers, crooked political leaders, discreditable lawyers, deceiving drug merchants, aberrant policemen, flesh trading women, delinquents and criminals. Some of these persons may be in mental hospitals and many of them in corrective institutions. These persons are constantly found conflict with the prison or institutional authories. This category of the persons are spread out in a very wide range with many types of the persons are spread out in a very wide range with many type of antisocial behaviour. Coleman (1974) identified five types of antisocial personalities.

Types of Antisocial Behaviours

The antisocial behaviour patterns are clinically diagnosed are identified into some types based upon the characteristics. Some of the types are (1) lack of understanding the guilt, (2) Impulsive behaviour (3) exploiting others for his unsocial behaviour, (4) failure or inability to establish interpersonal relationships (5) lack of ability to profiting from experience and (6) misusing the position.

These six types are generally considered as antisocial personalities. There are also other an unidentified antisocial personality patterns like impersonalization. We may discuss these briefly.

1) Lack of Understanding the Guilt

This behaviour pattern is clinically identified as antisocial. This type of persons refuse to understand and accept socially and ethically accepted values. They may appear to be acceptable orally, but in action they deviate and go against them. It is because of the low level of intellectual abilities or below the normal intelligence quotient. Generally the conscience level is not well developed in accordance with the demands of the society. Therefore the person is called as a social moron. This person pretents to be adhering the moral standard, but always goes out of it. The person may become aggressive and violent but never feels guilt of his behaviour. Since he lacks moral sense, fails to understand whether it is right or wrong. He may be involved in steeling and other illegal activities. He may show his hatred or ill will against the persons who take him easily and find fault with him.

2. Impulsive Behaviour

Persons who are classified into this type are often found to be most irresponsible. They lack tolerance and reveal frustration at some level. This type of person generally has hardened feeling in everything, he never respects the human rights, shows utter disregard for law and order. He does not bother about the needs and claims of other people. The person totally ignores truth and makes always false statements. Whatever he wants, not in the habit of earning and get it, but takes away or steals away others property. He drives away and remains often a law breaker. In going away from the law and order he is not caring the resulting effects. He makes his life as the present event and does not care the future and never learns anything from the past.

Immediate personal satisfaction is his motto and never hesitates to achieve it whatever takes place. The impulsive type of antisocial personality does not like to hold any responsibility . He does not continue in a job for long time and make going on changing often. He aspires always everything best, but meets with failures. Another important characteristic of this person is that he never trusts people.

3. Exploiting Other People for His Unethical Behaviour

This type of antisocial persons have the ability to convenience others by putting good show of themselves and obtain good opinion from others and make use of it for their won ends. In achieving their ends they go against socially approved behaviour and when something had occured they blame other people and escape form the punishment if any. They put up charming appearance and obtain the friendship of others and get good impression. They also have high sense of humour and put up pleasant out look. They have the knack of making others to believe that they are very much interested in the needs and problems or other people and exploiting others and capable of justifying their anti-social conduct and escape from blames and projecting, the blames on other people who have nothing to do with the occurrence of the faults. They may make many promises and raise hopes, but they will not successfully carry out as premised and finally put the blames on others and never feel sorry in the right sense.

4. Failure or Inability to Establish Interpersonal Relationship

The antisocial personality generally fails to build up cordial relationship with other people. The main reason is that he is very irresponsible and always makes reference to himself. But he is capable of winning the good will of others. The person's selfish attitude and the tendency to deny the view of others make him a cynical to contempt the virtues. In all his dealings the psychopathic never feels sympathy for any painful incidence to others. He is very much devoid of affection for others nor returns the affection showered by others. In this way he is very ungrateful person. Persons of this type may be causing very much nuisance and trouble to the family and others. He handles the sexual relationship in deceptive manners. As a husband he is very insincere and not responsible in his behaviour. He fails to maintain the conjugal relationship with the partner. In the occupational career the psychopathic is not keeping good relationship with other co-workers and always keeps himself aloof.

5. Lack of Ability to Learn from Experience

The antisocial type of person does not follow any of the rules and regulations in his every walk of life. He thinks that all the social and moral norms are not for him and thinks that he can acts according to his wish. The psychopathic does not accept the authority whether is it his profession or in a play on rejects any supervision over him and shows his feeling of rejection in his hostile and criminal behaviour patterns. With all that he is not branded as a professional criminal. Though he is punished for his criminal activities he behaves as if he is exempted from it.

6. Misusing the Position One is Holding

Persons occupy various positions in a society and they are expected to carry out their work according to the specifications. But the psychopathic persons often act differently and misuse the power assigned to them. Persons authorized to maintain the law and order have the power to enforce the law and order on those who violate them. The psychopathics attempt to enforce the law on innocent persons and penalize them. Mostly the aberrant police men take into custody innocent and unerring individuals whom they did not like and make them as law breakers forcibly and put them in prison. But these aberrant policemen fail to take action against the persons who really go against the law. These police men are psychopathics or antisocial persons. One of the antisocial behaviour patterns commonly found in these persons is the practice of illicit gratification. They become alcohol's and fail to carryout their assigned duties as public servants. In every occupational area there are antisocial elements.

7. Emotionally Disorganized

Emotional imbalance is one of the characteristics of antisocial personality. Mostly these persons are impulsive and behave in an excited manner causing damage to persons and properties. The psychopathics emotionally are described as shallow, cruel, immature short tempered, irritative, persons of mood and temperament and in the extreme level become aggressive and violent. Their moods may be fluctuating between mild expression of anger and violent expression of physical attacks. They have no control over their emotions. Very small matter may upset them and elate. These person do not show any regard for any social institutions like marriage and family life. Even if they are get married it is only short lived matter which normally end in failure. They are very stubborn, selfish and aggressive and do not cooperate for a peaceful coexistence in any affair.

All these characteristics and the symptoms described above are referring to the antisocial or psychopathic person's behaviour. But these characteristics are also found in different levels in other maladaptive persons, mostly in psychoneurotic persons.

The Causes of Antisocial Behaviour

The causes or the dynamics of antisocial behaviour are many and they vary from person to person and from culture to culture. What is the cause of antisocial behaviour in one culture is not the cause in another culture. Because it depends upon various factors. On observing the antisocial behaviour in some person and the type of behaviour in which they are involved may indicate what must be the cause of it. Antisocial is found generally in the primitive culture, in underdeveloped societies and also in highly civlised societies. The way in which individuals are reared and brought up, the learning habits and the physiological deficiencies all might have been the main causes of antisocial behaviour. Thus there are three important causes such as : 1) family background and bringing up, 2) deprivation in the early years and 3) physiological conditioning.

1. Family Background and Bringing up

If the family background is pleasant and highly adjustable the child may develop normal behaviour pattern. But if the background is not pleasant, and the parent child relationship is not compatible the child may develop feeling of helplessness or the feeling of destitute. There may be quarrels between the parents, either one may be of psychopathic personality. The husband or wife may be highly temperamental and also revengeful which may result not only in quarrels, but also in beating and separation. Children reared up in such situation naturally receive bad examples. The father in the family always expects that his son should come up high in status and the mother is too much of protective. The child pushed and pulled between these types of bringing up. Greenacre (1945) made a number of studies on this issue of faulty models. In his studies he has observed that the father of the children is highly placed person and commands good respect in the society and he expects that his son should follow his directions and get good impression from others. But the mother of the children is interested in loving her children and light hearted, not expressing her attitude openly and does not agree with her husband's attitudes. The real attitude prevailing in the family is concealed what is going on in the family. For outside world they a make a show that they are respected by all for their status. The son slowly becomes what he should be and lives a life of hypocracy and becomes a psychopathic person.

Two different types of parental behaviour, according to Buss (1966), result in producing psychopatic personality. In the parental models and learning there are certain variations. Meher (1966) states that it is also possible to produce moral behaviour and feeling of conscience in children by certain way of rewarding and punishing them. If the child commits any mistake he is published by the parents. But instead of punishing, the child is made to know and realize that such mistakes are wrong and he is advised that it will lead to punishment and hence he should not do it once again and he is excused for the mistake he had committed. By this means the child may develop certain amount of conscience. This means the child may develop certain amount of conscience. This type of parential model also prevails in the community instead of punishing the child severally. A severe punishment may make the child to commit the same mistakes and ultimately he develops antisocial behaviour in the long run. According to Wilkins (1961) antisocial behaviour in some persons is self-perpetuating. For example the businessmen and politicians make it as a life-style and carry on the behaviour consistently.

2. Deprivation in the Early Years

Deprivation of any type may cause depression and the feeling of helplessness in the child. If the child is neglected without parental care or lacks mother's care naturally he may develop psychopatic personality traits. If the parental care is lacking in three years the child misses many things in the developmental stage. The child misses the nutritional diet, love and affection of the mother, and the social relationship in the family. The child may also feel that he is isolated and develops the feelings of destitute, fear of meeting the peers and taking part in group activities. All these may contribute to the development of antisocial behaviour patterns.

Several studies were made on this problem. In one of the studies conducted by Beres and Obers (1950) very significant results were obtained. These authors made a systematic study of 38 adolescents. These children were institutionalized at a very young stage of three weeks and three years. At adolescent stage twenty one were found to be having personality disorder and only seven adolescents had developed required adjustments. These children totally deprived of direct parental care and domestic care and treatment. There was also delay in the immediate satisfaction of the needs. They were not able to have what they wanted. There was a very little chance for the development of conscience. They were not able to build up the long standing goals. There were no chances for them to take up any model and identification. There was also emotional deprivation of giving and receiving love and affection with others. Though the maternal and sociocultural requirements were not totally separated what they were enjoying was only artificial and manipulated emotional expressions. It was observed that there was gradual development of psychopathic personality traits.

3. Physiological Conditioning

Investigators are of the view that there must be some basic factors in the etiology of antisocial behaviour. The psychopathic is generally impulsive and whenever he faces some disagreeable situation, he begins to act out. He becomes aggressive for disciplines, at times becomes violent. These show that there is some imbalance between his inner and outer emotional reactions. It means some process in the nervous system becomes the root cause of the antisocial behaviour. Stoot (1962) was able to collect evidences that a conditions of non-hereditary abnormal at birth which may be stated as *congenital injuries* might have damaged the higher inhibitory centres in the nervous systems. This condition may make the psychopathic person more capable of damaging the inner controls under strainful conditions. But this condition is not traceable in the EEG instrument. Robins (1967) has stated that there is no evidence that abnormality or brain damage could be identified in the EEG recording. The EEG recordings on mentally retarded and on brain damaged persons do not really reveal the brain condition. The antisocial or psychopath is very rarely revealed in the EEG recordings.

It was also tested whether the psychopath could react to the conditioning in the same manner as the normal persons. Eysenck (1960) has observed that the psychpath is slow in reacting to the conditioning and also in normal socialization, and in the development of conscience. Hare (1968) and his coworkers observed the same type of relations in psychopathic persons and found that they lack the normal emotional reactions like fear, anxiety and slow in learning anything from punishments.

Treatment of Antisocial Personalities

The antisocial persons or the psychopathic personalities are not clinically diagnosed and classified as abnormal personalities. They function just like all other normals in most of the occasions, successfully deal with certain specific issues they differ very much from others and commit grave mistakes, cause damage to properties and injure persons. Mostly they act out their impulsive irresponsible and unethical, emotional immaturity, poor socialization in certain ways and situations. Therefore treatment for such persons based upon their behaviour is very difficult. Clinically any specific type of treatment is making them to participate in rehabilitation programmes. But these programmes were found to be not very much effective. Since the antisocial behaviour is based upon the developmental process and prolonged for long time it is very difficult to get rid of it as expected. What is felt more important, is to change the life style of the psychopathic personality.

In providing psychotherapeutic treatment to the psychopathic persons there are difference of opinions among the researchers. Bonay (1945) Thorne (1959) were of the view that the classical psychotherapeutic treatment was not very much successful with the antisocial behaviour. But behaviour therapy was found to be effective and successful with the antisocial behaviour. Bandura (1969) is of the view that learning principles were found to be successful in treating the antisocial behaviour. His three learning principles were mainly based upon change of behaviour modelling and rewarding the antisocial for imitating the behaviour. It was also observed that the antisocial behaviour was reduced in the psychopaths after forty years of their age. Coleman (1969) states that it is because that the psychopathic personalities become weak after forty years and their aggressive and violent behaviour patterns also become reduced.

The source and origin of antisocial behaviour is not yet correctly designed and applied. The organic defect of some defect is not the same in all individuals. It varies from person to person. In some cases, it is reported that the psychotherapeutic treatment has shown some improvement. In some serious and special cases brain surgery is recommended. Any treatment in the case of psychopaths shows improvement only after the age of forty years. It is said that the instinctive urge is strong in the early years and it gets weaken after forty years. There is also social pressure on them and they get better understanding about their behaviour. Every treatment programme should aim at these antisocial persons promoting a sense of responsibility, emotional balance, and stability in their live activities. They should accept moral and social norms. The antisocial behavioural attitude should be detected in children and it would be prevented without allowing them to develop along with them as and when they grow into adolescents and adults.

The prediction of the course of this disease at present time on full-blown psychopaths, according to Strange (1965) does not yield a positive result. Because the psychopaths essentially do not accept that there is something wrong with them. Since they did not develop normal conscience, they always think that they are blameless and believe that only others are wrong. Linder (1944) in his work "Rebel without a cause" states that psychoanalysis and psychotherapy treatments were found to be successful with the psychopaths.

CHAPTER 16

Criminal Behaviour

What is Criminal Behaviour?

Criminal means a person charged with and convicted of some crime. It is a person who commits crimes for a living. Criminal behaviour is a type of behaviour performing against the law and order. It may be any act like stealing or robbery, snatching away another man's prosperity, kidnapping a person for ransom, forcible rape, adultery, burglary, murder and similar act which is against society. Criminal activity also includes violating the accepted social and moral norms. Assaulting and hurting a person is also a criminal behaviour. Cheating other persons in any form with the view of getting some benefits, swindling or defrauding money or property are quite common types of criminal behaviour in any community. Therefore, criminal behaviour may be defined in a broader sense as the type of antisocial behaviour which is committed by a person violating the accepted ethical and social norms or principles and standards of conduct in any community which have a definite form and enforced through law and order. These criminal activities or violations are accompanied by some punishment based upon the level of severity and nature of the crimes.

The conception of criminal behaviour varies from time to time and culture to culture. What is a crime in one community or culture is not a crime in another community or culture. But some crimes like stealing, robbery, murder, cheating, forcible rape and adultery are universal in nature. To decide whether an act is a crime or not depends upon the laws prevailing in the country or culture. Certain laws in some countries are so severe as to punish the criminal with death sentence; such laws are relaxed as time passes on. What was punishable crime at one time becomes a non-punishable act at a later time. Since laws are man-made system for regulating the society it may be going on changing from time to time. For example, in Islamic countries the punishment for forcible rape and adultery is death. In other countries the culprit may escape from punishment for such crimes. There were cases against Mike Tyson, the boxing champion of United States, for forcible rape of some girls. He was not punished. In India even murderers are escaping from punishment. The court acquits murderers stating that there were no eyewitnesses. Thus for the same crime different types of judgements are awarded for the criminals depending upon the rigid way of dealing with the laws.

We know that any violation of law is a crime. Every human institution has its own laws. There are the legal laws, moral laws and religious laws. The violation of legal laws is called crime, the violation of moral laws is called immorality and the violation of religious laws is called sin. There is punishment in society for violating legal and moral laws. But violating the religious law is stated as the transgression of God's known will, or any principle or law is regarded as sin. Redemption is the process of deliverance from sin. Every religion has some process of redeeming the sin committed by the people.

Occurrence OF CRIMES

Crimes are committed by human beings in society. The increase of population in a society provides more chances for committing crimes. In the primitive society the crime rate was not so much. In the civilised and industrialised society the crime rate is very high. Increase of population, industrial and technological development provides ample opportunities for the incidences of crime. The American Bureau of Investigation has given an official figure and stated that the crime rate is higher in the United States than in any other countries in the world and the rate is increasing steadily. The Investigation Bureau has stated that the real crime rate may be still higher as there were many unreported cases.

A random sampling study was made by Ennis (1967) among ten thousand householders, and he found that there were many major crimes unreported. There were also many minor crimes, assaults, cheating, misguiding, petty thefts which were also not reported. Coleman (1965) presents the crime clocks based upon the statistics provided by the Federal Bureau of Investigation (1970) which indicates that for every 33 minutes one murder takes place in the United States. Forcible rape occurs enormously. After every 14 minutes one forcible rape takes place. The crimes of aggravated assaults take place after every 96 seconds and robbery takes place after every 91 seconds. The crime of breaking the building and committing theft (bunglary) takes place very often, one for every 15 seconds. If these types of crimes are occurring in the United States so frequently for every 15 and 19 seconds, what would be the crime rates in underdeveloped countries?

In India the crime rate is increasing in geometrical progression. The type of crimes are murder, homicide, genocide, group killing, kidnapping, kidnapping and killing, forcible rape, adultery, child abuse, a wife killing her husband joining with her paramour, husband killing his wife for her illicit contact with another man, theft, robbery, burglary, counterfeiting of currency notes and coins, forgery, misappropriation, impersonation, vehicle thefts, manufacturing illicit drugs and selling. Every time new types of crimes are invented depending upon the situations. In India many of the crimes are going unnoticed, unreported and unidentified. Actions are taken only when the concerned person reported the matter to the police. The government or the police do not take cognizance of the crimes not reported. Corruption or illicit gratification in India has become common occurrence.

In every government department, every day some officer or some official person is arrested on the charge bribery case. Without bribes in these days in government offices the public cannot get any of their grievances redressed. Sometimes some police officials issue statements with regard to the crime rates and the nature of crimes statewise. Among the crimes theft, robbery, burglary, forcible rape, and murder top the list in many states. The crime of genocide is increasing in Jammu and Kashmir, Manipur and Assam. The terrorist movements kill people in an organised manner. Organised killings for political purposes are also taking place in some states. In Maharastra, Andhra Pradesh and Tamil Nadu organised killings are often taking place. There are also suicide squads organised and trained by some terrorist movements, and also countries instigate them to kill as many people as possible by means of bombs exploding and by firing at the people with modern weapons. India is a country facing several such attacks by the suicides squads and losing thousand of men, women and children every year. This type of killing incidence is taking place everyday in some parts in India. What type of punishment can be awarded for this type of crimes? Killing such killers on the spot must be the only possible punishment.

Crime rates increase in India generally due to the increase in population and due to the themes of motion picture and television themes. The risky groups (adolescents and youths) in India are highly corrupted by the themes of motion pictures for crimes like theft, robbery, burglary, murder, dacoity, forcible rape and kidnapping girls. When such criminals were arrested and investigated, they state that they got this idea from some particular motion picture. It has been estimated that for more than 50 per cent of the crimes the ideas were borrowed form motion pictures.

Sex crimes are equally increasing these days. Obscene photos which are offensive to moral principles, screening pictures of sexual activities secretly, all contribute to sex crimes of various types. The crime of forcibly engaging female children, aged 12 to 14 or 15 in flesh trade is increasing nowadays in some states. In this crime of children flesh trade Tamil Nadu tops the list according to a statement issued by some organisation. The incidences of crime rates are not correctly available as many of them are not reported.

CAUSATIVE FACTORS IN CRIMINAL BEHAVIOUR

Criminal behaviour occurs due to various factors. Some of the causative factors are common to criminal behaviour, antisocial behaviour and delinquent behaviour. But certain factors are specific to each of them. For example, professional crimes and organised crimes are specific to adult persons. But some delinquents may be involved in these two criminal activities when they become adults. Scholars who studied criminal behaviour find the origin in heredity. Therefore, let us discuss some of the factors which lie behind the criminal behaviour. The causative factors may be discussed under three important factors like the biological (heredity), social factors and psychological factors.

Biological Factors

What type of persons commit crimes? Why do some persons commit crimes? Are there any specific biological and personality factors that are mainly responsible for the act of crime? In India, there is a belief that hereditary factors are the root cause of criminal behaviour. Certain groups of people commit all sorts of crimes traditionally. In the classification of communities, it is stated that criminal tribes live on committing the crimes like theft, robbery, burglary, way laying and looting, dacoity and cheating. The criminal tribe's motive is only to get money or some properly for their living. Since they live on such means of living their children or the next generation also adapt the same type of living. This type of life, taken up by the children from their parents and grandparents, is due to family and environmental backgrounds. But strictly speaking, biological factors are involved in hereditary factors.

In criminal or in antisocial behaviour hereditary factors cannot be ruled out. Hereditary factors play an important role in antisocial behaviour. But it is very difficult to conclude that the chromosomal abnormalities are carried on for generations in criminal behaviour or in the criminal tribal communities. Systematic studies were made on this issues to whether the chromosomal abnormalities are really responsible for the criminal behaviour patterns or not. The studies of Lombroso and his co-workers brought to light several interesting results with regard to criminal behaviour. Lombroso (1836–1909), an Italian criminalogist, has postulated the existence of a criminal type. It is known as *Lombrosian*, based upon the doctrine formulated by Lombroso that criminals are a product of hereditary and atavistic factors, and can be classified as a definite abnormal type. The studies of Lombroso-Ferroro (1911) is known as the Italian School of Criminology. Lombroso states that the criminal is a born type of person with the characteristics of a low forehead, very peculiarly shaped head and jaw, the eyebrows are together just above the bridge of the nose and projecting ears. These characteristics are very easily identifiable from any normal human being. These primitive physical symptoms indicate that he is a savage man and apparently predisposed to the person to a criminal. Lombroso's descriptions of a criminal and criminal behaviour were debated for a long period.

There were quite a number of studies carried out to see whether there could be any possibility of genetic evidences for this. Jacobs and his coworkers (1965) undertook an elaborate study on 197 abnormal persons who were in the Scotland Institution. The inmates of this institution were very violent, aggressive and dangerous criminals. In the chromosome testing it was found that about 3.5 per cent of them had the chromosomal abnormalities one X and two Y (XYY) chromosomes. But in the general population, according to the studies made by Sergovich (1969) the occurrence of chromosomes pattern was one in 250. Weiner (1968) investigated this problem in the security prison in Australia., Sergovich suggested from the results of his later studies (1970) that there was definite relationship between the chromosomal abnormalities and the criminal behaviour in man.

Weiner later on confirmed this view. Out of 34 tall prisoners four had XYY chromosomes. Of them two men prisoners committed murder, one had attempted murder and the other had attempted theft. Tallness is the characteristic of the extra Y chromosome.

Studies on this issue were continued and more evidences were produced associating the XYY chromosomes and criminal behaviour. The males who were with XYY chromosomes were found to be taller than the normal persons, and more aggressive, impulsive, and below normal intelligence. According to Montagu's (1968) study one Richard Speak was convicted on the charge of gruesome murder of eight nurses in Chicago in 1966. This person is a good example of XYY chromosome type. This person was tall, mentally retarded and had a peculiar facial shape. He was already arrested in 40 criminal cases. The investigators had the doubt whether Speak's criminal behaviour was solely rooted in XYY chromosomal abnormalities or the environmental factor of impoverishment and other factors combined in his behaviour.

It is generally observed that the chromosomal abnormalities of any type are found to be more abnormal in development and in behaviour than the males who are of normal type. However it is not experimentally established that all XYY chromosome persons are aggressive, impulsive and violent. Many males with XYY carry out the normal everyday activities without any problem, though at times they go astray. However, the prevalent views and the results of the studies that the XYY chromosomal aberration predisposes the individual to criminal behaviour cannot be totally rejected. The investigation made by Prince and Whatmore (1967) and Montagu (1968) suggested that the extra Y chromosome promotes the development of aggressive and violent behaviour pattern which leads the individual to criminal activities.

Social Factors

The social factors in criminal behaviour involve several sub-factors. The present-day society is becoming very busy and active in earning its livelihood. Everyone in a community or in a family wants to get into a job and earn for a better life. However well a society is organised with a strong government, maintaining law and order, the incidences of crimes prevail at some level. There is no society at present without the occurrence of crimes. The increase of crimes in society indicates that there are persons violating the accepted social, cultural and ethical norms and also going against the law and order which the government is enforcing.

A society may be classified into certain categories on the basis of the economic status of the families. These are high socio-economic status groups, middle socio-economic status groups and lower socio-economic status groups. Members of these groups have their own occupational levels and standard of living and they are committed to the values assigned to them. But due to some unknown reasons the members of these groups, mostly the youth, do not commit themselves to their responsibilities. Some in each group go astray due to economic conditions or personal factors, and involve themselves in criminal activities. Adolescents who go to schools are not able to maintain the standard assigned to them and they fall back. The intellectual level does not help them to cope up with the standard. They are not able to meet the demands of the academic standards in the schools. They become dropouts and feel disgusted with the academic works, they try to find out some job elsewhere. If they are not successful in finding out some job they get involved in some antisocial activities like stealing, forgery, cheating and in all possible minor crimes. Generally, the school or college misfits and dropouts take up some easy way of life. These young persons in their (alienation) going away from the conventional society and turn to mysticism, psychedelic drugs and communal living. This type of life of these misfits and dropouts created a new type of population called the 'hippie' society.

Many of these young dropouts keep company with criminals and take up the same job, and find out ways and means for their living by theft, robbery, burglary, shoplifting, kidnapping and various kinds of criminal activities. They also find their living places in some slums in cities and big towns and develop all sorts of antisocial behaviour patterns. These slum-living youths get closely knit together easily as they become like-minded persons and share in all types of behavioural patterns.

People living in villages live in close proximity, and their social life does not permit the youths to go astray and commit crimes. Even if anyone commits a crime like theft, cheating, assaults or sex crimes, he is taken to task and punished. The village community is closely knit and also very sensitive to the antisocial behaviour. The rural community mainly lives on powerful customs and traditions, hence criminal activities rarely occur. But the environmental conditions also play an important role in the antisocial behaviour of the people living in the particular area. Public properties which are not under the direct control of the authorities are taken away by the people who are living in the nearby areas. If any person started to steal away or some wood parts of some machine and makes money out of them, others are also tempted to the same thing in due course.

Home and family conditions also cause unhappy situations in certain communities. There may be a family quarrel and separation of husband and wife. The position of children then becomes very precarious. The children become delinquents. Everyday there are reports in newspapers about the incidences of separation, divorce, husband killing wife for her illicit affaris with another man or wife killing her husband for engaging men for cruel treatment to her. These incidences are becoming very common these days. What is the position of their children? They get involved in some kind of illicit transactions and unlawful drug trade. When these children become adults they become full-fledged criminals.

Criminals come from homes where there is no love and affection, no care for them or from homes where there is no discipline or control over the children. Even strict discipline becomes harmful for children. Many children run away from homes for fear of strict discipline. This becomes an everyday incidence and reported in newspapers. Boys and girls fail to do their school academic works satisfactorily, develop fear that their parents may scold or beat them and so abscond. Particularly girls who are very timid even commit suicide or get into the hands of flesh traders who raise hopes and confidence and engage them in prostitutions for making money.

A press report states under the heading of 'Children predated in flesh trade in India', that apart from adult women and adolescent girls involved in the flesh trade the innocent children also are found to be involved in it. It is estimated that about six lakhs of children in India are being predated in the flesh trade. Children constitute 15 per cent of the prostitutes in India. The children involved in sex trade are from six major cities of Delhi, Mumbai, Kolkata, Chennai, Hyderabad and Bangalore. It is not willingly that these children get into the sex trade. Either they are girls who have run away from their homes for fear of their parents' punishment or kidnapped by the sex traders while they were returning home. Some girls might have been illegitimate children. Many criminals who are arrested and punished are found to be either widowed or divorced persons. Most probably they are psychopaths.

Studies have been made on this problem, and the results mostly reveal that alienation or turning away from the social norms and rebellious attitudes of the young persons are common behavioural patterns. The pathogenic family patterns in every culture are unavoidable, however well organised a society is. There are broken homes, and absence of father in the family in many cases causes the family to be pathogenic. In the case of absence of both the parents in the family it may result in total confusion. The children become destitutes and ultimately resort to delinquency and get involved in antisocial behaviour. Even if they get some job in the normal course, they lack the required skills for performing the job. Academically, psychologically and socially they are found misfit, unable to carry out even the semi-skilled jobs successfully.

The economic factor in every society is found to be one of the important causes of crime. Most of the criminals arrested were found to be poor and unemployed. Therefore, poverty and unemployment, and rapid increase of population function in the incidences of crime. Although individuals are employed in some works they are not satisfied with the income. They find it difficult to run the family and therefore they quit the job and go in search of some other job which is not easily or immediately available. Thus they become unemployed. Many unskilled workers are poor and they are in the state of deprivation for prolonged periods gets frustrated. The only alternative is theft, or some criminal activity which could satisfy their needs. In the industrial society even rich men are not free from committing crimes. They try to make money by short-cut methods by producing and selling adulterated goods. The quality control board found many such cases and arrested and punished them.

Racial factors were found to be operating in the criminal behaviour. Actually no race or community or tribe is criminal by nature or by heredity. We have discussed this matter in the preceding pages. It is the social situation and environmental conditions that are prevailing around the racial and tribal groups. The racial or tribal behaviour may vary from time to time. The tribal people are neither rich nor possess anything in store for their living. They go out to collect food materials during summer season and stay in during winter, consuming the collected materials, food and other ingredients. They do not have any permanent income. It is only seasonal collection. They collect whatever is available to them. They do not consider it as theft, but a normal way of collection. Sometimes they get caught and are punished.

Psychological Factors

Clinical studies confirm that criminals are below the normal level of intelligence, have personality disorders and are neurotic persons. Subnormal persons commit crimes not with any definite aim or motive, but they are incapable of easily distinguishing right and wrong, good and bad, and lawful and unlawful. They think and assume that what they do is right and proper. Persons of below-normal intelligence are generally feeble-minded and there are several levels in it which are normally indicated as mentally retarded. In the case of delinquents there are more number of criminals mentally retarded than the delinquents who are of normal intelligence. Most of the criminals come from poor families and are not educated.

But all criminals are not mentally retarded. There are criminals who are of superior intelligence and are educated. What makes them to commit crimes? One of the factors might be the desire or motivation for better living. The economic deprivation motivates many intelligent people to acquire more money or property of some kind and develop all facilities in their life. They even learn certain skills in committing crimes. Once they taste the comforts of life by criminal means they try to specialise in certain type of crimes like burglary or forgery or misappropriation. These persons plan the methods very carefully to become rich for a very comfortable life. They do not commit very serious crimes like murder and kidnapping and then demanding huge sums of money. Since this type of crimes may lead to investigation and is likely to get arrested and punished, they commit the crimes which do not give any chance for suspecting them. Their motive is to make money in the shortest possible time and in the safest manner without any act of aggression and violence. These criminals are superior in intelligence. They use their intelligence only in terms of making money.

Clinical assessments show that many of the criminals are neurotics to some extent. The neuroses that are associated with criminal behaviour are kleptomania and pyromania. But some normal persons who are involved in criminal cases pretend to be mad and act in an abnormal manner to escape punishment. There is a court of law that if neurotics or psychotics are proved by the court to be insane they are not punishable. Generally, a psychiatrist is engaged to examine and declare whether the accused is insane or sane. But evidence should be produced to show that at the time of committing the crime the person was insane and because of this state he could not understand whether the act was a crime or not. Criminals who are insane are not held responsible for the act and therefore they are not liable to be punished.

Treatment of Criminals

While discussing about the criminal behaviour or criminals we may also recollect the subject matter that was discussed under the heading of antisocial behaviour or personality. Since the etiology of these two behavioural patterns is devoid of any clear-cut demarcation there may be some mistaken identity of these two. But, however, some distinction can be brought out. Antisocial behaviour or personality refers to the personality disorder involving a marked lack of ethical or moral development, whereas a criminal refers to a person charged with and convicted for committing a crime. The criminals are those who violate the state law and order and also go against the accepted social and moral norms, commiting all sorts of criminal activities. Therefore, they are punished according to the law. All the crimes we have discussed earlier are punishable according to the criminal law.

A systematic, rational way of dealing with the criminal was not in force till the beginning of the nineteenth century. The nineteenth century British philosopher, John Stewart Mill (1806-1873), had revised Betham's utilitarian philosophy and also written about the rights and freedom of the individual. It was James Mill (1773 - 1836) a Scottish philosopher, who expanded Betham's utilitarian philosophy and wrote the criminal law first. This awakened the various governments existing at that time and they began to formulate laws for charging the criminals.

But in the earlier days, in the primitive societies, the criminals were dealt with crudely by punishing with harmful returns, execution of physical torture, and social dishonour. These were the common methods of treatment used till the beginning of nineteenth century. In place of retributive punishment there were other methods of treatment, like deterrence and rehabilitation. In the European countries, according to Coleman (1954), only during the course of 150 years a standard procedure of dealing with the offenders was followed. It is by means of rehabilitation and retraining in socialisation. But implementing any such programme involves adequate financial assistance. Though imprisonment of these offenders was a common procedure of dealing with them, gradually the correctional procedure also was introduced. The community-based programme, Magee (1969) states, has been started as a revolutionary change in the programme and it may be applied as a scientific method of treating the offenders making use of the ideas of social sciences.

The course of action with criminal behaviour is almost like the procedures used in psychopathology. Therefore, the same type of treatment procedures may be applied in treating the criminals. The causes should be detected as early as possible and the treatment should be applied for the correction of an unhealthy way of life, of unwanted social conditions and providing adequate facilities for the offenders. The criminals are of various types and the crimes may have a vast range of area and therefore the individual offenders may fall under different categories. Thus it is a complex problem and no single procedure of treatment or any one generalised procedure can be successfully applied as a solution. The problem is based upon several factors like social, psychological, economic and environmental.

There are several aspects of treatment assigned to the criminal offenders. These aspects are based upon the severity of the crimes committed and the nature and type of crimes. The primary aspect is punishment for the offence. The second aspect is the nature of the crime. The third aspect is the correctional trends and the fourth is putting back in some condition or rehabilitation.

Punishment

Punishment means a penalty or sanction given for any crime or offence. It is an act of punishing or a state of being punished. It is a penalty imposed on a person for committing an unlawful act. In the primitive society punishment was very severe, mostly by death or social boycott or driving the offender away from the community and not having any contact with the offender. But as changes took place in society there were also changes in the procedure of punishment. The punishment is based upon the severity of the offence. The offences have social importance and punishments also are based upon them. The social importance of crime changed from time to time and therefore the type of punishment also changed. At one time stealing money or any property was considered as a very serious offence and when the offender was caught, the punishment awarded to him was death by hanging. But in these days such offences are not considered as serious and the punishment also is changed to a mild form. Sometimes the offender goes to court and gets release from any punishment.

In India before the British rule there were princely states, ruled by Rajas and Maharajas. It was a tradition that the king himself conducted the enquiry and when the person was found to be quilty he was given death sentence by hanging. For some minor offences, based upon the severity of the injury, the punishment was cutting an ear, leg or hand. In some cases the criminal was driven away from the state. In the case of theft, robbery, burglary in some of the Indian states, cutting off of body parts was a common punishment. In some of the semi-civilised countries beating or flogging and beheading were punishments for the offenders. In Russia, once the convicts were sent to Sibaria as a punishment of exile or banishment.

After the British rule came to India courts were set up and systematic enquiries were held and if a person was found guilty he was punished on the basis of the type of crimes ranging from simple imprisonment to death sentence by hanging. This type of punishment enforced by the British rule in India finds its root in the utilitarian philosophy of Jeremy Bentham (1748-1832), a British philosopher and jurist. According to him if punishment is certain then it should be swift and severe, so that others should avoid criminal behaviour. Bentham's conclusion is accepted and practised in most of the countries all over the world. Punishment for the offender usually must involve imprisonment. This is the most operative way of making the offender to realise his mistake and be free from further offence, and it is one way of removing his offensive ideas. Punishment serves three important purposes such as (1) revenge or retaliation by the society, (2) imprisonment protects the society and (3) punishment prevents or deters by setting up an example for others not to be offenders.

1. Revenge or Retaliation

It is in society where many members live that an the offence is committed. Society never tolerates offences and feels that the culprit should suffer. Revenge is an approach in dealing with the offender. It is a defensive approach by society in favour of the distressed. The criminal activity must put the idea that the guilty person most suffer. Studies were made on this issue and Henley (1971) has pointed out that many crime victims carry with them unnoticed and long-lasting psychological fears. In case the government or society does not put forth legal procedures for penalising the criminals the people in the society or group of individuals take law into their hands and deal with the offenders. This is happening in every country. The offenders are severely punished by beating and killing, illegal hanging and lynching. Sometimes the victim himself deals with the culprit and punishes him by beating or stabbing and killing.

2. Imprisonment Protects the Society

In punishing the offender by putting him in prison, society is protected. So long as the offender is in prison he is prevented from committing any crime. The property of the people in the society is safe. But it cannot be assured what he would not do it after the period of imprisonment. Imprisonment shall be followed by a rehabilitation programme. Otherwise the offender after the period, may commit the same crime. He may improve the old criminal skills or learn or invent a new type of criminal skill or reduce his criminal behaviour. Tougher convicts may assault new and younger ones and also may commit severe crimes like stabbing, and may be involved in other violent activities. In such cases the offender himself is not protected. Criminal activities inside the prison are becoming quite common in India these days. There may be communal, religious and racial conflicts. The prisoner himself is not protected. There is no security for life. When such offenders come out of prison they come out with more criminally inclined behaviour than before the imprisonment. There is more insecurity for the society than protection or security. Nixon (1970), the former President of the United States, stated that prisons are universities of crime where more than two lakhs of hardened criminals are graduated every year. Therefore we may state that putting the offenders in prisons does not correct them or make them learn any lesson.

3. Deterrence or Frightening

Deterrence is a way of discouraging a person from acting, and preventing from occurring usually by instilling a sense of fear, doubt or anxiety. Deterrences are made on the idea that punishment for committing crimes will deter or prevent the criminal offender in the future and also prevent others from committing such criminal activities. This is what expected in the efforts of deterrence. But there are certain factors limiting the effects of punishment. Punishment sometimes is delayed and also there is no surety of punishment for the crime one has committed. The person who has committed the crime and had imprisonment may not be having the feeling that he is guilty.

The nature of punishment should create a sense of fear in the offender. It could be done so if only punishment is awarded as early as possible without a long delay. The impact of punishment is lost due to unnecessary delay. Deterrent effect in the offenders will function only if the punishment for a crime is severe. In the case of homicide the rates in India is increasing in geometrical progression. The percentage of the rate for sex is higher than among other types of homicide. A husband kills his wife for being unfaithful to him, A man kills his paramour for not cooperating for illicit relation. A girl is killed for not loving the man. These types of sex crimes are reported everyday in newspapers all over India, the higher percentage being from Tamil Nadu. In some cases the offender is not arrested, in many cases the offender is arrested and committed to the court of law. But the punishment in most of the cases are simple imprisonment or the offender is acquitted. Very few are punished, but not severely like capital punishment. As a result of this type of punishment there is no scope for deterrence. There are such themes in motion pictures and a youth takes them as examples. If homicide would certainly result in death sentence, then there is scope for causing fear in others for committing such crimes. Homicide, forcible rape and other sex crimes are becoming common occurrences in India as there is no capital punishment enforced on these offenders generally. As result of this, punishment for these types of crimes does not cause any sense of fear in others, including the offenders.

Studies on this problem were made in many countries. Schwartz (1968) observed in his study that homicide rates in United States are as high as in states that still award capital punishment as in those states that have abolished it. But it is found that even though law enforces severe penalities for forcible rape, there is no expected effect on its incidence or in the humiliation of the victims. In some cases law shows its deaf ears. Law does not produce a deterrent effect on would-be-law breakers. There are published reports in newspapers that the offender admitted during police investigation that he had murdered a person but the court had acquitted him stating there was no eyewitness for the crime. This means that there are chances for the offender of any type to escape punishment. This may serve as an example for the other offenders to follow the same technique. Therefore, unless people are aware that the law is supreme and any violation would certainly result in severe punishment, it will not be possible to produce any deterrent effect on the offender or on others.

Rehabilitation and Re-Education

Rehabilitation is mainly making the person adapt to the situation. Rehabilitation generally means helping a person who is physically or mentally disabled, or has just been released from prison, to adapt to society or to a new job, by means of vocational guidance, retraining, re-education or by therapy. Rehabilitation may be also stated as the restoration to a former position or work. It is also restoration of once lost good reputation. In the case of treatment of criminals rehabilitation generally means the process of making the criminal adapt himself to a situation. This may be mainly putting the criminal in some physical work or training him for some unskilled or skilled works or educating him, if the criminal is educable, for some mental works.

Generally criminals in the prisons are treated rudely and severely. It is because the criminals themselves may behave rudely and refuse to carry out the orders in prison. They may be also wicked and violent in their movements. The habitual murderers may behave in an unruly manner in prison. There are incidences reported that the prisoner attacked the prison guards. Such prisoners are generally kept in strict confinements. The other prisoners who behave according to prison rules and carry out the orders, are given training or education according to the rehabilitation programmes. The rehabilitation programme also includes resocialisation and development of a sense of duties and responsibilities. According to Glaus (1968) imprisonment should promote redeeming characteristics without which imprisonment has no deterrent effect to criminal behaviour and also, it has no useful purpose for the criminals. Menhinger (1968) states that if imprisonment is a revengeful punishment, it would only lead to worse the situation. There are various ways of treating the offenders and different approaches in the treatment of the prisoners.

1. Indefinite Decisions of the Court and Releasing the Prisoner (Paroles)

The courts have become very liberal these days and reluctant in sending the offenders to prisons. The courts prolong the enquiries and also delay in making quick judgement in criminal cases. Making indefinite decisions in judgements are on the rise. In such situations the qualified offender in the rehabilitation programme does not know when he would be released from the prison. The rehabilitation authorities can plan the programme for an individual only when they come to know the duration of the imprisonment. They cannot plan any long term programme for an individual offender if he is suddenly released from the prison. If only the rehabilation authorities know the duration of each offender in the prison a substantial and beneficial programme can be planned and suitable training can be offered. Only then the prisoner can come out of prison with the satisfaction that he is benefited by his stay in the prison and may continue a normal way of life in the community, and committing any crime further may not incubate in his mind.

Further releasing offender on parole also causes problems in rehabilitation. The criminal may be undergoing some training programme which may be very much useful for him on going out after completing the prison term. If the offender was released on parole before completing the prison term, he is at a loss and not benefited by the rehabilitation programme. Now and then improvements are made in prison facilities and innovations are made in the rehabilitation programmes. The indeterminate sentences and releasing the offender on parole make him not to make use of the benefits of the rehabilitation programmes.

2. Approaches in the Treatment of Criminal Offenders

Several new methods of dealing with the criminals in prisons have been suggested and some methods have been put into practice to some extent. These new approaches were dependent upon the nature of the crime and the type of the criminal offenders. The treatment for the drug addicts must be something other than the treatment given other criminals. Offenders of theft, casual or habitual, are given treatments which should have deterrent effect. Bandura (1969) and others have tried with systematic application of behavioural modification techniques on juvenile delinquents and in adult criminals. The electrical shock approach also has been used in dealing with criminals for controlling the criminal inclinations.

Imprisonment causes different effects in different people. For some it is an incident in the life which causes degradation to their status and some feel that it is an insult and shameful incident and feel that they lose respect in the community. Imprisonment in some causes sexual aberrations. In the case of an offender who was married and had wife and children, his imprisonment put a heavy burden on his wife and children. If the offender is young and has committed a simple crime for the first time he is generally excused and sent out with a warning or with a mild punishment. But if it is a serious crime like homicide he is given a severe punishment.

It has been observed that imprisonment does not produce any rehabilitation effect in some violent prisoners. For such offenders different types of treatment should be given. In some Arab countries criminal offenders are beaten in public. In some cases a part of the body is cut off, like the fingers or hand, depending upon the nature of the crime. The punishment for serious crime like homicide is to behead the offender without causing any delay. This method of treatment has strong deterrent effect in others. This is according to the Islamic law. But in many countries in the world it is found that imprisonment has failed to achieve the object.

Imprisonment or punishing institutions in many cases do not reform the criminals, but allow them to become hardened criminals and enemies of society. Generally, the punishments are not proportional to the severity of the crimes committed by the offenders. Thus prison fails to reform the criminal offenders.

Prisons with Rehabilitation Programmes

There are prisons in India with several types of rehabilitation programmes. In some prisons there are textile mills where the prisoners who are sentenced for more than three or four years are employed in the mills as mill workers. They are first given training in various sections of the mill and after becoming proficient in the work they are placed as regular workers. When they go out they may get employed in some mills. There are also handloom textile programmes, blacksmiths, lathe industries, carpentry, furniture making, manufacturing small tools, bed making, mat weaving, weaving clothes, blankets, doormats and other materials required for homes.

In some prisons, there are open prisons where prisoners are not kept in lock-up rooms. They are left in open spaces for working. They work in paddy fields the whole day and sleep in dormitories. Prisoners are trained in agricultural farms and when they go out they are absorbed in some agricultural works. Having worked in some manually skilled areas when the offenders return home, they may be tempted to continue in the same work and make it their vocation. These kinds of rehabilitation programmes seem to be very beneficial for the convicts and there are chances to get over the criminal tendencies and settle in life peacefully.

Offenders who are mentally upset, psychotics, mentally retarded may have to be kept in separate institutions where they may be given suitable treatment and given some vocational training according to the level of mental development. If they are fit for any simple manual work they can be placed in suitable works in such a way as to make them self-dependant and self-suffucuent.

CHAPTER 17

Delinquent Behaviour

What is Delinquent Behaviour?

Delinquency means an offence or misdeed usually of a minor nature, especially one committed by a young person. Delinquency or a delinquent is always associated with juvenile delinquency. Juvenile delinquency refers to a child or young person guilty of some offence, act of vandalism or antisocial behaviour, or whose conduct is beyond parental control and who may be brought before a juvenile court. Therefore delinquency may be defined as the behaviour of offence, not acceptable to society, committed by adolescents or youths under 18 and above eight years of age calling for some kind of punishment or some kind of corrective or reformative action.

Delinquent behaviour includes staying away from school (truancy), disobedience, waywardness, running away from home, being not under the control of the parents and teachers, not amenable to any kind of discipline, being mischievous and violent among the peers, behaving in a manner injurious to others and to himself, acting against the well-being and happiness of others, using illegal drugs, homicide, eve-teasing and other serious criminal offences. It is very difficult to determine the incidences of delinquent behaviour as many of them are not reported. Generally, juvenile delinquency means antisocial or illegal behaviour by minors, usually individuals who are below 18 years of age.

Occurrence

The range of occurrence of juvenile delinquency is much more common in cities and slum areas of cities than in rural areas. Since the community is well knit in rural areas delinquency is controlled and prevented by the rural people. But in cities everybody is a stranger to every other person unless they live in close proximity in the same place for years. Therefore delinquent tendencies are much higher. The crimes committed by the young offenders are like the crimes the adults commit and many things that are within the reach of the young persons. In India there are quite a number of juvenile delinquent homes where the young offenders are kept and guarded. In every state in India there are about 10/15 such homes but the statistics of the inmates are not available as the institutions or the state government do not want to reveal them.

The statistics about the crimes committed by the juvenile delinquents are available in the United States. Quite a number of investigators have presented the statistics and nature of crimes. Roswell and Fishman (1968), Uniform Crimes Reports (1971), U.S. News and World Report (1970) and Valde (1971) have presented an alarming picture of juvenile delinquency. According to them, during the period 1960 to 1970 there were more than 110 per cent of arrests of the persons under the age of 18 years. The arrested persons were between 10 and 17 years of age. The type of crimes also were varied. Among the arrested juveniles there was one out of every three for robbery. One out of every five was for forcible rape, and one out of every 10 for homicide. There were more than 70 per cent of the offenders below 18 years out of more than 10,000 persons arrested. Most of the delinquents were males. One out of every 20 adolescents was arrested in United States in 1970. The more astonishing fact is that juveniles have committed about half of the total serious offences in the United States. The statistics of the female delinquents were also included in the reports. Female delinquents are generally arrested for various offenses like drug abuse, sexual offences, running away from home and stealing.

The male delinquents are arrested mainly for drug abuse, crimes against property, aggressive assaults, violence, sex crimes like forcible rape, eve-teasing, damaging public property etc. It is observed that the occurrence of delinquent behaviour differs among the delinquents of different socio-economic status groups. Specifically the occurrences of delinquent behaviour among those from slums are found to be higher and severe. In Hoover's (1968) study, it was observed that the delinquency rate among socially disadvantaged and lower socio-economic status delinquents was almost at the same level.

Causes Assigned to Juvenile Delinquency

In juvenile delinquency there are several factors or conditions operating. The delinquent behaviour depends mainly upon the environmental conditions that prevails in the life of a youth. The other important causes that may be assigned to the criminal behaviour of the youth may be biological factors, social, economic, racial and psychological factors. The culture to which one belongs to was also stressed as one of the causes of delinquent behaviour.

1. Personal Perversion

Personal perversion is associated with mental retardation and delinquent behaviour. Studies have been conducted to trace the causative factors of delinquency. Caputo and Mandell (1970) have observed that there is about one per cent of brain pathology cases. These individuals have the tendency towards violent behaviour pattern, and they are found to be often hyperactive, impulsive., emotionally unstable. Peer groups have a significant influence upon them. They face acceptance and rejection of their families. About five per cent of the delinquents are of low intelligence levels. The delinquent individuals are incapable of looking into the consequences of their behaviour and understand the results of their actions. These results are found in individuals who are mentally retarded males and sexually delinquent girls (Wirt, et al 1962). According to Blackhurt (1968) mentally retarded delinquent males often behave impulsively against persons. Less intelligent boys and girls who are not able to visualise their acts fall under the influence of bright psychopaths and delinquent gangs. These psychopaths and delinquent gangs have dominance over them and dictate their activities.

In some cases mental retardation and brain damage are combined and thus the characteristics of brain damage and mental retardation may be found in the delinquent behaviour. A delinquent need not be mentally retarded and low in intelligence. A youth of average intelligence may become a delinquent if he gets into the company of delinquents. The brain damage also may cause a tendency for delinquent behaviour. Delinquents may be mentally retarded, but all delinquents are not mentally retarded. But it is generally observed that most of the delinquents are either brain-damaged or mentally retarded. They deviate from the normal way of life and involve in destructive activities. They usually act in a perverse manner as a means of finding satisfaction by performing an unlawful act. This is an abnormal way of finding satisfaction. The person's satisfaction may be anything like stealing some materials that are not essential for him, setting fire for no purpose, destroying public properties for no reason. This tendency is personal perversion.

Delinquency is also associated with neurotic and psychotic disorders. According to Coleman (1974) about 10 per cent of delinquent behaviour is associated with neurotic disorders. The neurotic delinquent often behaves in the form of compulsive neurosis. He is compelled to perform some unlawful act, like peeping at others' activities through holes or windows, which has not any specific purpose, stealing things that are not required for his purpose, damaging some properties on his way, setting fire to some properties; if the delinquent is sexually perverted, he may indulge in stealing the undergarments of the girls, by such acts he finds deviant gratification. It is also believed that inhibition or over-inhibition induced by parents cause these delinquents to commit these perverted acts. But the perverted delinquent, before involving in these delinquent behaviours, meets with conflicts. Whether to do the act or not? But his impulsive tendency puts him in action, and after performing the act he feels guilty for committing such acts. It is because of his compulsive neurotic tendency that he cannot avoid such perverted desires.

The psychotic disorder is to some extent associated with delinquency. Several studies were conducted on this problem. Bandura and Walterns (1959) have found that about five per cent of delinquents suffer from psychotic disorders. These psychotic delinquents suffer from emotional frustration for a longer period and also socially withdraw themselves. These characteristics they develop out of violent behaviour with others. Wirt et al (1962) state that personality disorder is the main cause of delinquent behaviour though the antisocial tendency is there. These delinquents are mostly schizoid characterised by eccentric thinking, but they are devoid of delusions and hallucinations. This type of psychotic disorder is a mild type. The psychotic delinquents do not like others to see their activities.

It is also observed that a considerable level of delinquency seems to associate with characteristics of antisocial and psychopathic personalities with resentful character, impulsive, feelings of guilt and remorse, lack in personal relationships. They are not benefited by the past experiences. They are often involved in some meaningless activities since they lack conscience and contact with reality. These psychopathic delinquents may steal money and materials, though they do not require them. They live absolutely under the control of their impulses and excitements and without any idea about their future.

Generally most of the studies on delinquency were on male delinquents. But there were only few studies on female delinquents though there were quite a number of cases of female delinquents. Investigators like Cloninger and Guze (1970 a), Fine and Fishman (1968) have stated that there were many incidences of psychopathic personalities of girls in correctional institutions. Fine and Fishman (1968) have presented the psychopathic personality characteristics of 115 girls in a correlational institution in one of the states in United States. It was found that these psychopathic delinquent girls were very rebellious, impulsive, unstable and immatured.

2. Delinquents and Drug Abuses

It is a general characteristic of the delinquents to resort to drug abuses. It has become a fashion in these days for the adolescent boys and girls to adapt to drug-addicting habits. Once the adolescents become drug addicts their activities are directed to stealing money and other properties, damaging properties and involving in all sorts of sex crimes like forcible rape, eve-teashing, gang raping and killing the girls. Senior adolescents or youths easily get into the habit of getting addicted to the hard drugs such as heroin, morphine, cocaine and marijuana. Since the drugs are very expensive they will have to maintain them by stealing money. The delinquent youths under the influence of the drugs become very impulsive and are ready to commit crimes against persons, apart from stealing goods and valuable materials and selling them at lower rates.

3. Pathological Family Conditions

There are pathological conditions which cause several problems in the family. Family conditions or patterns produce both pleasant and unpleasant situations. There is no problem with a happy family. But conditions change adversely in the family situation due to quarrels between husband and wife, excess alcoholism, separation of husband and wife. All these may cause bad effects upon the adolescent boys and girls. The primary family condition that may lead the adolescents to delinquent tendencies is the broken home. Investigations reveal that very few adolescents are found in the correction institutions from pleasant families. According to Anderson (1968) the delinquent youths in correctional institutions are either without fathers or lack of father's care in the socialisation process of the youths. Those children who have lost the parental care from the age of four to seven were found in the correctional homes as delinquents.

4. Treatment of Parents

Parents play a crucial role in the development of their children in the form of showering love and affection on their children and in getting them well educated fit for lucrative occupations. But if the father does not take any interest in his son's future and the mother is very much dominant and stubborn in her decisions, the parents have failed to provide opportunities to their children to identify with their parents. These children grow into adolescents with some antisocial activities and get involved in criminal behaviour. It is because of the parents' restrictions that children seek interests outside the homes. Andry (1962) has conducted an investigation among many delinquent boys. Most of these delinquent boys have expressed that they are rejected by their fathers, but shown love and affection by their mothers, whereas the non-delinquent boys state that they are loved by both parents. The author also observes that a delinquent boy expressed his dislike for his father.

Parental treatment of their children sometimes turns them into being rude and inconsistent. Bandura and Walters (1963) have studied the background of some aggressively delinquent boys. In some cases the father's rejection has aggravated the feelings of the boys by the inconsistent dealings of both the parents. According to these authors such families have the pathogenic family pattern. The father is a hostile person and punishes the boy physically for being indisciplined. It results in making the boy hostile, resisting the existing disciplines and becoming an improperly socialised person. The boy gives in to his impulsive characteristics and becomes a delinquent.

5. Antisocial Parental Patterns

In the study of juvenile delinquencies it was observed that in many cases the fathers of the delinquent boys were found to be of sociopathic personalities. The investigations made by Glueck and Glueak (1969) and O'Neal et al (1962) reveal in many cases that the fathers of these delinquent boys are characterised by alcoholism, hostility, brutality, antisocial behaviour, frequent absence from home and failing to provide what is required for the family. Thus the parental model is unacceptable. This type of sociopathic or antisocial parents are the cause of delinquent behaviour in girls. There is disguised support for indiscriminative sexual behaviour which commonly occurs. In some cases there is actual incest with daughter. Scharfman and Clark (1967), in their investigation, have found serious such incidences of various types of early sexual activities among the delinquent girls. These authors have asserted that the main causative factors operating in the delinquent behaviour of the girls are broken homes and poverty or material deprivation, early sexual activities and overstimulting sexual situation, and harshly and aggressively demanding of discipline from the girls.

6. Estrangement or Alienation and Social Rejects

Cultural pattern and family pattern play an important role in the delinquent and antisocial behaviour of the young men and women in society. It is going away from the customary way of life in society. It is a feeling of state of being an outsider or a feeling of being isolated from a society. Psychiatrically it is a state in which a person's feelings are inhibited, so that extensively both the self and the external world seem unreal. The social condition or family situations tend to produce delinquents. The adolescent boys and girls in economically, socially and emotionally deprived families often tend to develop the feelings of alienation and helplessness. The young boys and girls are not able to identity themselves with the established values in society. They are very confused with the roles they will have to play and the duties and responsibilities that society has assigned to them.

When the youth comes out of his home, he finds everything outside is very gloomy and does not know into what job he can get into according to his mental and physical make-up. After observing how things are going on outside, he feels that the world is an illusion, not real. It is a cruel and hostile place, where there is no place for an honest person. The world is dominated by some useless old-fashioned persons who keep persons like him away from the world. The youth feels that these persons make unwanted discrimations and lay down useless and impractical conditions on others, specifically on the youths, and demand unachievable objectives. He either should submit and accept the demands of the elders unwillingly or should adapt a different way of life which is easily available for him. He gets into the groups which are drug addicts, becomes rebellious leaves home and becomes a misfit or drop-out. Once he resorts to the use of drug or alcohol he does not bother about accepted or non-accepted type behaviour. Whatever he does is right for him and so he becomes an aggressive delinquent.

In Indian culture society has different types of customs and traditions. The Indian society consists of innumerable number of castes and communities and each one has its own habits and customs that were adapted for centuries. In the case of a young person alienation does not affect him very much. He can manage somehow by doing some physical work with all his grievances. But a young girl who leaves her home due to broken home, or poverty, loss of love and affection, hostility, unavailability of support from any source for her livelihood, finds the world very unkind, unsympathetic and cruel. She develops the feelings of a destitute and helplessness. Thus the feeling of alienation is quite common among young girls in the Indian community. Once she leaves the home, there is no going back to her home or village or town. Her relatives would not permit her into their homes as she is a runaway. A runaway girl in the Indian community is considered to be an outcast. She has to go and beg some people for a job which is not easy for her to get it. Being a young girl every man has a suspicious look at her and she may fall a prey in the hands of lascivious men or she be cheated with hopeful words, or there may be forcible rape. Thus she becomes a delinquent by getting into promiscuous sexual behaviour. Thus delinquent behaviour among the girls in India is caused. It has been estimated that there are about 20,000 delinquent girls in Tamil Nadu. In other states like Maharashtra and Andhra Pradesh the number is very high. The main cause for these many delinquent girls are the estrangement or alienation and the customs and traditions of the castes and communities in India.

These delinquent girls are socially rejected and they become a separate community or constitute a new type of population. These girls are domestically trained in their homes and therefore they go in search of some job domestically oriented and not fit for any skilled works. Therefore they may either be engaged in some domestic work which is very difficult or go into flesh trade. In India girls who have become destitutes have very little choice and take up flesh trade. This has become an accepted trade in some states in India. This type of delinquency rate is rapidly increasing and no rehabilitation programmes are sponsored by any organisation for them.

Treatment of Delinquents

The delinquents are the offenders of committing some types of crime in society. The treatment for them is different from the treatment given to adult criminals. The delinquents are not punished by putting them in prisons where the adult prisoners are kept. Juvenile delinquents generally are sent to correctional homes or some rehabilitation centres. Some progressive and rational methods are adapted in dealing with the juvenile delinquents. They are also sent to reformatory centres. However, these juvenile delinquents are tried in separate courts. There are separate courts for young delinquents in big towns and cities in India. These courts try to understand the young offenders with the idea of helping them and not with the view of punishing them like adult criminals. The courts conduct the trials not by cross examinations and making them nervous and fearful. It is more like counselling to get an idea of what they have in their minds. Mostly it is a way of making the young offender confess his activities which are offensive. If the offences are of minor type the young offender is released with some warnings. But if the offences are of a severe type then he is tried with regular legal procedures and if the offence is proved he is sent to reformatory or corrective home or rehabilit-ation centre and kept under safe custody. These institutions are more like prisons but not with strict instructions.

In the case of minor offences the cases against them are dismissed and they are sent home with instructions to the parents and teachers to have a close watch on their movements and activities. The idea is that a young boy or girl should not indulge again in similar offensive activities. Sometimes they get into the company of other young delinquent gangs and secretly keep contact with them and run away from homes. This type of delinquent behaviour pattern is a common occurrence among the adolescent boys and girls these days. Therefore, the judges of the juvenile courts want that they should be watched for at least one or two years. Sometimes, in some suspicious cases the probation officials go and verify whether things are normal with them.

In the case of offences which need punishment the young offenders are sent to correctional centres where the treatment is very systematic with the view to bringing them back to the normal way of life. The young offender is encouraged for his good conduct. There are systematic physical training programmes, regular medical and health check-ups, good diet arrangements. Depending upon their physical and mental make-up trainings of various types are provided. Concentration is on his education which the offender has missed and also specific vocational training which may be useful to him for setting up his life occupation on returning home. Facilities are provided for social and recreational activities. The juvenile homes do not make any provision for the emotional deprivation of the offenders. The juvenile home officials act according to the principles laid down for running the home. They do not gratify the young offenders' emotional requirements. The strength of juvenile delinquents in delinquent homes is increasing rapidly these days. In Tamil Nadu alone there about 10 juvenile homes and in each there are more than 250 young delinquents under safe custody.

If the juvenile homes have adequate facilities such as educational and vocational training schools it will be of great help for the young offenders to further their education and develop the needed skills and find their means of living. It is also possible for the young offender in such a situation to have psychological counselling, Group therapy and interaction with group members. The important outcome is that the gang pressures and influences are turned in the direction of healthy socialisation rather than going back toward the same delinquent behaviour. The rehabilitation institutions or the juvenile homes which provide reforming facilities should make the offenders develop an interest or liking of the training they offer for the young offenders. Once they could make it successful, the offender has no chance for any offensive activities. The training programmes should be fully psychologically oriented.

In most of the cases the juvenile courts and the juvenile homes treat the young offenders liberally. Either the case is dismissed or the offender goes out on probation. Probation is a conditional suspension of a convicted person's sentence. Probation may be granted after the conviction or after some period of imprisonment or institutionalisation. In one of the studies made by Lerman (1971), it was observed that more than 80 per cent of the girls in a state home for girls (juvenile), in one of the states in United States were institutionalised for offences such as running away from homes, staying away from schools, beyond the control of their parents, illicit sexual relations and becoming pregnant. The author of this study has stated that institutionalised juvenile offenders actually have increased their juvenile behavioural problems instead of correcting and reducing them. The author has quoted a number of cases of this type of outcomes.

Juvenile or correctional homes may have different repercussions from culture to culture. Unless there is a deterrent effect in the juvenile homes on the offenders, juvenile or correctional homes will serve no purpose in some cultures. A person who is in the juvenile home for three years as an adolescent boy, becomes a professional smuggler when he grows into an adult. This is one of the cases observed in Tamil Nadu. There are also many unreported cases of this type of offences. Therefore, the rehabilitation programmes should be more effective, long ranged, aiming at the prevention of delinquency, provision for educational and recorrectional facilities for the disadvantaged youths.

CHAPTER 18

Problems of Alcoholism

What is Alcohol?

Alcohol is a colourless flammable liquid. It is an intoxicating drink produced by fermentation of sugars, especially glucose, and used as a solvent and in the manufacture of organic chemicals. Alcohol may also be stated as a colourless, volatile pungent liquid used in various forms as a fuel and an intoxicating ingredient in fermented liquors. Any such intoxicating liquor is alcohol. An alcoholic is a person affected by alcoholism. He is one who is suffering from an excess of drinking alcohol, one who has become chronic of drinking of alcoholic liquor. Alcoholism refers to the habitual excessive drinking of alcoholic liquor or it may be the resulting diseased condition. It is a state of continual heavy consumption of alcoholic drink resulting in physiological disorder. Thus alcoholism is a state of excessive alcoholic drinking resulting in behavioural disorder and also having an impairing effect in the brain.

Since alcoholism causes physiological and behavioural disorders, it has become a social and moral problem. In these days it has also become a health and psychological problem. Whatever problem it causes the rate of alcoholics is increasing all over the world. Any attempt to prevent it meets with failures. The reason is man wants to drink. There is a compulsive desire in man to have the effects of alcohol. Once a man experiences the effect of alcohol, he wishes to repeat it. He finds some kind of elation in it. Adolescent boys and girls and the youth are easily tempted to resort to drinking habits swayed by the themes of motion pictures and the Television plays. These days it has become a fashion to drink alcohol and smoke.

Alcohol has a long history. It is said to have made its first appearance in Masitonia some 5,000 years ago. It is as old as human civilisation. In many of the ancient cultures like the Eygyptian, the Greek and the Romans people made extensive and excessive use of alcohol. It is not possible to state when and where the first alcoholic beverages originated. Every culture, race, nation and tribe had its own way of preparing some kind of alcoholic drink and using them. In primitive culture some kind of alcohol was an important item that was served to all who participated in their congregations. The tribal people in India prepare their beverages from some plants and roots. It is considered to be one of the items in their feasts. To the people of many cultures it is some kind of food energy, and appetite, stimulant, a digestive aid, a useful sedative and a rejuvenation during fatigue.

Millions of people believe that alcohol relieves tensions and anxieties and most commonly used as a tranquilliser. At one stage it was believed to cure baldness and bad breath. People do not drink alcohol itself. It is convected into some palatable form like wine, beer, whisky, brandy, gin, vodka, cocktail or a mixture of consumable ingredient.

Why Do People Drink?

People drink alcohol not in its original form. The alcoholics drink because they are chronic and excessive drinkers of alcohol. But people in the general population drink for different purposes. Alcoholics take drink at all times. But other people who drink probably do it for keeping company or to greet a person for his achievement in certain area. Many among the general public associate it with food. The drinking habit of time varies from country to country or culture to culture. The English people take drinks, mostly a glass of wine of some type with their meals. In United States some particular kind of drink, mostly whisky, cocktail is taken just a few minutes before meals as an appetizer. The Russians take a glass of vodka before the meals. Similarly, so do the Japanese and Chineses. All over the world in most of the civilised countries people take a peg of whisky or brandy to arouse themselves.

In India and in other developing countries also people are developing this habit of taking some kind of drinks before meals. Generally, in dinner parties, given in honour of some eminent person, wine is supplied in small quantities just to stimulate or as an appetizer. These people are not alcoholics. They drink a little for the feeling of relaxation and warmth which may cause a pleasant feeling and mild mental and emotional stimulation and to be free from strain and stress. These types of drink are personally not harmful and socially not objectionable.

Extreme desire for drinking is not inherited. There are studies about alcoholics which reveal that about 40 per cent of alcoholics have relatives who ware either alcoholics or have some abnormal characteristics. Generally people drink when they are in a worried state. They want to escape from worry, anxiety, difficult responsibilities, misery, domestic problems for forgetting painful experiences and to compensate their failures in life situations. A timid person behaves boldly under the influence of drink, feels great and self-confident, the unhappy person feels cheerful. The frustrated person get rids of his frustration.

In Indian culture there are innumerable sects of people who use alcohol of varied types for different reasons, mainly for spiritual, or during religious festivals and in social and domestic functions. They enjoy drinking the beverages manufactured in their homes. Particularly, the tribals invariably use the home-made beverages on important occasions. Both men and women and also children take part in drinking. They are not alcoholics, but on occasions they drink.

Following the Gandhian principles the Indian state governments had introduced prohibition of alcoholic beverages of all types. Strict preventive measures were introduced. Foreign drinks and other Indian-made drinks were banned. Tamil Nadu was the first state in India to introduce prohibition when Rajagopalachari was then Chief Minister of the state. Following this some of other states also introduced prohibition. This resulted in large scale manufacturing of illicit drugs, mainly a kind of spirit called 'arrack', in concealed areas and sold to those who were interested in drinking. The drunkards violated the law and continued in taking the alcoholic liquors secretly. Drinks were extracted from palm trees, which is called 'kallu'. In rural and in tropical areas, wherever the palm trees were available, this drink was extracted and the rural people enjoyed it. This was also prohibited. The offenders of the prohibition order were arrested and put in prisons. But this did not cause any deterrent effect on the offenders. Thus the desire for drinking alcoholic beverages or liquors continues since it is associated with food and important ceremonies. People of all types take some kind of drink occasionally or regularly for some purpose of their own.

The Effects of Alcoholism

Alcoholism is a universal habit developed for various reasons. In each culture one justifying reason is provided for the consumption of alcohol. Whether it is taken for good or bad, it has its own effect which the drunkards need. The negative effects are several times greater then the positive effects. Though it reduces anxiety, worry, stress and unhappiness in the case of an individual, it becomes a very big social and psychological problem in the community. The bad effects of alcohol is not generally accepted. Those who define alcoholism underestimate the impact of alcohol abuses. O Leary and Wilson (1975) have stated that for every alcoholic five to six additional persons are exposed to the disruptive and destructive consequences of alcoholism.

The number of alcoholics is rapidly increasing in every culture, irrespective of education and ethical preachings. Alcohol abuses are associated with diverse social malaise and disruptions. Ullmenn and Krasner (1975) have observed that in United States 50 per cent of the first admissions to psychiatric hospitals are alcoholics. Wilkinson (1970) states that in more than half of the fatal and injurious traffic accidents at least one drunken driver is involved. Sanders (1970) has stated that a number of chronic and severe diseases have been associated with alcoholism. For example, heart disease, cirrhosis of the liver, throat or stomach cancer and alcoholic psychosis are caused by alcoholism. Blum and Braunstein (1967) have observed that homicides and suicides are more frequent among the alcoholics than non-alcoholics in the United States. Alcoholic mothers give birth to the children of irreversible birth defects.

There are also economic losses due to alcoholics, like absenteeism in industries and in workplaces, industrial accidents, reduced productivity, arrests, treatments and hospitalisation. There are more cases of separation and divorce from the wives of alcoholic husbands. The effects of alcoholism in Indian culture is becoming more and more severe and destructive. Every day there are reports in newspapers that the husband returns home in a drunken mood and beats his wife severely and the wife runs away from home. The man in the drunken state is ready to do anything with his wife. There are also cases of killing by cutting the throat. Sometimes the alcoholic husband even kills his children along with his wife, and goes to the police station and reports that he killed his wife and children. In slum areas and in rural areas these are the common occurrences every day in alcoholics homes. In Tamil Nadu there were reports that even policemen on duty were found in drunken state and behaved abnormally. These are all the effects of alcoholism. There are also serious unreported cases of the alcoholic effect in the community.

Classification of Alcoholics

Alcoholics are of varied types and they are classified on the basis of the nature of the usage of alcohol. There are two main systems of classification of the alcoholics. One classification was made by the Diagnostic and Statistical Manual of the American Psychiatric Association in its *DSM-II*, 1968 classification. There were physical and socio- – psychological complaints on the alcohol-related problems and the diagnosis was a differential type. Chronic or acute heavy drinking impairs brain tissues which is diagnosed as psychosis associated with organic brain syndrome. It is stated as alcoholic psychosis. This category is subdivided into delirium terminus, Korsakov's psychosis, alcoholic hallucinosis, alcoholic paronoid state, acute alcoholic intoxication and alcoholic psychosis.

If alcohol consumption is strong enough and interferes with health or personal and social functioning the syndrome is classified as alcoholism. This is placed under the general category of personality disorders. According to the description of *DSM-II* classification there are four sub-categories of alcoholism. They are (1) episodic excessive drinking which indicates high intoxication as often as four times per year, (2) habitual excessive drinking; this is the indication of high intoxication more than 12 times, (3) alcohol addiction, in which the person is dependent on alcohol, a psychological nature which is typical response to adversity of situation; this has a withdrawal symptom, and (4) the other unsignified alcoholism.

There is also another classification of alcoholics, made by Jellinek (1960). This classification is very widely referred in most of the studies. It is based upon the description of the nature of excessive drinking that may take place in different individuals and cultures. According to Jallinek there are four major types of alcoholism. The first type is Alpha alcoholism. The Alpha alcoholic consumes alcohol frequently to reduce emotional or bodily stress, but he has not lost control over his drinking, The second type is Beta alcoholism. The person suffers from physical problems such as malnutrition and cirrhosis of the liver. There is no loss of control in Beta alcoholic. The third type is the Gamma alcoholism. This is characterised by loss of control over drinking and increased tolerance to alcohol and symptoms of withdrawal. The fourth type is Delta alcoholism. This is characterised by loss of control. The Delta alcoholics are mainly found in wine drinking countries, mostly in France.

Theories of Alcoholism

Though there were several studies on alcoholism and on the attempts to identify the aetiological factors of alcoholism there were no accepted conclusions about it. There were confusions and disagreements concerning the causative factors of alcoholism. Nathan and Harris (1975) were able to indicate four major causative factors of alcoholism. They are mainly physiological, sociocultural, psychological and behavioural theories.

1. Physiological Theories

It has been observed that some people have some sensitivity to certain foodgrains which are able to reduce tension temporarily. Chafetz and Demone (1962) have stated that these grains have certain intoxicating effect, on the basis of which alcoholic beverages were derived. It is hypothesised that alcoholics differ from non-alcoholics in their metabolic functions. According to Smith (1949) the adrenal cortex is the place responsible for metabolic disturbances. Williams (1959) has stated that alcoholid abuse is associated with nutritional deficiencies. The study of Nathan (1976) reveal that there is active interest in alcohol consumption due to genetic factors.

Contrary to the popular belief, alcohol does not act as a stimulant, but rather as a general anaesthetic. It acts as a primary and continuous depressant of the central nervous system. The popular view is that the cortex of the brain is not sensitive to the effects of alcohol. But it is the area of the brain called reticular system that appears to be the most sensitive to the effects of alcohol. It is an important integrating centre of the brain. Alcohol attacks and paralyses the higher centres of the brain, thereby weakening their controls on the lower centres. When the controls are weakened the primitive impulses and emotions become free from control and make their expressions. At this stage the individual's concentration, memory and insight are lost, mood swings are accompanied by sensory and motor disturbances. Alcohol does not increase mental or physical abilities.

2. Psychological Theories

It is not easy to identify an alcoholic personality. Attempts have been made by many psychiatrists. The alcoholic's basic conflict has been considered variously as the outgrowth of too much of nurtured mother-child relationship, too much of deprived mother-child relationship and a repressed mother fixation. But some theories view that alcoholic behaviour is a form of motivated suicide by deep-seated guilt feelings or hostility. There are several interpretations offered emphasising its defensive mechanisms. According to Sigmund Freud (1930) alcoholism is the result of conflict of repressed homosexual desires. Adler (1941) states that it is the result of the feelings of inferiority. According to Schilder (1941) alcoholism is the result of interpersonal insecurities and inhibitions.

It was observed that many alcoholics have many behavioural traits in common. Winokur et al (1970) have stated that there are high incidences of depression in the personal and family background of female alcoholics. The characteristics that are found to be common in the backgrounds of most problem drinkers is personal maladjustment. But it is also observed that most maladjusted persons do not become alcoholics. In general it appears that depression and antisocial personality are the two clinical syndromes that most commonly go with alcoholism. Schaefer (1971) states that alcoholism is a conditioned response to anxiety. The individual finds in alcohol a means of relieving anxiety, resertment, feeling of stress of his life situation. Every time he drinks gets relief from tension and his drinking habit is reinforced. Finally he becomes a habitual drinker for coping up with his stress. But it is a danger to consider that alcohol always reduces tension and stress.

Some investigators have stated from their studies that family background appears to be related to alcoholism. Wood and Duffy (1960) have presented that a cold domineering mother is found to be warmer, but an alcoholic father has a miserable self-image. An alcoholic father is a highly undesirable parental model. Alcoholism generally occurs during the crisis period when changes in personal or social role result in confusion in relation to self-concept.

3. Behavioural Theories

The behavioural theories try to explain the aetiology of alcoholism effectively associating the sociocultural and psychodynamic theories.

The socio-cultural and the psychodynamic theories have certain deficits and fail to incorporate certain processes involved in alcoholism. Behavioural theories try to fulfil the deficiencies of them in. The important aspects involved in behavioural theories are the formation of concepts which carry empirical verification, identifying the antecedents and the consequences which influence the drinking values, and relating the development of treatment techniques for demonstrating the regulation of deranged drinking. The worthwhile return qualities of alcohol are divided into three categories and each one reveals what has become the basic principle of behavioural theories of alcoholism. Bandura (1969) states that alcohol consumption is a generalised response to aversive stimulation.

a) The reinforcing effects of alcohol are widely accepted as tension-reducing formula. Alcohol consumers hold the belief that it helps to reduce tension states, specifically approach avoidance conflict, fear of failure of efforts. The results of the experiments conducted on animals serve no evidence for tension-reduction hypothesis. Several investigators like Conger (1956), Smart (1965), and others on animals, and Braum (1959), Hershenson (1965) on human beings have conducted experiments to verify the tension-reduction hypothesis.

b) The effect of intoxication of alcohol is also considered as a reinforcing stimulus in the sense that the disapproved behaviour is legalised by the disinhibiting effect of alcohol. From this point of view it is viewed that intoxication acts as a discriminative stimulus. According to Mac Andrew and Edgerton (1969) the pattern of alcohol disinhibited behaviour may be culturally determined. These authors state that in the United States the alcoholics of some type display aggressive, dependent and unexpected sexual behaviour. The intoxicating effect sometimes violates the cultural norms.

c) It is also observed that sustained extreme use of alcohol is maintained by the individual's attempt to avoid unpleasant physical reactions secondarily. This type of behaviour is associated with the lower-blood-alcohol concentration levels. It is a state of physical dependence. Because of this development, alcohol use is negatively reinforced. The severe symptoms of the withdrawal syndrome is prevented at this stage because of its characteristics.

There were many researches, conducted to challenge the hypothesis that alcohol reduces tension. It is viewed that the alcohol used in animal experiments was an artificial alcohol. It is not as bad as the effects of real alcohol used by human beings. Therefore the results obtained in animal experiments are dubious and does not really verify the hypothesis. Experiments on alcoholics indicated consistently that alcohol consumed in other than in small doses actually increased the levels of anxiety and depression. Sobell and Sobell (1973 (a) have argued that the experimental results may be due to lower levels of anxiety among the institutionalised persons and therefore the effects observed were different from other alcoholics.

Some of the investigators like Nietzel et al (1977) state that alcohol-as-reinforcer theory fails to establish the result. It was observed that most people who encounter stress were not alcoholics. Among those persons who reduce their tension periodically by drinking alcohol, some become excessive drinkers. Further involving learning theories have certain limitations in tension reduction by resorting to alcoholism. Behavioural theories of alcoholism have become more complex as it emphasises more on social, interpersonal and environ-mental factors in the aetiology of alcohol abuses.

Stages of Alcoholism

Alcohol and the alcoholics pass through different stages. Alcohol is generally believed to be a tension reduction devise; whatever the purpose the drinker attributes he passes through certain stage. The stages varies depending upon the quantity of alcohol one consumes. According to Strange (1965) there are three stages such as prodromal stage, critical stage and alcoholic stage.

In the prodromal stage, even after using alcohol constantly for reducing tension and anxiety the drinker appears normal to his friends and does not show any abnormal symptoms in his behaviour. This stage is called prodromal stage. These symptoms indicate that the person is going in for a disease state. This means that in a party when others take one round of drink this person will take two or three rounds of drink. The drinker himself suspects his behaviour, but neglects the symptoms and thinks that nothing is wrong.

The second stage is critical in which the drinker starts losing control. At this stage once he start drinking, he will not stop. The duration between drinks becomes shorter and shorter and he becomes a chronic drinker and alcoholic in the real sense. At this stage the drinker goes against society and breaks the social or cultural norms. He builds up the defence mechanism to justify his behaviour. His abnormal drinking habits and the application of various defence mechanisms make it difficult to for him to maintain his existing job and he loses all his old friends. Thus, instead of reducing his tension and anxiety, alcohol turns him into a chronic alcoholic.

The third stage is the alcoholic stage in which the drinking has become regular every day and the habit has become chronic. The duration between two drinks has become very short, which is continued for several days without any break. He often feels that he has lost his family, occupation and friends and as a consequence he becomes a chronic alcoholic. There is a constant urge in him to drink more and more and as result of it he becomes unconscious. In the chronic alcoholic stage there occurs malnutrition and damage occurs in his mental activities, unless there is a proper rehabilitation programme for him.

Alcoholic Psychoses

Psychosis is caused by several factors which may be organic or functional types. In diagnosing the psychotic patients many of them are found to be alcoholics. Thus it is designated as alcoholic psychosis. It is observed that chronic alcoholism causes malnutrition in the nervous system. It is unavoidable that many alcoholics suffer from acute and chronic mental disturbances which are found to be organic psychoses. Persons who suffer from various other causes, particularly from tension and anxiety, turn to alcoholism as an attempt to reduce them and to make adjustments in society. Persons who reveal symptoms of manic depressive psychosis have a history of drinking habit. Some of the persons have other types of depressions at the time of admitting in hospitals. In many of the cases of paranoid psychosis the patients have shown strong tendencies for alcoholism. Among the various psychotic patients, schizophrenics have the tendency to reduce the emotional frustration, trying to avoid alcoholism. Generally, alcoholism is associated with psychoses. The alcoholic psychoses are of four types. These are pathological intoxication, delirium tremens, alcoholic hallucinosis and Korsakoff psychosis.

Pathological Intoxication

Persons who have very low tolerance for alcohol suffer from this type of reaction. Pathological intoxication occurs in persons who suffer from epilepsy, extreme fatigue and emotional strain. These persons cannot tolerate even a small dosage of alcohol. They show symptoms of pathological intoxication even if they consume a small quantity of alcohol. They suffer from this disorder even by consuming any mild intoxicating drink like beer. They develop hallucinations and are very much disturbed. Such patients become violent and threaten to commit suicide and die. They also go to the extent of murdering others. There may always be the fear that these persons may commit serious crimes like homicide, arson, sexual assault and burglary. This type of behaviour in the persons do not depend upon the amount of alcohol consumed by them. These patients may have the reaction even with a very small quantity of alcohol. But in some persons only a big quantity of alcohol consumption causes these reactions. This condition makes the psychiatrist infer that persons of psychopathic background may develop this state when they consume a small quantity of alcohol. These persons may be having some brain injury or mental illness like hysteria, epilepsy or schizophrenia.

Delirium Tremens

This is one of the alcoholic psychoses diagnosed and described. Delirium tremens is a condition of acute delirium that may occur as a result of chronic alcoholism, characterised by fearful hallucinations and delusions and by muscular tremors and exhaustion. Delirium is a mental state marked by confusions, activity incoherence, disorientation and hallucinations. It is a very serious behavioural disorder that is specific to chronic alcoholics. It is a special sentivity of the neural tissues to alcohol that sustains attack. The physiological facts are not yet clearly identified. Delirium tremens is a consequence of excessive drinking for a long period of time and it is very well known of all the psychotic reactions. It may occur also after an injury and or by a sudden stoppage of drinking but it has to be tested. It is also found that one or two days before the attack the person is found to be too sick for drinking. It does not occur suddenly in some cases. The person is very much agitated and restless just before the occurrence and finds it very difficult to sleep. He is in a state of nervous tension and suspicion. He feels that he has got into a group of people who are very cruel and the world is very unkind to him. He is alternatively passing through partial contact with his environmental and psychotic state of no touch. His attention, perceptions and understanding are not in a normal stage.

Most of the times he has hallucinations, of specific type and sometimes auditory types. All the visual hallucinations are not clear, and animals and vermin that crawl on the walls terrify him. He is in a state of panic and extreme excitement, he may scream in terror and also laugh. He gets confused and is unable to make decisions and choices necessary for his everyday living. By consciously avoiding drinking under hospital care the patient could return to normal activities. But however, by recurrent attacks, if the syndrome is severe, the patient may die.

Alcoholic Hallucinosis

Persons who drink regularly and consistently have slow development of auditory hallucinations. In these persons there is no development of delirium tremens. Suffering from alcoholic hallucinosis they often hearing voices accusing them. Mostly they have delusions of prosecutions. To protect their imagined prosecutions they become violent in their attempts. In this state the alcoholic gets very strange, acute sensory sensitivity and anxiety hallucinations. He considers that hallucinations are very serious. The voices he hears are strong persecutives and reproachful. These hallucinative voices accuse him and bring out his innermost weaknesses, specifically those related to sexual desires and activities. Because of this he is terribly afraid of the matter being brought to light and criticised. His hallucination is such that he believes some persons are going to attack him as he believes he hears the sounds of sharpening of their knives and footsteps. He is very afraid of these dangers directed to him and wants to escape from them. Since there is no chance of escaping from them he cries for help from others and as it is not available immediately he wants to die by committing suicide. The state may continue with him for a few days and even for weeks.

All these occur in the state of acute hallucinosis. But the patient does not suffer so much from other symptoms like illusions, restlessness and other characteristics. He is well adjusted as a normal person, he is consistent in his speech and movements. When he gets rid of his illness he can recollect the events which occurred during his illness and feels sorry for all that happened. It has been found that about one-fourth of the patients admitted in the mental hospitals with complaints of alcoholism have suffered from acute hallucinosis.

Many researchers are of the view that these symptoms we have described above are not the direct cause of alcoholism. It is developed from schizophrenia and paranoid personality, but pushed over the line by excessive alcoholic habits.

Korsakoff's Psychosis

There are also several other conditions caused by chronic alcoholism. Prolonged periods of malnutrition and avitamitosis are the conditions that are associated with acute alcoholism. One of the important conditions is the Korsakoff's psychosis. Korsakoff's psychosis is usually associated with chronic alcoholism and characterised by disorientation, gross memory defects and confabulation. Confabulation means filling up the memory gaps with false and often irrelevant matters. Patients with Korsakoff's syndrome show damage of mild line dienceplolic structures and to frontal cortex. Korsakoff, a Russian neurologist, published a paper in 1887 about a syndrome in which impaired memory was a major factor. This subject matter became a classic and the condition was later on named after him as Korsakoff's syndrome. Persons suffering from Korsakoff's syndrome (Psychosis) fail to recall many items or events of the past. If such an item is presented again or if it happens to be recalled the patient does not feel familiar with it. Patients of Korsakoff syndrome often deny that anything is wrong with them. They often show disorientation of time and place and fill up the gap in their memory with false information which they seem to accept as true. The main cause of Korsakoff's syndrome or psychosis is lack of vitamin B thiamine (B Complex). Alcoholics who obtain most of their calories from alcohol and neglect their diet often exhibit this deficiency.

These patients, if treated with thiamine (Vitamin B Complex), can be prevented from further deterioration of memory functions. If the treatment is started before the person has become a full-blown Korsakoff's case, the condition can be removed. Several researchers studied this aspect experimentally for several years. Mair, Warrington and Wieskrantz (1979) tested two of Korsakoff's patients for several years using a battery or behavioural tests. After sometime they examined the brains of these patients in detail. The brains of both the patients shown shrunken, diseased, mammillary bodies and also some damage in the dorsomedial thalamus. Other parts such as temporal lobes structure, the hippocampus and the temporal stem were found to be normal. In Korsakoff's patient, according to Mair and his

Cowarker's study there was also damage in the basal frontal lobe. Therefore, we may state that Korsakoff's psychosis is concerned with memory disorder related to a thiamine (Vitamin B Complex) deficiency, that is generally associated with chronic alcoholism.

It is also observed that some chronic alcoholics suffer from nicotinic acid deficiency showing many of the same symptoms. The liver is one that is much affected by ethyl alcohol. Any disorder of the organ may become serious in an alcoholic when the liver is severely damaged. There is some impairment in the brain function as a result of hormonal imbalance. The chemiogenic disorder is caused by excess use of Italian red wine. Generally, in Korsakoff's psychosis there is both physical and mental health impairment.

Treatment and Outcomes

Treatment for chronic alcoholism is a very complex problem. It requires multifaceted approach involving medical, psychiatric and psychological treatments. Unless the course of disease is assessed correctly any treatment for chronic alcoholism may not be successful. It is therefore very essential to know first of all to evaluate physical and psychological conditions. The effects of alcohol in individuals may not be the same. It may vary from person to person, depending upon the physical conditions. A person may take up alcoholism to reduce his tension and anxiety he is facing in the family or social situation and may become an alcoholic. In another case a person with personality defects or psychopathic characteristics might have turned to alcoholism. Therefore alcoholic psychosis is a double-edged sword. In treating alcoholic patients there should be different procedures with the characteristics of individualisation and flexibility.

One approach may be removing first the personality defects with the help of a psychiatrist, because it is this that makes him dependent upon alcohol. There may be brain damage in chronic alcoholic patient due to vitamin deficiency. The first step in treating the chronic alcoholic is to take away the patient from the condition of alcohol consumption and bring him to the normal physical health as far as possible. This involves supplying glucose to the body if it is an acute state. This involve also supplementation of good diet and also vitamin B complex which may restore his health. The important aspect of the treatment is the recovery of the patient from alcoholic state. It also involves physical rehabilitation and preventing the patient from strongly craving for liquor and making him adjust to the living situation successfully without drinking alcohol. Several treatment programmes are applied for recovery. Some of them are medical approach, psycho-social approach and aversion (approach) therapy.

1. Medical Approach

The first important step in medical approach is physical rehabilitation. This is done by deintoxicating or elimination of the harmful alcoholic materials from the patients and to create a withdrawal or aversion system. These can be performed only in a hospital situation. The treatment for the withdrawal symptoms and prevention of delirium tremens may be produced by administering the sedative drugs. These drugs help to reduce tension and anxiety, counselling and psychotherapy may help for deintoxication.

In the medical approach, first, it needs sedation and the administration of barbiturates effectively. There is likelihood of the patient becoming a drug addict. Of late *paraldehyde* is used as sedative in these cases. It is not so dangerous as other drugs and is also effective. With all these medical treatments the patients may have the psychological effect for drinking liquor. If this desire still exists, than psychotherepy techniques must be applied.

2. Psycho-social Approach

Treatments for alcoholic psychosis are of varied types even though certain approaches are put into use effectively. The individual psychotherapy approach was found to be successful for a long time. But the later developments for alcoholic psychosis seem to be more effective recovery of the patient from the disorders. The psycho-social approach is also stated as group therapy and socio-therapy.

3. Group Therapy

This generally involves convincing the person that he has some alcoholic problem and that there are ways and means of helping him to deal with the problem and get rid of it. It is not easy to get the alcoholic to accept for this treatment. In the rough and harsh give and take group therapy the alcoholic is compelled to accept the problem and realise the dangerous consequences. But it is not always possible to get the recognition from the alcoholic and treat him by group therapy and get the positive result in his drinking problem. The alcoholics sometimes may even turn to violence. In such a situation the wife and children of the alcoholics also are invited to be present in the group therapy situation. If this takes place in the case of few alcoholics jointly it may be also stated as family group therapy. The group therapy when conducted with the cooperation of the family members may be effective, but sometimes the alcoholic may fail to tolerate further humiliation in the situation. The family members also do not encourage it willingly.

4. Socio Therapy

In the therapeutic attempts to alleviate the alcoholic disorders or the maladeptive behaviour problem of the alcoholic it is also felt that a supportive measure should be followed. This involves changes in the alcoholic's life and in the life situations, more specifically changes in the community environments. As result of his drinking habits he becomes indifferent to his family, relatives and friends and loses his occupation. The persons who are around him are not as friendly as they were in the past and no longer supporting him. They feel that he has some physical ailments and he can get rid of it by some treatment. But since he has impairment of his mental functions it is very difficult for him to recover from it.

Further, there is every chance for him to get his pathological condition relapsed by living in high risk environmental conditions and by reducing the close relationship with his family members, relatives and friends. Kecho and Webster (1969) have observed in their studies that an alcoholic will not be abstained from alcohol unless the psycho-social treatment is reinforced upon him intermittently. It is not always possible to make the required changes in the life of an alcoholic if he is often given alcohol even after the psycho-social treatments. In such a case it is better to have a treatment of increased stress tolerance and also more, effective coping up techniques. By such approach the alcoholic may make an effective adjustment without alcohol. But he should be made to be cooperative for the treatment.

5. Alcoholic Anonymous (AA)

Alcoholics organisation is also called Alcoholics anonymous. The works of this organisation provided with appreciable success in dealing with the problem of alcoholism. This organisation was started by two persons in the year 1935 with a view of finding out a suitable procedure of treating the alcoholics. These two persons were Bob and Bill, who were once chronic alcoholics. Bill recovered from his alcoholic disorder by adapting a spiritual way of life. Bob with the help of Bill was able to recover from his alcoholism. Alcoholic Anonymous is an organisation composed of former alcoholics working for the treatment of alcoholism through personal, social and religious rehabilitation. This organisation started functioning as a psychotherapeutic scheme in which persons-to-persons and group relationships were stressed. The alcoholic organisation is not related to any religious movement. Its important work is treatment of alcoholics. The aim is to shift the burden of the individual's personal responsibilities from the alcoholics and make him realise that alcoholism is a bigger problem just like all other problems human beings face and he should not think that he cannot face it. The alcoholic is counselled that he is not incompetent physically, mentally and morally and the only behavioural aspect is that he cannot drink alcohol. In a group participation and in the individual person-to-person relationship, problems of alcoholism are easily resolved. The Alcoholic Anonymous organisation mainly functions on mutual help and assurance through participation in a group which is constituted of other persons who had similar experience of chronic alcoholism.

The Alcoholic Anonymous movement made it a policy of having family groups. If the husband is an alcoholic the wife also takes part in the meeting, similarly if the wife is an alcoholic, her husband takes part in the meeting, so also their relatives. They are collected together in a meeting and share their common problems and the experiences of their specific problems and they are given chance to gain better understanding about the nature of alcoholism. Everyone understands every other one's alcoholic problems and thereby find ways and means for resolving the problems. Since they find this type of meetings are fruitful the alcoholic's spouse's attendance at the meeting continues for several nights and weeks. If it is found relapsing, it should be prevented or stopped. These alcoholics are helped to see less drinking husbands and less-drinking wives. These meetings held the alcoholics that there are several factors behind their alcoholism and by understanding the causes, they find that they are relieved of their guilt feelings.

The Alcoholics Anonymous organisation is considered to be the most widely known self-help group in the world today. It was founded in the United States and it has more than a million members there. This AA organisation is functioning in more than 90 countries in the world. This organisation runs regular meetings at which newcomers make announcements that they are alcoholics and old numbers present their experiences relating to alcoholism and how their lives are better now. The group provides emotional support and counselling for the alcoholics and a social life for relieving the isolation. Continued watch is necessary to prevent taking even a small single drink. Otherwise, the person may resort to drinking uncontrolled over again. The Alcoholic Anonymous formulated 12 important religious and spiritual aspects which the members of self-help group were to take up (1952). The relatives of alcoholics regularly meet in Al-Anon Family groups for getting mutual supports in dealing with their alcoholic family members. A subsection of this organisation also was evolved for teenagers who have become alcoholics which is called *Alateen*. These young alcoholics also require support and understanding of their problems.

6. Aversion Therapy

The behaviouristic approach to study human behaviour has also extended to the therapeutic techniques. Behavioural scientists have been applying the techniques for the treatment of alcoholism for many years. The first approach was tried by Kantorovich (1930) as aversive conditioning. Aversion therapy is a form of behaviour in which punishment or aversive stimulation is used to eliminate undesired responses. It is a behavioural therapeutic procedure that pairs a noxious stimulus such as shock, with situations that are undesirably attractive, the intent being to make the latter less appealing. This aversion procedure is applied to alcoholics for curing the alcohol disorders, to make the chronic alcoholics avoid drinking liquor.

It is to be known that according to Voetglin et al (1940) aversion procedures are not new in the treatment of alcoholics. However, some recent developments have come up. Investigations have been made on the procedural variations on the supplementary therapeutic components and on the alternative aversive techniques, and found that these procedures had significant results on alcoholism. With regard to addictive problems aversion therapy for alcoholism falls under three approaches, such as chemical aversion, electrical aversion and convert sensitisation. These approaches vary according to design of the application on the basis of sophistication. These are (a) procedure involving case studies, (b) single group designs and, (c) control group designs. These designs also depend upon the nature of individual cases.

7. Chemical Aversion

Aversion to alcoholism is produced by administering certain chemical substances. It is mainly inducing of nausea by the use of apomorphine and ematine which may cause vomiting. The other chemical substance is succinylchaline chloride. These agents are most frequently used drugs for producing chemical aversion. In some cases these drugs are used repeatedly for conditioning.

The aversion therapy is receiving greater research attention in treating the alcoholics. Coleman (1965) states that the ancient Romans used this techniques. It was done by putting a live *eal* (a type fish) in a cup of wine and the alcoholic forced to drink this unpleasant tasty cocktail. The alcoholic would feel disgusted with it and afterwards reject the wine. Nowadays there are several types of pharmacological or chemical deterrent devices that are employed. In one of the studies on this problem Franks (1966) observed that in one approach the intramuscular injection of emetine hydrochloride, an emetic, was used. Just before the nausea takes place as a result of the injection the person is given alcohol. He develops severe vomiting sensation in seeing the colour of alcohol, the smell he feels and the taste – all make him reject the alcohol. On repeating the classical conditioning procedure a strong deterrent effect is advised.

Case Studies

Individuals differ in the effects of treatment which depend upon the severity of the alcoholic condition and physical factors. This resulted in adapting alternative approach of case studies. Raymond (1964) reported a case study of an alcoholic aged 63 years, who was a hospitalised male patient. He was successfully administered with apomorphine based on conditioning method. Then regular nausea reaction was produced. In between the reactions, intermittent choice trials were introduced, in which some selected non-alcoholic drink was given to him. This did not result in producing a nauseous feeling. This type of conditioning chemical aversion approach was supplemented with other techniques, like occupational and group therapy. Follow-up study indicated that there was absence even after three years. Another case study was reported by Gordon (1971) in which the chemical substance emetic was used along with alcohol and the patient reported feeling of nausea.

1. Single Group Design

The single-group design is considered to be the most comprehensive chemical aversion therapy. It is referred to as conditioned reflex therapy. This therapy was used by Shadal (1944) at the Shadal Sanatorium, Washington. There were potential clients tested in their desire to stop drinking. If their desires were of earnest one, then they were the persons on whom the aversion procedures were used, the expected effects and a short period of hospitalisation and booster sessions were required for one year. The treatment consisted of five trails of pairing of nausea with their favourable alcoholic drink. The participants were encouraged to talk among themselves about their alcohol-related experiences which could be characterised similar to alcoholic anonymous type. Group support for the abstinence was provided for this. After the patients were discharged a decision of complete abstinence was stressed on the patients and periodic treatments were arranged. The treatments were subjected to a series of evaluations. Voetglin et al (1940) reported the result of the first evaluation after three years of follow-up study of 685 patients of which 64 per cent of abstinence rate was found. Other investigators like Thiman (1949 a), (1949 b) have also presented similar results of one to three-year follow-up study on 245 patients and found 51 per cent as abstinence rate.

2. Group Aversion

Procedures were suggested for more efficient management of large numbers of patients. One investigator Beanbaum (1967) applied group aversion treatment. This is intended for increasing the suggestibility of the patients to conversion of Alcoholics Anonymous groups. The patients were taken from an institutional setting to the local Alcoholics Anonymous groups. There were some patients who had genuine aversion while others did not, but they had reduced their drinking. There were 231 patients included in the study. In the follow-up evaluation nearly 50 per cent of them abstained from drinking socially.

3. Control Group Designs

In the aversion therapy the control group designs are considered to be more sophisticated approach that has been made with the use of succinylcholine respiratory arrest technique. Several investigators jointly and independently made use of this technique. Madill, Camplell et al (1966) have taken 45 patients randomly assigned to one of the three groups. All of them patients and volunteered. The treatment group was given a one-trail pairing of succinylcholine-induced apnea with alcohol. The treatment group was given the induced apena but not paired with alcohol. But the placebo (neutral) neurotic group was given alcohol in the treatment room. Physiological changes were recorded and a fear-rating schedule also prepared. The results indicated that conditioning took place in both the treatment groups, but some conditioning also took place in the placebo group. All the three groups have shown significant pre-post reduction in alcohol consimption. The treatment group had almost the same effects as the other two groups.

4. Electrical Aversion

The electrical aversion treatment involves presenting the patient with slides of alcohol stimuli and actual glasses of alcoholic drinks followed by electrical shock. These two sets of stimuli were presented in scattered manner with neutral stimuli. The electrical aversion therapy may be also called shock therapy. Maguire and Vallance (1964) made a description of a portable shaking device. It was about a case study of 40 year-old male alcoholic. A follow-up evaluation was made after six months which indicated complete abstinences. Results obtained from a number of studies suggested that aversive techniques are not essential elements in successful treatment.

Electrical aversion technique is used mainly for the treatment of psychosis and also for treating sexual deviations in the case of alcoholism. It is mainly for avoiding or preventing alcoholic psychosis.

In using single group designs Blacke (1965) has explained a multiple-component-learning-based approach to alcoholism. The treatment stage included relaxation training, instructional motivation arousal about the negative effects of drinking electrical aversion and avoiding training. In this experiment the patients were given shocks half the time when they started drinking alcohol. The shocks were stopped when the patients started spitting out the alcohol. There were 37 patients, of whom 27 were males and 10 females. They were mainly from middle and upper socio-economic status groups who participated in this experimental treatment. The follow-up evaluation after six months indicated that there was 54 per cent abstinence and 52 per cent after one year. In the investigation conducted by Hsu (1965) a more extreme electric shock procedure was used. A satisfactory result was reported.

There were quite a number of experimental investigations conducted by many researchers using control group designs. Blake (1967) used relaxation training method in addition to the electrical escape-training procedures. The experimental group consisted of 37 persons. They were given the escape-training procedure and relaxation training for reducing the general anxiety. The control group consisted of 25 persons who were given the electrical avoidance training. These two groups were demographically similar in characteristics. An evolution was made after six months and the abstinence rate was considerably higher for both groups, 62 per cent for the experimental group and 60 per cent for the control group and after one year it was 59 and 50 per cent.

5. Covert Sensitisation

This is a hidden or disguised procedure adopted in treating the alcoholics. The procedure is by verbalisation of the bad effects of alcohol. Several investigators made case studies of the alcoholics and reported the results. They were by using covert sensitisation. Cautala (1967) used covert ensitisation therapy and Anent (1967) used verbal aversion therapy. In these procedures imagined stimuli were used instead of electrical shocks, and chemical substances for conditioning aversion to alcoholic stimuli. He has stated that his experiment with covert sensitisation procedure was found to be successful. This involves the elements of determination of the specific drinking pattern, training progressive muscle relaxation and the introduction of imagined drinking of a favoured liquor in a habitual setting immediately after the experiment of nausea and vomiting. Cautala (1970), in a recent study as a supplement to his previous studies of the imaginal aversion found that the person had developed a pleasant feeling and decided not to drink alcohol anymore.

In a single group design experiment, Anant (1967) has observed a well-maintained abstinence in the verbal aversion therapy on 26 alcoholics. Control group designs therapeutic procedures were applied by Ashem and Donner (1969) and others, using covert sensitisation technique. The authors compared the untreated control group which consisted of eight persons with alcoholics referred to a covert sensitisation treatment which consisted of 15 persons. In the treatment suggestions of sickness vomiting were stated immediately after the persons were given the signal that the taste of alcohol had been imagined. It is possible to have the feelings of relief and relaxation on the imagined rejection of alcohol. All the persons participated in the general activities of the treatment. The covert sensitisation treatment went on for nine sessions, each for 30-40 minutes. In the follow-up study, after six months of the treatment, 40 per cent (6 persons) of the treated persons were found to abstinents, while the control group participants did not stop drinking. But the results of covert sensitisation are not yet clinically determined.

CHAPTER 19

Drug Dependency and Addic

Dependence and Addiction

The earliest history of humankind is full of interesting and exciting incidences. Looking into the lifestyle of the ancient people we can see that they tasted, sipped, chewed, and swallowed all kinds of substances like animal, vegetable and minerals. From these experiences people have learned to consume some substances. Social habits and dietary norms evolved to protect people from consuming harmful substances. This long history of searching, testing and using different substances came not only from the needs for nourishment, but also from the needs for relief from pain, tension and anxiety, and also for the pursuit of pleasure. Various kinds of drugs and substances can fulfil these needs. But many of these drugs and substances may also cause dependency and also induce panic and psychotic states.

The drugs consumed by humans is so pervasive that man forgets himself and goes into translike state. One of the investigators, Leonard (1982), characterises human beings as "drug taking animals". Another investigator, Sieget (1989), states that we are not alone in this activity, but almost every species of animal is engaged in the natural pursuit of introxicants under this heading of drugs dependency and addiction. We shall discuss how drugs affect the nervous system and behaviour and also find certain toxins which affect the brain and cause behavioural disorders. Drug addiction and abuses have become very serious social problems in these days.

It is believed that the tribal people were the first to produce the drugs which were of hallucinogenic characteristics. These drugs are made from a variety of mushrooms by some tribal people in Siberia and in the far Eastern countries for inducing intoxication, inducing spirit and courage during the periods of festivals and clashes between the tribes. The substances had many of the effects that the modern hallucinogenic drugs have. According to Brekhman and Sam (1967) the ancient people made use of various narcotic drugs such as Luoscuamus and hemlocks.

Apart from alcoholic drinks there are several psychoactive drugs which are commonly used by people and associated with dependence and abuses. The kinds of drugs are narcotic drugs such as opium and its derivatives. The second mostly used drug is sedatives such as barbiturates, the third kind of drug is the stimulants such as amphetamines, the fourth kind is the tranquillilisers such as meprobamates and the fifth kind is the hallucinogens such as marijuana. Modern biological psychologists also include caffeine and nicotine in the list of drugs of dependence. But the American Psychiatric Association did not include these in their list of drugs. It is an accepted hypothesis that drug abuse and dependence may be practised at any age level. But to abuse and dependence of drugs are attributed mostly to the younger age groups, particularly the adolescents and the young adults. The physiological and psychological effects of drug abuses and dependence rely upon several factors according to clinical assessments. We shall discuss some specific drugs.

Narcotic Drugs

Narcotic is a Greek concept which means numbness, and is believed to relieve pain. It causes numbing of the sences, stupor and sleep. It mainly refers to opium and its various derivatives, and also anything that is equivalent to the drug. The other narcotic drugs that come under this are cocaine and marijuana.

1. Opium and Its Derivatives

Opium is a narcotic drug which leads to physiological dependence on consumption and building up tolerance. Its derivatives are morphine, heroin, parigeric and codine. Opium is obtained from a species of poppy which is botanically known as *Papaver somaniferum.* The drugs derived from this plant is used by human beings since ancient time. Roughly we may state that it was in human use for over 5,000 years. Galen (AD 130-201), a Greece-Roman physician, anatomist and physiologist, had codified existing medical knowledge, and his authority continued until the Renaissance. He was a disciple of Hippocrates and his writings were the source of information for both physical and mental illness, and he was frequently described as the father of medicine. Galen considered that opium was an important ingredient for many purposes. It resists poison and venomous bites, cures headaches, deafness, epilepsy, dimness, apoplexy, dimness of sight, loss of voice, asthma, coughs and jaundice, stone, urinary complaints, fever, etc. Opium derivatives are still used for some of the conditions Galen had mentioned.

Opium is also known as alkaloids which contains all greatest amount of bitter tasting powder and is found to be a sedative pain killer. It was because of this it was named as morphine, named after the Greek goddess Mopheus. Alkaloid is a group of nitrogenous basic compounds found in plants, typically insoluable in water and physiologically active. The common examples are morphine, strychnine and quinine.

The word opium is derived from the Greek word *opion*, which means vegetable juice. Opium is an extract of the juice of the seedpad of the opium poppy, *Papavar sominiferum*. Opium substance is such a powerful one that it protects the seeds of the plant from insects and most of the insects avoid the seeds, but eat the other parts of the plant. Humans used the opium as a drug for thousands of years. Opium poppies were cultivated and used from the Stone Sge period. It was from the lake areas of central Europe and Switzerland that opium was traded with the Eastern Mediterraneen countries (Seigel, 1989). Opium was used as a medicine also against diarrhoea in ancient Egypt, Greece and Rome. Later on, the Greek and Roman poets like Homer, Virgil and Ovid had mentioned in their writings about its sleep-inducing effects. The nineteenth century English writers administered opium for its effects of soothing the body and for its stimulation of imagination.

Morphine is derived from opium, separated from new opium and made into a powder form and used in patent medicines. It was also directly injected into the veins for relieving pains. It was also found that morphine could be converted into another powerful pain-relieving drug, named as heroin. It was substituted for morphine in cough syrups and in other patent medicines. Heroin is used for many maladies. Brecher (1972) considered it as God's own medicine. Heroin is found to be more addictive and more potent than morphine and it also acts more quickly and with greater intensity. Morphine and heroin are the derivatives of opium. All these have the effects of producing euphoria, drowsiness, sleep. These derivatives sometimes cause lack of coordination in behaviour.

A derivative of opium is herion which has an additional effect of a warm feeling of rush. The addicts of heroin are free from worries and fears and develop a great amount of self-confidence. But this state can continue only for five or six hours. After that the experience goes down and the mind and senses become dull. As these drugs press down the central nervous system they relieve pain. The addicts of these show increased tolerance and also there may be withdrawal symptoms. Human understanding about the process of addiction to opiates increased very much and it resulted in finding out a specific opiatic receptor in the vertebrate brains, a cell component to which opiates produce euphoria and analgesia. Since these receptors do not interact with opiatic alkaloids in that environment a search is made. According to Goldstain (1976) this search resulted in finding out an internally produced opiate. This opiate component is called endorphine. This internally produced opiate component functions in several species, including human beings. According to this theory human bodies can produce natural opiates. These components are the body's own pain relievers and also play a crucial role in addiction. The intake of exogenous opiate heroin may stop the natural production of endorphine. When the exogenous substance is not supplied, the person is left without opiates in the body and then there will be sudden withdrawal symptoms.

The withdrawal reaction symptoms may appear within eight hours of not having the heroin dosage. The person may have muscle tension, sneezing, sweating, becomes tearful and symptoms like influenza appear. As time goes on the symptoms become severe with uncontrollable muscle twitching, cramps, excessive flushing and sweating and increase of heart rate and blood pressure. The person is unable to sleep, vomits and has diarrhoea. These symptoms continue for three days and then gradually diminish in a period of eight to 10 days. The narcotics are illegal addicts. They deal with their activities in the underground. The drugs are costly and the addicts must spend for them. Either they must be rich or get money by some other illegal activities like stealing, prostitution, selling drugs, etc. It is found that the correlation between drug addiction and criminal activities is very high. The drug addicts generally become criminals.

2. Sedatives and Other Barbiturates

Barbiturate is a derivative of barbituric acid such as barbitane or phrneborbitone used in medicine as a sedative or hypnosis. Barbituric acid is a white crystalline solid used in the preparation of barbiturate drugs. Generally, it is stated that barbiturate is a class of synthetic selective drug that is addictive and in large doses it can cause death, because the diaphragm relaxes almost completely. It is also observed that barbiturates have their effects on the cortex of the brain, on the reticular activating system of the brain stem and on the vagus nerve that spreads out to a large part of the viscera.

Barbiturates are synthesized as a helping dosage for sleep and relaxation. It was produced first in the beginning of twentieth century, but within a short period hundreds of derivatives of barbiturates have been produced. It is a safe and effective drug if carefully prescribed and used. They are administrated in two ways. One way is for short-term acting and the other is for long-term acting. The short-term acting barbiturates are for quick sedation and sleep. The short-acting drugs are considered as addicting. In the beginning these drugs are viewed as highly preferred and prescribed very often in most of the hospital cases. But around the 1940s, there was a protest against the use of these drugs very often in most of the cases as it was found to be addicting. As a result of it the frequency was reduced.

The derivatives of barbiturates are pentobarbital, secobarbial and emobarbital. These are used for relaxing the muscles. A small dose of these causes a mild euphoric state. Heavy doses make the speech unclear and there may be unsteady steps. The person's understanding and judgements may be impaired. The person who uses this drug loses control over his emotion, gets irritative and violent before going into deep sleep. The prolonged excessive use of this drug may result in brain damage and personality disorders.

Drug users may abuse the drugs of barbiturates. These drugs are abused by the drug addicts and they are distinguished into three types. Sheder et al (1975) and Liskow (1982) have described the three types of drug abuses. The first type of group is identified as illicit drug abusers. This group consists of mostly adolescents and youths. These individuals are usually males and antisocial elements. This group uses the drugs for changing its moods and consciousness. For having the better effect of the drugs this group mixes other drugs into this drug and they feel free from tension and stress.

The second group mostly consists of middle class people of middle age who are said to be respectable persons. They begin to use the sedative drugs on the advice of physicians for avoiding sleeplessness and anxiety. Then they start using larger and larger doses and become addicts.

The third group of persons are health professionals, physicians and nurses. These people get the drugs easily and use them often for self-medicating, for tension and anxiety-related problems.

3. Stimulants: Amphetamines

Barbiturates are used for depressing the central nervous system, but the other kinds of drugs which stimulate the action of the central nervous system are the amphetamines and cocaine. These have some chemical effects which stimulate or make the activities of the central nervous system to function rapidly. The Chinese-American physician, Chen, was able to find a remedy for treating asthma by studying the ancient Chinese descriptions of various drugs. He found a medicine called *mahuang* as an effective drug. It is a desert shrub. After making a systematic study Chen was able to separate an alkaloid from the plant shrub which is called ephedrine which was found to be highly successful in treating asthmatic patients. Synder (1974) states that a systematic study of the plant, which is a woody plant having several stems, resulted in finding a synthetic malstite, the amphetamines.

Amphetamine is a synthetic colourless volatile liquid used medicinally, mainly for its stimulant action on the central nervous system, although it also stimulates the sympathetic nervous system. It can have unpleasant or dangerous side effects, and drug dependence also may occur. Amphetamine derivatives are Banzedrine, Dexedine and Methadrine. These drugs produce effects quite similar to the effects of norepinaphrine in the sympathatic nervous system. These can be addicting and they are taken orally or intravenously.

The effects of these drugs are mainly heightened wakefulness and inhibition of intenstinal functions. Appetite is reduced. There is increase of heart rate. There is constraint of blood vessels and also in the skin and mucous membrance. In this state of effect the individual becomes alert, euphoric and more outgoing. He is in possession of seemingly limitless energy and self-confidence. Heavy doses make the person nervous, agitated and confused. The person also experiences palpitations, headaches, dizziness and sleeplessness.

The person who takes heavy doses of the drugs, sometimes becomes so suspicious and hostile that he can be dangerous to others. It was also observed in some persons who took high doses over a period of time that they were induced to a state quite similar to paranoid schizophrenia and the corresponding delusions. This state may persist in the person even after the effects of drugs are exhausted in the body. It is believed that a large amount of amphetamine may cause brain damage when frequently used. The chronic abuse of amphetamines can cause mental disorders called ephetamina psychosis. It was also observed that excess usage of amphetamines may lead the person to suicide, homicide, assault and other acts of violence. In the studies made by Ellin Wood (1971) it was found that 13 persons who were under the influence of amphetamine intoxication committed homicide and most cases of homicidal acts were directly related to amphetamine-induced paranoid thoughts.

4. Cocaine

Cocaine is an addictive narcotic drug derived from coca leaves or synthesized and used medicinally as a topical anaesthetic. It is a pain-reducing stimulating and addictive alkaloid, obtained from coca leaves, which increases mental powers, produces euphoria, heightens sexual desire and in large doses causes paranoia and hallucinations. Cocaine like the opium is a plant product discovered and used by ancient man. Jarvin (1967) in his study has stated that the Indians of Peru chewed coca leaves. It was the Spanish explorers on their voyages who found this in the Andean uplands and introduced it in Europe. The Peru Indians used the leaves to relieve their hunger, fatigue and the general burdens of a miserable life. The effects of the cocaine leaves were also mentioned by eminent writers like Sherlock Holmes as sex stimulants.

Cocaine like the opium is used in various ways by swallowing, sniffing and injecting. It hightens the euphoric state for up to six hours and the user experiences peace and contentment. Davison and Neale (1997) state that at one stage Sigmund Freud himself used cocaine to combat depression. Freud was very much convinced by the wonderful effect of cocaine and he had prescribed it to his friends who were suffering from some painful disease. He published the effects of cocaine in one of his research papers. One of the traders using the coca leaves has produced the coca-cola, the recipe and introduced it in the international market.

Cocaine, in addition to its pain-killing effects, also acts speedily on the cortex of the brain like other drugs. It increases sensory awareness and induces euphoria for 30 minutes. An overdose may cause nausea and insomnia and terrifying hallucinations of insects crawling beneath the skin. Chronic overdose results in changes in personality characteristics, which includes irritability, affecting social relationships. According to Kozel, Grider and Adams (1982), as the users take more and more larger doses of the pure form of cocaine, they more often go rushing to emergency wards of psychiatric clinics and may die of myocardial infarction, mostly due to heart attacks. As cocaine is easily available in the open markets or secretly, people rush and buy for their purposes. Cocaine contains strong vaso-constricting properties which may cause great damage in pregnancy.

Cocaine is used by human beings in various forms like opium. It is used in pipes for smoking, used in cigarettes, sniffed, swallowed in some form, injected into the veins like heroin. Some heroin addicts mix cocaine with heroin in some combination and taken orally, which is known speedball in the United States. Cocaine, till recently, was believed not to be an addictive. But recent studies indicate differently. If the addict ceases the use of a cocaine, Gawin and Kleber (1996) state that the person experiences severe withdrawal syndrome. According to them there are three states the addict passes through, such as crash, withdrawal and extinction.

Crash refers to the initial dysphoria or a feeling of being ill at use followed by a crash in mood and to the state of sleepiness and crash of activity. But crash generally means break or fail or collide. This means that the addict reaches the state of breaking down or dispensing with activities. This state may continue for a period of nine hours to four days, depending upon the length and intensity of the preceding addition. After few hours of abstaining from the drug the desire increases so strongly that cocaine should be used. Otherwise the person becomes very miserable, depressed, cannot sleep and confused. The craving for cocaine is gradually reduced. The person is almost a paranoid, may be also thinking of suicide. The person feels fatigue and has a desire to sleep.

The second state is the *withdrawal* which may take place from one to 10 weeks. There is a development of returning to normal. The desire for cocaine is very little and the person understands the negative consequences of the use of cocaine. But within a short period the craving for cocaine increases and the memories for the use of cocaine become very vivid. Desire may be aroused to plan and get the drug. If there is any easy way of availability, the person may give in to temptation.

The third state is the *extinction*. Extinction generally means annihilation or destruction. In this context the individual who is an addict of, cocaine stops taking it and this is indefinite. If there is no going back to the use of the drug the person experiences a period almost near normal. But there may be chances for the person in certain situations to think of the drug after few months.

5. Tranquillisers: Meprobamates

Tranquilliser is a drug that calms a person without affecting the clarity of his consciousness. Generally a tranquilliser is a drug, which is commonly administered in the physician's clinic or in a hospital where treatment for some disease is given without causing the patient to go into deep sleep. There are several drugs used for this purpose.

Meprobamates is one of the mild tranquillisers administered in the treatment. It is a white bitter powder used as a tranquilliser. Apart from, possibly alcohol the psychoactive drugs most commonly used for coping are the minor tranquillisers such as libraium, miltown, and valium. In the community many people use alcohol in moderate quantities for reducing tension, worry and anxiety and for facilitating social interaction. But it is mainly taken under medical supervision. The mild or minor tranquillisers, when taken on the medical prescription are found helpful in alleviating anxiety and tension, mostly in relation to life stresses. Just like alcohol the minor tranquillisers are potentially dangerous as there are possible side effects. These may by taken on the ill advised recommendations which may cause physiological dependence from continued use. Motor disorganisation, drowsiness are found to be the side effects of the use of minor tranquillisers.

There are also evidences that meprobemates have been found to be involved in an increasing number of suicide attempts. Further, mixing mild tranquillisers with other psychoactive drugs may have other undesirable effects. For example, a medically prescribed barbiturate for sleeping may be of greater potential effect than what is intended when taken with alcohol and tranquillisers. The practice of mixing the prescribed drug with other tranquillisers is more prevalent. The other dangerous practice that prevails among many husbands and wives is the use of the other person's prescription of drugs and tranquillisers. The prescribed drug of minor tranquillisers in heavy dosages may build up tolerance and physiological dependence. But stopping it abruptly may result in serious withdrawal symptoms (Greenblatt and Bhadar 1971). The most valuable groups of tranquillisers are derived from phenothiaziane and ravwolfia according to the studies of Hoach (1957). The drugs of rauwolfia group, when administered to the person, causes calmness by depressing certain centres in the hypothalamus area. The phenothiazine is a new synthetic chemical group of drug tend to block the reticular activating system (RAS) in the brain stem. The blocking of the RAS makes the person to become less emotional and more tranquillised.

The Hallucinogens (HSD) and Marijuana

Medical scientists in their anxiety to treat the mental illness put more efforts on biochemistry and invented some new drugs and tools. The most interesting results yielded in their efforts have been a group of drugs known as hallucinogens or psychotomimetic drugs. These drugs cause hallucinations and other psychotic-like symptoms in normal persons. These drugs, unlike sedatives and opiates, do not cause confusion in the consciousness of the patient. They have been used by primitive people for centuries.

Hallucinogen is a drug or medicine which, when taken by the patient, may produce in him hallucinations. The lysergic acid dietaylamide (LSD) is an alkaloid derived from a fungus. It can cause hallucinogenic and psychotomimetic effect in the patient. Mescaline is one of the psychotomimetie drugs, a chemical derived one from the *Peyotl cactus.*

Peyotl cactus is spineless globe-shaped cactus (fruit) of Mexico and the South Western US. Its button-like tuberless contain mescaline and are chewed by certain Indian tribes for their hallucinogenic effects. It is a colourless alcoholic spirit distilled from the fermented juice of certain agava plants. Mescaline is chemically similar to the amphetamines. It is also believed that it produces its effects by interfering with the bodily functions of epinephrine, and disrupts the normal functioning of the autonomic nervous system. The results of the effects of this drug are the distortinon of perception, emotional disorder and confused thinking (Time, 1963).

In need of immediate effect mescaline is administered orally or intravenously. Heavy doses of this drug produce temporary psychotic-like reactions somewhat similar to schizophrenia. It is common to have visual hallucinations in this state and sometimes followed by synesthesia in which auditory stimuli are observed. The patient tends to see colours in the environments more vividly than the actual colours. There is also change in the emotional reaction in the person of normal personality in the direction of depression. There is distortion of thought process in the direction of delusions. The physical change of the mescaline effects is the increased output of urine and disturbance of the functioning of the liver. If the dosage of mescaline drug is prolonged the person can develop physiological tolerance. But if the usage of the drug is stopped there will be negative effect emotionally and physiologically.

Lysergic Acid Dietaylamide (LSD)

LSD is a crystalline compound prepared from lysergic acid, used in experimental medicine and taken illegally as a hallucinogenic drug. The informal name is illegal hallucinogen acid. LSD is an alkaloid derived from a fungus that attacks the rye plant. The rye is a hardy widely cultivated annual grass having soft bluish green leaves, bristly flower spikes and light brown grain. The grain of this grass is used in making floor and whisky. Whisky is distilled from rye. LSD is needed only in minute doses to produce psychotic-like symptoms. Usually LSD is administered orally and the result is obtained a little late. The symptoms for LSD are quite similar to schizophrenia paranoid.

The physiological effects for LSD are many. The often appearing effects are paralysis and motor ataxeas. The other physiological effects are depression in blood pressure and in respiration. The most common clinial effects are increase in body temperature and also blood sugar.

There are also some psychological effects caused by LSD. These include feelings of depersonalisation, symptoms of catatonic change in mood, paranoid delusions and also visual and auditory hallucinations. These psychological effects and changes are seen in the normal personality state of the person as in the mescaline state. There is some impairment in the ability of creative artists. Writers of various themes also meet with some difficulties in organising the subject matter in a coherent manner. Experimenters who used LSD drugs in the earlier days believed that they produced actual schizophrenia temporarily. Many of the therapists tried to use LSD and mescaline drugs as aids to psychotherapy. But the effects were found to be mixed and not specific (Strange, 1965) In some patients the LSD drugs helped to get rid of resistance. In the case of strong emotions therapists found that mescaline had better effect than LSD. However, the tranquillisers were more useful for the therapists.

Several studies have been conducted on the use and effects of LSD. Rorvik (1970) and others from their results of the studies have concluded that LSD may cause chromosomal damage to the patients, and the drugs act as a carcinogenic agent and as potential cause of congenital malformations. But the studies of Aasa, Laestadius and Smith (1971) and others have not confirmed this result at the moderate dosage levels. Further, the persons who use LSD do not develop physiological dependence nor develop tolerance. Further, it was observed that some chronic LSD users have developed psychological dependence and also sociological reliance.

There are three functional advantages attributed to the use of LSD. The three important advantages are curiosity and pleasure seeking, escaping from the burdens of reality and improving the self. There are also other advantages and benefits stated by the users of LSD.

Curiosity and Pleasure Seeking

Experiments have been conducted on the use of LSD in the case of other drugs. These experimenters are over-inquisitive on the alleged effects of the drug such as increased sensory awareness, possibility of getting satisfying experience and mental alertness. It provides a passive pleasure-seeking experience. The AMA's (1968, b) description of the effects of LSD are highly fascinating. The LSD patients receive new sensory experiences like sounds, shapes, colours and smells. All these are flooding in their senses. There are also new thoughts appearing about their contact and relationships and also their secret thoughts appear in their minds. The LSD users often enjoy these floodings of sensory experiences and thoughts.

Escaping from Burdens Of Reality

The use of LSD normally takes away the user from the world of reality. The person's desire is to get rid of the tension and stress he is experiencing every day. The LSD users fall under different types such as drug-depending types and disenchanted types. Blacher et al (1968) made a very intensive study of 21 chronic LSD users of middle class youth. These youths before the use of LSD had adapted the accepted customs and traditions. After addicting to LSD they were frustrated and were angry with their parents and with their general life situation. The use of LSD often made them adapt to a life of their own choice. The use of LSD resulted in repeated intensive emotional experiences which yielded special learning environmental situation.

1. Improving the Self

Persons who have sought self-improvement desire to use LSD. These persons believe that LSD can lead them to a better personal insight, increased sensitivity, mystic experiences and for a better understanding of human beings and the world. It has been observed that persons of this category are mostly writers, painters, poets, composers, and artists who are often thinking of producing something new. They resort to the use of LSD drugs and find their new world of imagination and enjoy in it. Some investigators have stated that some well-known writers and artists have claimed that they had improved their creativity which was inspired from the use of LSD. AMA (1968 b) reported that objective observations recognised only a few cases. Rinkal (1966) state that a well-known American painter gave a negative reply when he was asked whether he had any improvement of his LSD experience. Thus the positive and negative replies to the LSD experience depends upon the users' attitude that they have developed towards the LSD.

2. Marijuana

Marijuana is classified as one of the psychoactive substances, the use of which constantly results in disorders. It is a drug derived from the dried and ground leaves and stems of the female hemp plant *Cannabis sativa,* which produces euphoria and hallucinations and reduces inhibitions. This does not cause physiological dependence. It is mostly smoked in cigarettes and similar things. It is also chewed. Tea is prepared out of this. Another drug called hashish is also prepared from cannabis plant. Hashish is very much stronger than marijuana. This is produced by removing and drying the resin from high quality cannabis plants. Marijuana and hashish have been known and used for thousands of years.

Marijuana was first traced as a drug by human beings in ancient China. It was found in the list of the herbal compendiums of the Chinese emperor Shan Nung lived in 2737 B.C., according to Blum (1969) and Cullistion (1970). Meglothlin et al (1970) state that marijuana was used by the lower socio-economic status people in the United States till the first quarter of the twentieth century. These people used this drug in entertainments and in related fields. But marijuana took a dramatic increase among the youth of the United States in the middle of twentieth century. In one of the surveys made by Gallup, (1971) about 42 per cent of the college youth have used marijuana. Other studies indicated that more than 50 per cent of the youth, including 10 per cent of high school students used marijuana (Kaplan, 1970).

It was found in the American history that marijuana (*Cannabis saliva* plant) was cultivated extensively not for using as a drug, but for its fibres. This was used in manufacturing cloth and rope. But the medical properties of cannabis were traced only in the nineteenth century. The medicine derived from this plant was administered to treat rheumatism, gout, depression, cholera and neuralgia, and also smoked for pleasure.

3. Why People use Marijuana

Marijuana is now used all over the world for its effect. The youth of the present generation are very much enchanted by marijuana. Along with hallucinogens, marijuana is considered as a drug of the young. Since it is believed that it has a magic effect it has become very popular even among persons below 40 years. Marijuana attracted the college students and young adults for its pleasure-giving effects. Persons who taste marijuana often praise it and state that they enjoy very pleasant feelings. They claim that they are lifted to the stars and relax even better than taking common alcohols. They generally find that the world has become larger and time is spent with pleasure, perceptions are bewitching. They also find the feeling of serenity and detachment. The user often feals that he is a creative artist.

Many marijuana users feal that it is possible to escape from everyday monotonous way of life and the social life in which showing the interest of others increases the joys. Freely mixing with others, touching, conversing and listening to music are all the effects of marijuana. When the penalties in United States for the marijuana users were reduced, people from all walks of life joyfully started to use marijuana. One of the derivatives of marijuana is the sweet scent attracting people in all common places where people assemble.

4. Effects of Marijuana

Since marijuana attracted the attention of the general population a great amount of researches started just like on all other drugs. It has been done with all risks. Medical and chemical scientists are of the view that the more information they collect about the drug the less benefits they observe. It is found to be true also in the case of marijuana. It is because an opinion which has been prevalent for some time is expressed in the "stepping stone theory" of marijuana use. According to this opinion, marijuana is dangerous and can lead young people to become addicted to still harder drugs like heroin.

Just like all other drugs, marijuana also has intoxicating effects. The effects of drugs depend upon the potency and the quantity of the use. One important effect of marijuana is that smokers of marijuana feel relaxed and become sociable. Heavy doses of marijuana cause rapid changes in emotion, make dull attention, distortion of thoughts and memory damage. Extremely strong doses have been found to cause hallucinations and other effects that are similar to LSD. In this state the individual becomes extremely panicky and the frightening experience will not end.

The psychological effects of marijuana are found to interfere with a wide range of cognitive functions. Test results show that there were intellectual impairments, such as loss of short term memory, diminishing of complex psychomotor skills necessary for driving, arrest of highway drivers for accidents. Heavy marijuana uses resulted in more separations, divorce and delinquency, increased tendency to consult mental health professionals, loss of stable employment, and prostitution among women.

The physiological effects of marijuana result in increasing the heart rate moderately and slowing down reaction time. But it does not affect the respiratory rate and blood sugar. The other effects are eye irritation, dry mouth, and increasing appetite. The heavy doses of marijuana may cause lethargy and passivity and hence there is hallucinogenic effect. Marijuana does not cause physiological dependency, but it causes psychological dependence which makes the person aspire for it.

Treatment of Narcotic Drugs

We have discussed the treatment for alcoholism in detail. The treatment for drugs is also almost similar to that of alcoholism. In the treatment for alcoholism the procedure involves physically and psychologically helping the person to a withdrawal period. But often the withdrawal is not generally complete. On completion of withdrawal the treatment for the person is to make him adjust to his community and abstain from the use of the narcotic drugs.

Withdrawal reactions are from mild bouts of anxiety, nausea and restlessness for several days to more severe bouts of delirium and madness depending upon the purity of the heroin that the person was using. A person who is higher an ampetemines can be brought down by appropriate doses of one of the phenothiazines, a drug used to treat schizophrenics. The uses of barbiturates for withdrawal reaction from these drugs are severe and also fatal. Withdrawal from these drugs can be best done gradually and slowly and should be done under careful attention of a physician (Honigheld and Howard, 1978). The process of detoxification is the first step the therapist can help the drug user to function on his own without the drug.

There are two drug therapy programmes for heroin users. They are the administration of heroin substitutes and heroin antagonists. In the first one there are methadone and methadyl acatate. These two are synthatic narcotics, developed by Dale and Nyswander (1966) which take the place of heroin by administering, these which are also narcotics. The heroin addict is converted into a methadone addict. This could occur in the patient as methadone is cross dependent with heroin. These act in the same central nervous system receptors. This replaces the original dependency. After sometime, by discontinuing the methadone, the result is withdrawal reactions in the patient. Jaffe (1985) states that the patient gets away from drug dependency. This patient should go to the clinic once a day and swallow methadone and three times a week should take methadyle acatate in the presence of a staff member.

The methadone treatment is found to be successful in many cases. Cooper et al (1983) have observed that many methadone users could manage to hold their jobs, committed no crimes and stayed away from illicit drugs, but some of them did not get the benefits and some abused alcohol. Since methadone does not induce an euphoric high, many of them return to heroin, if it is easily available to them. Honigfeld and Howard (1978) observe that when methadone is injected instead of orally taken, its effects are similar to heroin.

The other synthatics, eyelazocine and naloxone are found to be heroin antagonists. When the addicts gradually withdraw from heroin they are given increasing dosages of any one of these drugs, which prevents them from heroin experience. The drugs have the same effects as heroin has. These antagonists change the whole nature of heroin. The addicts should go to the clinics regularly for promoting motivation and responsibility on their parts. But they may have craving for heroin for sometime.

One of the physically addicting drugs is cocaine, which is required to ease the symptoms of withdrawal and also the attack of physical basis of the addiction. The drug, tricydic antidependutes, being explored successfully to some extent. In these cases the psychological approaches are also employed in which the operant conditioning and cocaine anonymous are widely used on alcoholics. In any drug abuse case, generally the patients are encouraged to check up the effects of cocaine in their lives and try to meet in more healthy ways whatever requirements are there in the case of drugs which are harmful.

1. Psychological Approaches

People of various categories prefer drugs for several reasons. There may be physical reasons and also psychological reasons. Though in most cases their drug consumption is controlled by physical addiction, their resistance is influenced by the drug and therefore it draws the attention of those who hold the responsibility of removing the drug from their habits. But drug abuses cannot be dealt with only by some kind of chemotherapy. It is very difficult to maintain abstinence from drug addiction. The cause is attributed to environmental stimuli which could influence the recovering addicts primarily. The secondary reinforces are the neighbourhoods, those who need, and others with whom the person used to take drugs. Wikler (1980) states that alcoholics, drug addicts and cigarette smokers have the same type of experiences.

Generally drug abusers are treated by psychiatrists, psychologists and other mental health workers in their counselling rooms just like all other human maladjustments. There are several kinds of psychotherapies applied to drug abused disorders. Kiskow (1982) says that the expected successful results produced by psychoanalytic, behavioural and humanistic therapies in helping people for dissociating their drug dependence are well known though there may be certain variations and defects. The most widespread psychological approach to deal with heroin addiction and other drug abuses is the self-help residential homes or small group congregation. This is modelled after Symanon, a therapeutic community of former drug addicts. There are also other such rehabilitation homes, having certain common features.

According to these homes, drugs of any type are not available in the total environment. The addict is made to accept the responsibility for the problems, his drug habits, and compelled to take charge of his life. An addict is honoured as a human being and not as a criminal in the setting, and is not isolated from the previous social contacts. This type of self-regulating residential communities may help a large number of members for keeping themselves away from the drugs.

2. Prevention

The most accepted and the best way of dealing with the drug abuse is to prevent it first of all. Davison and Neale (1980) state that in the United States in recent times, the well-known sports and entertainment personalities urged their audience not to experiment with illicit drugs, especially cocaine. But the message brought to light in 1990 is that mind-altering drugs interfere with psychological functioning and with the achievement of one's personal best that these drugs are harmful to the body and can even cause death unexpectedly.

It seems that at present marijuana is a more serious drug in usage. There was a strong protest for this message from the young people of United States. They have also brought political and social pressures to this view.

CHAPTER 20

Mental Retardation

What is mental Retardation?

People are born and brought up more or less in the same manners in a society. But they differ in their behavioural patterns. Some may behave in a very brilliant manner, some may be average, but some may behave in a different manner. Generally persons in a society may make good or poor personal and social adjustments according to their strength and weakness of their personality and psychobiosocial make-up and development. A person, who is intellectually weak may perform activities erroneously and may also cause problems to himself and to others. Mental deficiency may prevail in any society and it is based upon heredity and environment, and psychobiosocial make-up. The level of mental deficiency may vary in individuals. The term used to indicate this is called feeble-mindeness. According to this, mentally deficients are classified into three categories as idiot, imbecile and moron. But this term feeble-mindedness is considered to be an old term and now mental deficiency is used.

Mental deficiency or retardation is defined in various ways. In order to have a clear understanding, the American Psychiatric Association (1968) has designed its own definition. According to them mental retardation is a subnormal general intellectual functioning which originates during the developmental period and is associated with impairment of either learning and social adjustment or maturation or both. According to the statistics of the Association, the incidence of mental retardation in the United States is about 6.5 million persons which is three per cent of the total population in 1968 (Albee, 1968).

But the American Association of Mental Health made a classification of the various levels of mental deficiency and found a suitable concept called mental retardation. The 1973 classification *DSM-III-R* dropped the concept mental deficiency and recommended the concept *Mental Retardation* with suitable definition. Accordingly mental retardation is defined as the state, significantly subaverage general intellectual functioning existing concurrently with deficits in adaptive behaviour and manifested during the developmental period. Mental retardation may also be defined as the condition of low intellectual development requiring special education and employment. This is also called mental handicap, mental subnormality and mental deficiency. At present the concept mental retardation is used and the synonymously used concepts such as feeble-mindedness, mental defecitness, mental handicap, mental subnormality and mental deficiency are dropped to avoid confusion.

The general intelligence may be defined as the capacity of the individual to perceive, think, understand objects outside of him and to react to the situation without confusion, and perform his activities successfully to adjust himself in a social situation without any conflict. It may be also defined as what psychologists measure with their intelligence tests. Intelligence also may be defined as the composite intellectual capacities and abilities used by person for comprehending the outside world of reality.

Intelligence Tests as criterion for classification

A person is rated as highly intelligent when he faces more complex levels of situations and problems and is able to understand and solve them without much difficulties. Intelligence tests are used to measure the various levels of intelligence. Some of the mental abilities included in the intelligence tests are mainly the verbal abilities, vocabulary, arithmetic abilities, logical reasoning, spacial relations visual comprehension of geometrical forms. If a person is deficient in all or in many of these mental abilities, he is said to be mentally deficient or defective in his attempts in solving his problems of life. But in the conventional intelligence tests certain factors such as personal and social adjustments, facing conflicting situations and participation in group activities for testing whether a person is socially acceptable were not included.

An individual's intelligence is measured in terms of Mental Age (M.A.) and Intelligence Quotient (I.Q.). A person's mental age is the level of his mental development which should be revealed as equivalent to his actual age. The actual age is stated here as Chronological Age (CA). A person's Intelligence Quotation (IQ) is the ratio between his Mental Age (MA) and the Chronological Age (CA). It is hypothetically determined that the IQ may range from 0 (zero) to 200, and the average is 100. The ratio is multiplied by the average. Thus the formula to assess is:

The mental age of an average child is the same as his chronological (life) age. The mental age of the person is obtained from the intelligence test score. In order to avoid the fraction in the formula, it is multiplied by the average 100. We get the IQ without fraction. It has been estimated that about 50 per cent of the total population have the intelligence quotient between 70 and 110, which is supposed to be the average range of IQs. The bright or superior group has been estimated as 25 per cent, whose IQs is above 110. The IQs of about 25 per cent of the people fall below 90. These twenty five percent of the people vary in their IQs considerably. These are the people who come under the category of mentally retarded and we are more concerned about their behaviour.

Among the 25 per cent of the people those who obtain the IQs between 80 and 90 are called dull. Those who obtain the IQs between 70 and 80 are stated as borderline category. Those whose IQs fall below 70 are classified as feeble-minded. These feeble-minded persons constitute about three per cent in a population. This is supposed to be the earliest system of classification. According to this the feeble-minded persons fall under three categories as idiots whose IQs fall below 25, the second category is imbeciles whose IQs fall between 25 and 50. The third category is morons, whose IQs fall between 50 and 70. It has been considered by the professional workers in the field of mental health that these concepts, idiots, imbeciles and and morons, are derogatory for indicating the feeble-minded persons. They prefer to use different concepts (APA, 1952).

Classification of Mental Retardation

Therefore the system of classification made by the American Psychiatric Association (1952) has been designated the borderline and the feeble-minded cases as the mildly dificient (morons), the moderately deficient (imbeciles) and the severely deficient (idiots). The levels of IQs also were revised and varied. Accordingly those individuals whose IQs are between 65 and 80 at maturity with an MA of from 10 to 13 years are described as mildly deficient. The mildly deficient may benefit in school work, but his progress is slow and he has to repeat each grade. These mild deficients may be taught to do simple routine work without close supervision. They can make their living by taking up unskilled factory works.

The moderately deficient individuals have their IQs ranging from 50 to 65 and their MA at maturity may be from eight to 10 years. They are not well in doing their school work. Special classes should be offered to make up their slow learning. They do their work under close supervision in simple physical works. They do not learn to avoid common dangers of life. Those who are a little higher in this category learn to perform some useful work under supervision. Those who are on the upper limit of this category may learn to dress, wash and feed themselves. But they should not be left free without close supervision.

The severely deficient individuals have their IQs ranging from zero to 50 with an average of MA at the maturity level from one year to eight years. The upper limit of this category can be profited from the special classes in schools. These persons cannot avoid even common dangers of life. They may even put their hands in fire, walk into deep water and also stand in front of a moving motor-car. They do not learn to wash and dress themselves and most of them do not learn to feed themselves or care for their bodily needs. They can talk only a few monosyllables. They may be considered as abnormal, because they are not able to make any possible adjustment even in simple life situations without the care of some person.

There are children or adults who are not actually feeble-minded, but do not score high on intelligence tests. It is because of their emotional disturbance. They are called mentally retarded. They are different from the feeble-minded persons in their behaviour. The higher level of mentally retarded persons may be given suitable training through psychotherapeutic treatment and make them socially potential human beings.

Several studies on mental retardation have been made, and on the basis of those studies mentally deficit persons were classified on the basis of the IQ levels. According to the correct Diagnostic and Statistical Manual of the American Psychiaric Association, *DSM-III* four levels of mental deficiencies were recognised. Each level has a specific subaverage range. Robinson and Robinson (1976) described the four levels of mental retardations. They are (1) Mild mental retardation, (2) Moderate mental retardation (3) Severe mental retardation and (4) Profound mental retardation. This classification is based upon the scores of the intelligence tests and the IQs of the individuals. The scores were standardised in such a way that the mean was 100 and the standard deviation (SD) was 15. The SD is the dispersion score, which is deviating from the mean, the normal level. It was found that two-thirds of the population fell between 85 and 115. This is one SD dispersion on either side. But the deficients were decided with two SDs below the normal whose scores fell on 70. It was assessed that about 2.5 per cent of the population have the IQs below 70. These people are considered as mentally retarded.

1. Mild Mental Retardation

The mentally retarded people constitute 85 per cent of the total mentally retarded people whose IQs range from 50-55 to 70. As they are, there is not much differences between them and the normal children. Only when they go to schools and perform school activities their retardation is observed. When they reach their late teens they perform the academic activities at a lower level compared to the normal children. When they reach the adult stage they can manage unskilled works along with the normal people. But these persons always need help in social and financial matters. They can get married and give birth to children. It was observed that most of the mentally retarded persons had some brain pathology or abnormality.

2. Moderate Mental Retardative

These people constitute about 10 per cent of those whose IQs fall below 70. The IQs of these people range from 35-40 to 50-55. These people are subjected to frequent brain damage and other pathological conditions. The moderately retarded people have physical defects and nervous disorders, and their motor skills such as grasping, running and climbing are affected. In the childhood and early adolescent period these individuals are given special classes in which the individual's self-care skills are stressed and not the academic achievements. These persons can be taught to travel along in known areas. But many of them need institutionalised. They can do some unskilled works, but under supervision. They must be under the care of some persons, otherwise they may get into troubles. The retardation of these persons may be identified in the infant stage or during the childhood period.

3. Severe Mental Retardation

These persons constitute about three or four per cent of those who fall below the IQ of 70. The IQ of them range from 20-25 to 35-40. These individuals generally have physical abnormalities by birth.

Their sensory motor controls are limited. Most of them need constant supervision and help from others. Children of this category require constant help for learning to speak. As an adult the severely retarded may be friendly but, he finds it very difficult to communicate anything meaningfully. They may be engaged in very simple and small activities, but often remain indifferent. The severe brain damage makes them very possessive. Most of them need institutionalisation.

4. Profound Mental Retardation

According to the assessment made by Robinson and Robinson there are about one to two per cent of the mentally retarded falling under this category from the people whose IQs are less than 70. The IQs of the persons whose mental retardation is below 20-25 require close supervision and care should be paid all the times. Proper training and practice may improve their motor skills. There may be physical defects and neurological impairment in most of them. The death rate of these retarded individuals is very high in the childhood period.

Classification from Educational Field

The mentally retarded persons were also studied by educational psychologists from the educational point of view. This classification is also quite similar to the classification of *DSM-III-R*. But it is with aiding instruments and tools and are with institutional programmes for the mentally retarded. They made the classification of the mentally retarded as educable and trainable. According to them the educables are mildly retarded and the trainable are moderately retarded.

Classification of Mental Retardation based upon the APA, 1968

The classification of the degrees of mental retardation made by the APA in 1968 varies from the classification of the mental retarded that we have discussed in the preceding pages. The 1968 APA classification significantly varies from that of the 1952 classification. The 1968 classification identifies five levels of mental retardation such as (1) borderline mental retardation, (2) Mild mental retardation (3) Moderate mental retardation, (4) Severe mental retardation and (5) Profound mental retardation.

This classification system is based upon the IQ levels just like all other classifications. But this classification system went one step further, that the IQ as a single criterion does not include sufficient information in the measurement of the individual's capacity. the measurement should also include the individual's early development, the present level of functioning academic and vocational achievements, motor skills and social and emotional maturity (APA, 1968). The 1968 APA classification system in its assessment of the mentally retarded included also other variables.

1. Borderline Mental Retardation

The borderline mentally retarded persons generally do not differ much from the normal intelligent persons. But it is found that these persons are slower in learning school work. They have only a limited capacity to understand complex learning materials and ideas. The backwardness is generally observed in verbal learning. But these persons do not fall back in motor activities from the normal persons. Generally the borderline mentally retarded persons show their deficiency more in the rate of learning than in retaining what they have learned. Most of them make adequate adjustments in the community. But they require some help and guidance from others. These persons' IQs range from 68 to 83.

2. Mild Mental Retardation

Among the catagories of the mentally retarded persons the mild mental retardation group constitutes the largest in number after excluding the borderline catagory of mentally retarded persons. The IQs of these persons range from 52 to 67. Their level of intelligence at the adult level can be compared to the average of 12-year-old children. The adult's social adjustment is to that of the adolescent. But their level of imagination, inventiveness and judgement fall behind that of the adolescents. They do not exhibit any sign of brain pathology and physical deformities. Since they are with limited mental capacity they cannot anticipate the consequences of their activities. Therefore they need some supervision. If their level of mental ability is diagnosed earlier with their parents' assistance and special educational programmes they can be made socially adjustable, get through simple academic and occupational activities. By these means they can be made sellf-supporting persons.

3. Moderate Mental Retardation

The individuals, whose intellectual attainment is found to be equivalent to that of four to seven years old child, in their adult life, are classified as moderately mentally retarded persons. The IQs of these persons range from 36 to 51. There may be some whose IQ fall at the extreme height may show some brightness at the intellectual level. These persons can be taught to read and write at a smaller level. Some of the moderately retarded persons manage to speak well and coherently. The understanding of these persons is very limited and their rate of learning is very slow. Their physical appearance is generally with some deformities and they exhibit low motor coordination. Some of them behave aggressively and violently. A few of them appear pleasant and also senseless. But with early diagnosis and with parents' cooperation and adequate training programmes, many of them can be made to live on their own to some extent.

4. Severe Mental Retardation

Persons who are under this category have been found to be handicapped in several areas. The IQs of these persons range from 20 to 35. Generally they lack in motor and speech development to a considerable extent. The common defects are found in sensory areas and in motor coordination. These persons can learn a limited level of personal neatness and clean habits. They cannot help themselves at all levels. They need the help of others to have their things done and also supervision may put them in the correct path. But some can be trained in simple occupational works to help them by close supervision and educational programmes.

5. Profound Mental Retardation

This category comprises severe mentally dificient persons. These persons cannot master or learn any of the tasks, however simple they are as their IQ is very low, below 20. They can develop their language ability only to the rudimentary level. The profoundly mentally retarded persons are generally found with severe physical deformities, brain pathology, and their growth also is retarded. They suffer from convulsive attacks, deafness, and also mutism. These persons must be under the care of someone at all times, otherwise they may get into trouble. Their life expectancy is very short.

These five categories of mental retardation was made by the American Psychiatry Association in 1968. This classification system is done very extensively. According to it except for the borderline mental retardation and the mild mental retardation, the other categories need to be diagnosed sufficiently at a very early state, and proper training and educational programmes should be provided for them under strict supervision, otherwise, because of their physical deformities and metal retardation, abnormalities may develop in them.

Causes of Mental Retardation

The cause of mental retardation can be determined to some extent from the categories of mental retardation we have discussed in the preceding sections. The causes may be both biological and psychological and also both combined. In the earlier days it was strongly believed that heredity was the sole cause of mental retardation. Later on the research findings indicated that the brain pathology caused by infectious diseases was found to be the cause of mental retardation. There are also other physiological causes behind mental retardation.

The etiology of mental retardation varies time to time on the basis of research findings. The causes assigned to mental retardation are mainly biological and psychological. The biological factors play an important role in causing mental retardation. Mental retardation or mental deficiency in the true sense is the result of one or more biological or organic or soma togenic factors. These bodily factors interfere in the functioning of the central nervous system. It was observed that in many cases the brain has been injured of damaged and as such has failed to function normally. Strange (1965) observes that the shock or the failure of functions in genogenic (genes), chemogenic (chemical changes) and histogenic (bodily tissues) factors causes mental retardation. These factors are capable of causing mental retardation, independently or in combination. But it is not yet discovered which specific factor causes mental deficiency and therefore it is labelled as feeble-mindedness of some type and referred to as unknown somatogenesis. In the earlier days the classification of these organic factors was made as endogenous (genogenic) or exogenous (chemogenic or histogenic). If any of the factors do not come into these categories they are named as unknown factors.

Authors explain the causes of mental retardation with varied concepts and descriptions. But however, the substances are the same. We shall discuss the causes of mental retardation taking into consideration the factors such as genogenic, chemogenic and histogenic factors.

1. Genogenic Factors

The development of mental abilities is determined by the genetic and chromosomal factors. This is generally stated as heredity. The heredity factors such as genes and chromosomes play an important role in both simple and complex manner in determining the level of mental abilities of intelligence. In the case of mental retardation a dominant single or a pair of genes may cause impairment in the functioning of the brain. Mental retardation in some cases is caused by many recessive genes combined together. This mechanism occurs because mental deficiency is found to run in families. This is true particularly in the cases of borderline and mild mental retardation. The varied levels of intelligence is strongly influenced by many of the genetic factors.

Apart from the genes and chromosomes, the socio-cultural and the economic deprivations in which the family is involved and also the nutritional deficiency to which the early childhood period exposed are also found to be the causes of mental retardation. Coleman (1974) states that these deprivational factors have such a strong influence upon the mental retardation that even the inheritance of above-average intellectual potentialities do not prevent the below-normal or subaverage mental functioning. But the genetic factors have a strong influence in causing the rare type of mental retardation like the pheylketo-nuria (PKU) and Down's syndrome of mongolism.

It was observed in the studies made by Tijo and Leven (1956) that severe mental deficiency can be caused by the genetic failure in the reproduction of chromosomes within the cell nucleus. In one of the biological studies the number of chromosomes were found to be 46 instead of 48 which were found in the earlier studies. Mental deficiency occurs when children are born with more chromosomes (47) or with less chromosomes (45) then the normal bumber in 46. Thus mental retardation is associated with genetic-chromosomal defects. The defects may be moderate to a severe level.

2. Histogenic Factors

Individuals are prevented from reaching a normal level of intelligence by some damage caused in some bodily parts. Isacson (1970) has found in his study that one in thousand children suffered from brain damage. This prevents the child to reach the intelligence of a 12 year-old child. Damage may occur to the brain of the child during pregnancy if the mother got into some accident before birth or even after birth which results in impairing the development of intelligence of the child. Mental retardation may be caused by brain injuries to the child during the time of birth. Infectious disease may cause damage to the brain and may result in producing mental retardation. The birth of the child may be difficult and prolonged which may cause damage to the brain and affect the development of intelligence. Most of the brain injuries during birth are minor and do not damage the brain. But there may be severe birth injuries which often result in producing mental deficiency like feeble-mindedness or may cause paralytic conditions. In these days there are frequent automobile accidents and head injuries are caused. Further, diseases like syphilis in the family can cause impairment to the brain and the development of mental abilities may be affected before birth and after birth. The child's brain may also be affected by some virus disease. Infectious diseases and toxic substances are very much associated with mental retardation.

The foetus of the mother might have been infected with some virus diseases like German measles which can affect the brain and cause damage. The damage can be very severe when a virus infection is caused during the period of first eight weeks of pregnancy. If the disease is syphilis the mother may suffer from infection of different levels of brain damage. The other toxic substances like carbon monoxide and lead may cause brain damage to the child during the period of pregnancy and after birth. Taking some medicines or drugs during pregnancy by the mother for the sickness may damage the brain of the child and the child may be born with very low weight. The development of this child, both physically and mentally, is very much affected. Such children may live for a few years without any movements, without any sensation and die after four or five years. Any disorder caused by infectious disease or poisonous or toxic substances may be reduced to some extent if early diagnosis is made and blood transfusions are carried out.

3. Chomogenic Factors

Chemogenic factors are mainly concerned with the chemical functions of the body which are also responsible in producing mental retardation. Factors such as anoxia, toxic chemicals in the body of the mother at the time of pregnancy and the consumption of poisonous substances during infancy are the important factors causing mental retardation. Anoxia is a condition of insufficient oxygen that affects the functioning of the brain. Anoxia is injurious to the brain. Infants who suffer from anoxia for a prolonged period show higher level of incidences of mental retadations whereas those without anoxia are free from this defect. Generally poisonous substances damage the brain of the infants.

Another important factor that affects the infant's physical growth and mental abilities is malnutrition. Infants who suffer from rickets also reveal the psychotic symptoms of pellagra. The non-nutritious diet of the mother during the period of pregnancy affects the physical growth and mental development resulting in behavioural pathology. Harrell (1955) and his associates found in their studies that the diet to the mother during pregnancy period is important in the development of intelligence of the child. In their study two groups of pregnant women were selected. One group was given the food supplement equal to that of the higher income group and the other group was given placebo (sugar pills). The children of these two groups of women were tested after a few years of birth. The children of the mothers who received the vitamins and minerals were found to be higher in their Intelligence Quotient (IQ) than those children whose mothers received only sugar-coated pills. Therefore nutritious food during pregnancy for the mother determines the level of intelligence of the children.

4. Socio-Cultural and Environmental Causes

In recent studies on mental retardation emphasis is made on social and cultural factors and on the influence of the environmental factors. This result was obtained in the studies of school children belonging to different levels of social and cultural groups. Results of the studies state that about 10 to 30 per cent of the school-going children were mentally retarded in socially and culturally disadvantaged groups. But at the same time the school going children from socially and culturally well advanced areas were found to be only one or two per cent of the mentally retarded. The study made by the Presidents' Committee on Mental Retardation (1970) revealed that out of 6.5 million mentally retarded persons in the United States on the whole 75 per cent of them were from the slums of the rural and urban areas. But it was also observed that the high level of mental retardation among the socially and culturally disadvantaged was partially attributed to the hereditary factors as the parents of these children who were low in intellectual potentialities, were mostly from the lowest socio-economic states areas.

Researchers involved in determining the causes of mental reterdated realised that hereditary is one of the many factors functioning in it. This has been tested by Beratz and Baratyz (1970), Herzog and Lewis (1970), and Hurleg (1969) in their investigations. The American Psychological Association (1970) states that mental retardation is mainly a psychological and psycho-educational problem. It is a deficiency in the individual to adjust to the needs and demands of society's expectations and the difficulties of the individual in learning, problem solving and abstract thinking, and adapting to the new situations. This finding does not exclude the possible influence of genetic and the biological factors. This view simply accepts the fact in most of the cases of mental retardation, that is, in about 85 per cent of the cases the neurological and physical impairment has not been experimentally verified. Efforts must be taken to prevent mental retardation by putting greater pressure on the role of environment factors for enhancing the mental development.

Types of Mental Retardation

Though the roles of environmental factors have been emphasised in the preceding section as one of the causes of mental retardation, mental retardation is mainly caused by genetic and biological factors. These causes and types are clinically recognised. The more common types of mental retardation are the mongolism or Down's Syndrome, cretinism (thyroid deficiency), cranial anomalies or micro-cephaly and macrocephaly, and phenylketonuria (PKU).

1. Mongolism or Down's Syndrome

Mongolism is associated with severe and moderate mental retardation. Mongolism is a form of mental retardation associated with chromosomal abnormalities. Mongolism in others words may also be stated as a form of feeble-mindedness or mental retardation, characterised by a distinctive oriental physical appearance and caused by a genetic observation called trisonism. Trisonism is a condition in which one of the pairs of chromosomes is, in fact, a triplet. One occurrence of trisonism in an individual givens him 47 chromosomes instead of the normal 46 chromosomes. It is also said that mongolism is a chromosomal abnormality resulting in a flat face and short nose, stubby fingers, a vertaial fold of skin at the inner edge of the eye, a long tongue with deep fissure in it and mental retardation. It is also called Down's Syndrome because it was Langdon Down, a British physician, who first described it in 1866-1867. Later on, in 1959, Jerome Lejeune, a French geneticist, and his co-workers identified its genetic basis. This has been recently revised by Traffer (1988). Mongolism or Down's Syndrome is also called savant syndrome or idiot savant syndrome. Kolb and Whishaw (1996) state that there are several hundred reports on Down's Syndrome and they are similar, but there are some narrow ranges of special abilities and the triad (chromosomal abnormalities) of symptoms of retardation. The term idiot savant was evolved by combining mental retardation as idiot-wit-savant or knowledgeable persons. The savant syndrome is generally found in males, six times more than in females. Certain specific skills in these persons may appear suddenly and also disappear suddenly. The savants often display the time calculations without any watch or clock. A savant can give the correct time, can tell the birth date of a person, and arithmetical calculations. The savant may also reveal musical ability, can play a musical note on hearing it once. He can reveal his skills in sculpture, drawing and feats of memory.

According to Smith, Bierman and Robinson (1978) there was about four per cent of recognised pregnancies with spontaneous abortions. Only half per cent of the babies who were born had chromosomal abnormalities. A sizable proportion of these babies die as soon as they are born. Of these babies who are alive, the largest percentage of them have the Down's Syndrome or Trisomsy -21. Trisomsy-21 is a condition in which there are three rather than the normal pair (two) of chromosomes without the cell Mucleus. Down's Syndrome or mongolism occurs roughly one out of 800 to 1200 live births.

It is also suspected that certain environmental factors seem to complicate this disorder. Generally it was observed that the mothers of the mongoloid children were older than the average mothers. The reason according to medical reports is that probably the metabolic system of the mothers might have become exhausted or the mothers might have developed chromosomal imbalance. Hejeuna and Tinpin

(1961) state that monogolid persons have the disturbance of truptophan metabolism. According to Strange (1965) it is assumed that the genes in the extra chromosome produce an over-production of certain enzymes that disturb the normal metabolism and also disrupt the growth and development of the brain and certain bodily parts and organs. Due to this disorder Benda (1970) states that every year about 12,000 persons are born with Down's Syndrome in the United States. But very few of them have all the characteristics that are common to the mongoloid persons. About 50 per cent of these children have cataract which are not compatible, but make their appearance when they reach the age of seven or eight years (Falls, 1970).

Persons with the disorder of Down's Syndrome have the IQs of the mild (65-80) and moderate (50-65) range of mental retardation. Children of Down's Syndrome have heart problems about 40 per cent. It is found that one in every six mongoloids dies during the first year of its life and the death rate after 40 is high. They mostly suffer from Alzheimer's disease. The mongoloids, in spite of their mental retardation can read and write and also do arithmetic works. Hervey et al (1977) have observed in their searches that certain individuals have faulty formation of the x chromosome, the x chromosmome actually breaks into two which is called the fragile x syndrome. The fragile x syndrome is associated with facial features like large under-developed ears, a long, thin face, broad nasal root and enlarged testicles in males. Further, a more important development is that most of the male mongoloids and one-third of the female monogoloids with fragile x syndrome have moderate mental retardation. Many of them are deficits of attention. Women may not reveal any of these symptoms outwardly, but carry them and transfer them to their children. Begman et al (1987) state that among the mongoloids many of those who are mentally retarded have learning disabilities, speech and language difficulties.

Following the Down's Syndrome, studying the disorders Dykens et at (1988) have observed that the fragile x is the second important cause of mental retardation on the basis of chromosome abnormalities. Fisch et al (1968) in their recent studies have noticed that there are cases of autism as to the cause of mental retardation. Lejeure (1970) and Robinsom (1961) ascertain that 97 per cent of the persons with Down's Synsrome have 47 chromosomes instead of the normal set of 46 chromosomes.

The main end result of the chromosomal abnormalities is the disorder in the growth process. The growth condition is irreversible once mongolism occurrs. There is no curable treatment at present available, but there are some preventive techniques which seem to be very much valuable. Parents are given counselling with regard to the chromosome abnormalities to avoid Down's Syndrome in their children.

2. Cretinism

Cretinism is a form of feeble-mindedness or mental retardation, resulting from hypothyroidism in childhood. Cretinism is a condition starting from thyroid deficiency in the early life of an individual and characterised by mental retardation. Cretinism may be also stated as a condition arising from a deficiency or thyroid hormone which is present from birth, characterised as a disorder that is caused by the state of thyroid deficiency or it may be called hypothyroidism. A child may be born without a thyroid gland or with a thyroid gland which does not secrete the hormone, thyroxin, sufficient enough for the normal functioning of the body. If the child is born without the thyroid gland at birth, it is stated as a disorder known as somatogenesis or genogenic which stems from defective genes. But if the child is born with a thyroid gland and fails to secrete the hormone, thyroxin, the condition is called chemogenic disorder which is caused by chemical changes in the body.

If any of these symptoms is observed in the child there should be suitable treatment for the disorder. Otherwise the child grows with many physical defects. Pickering and Fisher (1958) in their studies have observed that there was brain damage caused by thyroid deficiency and was very much marked during the prenatal period and also early postnatal period. Thyroid deficiency is also called myxedema in adults characterised by mental dullness. George Murry in the last quarter of the nineteenth century had discovered that the injection of thyroid gland extract was able to cure this disorder in adults.

Cretinism was once considered as a disorder due to here-ditary in some families. Particularly people who live in mountain vallyes are subjected to cretinism. It was observed in the valleys of central Switzerland and other geographical areas of the world that there was iodine deficiency which resulted in stemming the cretinism. Women living in such areas give birth to children with defective thyroid glands, which become underdeveloped and results in shrinking of bodily parts. The first cause of cretinism may be stated as the result of iodine deficiency in the diet and water of the mother, and also the area where the crops grow. The second cause may be thyroid deficiency which occurs in birth injuries or due to infectious diseases.

With regard to intelligence quotient, Strange (1969) states that it may range from below 25 to around 75, which is from severe mental retardation to mild level of mental retardation. The cretins, while playing with other children, are very stubborn and show much resistance, but many of the cretins have unemotional disposition and are habitually silent. They may become gradually very bad and at the age of puberty appear like wrinkled aged persons if there is no hormone therapy. In these days the child is given a thyroxin pill every day. This controls the physical and mental symptoms in the child. His intelligence also may turn to normal. Thus he is rescued from becoming mentally retarded by giving harmone therapy. To what extent this treatment is successful first of all depends upon the age at which the onset of this problem has taken place, the severity of the disorder and the duration the person has suffered from cretinism.

The studies conducted by Smith et al (1957) on cretinism reveal that early treatment is very essential, and if the children are not given treatment before they complete their first year of age they may have permanent impairment of their intelligence. If the cases are of long standing the thyroid treatment may have some improvement. But if the damage has taken place in the nervous system and in the physical development it can never be set right. Hypothyroidism in severe cases may cause deep depression which is the indication of psychotic problem. But hypothyroidism is a very rare condition these days, because of the use of iodised salt.

Cranial Irregularities

A number of physical conditions are associated with mental retardation. Apart from the genetic feature and thyroid deficiency, there are also physical conditions like the head size and shape which are greatly altered. The causes assigned have not been clearly stated. The craniosynotosis is a common form involving the central line of junction of two parts of the skull which runs from the front of the skull to the back side of the skull (Koch, 1967). The head has a narrow appearance. There is no chance for the head for broadening. the brain growth and development may remain in an unusual shape within the skull, and the joints may be expanded for allowing the brain to grow by early surgical treatment. The head size and shape can be altered in the cases of microcephaly, macrocephaly and hydrocephaly.

1. Microcephaly

Microcephaly is a condition of having an abnormally small head or cranical capacity. It is small headedness. It is a very rare type of feeble-mindedness. It is a type of mental retardation caused by impaired development of the brain and as a result of it the cranial part of the head fails to reach the normal size of the head. Greenfield and Wolfson (1935) studied these aspects and stated that in all cases of microcephaly that have been observed that the development of the brain was prevented at the fourth or fifth month of the foetal stage in the mother's stomach. They have stated that this condition is very rare. In the microcepahaly state the parts of the brain are totally missing and the remaining is undersized. Somehow, for reasons not known the children of this category do not have the normal development of their brains.

The children of microcephaly are temperamentally found to be happy and put up an appearance of smartness. They look active and their attention may shift rapidly from one thing to another. They are placed under the category of severe mental retardation as their IQs are around 25. These children rarely reach maturity. Normally they die in their early years of life. There is no medicine or successful treatment for this type of mental retardation.

2. Macrocephaly

It is a condition of having an abnormally large head or skull. The abnormal development of head size is due to unusual growth of the glial or supportive tissue cells of the brain. The brain cells fail to develop to the normal size because of the overgrowth of the glial cells. The symptoms are visual impairment, convululstion and some neurological symptoms. These are caused from the abnormal growth of glial cells.

3. Hydrocephaly

This is a condition in which there is accumulation of cerebrospinal fluid within the ventricles of the brain, because of its normal outlet has been blocked by congenital malformation or disease. In infancy it usually results in great enlargement of the head. This condition also causes damage to the brain tissues. In some of the congenital cases of hydrocephaly the head is already enlarged before birth or it may enlarge after birth. These children are at normal level until blocked by the cerebrospinal fluid. The accumulation of the fluid in the ventricles of the brain results in the death of the brain tissues. The child's behaviour may be severely damaged if early treatment is not provided.

The clinical description of hydrocephaly depends upon the level of neural damage which in turn depends upon the age at which there is the onset of the condition, the duration and the level of severity of the disorder. The important system is gradual enlargement of the upper part of the head which is disproportionate to the face and to the other parts of the body. The skull is found protruding and the face gives the normal appearance. The level of the mental abilities get impaired. There is also the loss of eyesight and sense of hearing. In the advanced stage the impairments become very severe.

These conditions may be reduced or arrested to a minimum level if early suitable treatment is provided. Laurence (1965) states that the brain damage can be also controlled if early treatment is offered. But some cases are not responding to treatment and they result in death.

Phenylketonuria (PKU) or Phenylpyruvic Oligophrenia

This is a congenital metabolic disorder characterised by the abnormal accumulation of pheny lalanine in the body fluids, resulting in various degrees of mental deficiency. The phenylalanine is a colourless soluble crystalline optically active amino acid that must be introduced into the body by diet. Phenylketonuria is an enzyme required to break down phenylalanine, an amino acid which is existing in protein foods. If this condition is not detected and treated the amino acid, phenylalanine, develops in the blood and causes injury to the brain.

Several studies have been made on this problem. Partington (1961), in his study, observed that this disorder generally makes its appearance after birth when the child is between six and 12 months old. In the early weeks of its life there are certain symptoms like vomiting, some strange odour, infantile czrma and seizures. The appearance of the first symptom, vomiting, is the indication of mental retardation depending upon the severity of the disease. Mental retardation may occur from moderate mental retardation to severe mental retardation. The severity of the brain damage may also cause many neurological disorders, change of colour in the eyes and skin and in coordination in motor activities.

The chemical accumulation, the phenylalanine, in the body impairs the physical development of the child, specifically the brain. If the baby's blood is affected by this chemical substance, amino acid, 40 times more than the normal amount of blood is excreted in the urine. This condition occurs because of this process called phenylketonuria (PKU). The PKU patients reveal from severe to profound mental retardation and the IQ of these patients may be around 20.

Studies made by Wolf, Griffiths and Mongrieff (1955) brought to light that PKU may be diagnosed by putting a few drops of feric chloric on the baby's diaper. If there is any change in the colour of the baby's urine to green, then the child has PKU disorder. Then the physican should immediately treat low phenylalanine which may result in saving the child from becoming mentally deficient. The PKU according to Strange (1965) is a truly hereditary condition, mainly gene-controlled, which may lead to severe mental retardation if there is no immediate treatment. It is also observed that changing by the environmental condition and by providing special diet the child can be prevented from mental retardation or feeble-mindedness. Since this method of treatment seems to be successful the medical scientists can discover suitable dietary system or medicines for this type of diseases which are considered to be so far incurable.

Amaurotic Disorder or Amaurosis

Amaurosis is a disorder occurring without any observeal damage to the eye resulting in blindness. It is also called amurotia family idiocy. This is caused due to genetic irregularities. It is mainly characterised by degeneration of the brain cells. The important symnptoms are mental retardation and blindness. This disorder does not always show its existence in the childhood period. According to Strange (1965) it has three forms. The *infantile form* of this disease appears in the third month of the child's life. The second form is the *juvenile form* which may appear when the child is in his sixth year of life and it may continue till the twelfth year of his age. This form of *amautic disorder* also results in mental hetardation, blindness and the patient may die within two years. The third form occurs in adult stage. This form of disorder does not make its appearance at puberty but in the late thirties.

Treatment of Mental Retardation or Deficiency

Mental retardation, mental deficiency and feeble-mindedness are synonymously used in the study of mental abnormalities. The treatment for any of these is a complicated issue as mental retardation is mostly hereditary or an inherited problem. It has also been discovered that it is the result of genetic irregularities or chromosomal anomalies. There is no curable drugs or treatment for mental retardation. Unless treatment is given in the very early babyhood period on observing any of these disorders by way of dietary food or some drugs, it will not be possible to protect the child from becoming a severe mental retardation. The environmental changes or training may only reduce the severity of the disorder. Some progress has been made by the use of neurosurgery, but this is applicable successfully only in the case of head injuries. But for any treatment with drugs or surgery or of any other technique, it requires much early diagnosis of the disorder.

Many mentally retarded persons in United States are admitted to the institutions where mentally retarded are given training and education. The President's Committee on Mental Retardation (1970) has felt that such institutions are overcrowded and no expected result is achieved. Though there were some negative side in some organisations, there were some benefits for the mentally retarded persons. The mildly retarded persons were provided with some training classes. They were capable of achieving academically oriented tasks like reading and writing to some extent. They were trained in some social skills in such a way that they can function independently, and also were useful to community.

The training programmes for the moderately and severely retarded have only some limited programmes. The main objectives for these retarded persons were the development of self-care without any assistance and also to function to assist others in the family. They were put in simple physical works. Dybwad (1968) and Cleak, Kiviz and Rosen (1969) have observed the performance of these retarded persons in simple job skills in a special programme carried out in an institute.

In some institutions the conditioning methods were used for training the mentally retarded. The mentally restarded persons who were admitted to the institutions for treatment fell under two categories as infants and children and the other category was adolescents. In both cases there was physical impairment and they failed to adjust socially. These retarded individuals needed institutional training for the development of their activities in various areas. Studies show that mentally retarded children in some pleasant home situations can show better emotional and mental development, even much better than the institutions of the mentally retarded. Conterwell and Conterwell (1960) have compared two groups of mental retarded children. In one group 32 mongoloid children kept at home for a period of two and a half years after birth and the other, the control group was kept at the institution after birth and found that the retarded children reared at homes were better than the children who were kept at the institution. The home children had superior physical development, higher IQs, and higher intellectual abilities than the children placed in the institution. They study made by Lyle (1959, 1960) also had similar results.

Treatment to mental retardation involves primarily prevention. This is a universal problem. This problem involves the chromosomal irregularities or the genetic factors, thyroid deficiency and other nervous and cerebral damages, chemical, neurophysilogical, psycho-social and dietary conditions. Therefore, the treatment and prevention of mental retardation becomes a multidisciplinary problem, mostly referring to the development of the retarded individuals.

CHAPTER 21

Mental Health

Introduction

Human life is assailed by various forces, and human beings face various types of problems during the course of their lifetime. Some of these incidences may be simple and within the control of the individuals. In such cases the individual successfully deals with the situations and the problems. But there may also be severe and violent incidences which may be beyond the control of the individuals and they will have to struggle seriously to deal with them. If the situations and problems overcome the individual's capacity and efforts there may be some difficulties. Recurrent occurrences of failures in meeting with the situations and in solving the problems result in some kind of dejection and disinterestedness. Psychologically this state is called mental depression. If further similar incidences continue, with continued failures the individual gets frustrated. Thus the feelings of rejection, depression and frustration become the beginning of mental illness or ill health. The mental illness or ill health is not a sudden occurrence. It occurs only after a prolonged period. We discussed the various aspects of mental illness under the headings of neuroses or psychoneuroses and psychoses. Man does not want to be mentally ill. He must maintain his mental health just like he maintains his physical health.

Mental Hygiene and Mental Health

The concept, mental health, is a recent development. A person is mentally healthy if he solves his problems without much difficulties, meets the social situations successfully and makes adjustments with other people. Mental health is synonymously used with mental hygiene. Therefore, mental health or mental hygiene may be defined as the scientific field primarily concerned with healthy personality development and prevention of mental disorders. Till the beginning of the twentieth century mental illness was equated with physical disease and therefore it was considered as a medical problem. Charcot and Kraepelin have stated that mental disorder is a somatogenic problem and therefore mental disorders are associated with physical disorders. It is believed that some germ or virus or poison causes some mental disorder and if possible it can be found and cured by correcting. But this is not done in the case of functional psychoses. If a person's behaviour is found to be maladaptive, he is described as mentally ill and his behaviour is called abnormal. He may be stated as a neurotic or psychotic person.

Strictly speaking mental illness is no more than a learned maladaptive behaviour. Similarly, mental health may be described as a behaviour which is adaptive socially and that makes the person adjust himself suitably with the society. We may state that if a person is not suffering from any type of neurotic or psychotic disorders or any type of organic or functional disorders, carries out his everyday activities without causing any problem to himself and to others, and solves his problems with all success he is said to be normal and he may be described as a person who maintains a sound mental health. A mentally sound, healthy person is active, sensitive, social, logical and reasonable, who is willing to listen to what others say about their problems. Mental illness or mental health is not a characteristic that a person has or does not have. These concepts are used to describe the different levels of maladaptive and well adaptive behavioural patterns. It is also observed that some normal persons, also mentally healthy, behave in a deviating manner and make the persons around him humiliated. We do not call him as mentally ill or suffering from mental illness.

Different views were expressed by authors who studied mental illness and abnormal behaviours. Szasz (1920) (1960), a psychiatrist, in his work, *The myth of mental illness* has stated that it is not correct to associate mental illness with medical model. He vehementally attacked such an idea using mental illness. According to him abnormal behaviour is not due to mental illness and it is not the correct term for most abnormal behaviours. He states that abnormal behaviour results from the problems one faces in the living situations and not from organic causes or brain damage. If a person's patterns of behaviour do not meet the minimum demands of society he is one socially maladjusted. It is not fair on our part to describe his behaviour as deviant. The roots of a person's behavioural disorder rests in the poor habits of adjustment and his learning in early life.

Actually he does not suffer from any disease of the brain. Szasz stresses that mental illness is only the description of learned maladaptive behaviour. If it is so, mental health is the description of learned socially adaptive behaviour.

It is often said in society that prevention is better than cure. This theory was not applied for a long time in the case of behavioural disorders. It was in the first quarter of the twentieth century that Beers wrote a book out of his personal experience on the importance of preventive measures. Therefore, in this way a new science, mental hygiene, was born. Beers spent the rest of his life in developing the field of mental hygiene, and a national organisation for mental hygiene was started in the year 1909. Today it is called the National Association for Mental Health which was extended to a very wider area to serve the various groups of people.

The essential idea of this mental health organisation is to prevent the behavioural disorders in the community and to maintain the normal personality. This has created an awakening in the mental health field. Organisations were founded for different groups to provide facilities in meeting mental health problems and to develop normal personality patterns. The community centres have associations for maintaining normal mental health. These associations had made it a policy of spreading out information about the ways and means of maintaining mental health and also how to prevent mental diseases among the community members. There were also special trained groups doing the services. The services were rendered to various age groups, like the youth groups, retired and elderly persons and the delinquent groups. Those who were patients in the mental hospitals and returned to homes also were benefited by the services of the associations. Generally all types of citizens were receiving the services.

The most important function of the mental health association is to make the general public to understand the procedure of maintaining a healthy personality and to prevent the mental disorders. In short, it is educating the people for normal mental health.

Generally hygiene means the science that is concerned with maintenance of health. Mental hygiene means the branch of science which is concerned with maintenance of mental health. Maintaining mental health is as important as maintaining physical health. Mental hygiene may also be defined as a system of principles for preserving mental health. In this way mental hygiene is a positive science as it is mainly sought to maintain conditions which promote mental health and prevent mental illness and to make people become aware of health consciousness, by providing help and guidance in a regular programme for building up the mental health and normal personality. Mental hygiene provides people with correct information for developing a standard mental health which everyone should follow and achieve. Since it is an ideal mental health programme it may also be called a normative science. Mental hygiene seeks to apply the principles of mental health programme for promoting sound mental health and make them happy in their life.

So long as a person is with a sound mental health he does not bother about anything. Once something wrong happens in his personal or social adjustment the problems arises. The level of mental health mostly is involved in an individual's adjustment problem. Everyone wishes to live happily and to lead a harmonious life, execute his work efficiently and receive appreciation and rewards, be cheerful with others in the interpersonal relations. All these may take place if only the individual is healthy in all respects. Health may refer to several states of the individual such as sound physical, mental and social emotional and intellectual aspects. All these aspects are interrelated in the successful function of an individual's total behavioural pattern. If any one of these aspects is damaged in some manner then the individual's personality equilibrium is impaired to some extent. Once it is impaired and disorganised then the individual faces problems from several sources. Therefore, it is very essential that everyone should maintain all the aspects in a healthy manner for maintaining a sound mental health.

Mental health is an individual's problem and also a social problem. Therefore, it should not be left uncared for. An individual who has lost his mental health may also become a psychopath or a sociopath. A psychopath or a sociopath may turn into an antisocial element and may cause problems to himself and to others. Therefore, it should not be neglected. Efforts must be taken to prevent such incidences. There are several values and issues in the mental health problems which should be made explicit. The definition of mental health is implied to include many life areas not traditionally thought of in that manner. Educational, social, employment and economic problems also should be viewed as legitimate mental health concerns, because each variable affects an individual's well-being and quality of life. If a child does not get proper nutrition his mental health may be impaired. If a child does not receive adequate education his mental health is affected on seeing his peer friend well educated. Thus we may define mental health as a set of behaviour and resources that must be available to an individual so that he has the necessary alternatives for coping with multifaceted problems of living.

Economic, educational and social variables are viewed as having an equal effect on mental health as the psychological factors have. If a child grows up with a belief that he is incompetent (a psychological problem) he is likely to have his mental health impaired. His adjustment behaviour is affected by poverty (economic problem) which stands in the way of getting an opportunity for learning. Similarly, the urban problems like getting a job and opportunities for training, having sufficient money for getting into a trade are all psychological factors which impair the copying behaviour of the individual that may in the long run damage the mental health.

Preventive Measures

The development of science and technology not only promoted industrial development and inventing efficient machines and tools, but also affected the life and happiness and unhappiness of human beings. Similarly, modern social sciences also play an important role in human life. Psychologists are not falling behind the progress of modern sciences. Several new fields have emerged in modern psychology. The advancements in psychology, psychiatry, biological psychology, physiological psychology and neuropsychology have established their advancement and sophistication that these areas can deal with very minute aspects of human behaviour associated with the functions of brain tissues. All these advancements are directed and put into action in preventing, assessing and treating the abnormal behaviour or mental disorders. The medical sciences have invented and discovered many new medicines, methods of treatment and antitoxins to deal with various physical diseases. On the other side modern human sciences have formulated new principles and techniques to help and prevent maladaptive behaviour and promote mentally healthy world of people. Attempts to put into practice the new techniques are made at national and international levels. At the national level efforts are made at community levels.

In the case of abnormal behaviour the causative factors are directly implicated in the prevention of abnormal behaviour. The metabolic deficiencies and the sociocultural deprivations underlying certain mental retardation and maladaptive behaviour. Though the understanding about the psychoses for successful dealing is limited with the advancement of knowledge in this field, it is possible to deal with the maladaptive behaviour and prevent mental illness and unhappiness that prevail in the communities. The waste of human potentialities in various ways can be prevented and can be utilised for the happy and harmonious life of the people. It has been observed that society is the cause of all human abnormalities by putting human beings to severe stress and the same society can also serve as a therapeutic factor in alleviating human suffering and maladaptive behaviour. Mental health field has a long history. In the eighteenth century and in the earlier period of nineteenth century the treatment was very crude and inhuman. Mental patients were put to a lot of humiliations and treated like hardened criminals. Beating brutally was the common treatment. Evil spirits, devils haunted in these patients and by beating they thought it was possible to exorcise them. It was felt by progressive medical scientists that revolutionary changes were required in dealing with the mental patients.

The first mental health revolution took place during the period of Philippe Pinel (1745-1826), a French physician who was the chief of the Lia Bicatra Mental Hospital, and who instituted humanistic treatment to mental patients. He released the mental patients from the chains and confinements. He advocated that mental patients should be treated kindly like ordinary physical patients.

Pinel was against the practice of treating the mental patients like animals and criminals. Selling (1943) has stated that the change in the nature of treatment of mental patients has a tremendous effect upon the patient's discipline. Zihborg and Henry (1941) have observed that many wonderful changes have taken place in the behaviour of the mental patients. Strange (1965) has stated that at one stage Pinel himself was suspected as a madman for making unconventional changes in the mental hospital.

The Second Mental Health Revolution took place in the last quarter of nineteenth century and the first quarter of the twentieth century. Sigmund Freud was the champion of this movement. He was an Austrian neurologist and a psychiatrist from Vienna (1856-1939) made systematic attempts to explain many problems of somatogenic disorders and factors related to hysteria and mental disorders. He had written and published more than 25 volumes on mental health problems. He used hypnotic and free association methods in treating hysterical and neurotic patients. With his accumulated materials and experience in the year 1900 Freud published his famous book, *The Interpretation of Dreams*. He lived and saw that his psychodynamic approach to the study of personality and psychoanalysis as the therapeutic techniques have spread out throughout the world. Freud made magnificent contributions to psychology, psychiatry, neurology, art, literature and science. Edwin Borings (1950) an American psychologist in his book, *History of experimental psychology,* wrote about Freud. He said that in Sigmund Freud, he met a man with the attributes of greatness. He was a pioneer in the field of thought, in a new technique for the understanding of human nature. William McDougall (1926), a British philosopher and psychologist, has stated that Freud has quite unquestionably done more for the advancement of our understanding of human nature than any other man since Aristotle.

Freud lived and died only for curing mental disorders and for inventing new techniques to deal with the mental patients. The monumental contributions made by Freud for mental health followed immediately after the humanitarian reforms in the mental health field made by Philippe Pinel. Freud's followers continued his treatment techniques and developed his psycholoysis in various ways and made it as a leading profession in the United States. Therefore Freud's psychoanalysis and therapeutic technique has emerged as the Second Mental Health Revolution in the history of mental health movement and also considered as one of the two major schools of psychology in the United States.

The recent development of the idea about mental illness is that community is totally the causative factor of mental illness or mental disorders. There are several factors operating in mental ill health, which are found only in the community settings. There is no single factor that can be attributed to mental illness or mental disorders. A number of forces, events and circumstances have jointed to create a torrent of conditions and mental disorder. Therefore, the scope of mental health field has been accounted for the development of new theories and new treatment approaches. Thus the most recent revolutionary development in psychology and the mental health field in general involves a variety of approaches to behavioural and social problems that implicate the community for both as a causative factor and a potentially therapeutic agent. This development according to Hobbs (1964) is a third mental health revolution. The outcome of the third mental health revolution is the emergence of community psychology (Rajamanickam, 1999).

Why is this third mental health revolution in psychology and in mental health field? Many reasons have been attributed to this state of affair. This spirit was developed among a group of psychologists in the United States around the 1950s out of dissatisfaction they had developed against the progresses in the field of clinical psychology and psychotherapy. Eysenck (1952) reviewed quite a number of cases and reported improvements made by the psychotherapeutic techniques. He collected the results of the studies and treatment conducted from 1900 to 1950. He strongly stressed the point that among the patients who were treated by psychotherapeutic techniques two-thirds of them improved regardless of the treatment. He stated that we can come to such conclusion only by comparing the recovery rates of the patients who had similar problems and treated by other methods. He compared two groups of patients, one treated by medical methods and the other by psychotherapeutic methods. It was found that patients treated by psychotherapeutic methods were in no way better than the hospital system. There was a strong protest against Eysenck's criticism. However, the dissatisfaction against the psychoanalysis and psychotherapeutic techniques increased for reasons that it takes longer time to cure the patients and is also expensive method.

Many in the mental health field doubt the overall effects of psychotherapy. Even those who have accepted that psychotherapy is effective, felt with all this that the present approach to the problem will not alleviate the overwhelming mental health needs of the society. Thus the strong faith that psychotherapy and psychoanalysis had built and held till 1950, enjoying a professional status in the United States, has become unnerved by the intriguing article published by Eysenck. Those professionals who were practising psychoanalytic techniques were now calling for a new method for dealing with the widespread mental health work. They felt that it was not a good decision to give up the well established psychotherapeutic techniques all of a sudden when there was no well organised and qualified alternative sources.

Now, since many began to doubt about the effects of psychotherapy and its other disadvantages, other therapies started gaining importance. The most important of them were behaviour therapy and the recently emerged, Aaron Beck's (1967,1985) 'cognitive therapy' which also stated as is 'cognitive behaviour therapy'. These two therapies started gaining importance after Eysenck's criticisms. Coleman (1976) has stated that until 1960 Watson's behaviour therapy could not come into its own position. The major cause for this long delay has been the dominant position held by psychoanalysists in the field of mental health. After 1960 behaviour therapy techniques have been applied on various types of maladaptive behaviours. During this period a group of psychologists who were dissatisfied with psychoanalysis and psychotherapeutic techniques and also who were actively engaged in promoting mental health programmes for the community at large met at Boston conference and have shown much interest in the establishment of a section of community psychology within the American Psychologists Association. Several training programmers also were started in the universities and also defined what community psychology is. Hersch (1969) fixed May 1965 as the birthdate of community psychology. Thus a third force in the mental health field has emerged which may be called third mental health revolution.

The mental health movements, instituted by Dorothea Dix in the beginning of nineteenth century, stressed towards changing the attitude of the general public toward mental patients. This view has been mostly incorporated in the aims of the third mental health revolution, that is, in the community psychology, and of the important aims of community psychology to safeguard the right and liberty of the individual person and also to make the individual liberty to be consistent with the larger community. The larger community, in spite of maintaining the regard for the individual difference, also provides facilities for the network of the social system by which all the resources are available to all its members. The individual has the right to enjoy the resource of the society in which he is a member or lives. Therefore, community psychology as a mental health movement is interested in all the people who live in a society who should have the right to material, educational, physical and mental health, and also psychological resources or wealth. In this way, it appears that community is an action-oriented mental health reform movement largely interested in the creation of a healthy society with physical and mental well being of individuals.

Intervention and Preventive Approaches

Community mental health movement's interest and commitments are to conceptualise human behaviour and social problems in terms of collective behaviour and advancement of community mental health by means of preventive approach and to develop human potentialities. While thinking about the remedial measures for mental health problems the mental health scientists confront the fact that the strategies for affecting a generalised and sustained social change in the community are more for the future generation than for the present community, because a sustained social change is programmed by the community. Mental health programme will not take place overnight. It will take decades for identifying the community as a causative factor and also as a potential therapeutic agent. But a cardinal characteristic of community mental health movement has been emphasised in interventions that are sought for prevention, rather than for amelioration of mental illness. The concept prevention appears to be simple, but the concept as applied to community mental health has a deep meaning with it. Generally intervention means modification. It is to take decisive or interactive role in order to modify or determine events or their outcomes.

The mental health programme in the community is not to attend on the single person and curing the mental illness. Instead, it is intended to deal with people of all types who are suffering from mental illness. It is not giving treatment to cure mental illness, but preventing people from mental illness or any other disorders. This prevention programme has reduced the stress in the community. The idea of preventing mental illness rather than treatment to the patients was first proposed by Adolph Meyer (1866-1956) in 1900. He was the most influential psychiatrist of the twentieth century. An eminent community mental health scientist, Rappaport (1977) states that community mental health field must owe very much to Meyer for originating the preventive ideology. He was very keen on educating the general public regarding the nature and causes of mental illness with the idea of preventing mental illness instead of treating mental illness. He wanted to introduce the preventive approach many years before the community mental health movement started. Somehow his ideas were not accepted at that time.

At the time when Meyer was advocating the preventive approach in the first quarter of the twentieth century, psychodynamics and psychoanalysis were getting importance and Freudian techniques were receiving great glamour. Young psychiatrists and psychoanalysts have shown much enthusiasm in them. As a result of this situation Meyer's preventive movement did not come into force in the mental health field till the 1950s. Around the 1960s Garland Caplan (1964) used this concept in mental health field and formulated three types of preventative approach. They are primary prevention, secondary prevention and tertiary prevention.

1. Primary Prevention

Primary prevention is the major approach in the mental health field as formulated by Caplan. The important process involved in primary prevention is reducing the incidence of mental disorders of all types in the community and eliminating disorders by modifying the pathological components of the prevention and any new cases must immediately to attended to. Primary prevention involves altering or eliminating the conditions that cause disorders before they develop into seriousness. Primary prevention according to Caplan includes all measures formulated to promote healthy a atmosphere and to foster affective coping behaviour at various levels like physical, psychological and socio-cultural.

Primary prevention does not deal with specific individual's case, but it tries to reduce the causative factors of mental illness of the whole community. It mainly finds out the environmental factors that are harmful and also the environmental forces which are useful for fighting the adverse forces. Primary prevention may help us to understand the cause of mental disorders. By this means any individual may have the idea about the environmental forces that predispose to a particular type of mental illness. The three types of supplies that the individual needs to avoid mental disorders are physical, psycho-social and socio-cultural supplies. If there is any deficiency in the quality and quantity of the supplies, then, it causes disorder of some type. Malnutrition is caused by excess of wrong food or insufficient food.

Thus the physical supplies refer to food, adequate shelter and other fundamental requirements for physical growth and good physical condition of the body. Physical health conditions are with the family types which include the number of children a family can have or no children at all.

The psychological needs mainly include emotional adjustments in the family, opportunities for learning, development of physical and intellectual competencies, and development of various skills. The psychosocial supplies refer to social interaction and emotional stimulation. The interaction is with other people, families and peer groups. Emotional disorder may be caused by the failure of enjoying the love and affection of other people. If the relationship is not healthy, harmonious and cordial there may be mental disturbance which may lead to mental illness.

The socio-cultural supplies also function in the promotion of mental health. It refers to the influences exerted by the culture or community. Socio-culture determines the individual's mannerism and the way of life he has to adapt. An individual born in a disadvantaged society meets with many obstacles in the development of his personality. An individual in one culture may find more chances and opportunities, but in some culture he is denied. Such negative attitudes may affect a person's mental health. All these needs are not equitably distributed in a society to provide equal opportunities for every one of them.

2. Secondary Prevention

Secondary prevention as formulated by Caplan is to reduce the rate of psychological disabilities that are prevailing in a population. It is mainly lowering the prevalence of a specific disorder. Prevalence generally refers to the rate of established cases of disorder at a given point of time. It takes quick steps to reduce the duration of disorders that have already occurred. It tries to alter the factors that lead to new cases. Secondary prevention generally tries to make early diagnosis and provide treatment and lower the prevalence of specific disorder. Therefore, reducing the prevalence of any disorder can be made only by removing the causes of disorders and reduce the rate of new cases and lowering the old case by treatment. The essential function of secondary prevention is detecting the existing disorder rapidly.

For the community mental health personnel the community is the client and therefore the diagnosis and treatment should be as rapid as possible and make significant improvement in the mental health of the community. Zax and Cowen (1969) are of the view that secondary prevention should be diverted upon the elementary school students, because it is they who show more maladaptive behaviour between early school period and later life. It is believed that for the educational and parental growth the school should be the primary object for carrying out the programmes to the maximum efficiency.

3. Tertiary Prevention

Tertiary prevention is directed on the individual who has suffered mental disorder and has received treatment and is now trying to readjust himself to the community life. The goal is to eliminate the residual effects of mental illness and to strengthen the individual so that he can contribute to the quality of life in his community. It is also to rehabilitate the recovered mental patients. This is the primary aim of tertiary prevention.

But it is to be noted that primary and secondary preventions also carry out the same service. Caplan believes that it is also possible to have a variety of large-scale efforts to reduce residual effects.

One programme involves public education about the nature of mental disorders. People living with the mentally ill are familiar with the person's behaviour. During hospitalisation change in behaviour is not noticed. What is his behaviour when he returns home? Programmes of public education and consultation with family members can help to understand him. The mental patient has missed his social setting for sometime. It is difficult for him to readjust when he returns home, with family, at work and the social peers. Hospitals can make significant contribution towards territory prevention. Further, there should be some institution between the sheltered hospital and the community.

Another approach is occupational rehabilitation of the patients on returning home. In this programme the patient's job aptitudes and capacities are assured. Retraining is provided when new skills are required to fit the patient into the local market. Locating job opportunities for the discharged patient is another service of rehabilitation.

Public Education for Mental Health

Public mental health education is found successful in improving the community standards. But public education in mental health matters is a very difficult undertaking. Public health mental hygiene is the application of the scientific knowledge about mental health and mental illness in the lives of the population. But mental illnesses have been associated with mystic-religious fantasies in the past.

The current attitude towards mental health education in most of the places has become critical. There are several lines of action to be carried out if we are to build a solid base for mental health education.

We must become more alert to the dangers of untested assumption and more critical of subjective values.

Principles of Mental Health Education

The principles of mental health education for educating the public was discussed in the conference of mental hygiene practice held at Helsinki in 1959. In this conference a key aim of educational effort was put forth. Accordingly, the basic mental health principles should be regarded by the public as common knowledge. Mental health education programme becomes more effective when it is made a part of general education through the existing educational channels. Such programme needs the support of the community.

The conference considered three main types of educational activities. These are (1) The small groups should be used for defined purposes, (2) Incidental educational function of certain professional people in their daily work, (3) Mass media of communication.

According to the decisions made by the conference the aim of the mental health educational programme should include the following: Attempts should be made to change any attitudes and behaviour that are likely to arouse emotional problems in others. People with emotional problems should be provided with information. The programme of mental health education must be planned with regard to the individual's life circumstances and for the community atmosphere.

There are many sides to mental health educational programmes. The primary responsibility rests on different people and organisations in different countries. In the USSR mental health education is made part of the function of health education. The mental health educational process is more complex. It is a matter of relationship between the presenter and the recipient. There is a great need to expand the use of learner participation. For the great bulk of educational programmes passive techniques have to be employed. Many of those who are acceptable culturally and professionally can take part in the mental health educational programmes.

Individual Anxiety and Mental Health Education

One of the major aims of mental health education is to alleviate excessive anxiety that is prevalent among the public. It is a healthy condition of survival that human beings should be ensured with an adequate food supply. It is the task of mental health educators to help people to have no or less anxiety about the possible starvation in a community when there is shortage of food. In certain communities, people seriously worry over possible starvation, feel irrational anxiety and it is a fit subject matter for mental health education. Is it legitimate or possible to alleviate anxiety by authoritative means? There is no agreement that this could be a satisfactory educational technique in this field. Mental health issues are so complex that they cannot be resolved by this means. It is extremely difficult to decide what facts can be put forward in the authoritative form and what the areas on non-authoritative type of presentation are, where accidents occur and addiction of alcohol drugs and tobacco are concerned. Health educators attempt to stimulate response by playing to open fear and pity.

Mental health promoters face the dilemma as to how to make the public realise that mental hospitals are bad. By this means the public are discouraged from seeking specialists' help at the beginning stages. In the case of learning by the children in school, the role of anxiety is not understood by many educationalists. Generally children's anxiety tolerance is very low. In the world today there is a raised level of anxiety due to changing ways of life. As more and more people become separated from the support of the traditional values, the factor of anxiety becomes important which should be alleviated.

Learning may be inhibited by anxiety. Many devices and techniques have been advocated for turning the aroused anxiety to positive account in the learning process. Many empirical methods have been proposed for dealing with anxiety.

Mental Health Education in Small Groups

Many mental health educators consider that group discussion is their most valuable educational method, whether the group consists of mental health patients or parents of children and whether they are conducted by public health workers, teachers, police or clergymen. In principle, all group discussion topics should be general to the needs of the groups. All information dealt within the groups must be understood by the members. Therefore, educators who take part in discussion of group activities must be competent in the field of group dynamics.

Mental Health Education to Schools

Children in schools generally play in groups and in casual social groups. Some kind of human relationship techniques are taught to them. But they are rarely systematic. The basic lessons for social contact, not traming on the right of weaker child, sharing an adult's affection and material goods, discouraging greediness and so on may be taught by direct means. It will not be possible to change the attitude in this area until they have passed through conventional control of behaviour taught by schools. The primary mental health educational objective in this connection should be to introduce into schools a greater degree of conscious consideration of the principles underlying items of behaviour.

To carry out these objectives it is necessary to secure more awareness among the teachers and more objective examination of these matters, which may be comprehensive programme of mental health and human relations education of the teachers. At secondary or high school levels the objective would be very different. The method ranges from adaptation of the usual techniques for teaching science to a sophisticated use of the humanities to further human understanding. A great deal of psychology and human relations could be introduced into school courses in direct ways that might be expected to have an opinion effect. One aspect of mental health, in the schools' opinion appears to be deeply divided, that is, the role of teachers in the therapy of the disturbed children. Teachers should be capable of handling certain amount of emotional disturbances in the classroom.

Glossary

Aberration : It is a deviation from what is normal, expected or usual or it is a departure from morality, or truth or any norm set forth and accepted. It refers to a lapse in control of one's mental faculties.

Abnormal : Anything not normal. It is deviating from the usual or typical. It refers to an informal behaviour also departing from the rule.

Abnormality : It is an abnormal feature or characteristic or event. Generally it refers to mental malfunction.

Abnormal psychology : It is a branch of the field of psychology which studies the behaviour patterns that diverge widely from generally accepted norms, especially those of pathological in nature or disorders, their diagnosis, classification, their treatments and the theories that explain them.

Abnormal sexual behaviour : The sexual behaviour which is characterised by maladaptive behaviour in the individual or in a group.

Abreaction : This refers to the release and expression of emotional tension associated with repressed ideas by bringing those ideas into consciousness.

Acetylcholine : It is a chemical substance secreted at the ends of many nerve fibres, especially in the autonomic nervous system, and responsible for the transmission of nervous impulses.

Acromergaly : It refers to progressive disease associated with the pituitary gland, characterised by permanent enlargement of the skeleton; hands, feet and face, a chronic disease, caused by excessive secretion of growth of hormones by the pituitary gland.

Acrophobia : It is an abnormal fear or dread of being at great height. Generally it is an abnormal fear of high places.

Acting-out : It is the expression of overt behaviour for reducing anxiety, hostility and other unpleasant feelings and emotions, thus functioning of a depressive mechanism.

Activation aronoal : A proses of organisation of the bodily energy to meet the emergency situation or to achieve the goal.

Achromatopsia : This refers to the lack of colour vision, but not black and white.

Acquired Immune Deficiency Syndrome (AIDS) : A highly infectious disease characterised by the loss of immune function that is spread out by human immunodeficiency virus (HIV).

Action pattern : A type of complex behaviour which is different from a simple movement.

Action potential : This refers to electrical message of a neuron, also called nerve impulse.

Activated effect : A change in behaviour temporarily, resulting from the administration of a hormone to an adult animal.

Acupuncture : It is the insertion of a needle at the particular points on the skin to reduce the pain.

Addiction : The condition of being abnormally dependent on some habit of compulsive dependency on narcotic drugs.

Addison's disease : A state that result from an under-secretion of the adrenal cortex, having the symptoms of bronzing of the skin, general weakness and sometimes psychotic behaviour.

Adipsia : A condition in which a person refuses to drink.

Adrenal cortex : It is the outer covering of the adrenal gland. There are three layers and each of the cellular layer of the adrenal cortex produces different hormones.

Adrenal gland: An endocrine gland laying just below the kidney.

Adrenel medulla : The inner core of the adrenal gland. The adrenal medulla secretes epinephrine and norepinephrine.

Afferent fibre : An axon that carries nerve impulses from a sense organ to the central nervous system or from one region to another of interest.

Agnosia : It is an inability to recognise objects, occurs after damage of a particular location of the brain.

Agraphia : This is the inability of a person to write.

Alexia : A person's inability to read.

Agoraphobia : It is a combination of fears centring around being in wider open spaces and leaving the home.

Alcoholism : It is a behavioural disorder in which the consumption of alcoholic beverages become excessive, impairs physical and mental health and also affects the social and occupational functions.

Alkolid : Any of a group of nitrogenous basic components found in plants, typically insoluble in water and physiologically active. The examples are morphine, strychnine and quinine.

Alcoholic Anonymous (AA) : It is a club organised mutually for ex-alcoholics whose aim is to refrain from all kinds of drinking. It is a highly successful group therapy by laymen without any professional assistance.

Alzheimer's disease : It is a presenile progressive impairment of the brain followed by severe behaviour disorder.

Ambivalence : Presence of two opposite emotions like love and hate in the same person or situation.

Amine acid : One of the large types of organic compounds important for building blocks of proteins.

Amnesia : Partial or complete loss of memory, is a functional like hysteria or organic, resulting from the damage of the brain.

Amphetamines : A group of stimulating drugs that produce increased levels of energy. In large doses it may result in nervousness, sleeplessness and paranoid delusions.

Analgesia : Insensitivity to pain without loss of consciousness. It is found sometimes in conversion disorder.

Anoxia : It is a condition of difficult of oxygen that affects the functioning of the brain.

Antihistamine : A drug that neutralises the histamine produced by the body during the time of allergic reactions.

Antisocial personality : It is also called sociopath or psychopath. The psychopath personality is apparently charming and a habitual liar. He has no regard for others, feels no remorse for hurting others, has no sense of shame for his outrageous objectionable behaviour, unable to form relationships and take responsibility and never learns from punishment or experience.

Anxiety : Psychologically it is an intense state of apprehension or worry occurring in a variety of nervous and mental disorders. Generally it is a state of uneasiness or tension caused by apprehension of possible future misfortune, danger, worry, etc.

Anxiety disorders : A type of disorder in which fear or tension disturbs the normal functioning. This may include phobic disorders, panic disorders, obsessive compulsive disorders.

Anxiety state : A class of psychological disorder, includes recurrent panic states, a generalised persistent anxiety disorder. This can be assessed by self-report, measuring physiological arousal and observing the overt behaviour.

Aphasia : Loss of ability to understand language concepts due to damage of the brain.

Aphonia : Loss of voice as a result of conversion disorder, either functional or organic.

Apoplexy : It is a cerebral haemorrhage generally called stroke.

Arteriosclerosis : This refers to the thickening of the walls of the arteries, hardening of the arteries.

Asthenia : Kretschemer's description of the bodily type which is tall, slender and week physique.

Aura : Bodily sensations experienced by an epileptic patient just prior to a seizure.

Autism : Fantasises of self-fulfilling as a source of pleasure, in thoughts and perceptions mostly in childhood period.

Asthma : It is a psychophysioiogical disorder indicated by narrowing of the air passage and increased secretion of mucus which often cause breathing difficulties and wheezing.

Asylum : An establishment for refuges as a place for confinement for the mentally ill established in Europe prior to the starting of mental hospitals.

Aversion therapy : A behaviour therapeutic procedure that pairs a noxious stimulus, like a shock with the situation that is undesirably attractive, with the idea of making the later less attractive.

Aversion stimulus : The stimulus that elicits pain, fear or avoidance.

Avoidance learning : An experimental procedure in which a neutral stimulus is paired with an unpleasant stimulus so that the individual learns to avoid the neutral stimulus.

Autonomic nervous system : The part of the nervous system that regulates internal organs, consists of primarily of ganglia connected to the brain stem and spinal cord and subdivided into the sympathetic and parasympathetic systems, which are functioning in a diverse manner.

Barbiturate : Synthetic sedative drugs, usually addictive. Large doses may cause death since the diaphragm is completely relaxed.

Basic neurotic anxiety : This concept is used by Horney which is referred to a child's feeling of anxiety when he/she is left alone to feel isolated and helpless in a world which he/she perceives to be hostile and threatening.

Behaviour-genetics : The study of individual differences in behaviour which are attributed in part to the differences in genetic factors.

Behaviour modification : Technique used to change the undesirable behaviour pattern, is also called behaviour therapy.

Behaviour therapy : One of the techniques of psychotherapies; thought in terms of classical and oprant conditioning to deal with the clinical problems.

Behavioural medicine : A recently developed area of behaviour therapy that is applied to psychophysiological disorders.

Behaviourism : A school of psychology founded by J.B. Wetson who proposed that only observable behaviour is the proper subject matter of psychology.

Bender gestalt : A psychological test composed of lines and dots that are to be copied by an individual on whom the test is administered. This is used in diagnosing the psychotic problems.

Benzedrine : This is used as a stimulant of the amphetamine group like the dexedrine, producing the psychological effects and also bodily effects.

Bromism : It is a toxic condition caused by the use of exclusive bromides.

Brain stem : Part of the brain connecting the spinal cord with the cerebrum. It consists of pons and medulla oblongata.

Brainwave : The fluctuating function of the parts of the brain caused by the spontaneous firing of its neuron. The EEG can record these.

Bronchioles : The small subdivisions of the bronchial tubes that lead from the trachea to the lungs. When filled with fluids may cause hard breathing.

Broca's aphasia : Chiefly defect of speech, results from a lesion to Broca's area of the brain.

Broca's area : The region of the left frontal lobe involved in the production of language damage in this area of the brain is Broca's aphasia.

Cancer : A type of malignant growth or tumour caused by abnormal and uncontrolled division of the cell, may spread out through lymphatic system or bloodstream to other parts of the body.

Catalepsy : A condition of muscular rigidity that can continue for abnormally long times.

Catatonic : It is a type of schizophrenia indicated by catalepsy stupor and excitability for sometime, with stereotyped movements.

Catharsis : It is a function of purging, used by Sigmund Freud for describing talking out of the problems by the patients.

Cerebrotonia : A personality type assigned by Sheldon which correlates highly with the ectomorphic body type characterised by alertness and inhibition.

Character disorder : It is similar to conduct disorder. This is indicative of 'act out' of the persons who are hostile and antisocial impulses.

Chemogenic factor : Behaviour stemming from chemical changes and disturbances in the body:

Chlorpromoazine : A derivative of phenothianine tranquilliser.

Claustrophobia : An irrational fear of closed places, rooms etc.

Client-centred therapy : A non-directive psychotherapy designed by Roger.

Climaeteria : A period of change in the life of men and women.

Clinical psychology : A branch of psychology that is concerned with an individual's emotional disturbance and diagnoses, a type of mental illness and treating the behaviour disorders. .

Cocaine : A sedative drug derived from the leaves of coca plant, produces violent hallucinations, not causing physiological addiction.

Collective unconscious : It is an inherited collection of racial wisdom and models. This was postulated by Jung in addition to Freud's individual unconscious.

Coma : An unconscious state in which all kinds of reflexes and behaviour are stopped, a very serious condition that often results in death.

Conversion reaction : It is generally called conversion hysteria, it is a bodily reaction like anaesthesia or paralysis as a symptom of neurosis.

Cortin : Hormone secreted by adrenal cortex.

Cretinism : A type of feeble-mindedness caused by hypothyrodism.

Cyclothymia : Fluctuating in mood of a person ranging from elation and excitement to depression and inactivity occurring in a cyclic manner with a period of intervention.

Delirium: Mental condition characterised by confusion, activity incoherence, disorientation and hallucinations.

Delusions : Belief opposed to reality, but firmly held in spite of evidence of its falsity, characteristics of some type of psychotic disorders.

Delusion of control : Belief that one is manipulated by some external forces or creature from outside.

Delusions of grandeur : An irrational belief that one is an important and very powerful person with all attractive qualities.

Delusions of persecution : An irrational belief that, one is being plotted to kill him by some persons.

Delusional jealousy : An irrational belief that one's spouse is very unfaithful. The individual person may collect small pits of evidences to justify the blame.

Dementia : A mental impairment that follows actual degeneration of the brain tissues.

Demoetia praecox : The term formulated by Kraepelin to describe a mental disorder, now called schizophrenia.

Dendrite : Tree branch-like process at the receiving end of the neuron.

Depression : An emotional state characterised by deep grief and sadness and apprehension, feelings of worthlessness and guilt, withdrawal from others, loss of appetite, sleep and sexual desire or loss of interest in pleasure giving activities, indicated by lethargy and agitation.

Diagnosis : Identification of diseases from the examination of symptoms.

Displaced aggression : Aggression towards a person or object other than the object of the frustration of the aggressor.

Down's syndrome (Mongolism) : A type mental retardation caused by an extra chromosome. The child's IQ falls below 50.

Dream interpretation : The method used by Freud to analyse the dreams.

Drive : An internal physiological tension impelling an organism for activity.

Drug abuse: The use of a drug to a greater extent that it interferes with one's health and social and occupational adjustments.

Drug addiction : The use of drug in an abnormally continued manner, resulting in physiological dependence upon the habit forming the drugs.

Drug dependence : The use of a drug abnormally resulting in a physiological dependence on it, indicating the symptoms of tolerance and withdrawal.

Dyfunction : Disturbance in the functioning of an organ, organ system and behaviour.

Dysocial personality : A behaviour pattern indicated by criminal activities, but with a good ego strength.

Echolalia : The immediate pathological repetition of words of others, a speech problem often found in children of autistic.

Ego : Freudian concept to describe personality, which consciously tries to cope with reality and with the unconscious and super ego. This is quite similar to the concept of self.

Ego ideal : It is a Freudian concept used to describe a person's desire to become like one who is admired and a desire to identify with him/her.

Eidetic image : Sulliran used this concept to describe the thought process of the people who imagine especially those that were experienced in childhood, imagined and unreal, but so vivid and sharp that they may be mistaken for reality.

Electroconvulsive therapy (ECT) : A method of shock treatment by the use of electricity to produce a grand mal-like seizure.

Electroencephalography : (EEG) : Recording the brainwave patterns by an instrument called electroencephalograph and interpreting them.

Empathy : The power of understanding and getting into the feelings of another person.

Encephalities : Inflammation of the brain tissues caused by a number of agents like the virus insects.

Endrocrine glands : Ductless gland that secretes hormone directly into the bloodstreams. The secretin of some endocrine glands is increased during emotional state.

Endomorphy : Sheldon's body type of personality classification: This is highly correlated with viscerotonia, which is characterised by fat, round physique with large visceral cavity.

Enuresis : It is bed wedding, may be the organic or functional type of psychosis.

Eonism : Refers to sexual pervertion. The individual gains his gratification by dressing in the clothes of the opposite sex, also called transvestite.

Enzyme : A group of complex proteins that are produced by living cells and act as catalysts in specific biochemical reactions.

Epidemiology : The branch of medical science concerned with the occurrence, transmission and control of epidemic diseases.

Epilepsy : A disorder of the central nervous system characterised by periodic loss of consciousness with or without convolutions. In some cases it is due to brain damage, but in others the cause is unknown.

Epinephrine : Hormone secreted by the medulla of the adrenal glands, also called adrenaline.

Erogenous : Sensitive to sexual stimulation. The area of the body arousing sexual desire or giving sexual pleasure.

Eros : Freud used this concept to indicate all positive strivings and behaviour which include libids originally Eros, refers to the Greek God of love, son of Aphrodite. For Freud it is life instinct, also refers to a group of instincts, like sexual, that governs the acts of self-preservation and that tends towards uninhibited enjoyment of life.

Estrogen : The female sex hormone produced in the ovaries which stimulates the development and maintenance of secondary sex characteristics.

Etiology : A branch of science which studies the various causative factors of diseases and disorders.

Euphoria : A feeling of great election, feeling of well-being.

Exhibitionism : A type of sexual perversion in which sexual gratification is obtained by exposing one's sex organ to an unwilling person.

Existentialism : A branch of philosophy founded and expressed by Kierkeguard, a Danish philosopher and theologian. He rejected the organised Christianity and anticipated the existentialists in emphasizing man's moral responsibility and freedom of choice. According to existentialism an individual loses his existence when he refuses to use his freedom.

Exogenious : Having an external oregin, caused by chemogenic or histogenic factors.

Exorcism : It is believed in ancient and medieval periods that mental illness was caused by evil spirits or demons. This is one of the techniques practised for casting the evil spirits out of the mentally ill persons.

Expanded consciousness : Producing some sensation by psychedelic drugs to make the individual to feel a new type of experience.

Experimental neurosis : Producing neurotic behaviour in animals by if conflicts and other types of stress.

Extinction : Allowing the conditioned response to disappear gradually by not reinforcing.

Extrapunitive : The tendency to direct the hostility outward caused by frustration.

Extrovert : Personality type formulated by Jung, characterised by the behaviour of a person who turns outward to other people, objects and situation instead of inward to his own thoughts and affairs.

Fantasy : A type of imagination, not restricted by reality, generally a wish-fulfilling daydream.

Female sexual arousal disorder : Previously it was called frigidity. It is the inability of a female person to reach the lubrication swelling stage of sexual excitement, the inability to enjoy a subjective sense of pleasure during the sexual activity.

Feeble-mindedness : A condition of mental deficiency or mental retardation, below the level of normal intelligence characterised by the inability to meet the personal requirements and the requirements of the society, gets into trouble if there is no close supervision. It is classified into three types as idiots, imbeciles and morons.

Fetishism : A type of sexual perversion in which the individual finds satisfaction from some objects (mainly inanimate objects) like the person's hair, handkerchief, blouse, panties which symbolise the person to whom it belongs to.

Fixation : A strong attachment of a person to another person or an object in early life, a defensive mechanism.

Free association : It is a method of treating the mental patients. Freud used this technique in which the patient is allowed to feel free and to speak out everything that are stored in his unconscious mind.

Frustration-aggression hypothesis : It is stated that all aggressive behaviour stem from the feeling of frustration but not all frustrations lead to aggression.

Fugue : It is a neurotic behavioural symptom, in which the individual makes a flight from home and starts a new life elsewhere.

Functional Psychosis : A condition in which the individual's emotion, thought and behaviour are disturbed without known pathological changes in tissue condition of the brain.

Galvanic Skin Response (GSR) : The electric conductivity makes change in the skin due to increased activity of the sweat glands when the sympathetic nervous system is activated.

Genotype : An individual's physiological genetic constitution. The total characteristics of the genes owned by an individual.

Gerontology : Study of the problems of the aged made by interdisciplinary approach.

Gestalt therapy : It is a humanistic therapy formulated by Fritz Perls.

Grand Mal : A type of epileptic seizure indicated by loss of consciousness and muscle contraction.

Graves disease : A state of extreme hyperthyrodism, resulting in irritability, anxiety, apprehension and neurotic and psychotic symptoms.

Group Psychotherapy : A system of treatment in which one or more member of therapies are applied to treat several patients at the same time.

Groupcentered therapy : It is similar to client centred Roger's nondirective therapy used in a group.

Habituation : It is a process that an organism responses to the same stimulus with repeatedly as result of temporary leison.

Hallucination : An individual perceives sensory responses without ,any relevant and adequate real stimulus outside; for example hearing some voice without any auditory stimulus, causing due to some psychotic disorders.

Hallucinogen : A drug or a chemical substance which produces hallucinations, the hallucinogenic drugs such as L.S.D, Mescaline which are called psychodelic.

Hashish : Dried leaves of cannabis plant, very strong in its effect.

Hebephreneia : A branch of schizophrenia characterized by giggling, hallucisation and delusion, a psychotic disorder.

Heroin : An extreme addictive of narcotic drug derived from morphine.

Hetrosexual : One who desires to have sexual relations with members of opposite sex.

Histogenic personality : An individual who is overtly dramatic, acts with emotional excess, becomes impatient with minor annoyances, immature, dependent on others, often sexually sedative, earlier it was called as hysterical personality.

Homosexuality : Sexual activity directed towards the same sex.

Holism : A theory that holds the view that an organism can be understood only as a whole and not as the sum of its parts.

Homeostasis : Maintenance of equilibrium among various chemical and other regulatory mechanism of the body.

Hormone: A chemical substance produced by the endocrine glands and released directly into the blood for controlling the functions of the body.

Huntington chorea : A presenile dementia which is fatal passed on by a single dominant gene characterized by the symptoms of spasmodic jerking of the limbs, psychotic behaviour and mental deterioration.

Hypertension : A condition in which the blood pressure is higher than the normal.

Hyperdyrodism : It is over secretion of thyroid gland which results in increased physical and mental functions.

Hypnosis : An induced translike state, the behaviour resembling sleep, characterized by increased suggestibility.

Hypnotic abreation : The reliving experience under hypnotic state.

Hypniotism : It is a method or technique, which Braid had used to the study of trance state, called hypnosis.

Hysteria : A type of psychoneurosis characterized by dissociation, or conversion reaction.

Hypomania : A state of mood elevated above normal.

Hypothalamus : Collection of nuclic and fibres in the lower part of the diencephalon connected with the regulation of visceral process, such as metabolism.

Id : Freud used this concept to explain the energy of instinct characterised by completely unconscious, impulsive drives and motives. It is primitive in nature.

Identification : It is a defensive mechanism in which individual affiliates or associates himself with the qualities of another person and gains vicarious pleasure from the success of the another person.

Idiopathic : A disease not caused by another disease. The idiopathic is an epilepsy, not caused by any injury to the brain.

Idiot : The earlier classification of feeble-mindedness referring to the lowest level of intelligence.

Idiot savant : A person is with rare form of feeble-mindedness or mental retardation. Such a person is extraordinarily talented in one or few areas of intellectual achievements.

Illusion : It is a mistaken perception of a real object such as the rope appears like a snake or a shell appears like a silver coin.

Imbecile : The second type of earlier classification of feeblemindedness. This is the middle category, falling between idiot and moron.

Incest : Sexual relationship with close relatives with whom marriages are prohibited, mostly between father and daughter and brother and sister, mother and son.

Incidence : Occurrences of new cases of disorders in a given area in a given time.

Infentile autism : A type of schizophrenia mostly in childhood period, marked by withdrawl from social participation, with wish-fulfilling fantasy.

Infectious disease : A disease is caused when the microorganisms such as insects, bacteria, virus invaded the body and multiplied and attack a specific organ or the whole system and cause severe damage to the whole body, for example, pneumonia, tubercubosis, etc.

Insanity : Mental disorder, a concept used in legal matters, the term denotes that the person does not know right and wrong, good and bad and needs to be in legal custody till he gets cured.

Insight : The capacity to understand one's own and another's mental processes.

Insulin coma therapy : The state of insulin-produced coma or unconscious state in the treatment for schizophrenia.

Intelligence : A comprehensive mental capacity to understand and solve difficult problems without much difficulty or struggle.

Intelligence quotient (I.Q) : The ratio between mental age (M.A) and the chronological age (C.A) and multiplied by 100. It is a measure of the intelligence of an individual derived from the result obtained from a specially designed intelligence test.

Intelligence test : Any of a number of tests designed to assess the stage of mental development of a person.

Intelligent : Indicating intelligence in performing progressively difficult activities. A person who is extraordinarily performing activities is called intelligent.

Introversion : Jung used this concept to describe a person who turns inward to his own thoughts and feelings rather than turning outward to other people and things.

Involutional melancholia : A mood disorder characterised by profound sadness occurring in the middle age of a man.

Jacksonian epilepsy : A type of epileptic attack in which a particular part of the muscle is involved.

Jaundice : It is also called jeterus, yellowing of the skin and whites of the eyes due to the abnormal presence of bile pigments in the blood as in hepatitis. It is a mental state of bitterness.

Juvenile : Adolescents, young, youthful.

Juvenile delinquency : Antisocial or criminal conduct by juvenile delinquents.

Juvenile delinquent : Adolescent or child or young person guilty of some offence, act of vandalism or antisocial behaviour or whose connect is beyond parental control who may be brought before a juvenile court.

Juvenile paresis : General reasis in children normally congenital in origin.

Klinefelter's syndrome : Mental retardation associated with sex chromosome irregularity.

Korsakoffs psychosis : Type of psychosis usually associated with chronic alcoholism, characterised by disorientation, memory defect. This occurs most often in alcoholics who neglect nutrition of food.

Latent content : Sigmund Freud in interpreting the dreams used this concept to indicate the repressed sex desires in the unconscious mind, the latent content is irrational and always tries to come out in a disguised form.

Lesbian : Homosexual activity among females.

Lesion : Structural changes in bodily part resulting from injury.

Libido : Freud used this concept to explain the psychic energy. It is sexual energy, part of id, also sexual urge or desire.

Lobotomy : It refers to brain operation in which the nerve pathways between the frontal lobes of the brain and the thalamus and hypothalamus are cut in the hope of effecting beneficial behavioural change.

Longititudinal research : Research or investigation information about the same subject or subjects or population repeated many times or years with the aim of determining how the information or results change.

LSD *(lysergic acid diethylamide)* : A drug synthesized in 1938 and discovered to be a hallucinogen in 1943. It is a crystalline compound prepared from lysergic acid used in experimental medicine and taken illegally as a hallucinogenic drug. It has psychosomatic effect.

Macrocephaly : A type of feeble-mindedness characterised by a large head and defective brain resulting from excessive growth of glial cells in the brain.

Mania : An intense emotional state, with excitement and activity of a bipolar disorder according to *DSM-III-R*.

Menic depressive psychosis : It is a major behaviour disorder characterised by wide fluctuation of mood, altering euphoria and profound sadness, a bipolar disorder according to *DSM-III-R*.

Manifest content : Freud used this term in his study of dream analysis. It is the actual ideas and thoughts and images of a dream as reported by the person who had the dream.

Marijuana : A drug derived from drived and ground leaves and stems of the plant *Cannabis indica* produces euphoria and hallucinations and reduces inhibition without causing physiological addiction.

Masochism : It is a type of sexual perversion characterised by pleasure drived from pain. The prevented often gets gratification by being beaten.

Masturbation : It is self-stimulation of the genital organ.

Meningitis : Virus infection membranes, covering the brain and spinal cord.

Menopause : The stopping of the menses in women.

Mental age : The level of mental ability of an individual as determined by a standard intelligence test, expressed in numerical value (M.A.).

Mental retardation : Sub-normal mental ability level of an individual characterised by the inability to adjust himself in social situation and unable to solve the personal problems and causing problem to himself and to the society.

Mental deficiency : Similar to problem-mindedness or mental retardation.

Mescaline : A drug which can cause hallucinogenic effect, derived from peyotl cactus.

Mesmerism : Anton Mesmer used this as a techniques for treating the neurotic patients, similar to hypnotism.

Mesomorph : Sheldon's body type correlated with somatotonia characterised by normal body muscular physique.

Metrazol : A drug which is injected to cause grand mal-type convulutions for treating the psychotic patients.

Microcaphaly : The condition of having an abnormally small head or cranical capacity, opposite of magracephaly, a form of feeble-mindedness.

Midgat : An abnormally undersized person; with large head and short arms and legs (dwarf) whose skeleton and features are normal proportion.

Migrainae headaches : It is severe, often occurring headaches specially on one side and accompanied by nausea.

Moderate mental retardation : The level of limitation in mental development measured on intelligence tests and the IQ is between 35=40 and 50-55.

Modified leucotomy : An area near corpus collosum to relieve obsessive-impulsive disorders by surgical means, it is a technique.

Mongolism : A form of mental retardation generally caused by an extra chromosome. The IQ of the person is less than 50. The physical characteristics are distinctive, the most noted one is the slanted eyes.

Mood disorder : These are disabling disturbances in emotion.

Moron : The third category of feeble-mindedness supposed to be more intelligent than the other two categories, idiot and imbecile.

Morphine : A narcotic drug, addictive alkoloid extrated from opium, used as a sedative.

Multiple personality : A rare psychotic disorder in which the person may at different times claim to be a different person often with amnesia for his other personality.

Mutism : The inability or refusal to speak.

Music therapy: The use of music in psychotherapy as an aid.

Myocardial infarction : Chest pains caused due to insufficient supply of blood and thus oxygen to the heart and myocardial infarction or heart attack in which blood and oxygen supply is reduced and heart muscles are damaged.

Myxedema : It is a severe, mental impairment and physical defects resulting from extreme hypothyrodism in adult persons. In children it is called cretinism.

Noreosynthesis : A psychotherapeutic technique for treating the patient who is under the influence of drug such as sodium pentothal.

Narcotic : A sedative drug of addictive such as morphine and heroin. The moderate dose may relieve pain and induce sleep.

Neo-Freudian : It is a term used to the followers of psychoanalysis, those who practised psychoanalytic methods after Freud are called New-Freudians, mostly Horney and Fromm.

Neurosthenia : A form of neurotic disorder indicated by feelings of general fatigue and weakness, the synonymously used term is asthenic tension.

Neurology : A branch of medical science which studies the functioning and the diseases of the nervous system.

Neuron : A single nerve cell.

Neurosis : A large category of neuropsychotic disorders characterised by unrealistic anxiety and other related problems such as phobia avoidances, obsessions and compulsions.

Neurotic anxiety : It is an irrational fear, as a result of painful experiences the individual had earlier.

Nicotine acid : It is one of the B-complex vitamines, known as niacin.

Non-directive therapy : It is Roger's system of psychotherapy, Roger used the term, client-centred therapy.

Noraghinephrina : The hormone secreted by medulla of the adrenal glands.

Nyphomania : It is a condition of extreme desire in a woman for sexual activities with men.

Nuciesus : It refers to a mass of nerve cell bodies within the brain or spinal cord by descending nerve fibres connected with ascending nerve fibres.

Obsession : An intense sand often occurring thought process that is irrational and uncontrollable to the person experiencing it.

Obsessive-compulsive neurosis : An anxiety disorder in which the mind is filled with personal persistent and uncontrollable thoughts and the individual is compelled to repeat certain acts over and over causing distress and interference with everyday activities.

Occipital lobe : The posterior part of each cerebral hemisphere, located behind the parietal lobe and above the temporal lobe which is responsible for a reception and analysis of visual information.

Odipus complex : Sigmund Freud used this concept to explain the desire and the conflict of a small male child who wants to possess his mother sexually and to elimate his father, the rival. The dread of punishment from the father makes the boy suppress these impulses. Girls have the same type of sexual desire for the father which is repressed and is called Electro Complex.

Operant behaviour : A voluntary response is operating in an environment and modifies the environment, so that the goal is attained.

Opium: A narcotic drug derived from a species of poppy, produces a feeling of well-being in the user of heroin, morphine, laudanum and opiates.

Organic factor : That which causes damage or destruction of the bodily organs or tissues, specially the brain.

Over compensation : It is a defensive mechanism by which the person replaces excessively one activity for another that has not given the required satisfaction.

Panic disorder : It is an anxiety disorder in which the person receives sudden attacks of jarring symptoms such as difficulty in breathing, heart palpitations, dizziness, terror and other feelings of extreme fear.

Paranoia : A psychotic condition, the symptom of which is a systematised delusion.

Paranoid (disorder) : A disorder in which the person has persistent persecutory delusions, delusional jealousy, unproved conviction that his/her mate is unfaithful.

Parasympathetic nervous system : A branch of autonomic nervous system which is responsible for controlling many of the internal organs and it is active when the organism is not aroused. It functions opposite to sympathetic nervous system.

Parietal lobe : The middle part of each cerebral hemisphere, situated behind the central sulcus. It is the receiving area of sensations of skin.

Pareis : A syphilitic infection of the brain. This is also called general paralysis.

Parkinson's disease : It is a presenile psychosis characterised by severe and uncontrollable muscle tumours. It is named after the founder.

Pathology : A branch of medical science, mainly studying the anatomical, physiological and psychological deviations of a disease or disorder and the study of the abnormalities.

Pedophilia : A desire to obtain sexual gratification by having contact with youngsters who are under age.

Pellagra : A disease caused by extreme deficiency of the vitamin .nicotinic acid, this may result in violent psychotic behaviour.

Petit mal : An epileptic attack in which the sufferer looses consciousness for a few seconds, not going into convulsion.

Peyotl : The cactus plant from which a drug mescaline is derived.

Phallus : It is symbol of the penis. Freud used this concept in his studies.

Phenomenology : It is a philosophical view applied in psychological experimental studies. According to this view the phenomena of subjective experience should be studied deeply because behaviour is determined by how people perceive themselves and the world instead of subjectively describing the reality.

Pharmacology : The branch of chemical science which mainly studies-about drugs and medicines.

Phenobarbital : One of the drugs in the family group of barbiturates which produces lasting effect.

Phenothiazine : The name of a group of drugs that relieves psychotic symptoms and considered as neuroleptics. It is a tranquilliser.

Phenylalanine : It is a chemical substance found in all proteins. The phenylketonuria is caused when phenylalanine is not systematically metabolised.

Phenyliketonuria (PKU) : It is a genetic disorder caused by the deficiency in liver enzyme characterised by abnormal accumulation of phenylalanine in the body fluids, resulting in various degrees of mental deficiencies.

Phobia : An unpleasant event which causes irrational fear held by a person who is suffering from neurotic or anxiety disorder.

Physiological paradigm : A wider theoretical point of view, according to which the mental disorders are caused by aberrant somatic processes.

Physiology : A branch of science which studies the functions and behaviour of living cells, tissues and organs and the physical and chemical aspects of the organism.

Pick's disease : It is a presenile psychosis generally caused by progressive brain deterioration, resulting in loss of memory loss concentration .and inability to think abstractly and finally ends with psychosis and death.

Placebo : This is a Latin word, which means, an inactive substance administrated to a patient who insists on receiving medication or who would benefit by the psychological deception of the efficacy of an active drug. The patient has satisfaction that he has been given the correct medicine.

Play therapy : The use of play as a means of therapy in treating the patients, in which what is troubling the child is uncovered by establishing rapport.

Pleasure principle : It is a Freudian concept. According to this principle the id is an instinctual function which needs immediate gratification either in the real situation or in the wish-fulfilment activities of dream or fantasies.

Plethysmograph : It is an instrument generally used by the physicion for the measurements of the level of blood pressure existing in a person's body.

Pneumonia : A highly infectious disease. It is the inflamation of the lungs, may affect one or both the lungs. In this disease the air sacs in lungs become filled with fluid which causes difficulty in breathing or breathlessness. It is caused by the bacteria called penuma cocal.

Pons : An area in the brain, containing nerve fibra tracts connecting the cerebellum with the spinal cord and with motor areas of the cerebrum.

Posthypnotic -suggestion: The suggestion given to the patient during the time of hypnosis which should be carried out after the patient is not hypnotised.

Prognosis : A prediction of the cause or outcome of a disease or disorder, for the chances of recovery from the disease.

Projection : A defence mechanism in which the person projects his own undesirable unconscious feelings and motives on others.

Projective techniques: A type of psychological tests which makes the person respond in such a way that he reveals his own personality characteristics.

Projective test : A psychological assessment method employing a set of standard vague stimuli or questions on the idea that the given material will make the person reveal his unconscious motives and fears.

Psyche : The mind or spirit or soul which is different from the body. In psychoanalysis it refers to the total characteristics of the id, ego and super-ego components.

Psychasthenia : Any neurosis characterised by phobias, anxiety or obsessions and compulsions, originally it means weakness of the will, not a strong mind.

Psychedelic : The drugs which expands the mind such as LSD which often results in hallucinations.

Psychiatrist : Physician with a degree of M.D. who has taken specialisation in post-doctoral training in the diagnosis, treatment and prevention of mental and emotional disorders.

Psychiatric social worker : A medically trained person engaged in the collection of relevant information from mental patients, from their family and friends and to work as a middle person between them and the patient.

Psychiatry : It is branch of medical science which deals with mental illness or disorders.

Psychoactive drug : A chemical substance having psychological effect which can alter the mood and thought process. Valium is a drug of this type.

Psychoanalysis : The concept formulated by Freud to name his theory of personality and the method of treatment of mental patients by associating the free association method and hypnosis.

Psychobiology : Meyer's conception of psychology is psychobiology, who emphasised the organic aspects and wished to make it and a multifactor approach to the study of behaviour, which later on was called psychobiosocial study of behaviour.

Psychodynamics : It is the study of the emotional and motivational states that become the causes of maladoptive behaviours of an individual.

Psychogenesis : Psychological in origin, different from somatogenic origin.

Psychomotor epilepsy : A type of epilepsy in which abnormal behaviour changes into convulsion.

Psychoaeurosis : A very wider category of mild mental disorders such as phobia, compulsions, conversion hysteria and other neurotic disorders.

Psychopath : It is acting out of a person who is an antisocial person, who acts devoid of conscience.

Psychopathology : It is a study of science that deals with behaviour disorders, considered synonymously with abnormal psychology.

Psychopathologists : Professionals dealing with mental health, conduct research into the nature and development of mental and emotional disorders.

Psychophysiological disorders : Disorders with physical symptoms that involve tissues damage in the organ system, which are produced by autonomic nervous system in physical stress.

Psychophysiology : A branch of science that mainly deals with bodily changes resulting in psychological effects.

Psychosexual : According to psychoanalytic theory the individual's development passes through several stages, each stage is characterised by the bodily area producing maximum erotic satisfaction, each stage finds the instinctual gratification intensely.

Psychosis : It is a major mental disorder characterised by loss of contact with the world of reality, the individual's emotion and thinking are impaired. Psychoses are of two major types, functional psychoses and organic psychoses.

Psychosomatic disorders : A physical impairment such as peptic ulcer that is caused by prolonged emotional conflict.

Psychosurgery : A surgical technique in which the neural pathways in the brain are cut for making change in the behaviour of the patient.

Psychotherapy : The mentally troubled individuals formerly were helped by verbal means of changing their feelings, thoughts and behaviour for reducing their severity of the illness for achieving better life satisfaction. Counselling and interview techniques are applied by the clinical psychologtis in treating the patients of behaviour disorders.

Psychotic depression : Deep feeling of sadness and unreasonable feelings of unworthiness in which there are delusions.

Pyknik : Kretschmer's classification of personality type on the basis of physique. Pyknik is to indicate a fat, round body built with a larger visceral cavity.

Pyromania : It is a compulsive neurosis and the individual is compelled impulsively to set fire to properties; he is often sexually perverted and his gratification takes place only when he sets fire and watches the flames.

Random assignment : A procedure of assigning a population subject to groups for an experiment for investigations, in which each subject is given an equal chance of being included in the group investigation.

Rape : Forcible sexual intercourse or other sexual activity on another person. Forcible rape is the legal term, statory rape is sexual intercourse between an adult male and with an unwilling person.

Rapport : A state of mutual understanding between two persons, mostly a therapist and a client:

Rationalism : A system of philosophy which makes its basic principle that reason and logic are the source of knowledge, wisdom and truth, it is opposed to empiricistic philosophy.

Rationalisation : It is a defence mechanism, a suitable reason is unconsciously invented by the ego for protecting itself from facing the real reason or situation for an action, thought and emotion.

Raynaud's disease : It is a psychophysiological disorder in which capillaries, the fingers and toes are subjected to spasm and characterised by cold moist accompanied by pain which may spread to other parts.

Reaction formation : Defence mechanism in which an unconscious and unacceptable feeling may cause anxiety and is converted into its opposite by which it can become conscious and expressed.

Regression : A defence mechanism in which an individual goes back to his earlier childhood days often and behaves in the vain to cope with a stressful situation and with his own feelings.

Repression : Freud's basic defense mechanism in which the desires and thoughts not agreeable to the ego and superego and are pushed into the unconscious mind.

Resistance : Defensive efforts of the unconscious part of the ego during the period of treating him by psychoanalysis, avoiding to reveal the desires and thoughts.

Reticular activating system : (RAS) : The central part of the brain stem that activates the cerebral cortex.

Rickets : Bone malformation in children due to vitamin deficiency.

Rorschach test : It is a projective test in which the subject is asked to interpret a set of the inkblots presented in cards.

Rubella : An infectious disease, if contacted by the pregnant woman during the first three months of her pregnancy, has a risk of getting mental retardation and physical deficiency in the child when born. It is generally called German measles.

Sadism : A type of sexual perversion characterised by the desire to inflict plain on others for the purpose of obtaining sexual pleasure.

Satyriasis : An abnormal extreme desire in a man for coitus with woman.

Schizoaffective disorder : When it is difficult to determine whether the person is suffering from an affective disorder or schizophreniform of disorder diagnosis is to be applied.

Schizoid personality : The patient is emotionally isolated and indifferent to praise, appreciation, criticism and to the feelings of others, he is generally alone, with few close friends.

Schizopheonia : A type of psychosis, functional in nature characterised by autistic thinking and withdrawing from the society.

Schizophreniform : It is a taxic psychosis indicated by social withdrawal and apathy.

Schizophrenogenic : It is genetically causing schizophrenia through family.

Sedative : Drug that could slow down the bodily activity mainly the central nervous system. It reduces the pain and tension and produces relaxation and sleep.

Self-actualisation : It is applying the potentialities of a person to the fullest extent for fulfilling his highest motives and desires to maintain and promote the goal-achieving effects.

Semantic differential : A self-report inventory or test which requires the subject to rate each term or concept. Each concept has the polar adjective with opposite meanings at both ends like, good-bad, right-wrong, etc.

Senile dementia : A condition of psychosis occurring in old age due to progressive deterioration of the brain marked by impairment of memory, inability to think abstract matters, loss of control of impulses, lack of personal hygiene.

Sociogenic factor : A disorder causing from interpersonal relationships like being in groups, family, peers and fellow workers.

Somatopsychic : Psychosomatic, emotional disturbances resulting in physical disease or disorder.

Somnambulism : It is sleepwalking, translike behaviour of certain hysterical type.

Stress : Mental or emotional or physical tension caused due to unsuccessful efforts to achieve a goal.

Stroke : Sudden appearance of neurological symptoms as a result of severe interruption of blood flow.

Stupor : A type of mental condition marked by confusion, inactivity, disorientation and lack of responding to stimulus.

Sublimation : Freud formulated the concept while studying the nature of unconscious mind. It is a type of mechanism in which the real sex-motives or desires are suppressed and sent to the unconscious level. But they however come out in some disguished form which are socially accepted. The real sex motives appear in the conscious mind in the non-sexual forms.

Substance abuse : The use of a drug for a long time to the extent that the person is often intoxicated throughout the day and fails to attend important works and abstains, but there is no physiological dependence.

Substance dependence : The use of a drug has become chronic which results in physiological dependence on it. This is made evident by tolerance and withdrawal symptoms, the state is also called drug or substance addition.

Substance disorders : The use of drugs like alcohol and cocaine are abused to the extent that behaviour becomes maladaptive, social and occupational functions are impaired and control is lost – such condition leads to substance disorders. Dependence on the drug may be psychological like substance abuse or it may be physiological like substance addiction or dependence. Therefore it may be psychological disorder or physiological disorder.

Suggestibility : A state under hypnosis in which a person will accept the suggestions of another person and act accordingly.

Suicide : The act or instance of killing oneself intentionally; the self-inflicted ruin of one's own life or prospects or interests.

Super-ego : Freudian concept used in the study of personality and unconscious. Super-ego is the same as the conscience but without involving morality.

Sulcus (Fissure): A small cleft produced by folding of the cerebral cortex separating the nearly gyrior convolutions.

Sympathetic nervous system : It is a branch of autonomic nervous system that acts on bodily systems, like spreeding up of the contractions of the blood vessels, slowing down of the intestines, increasing the heart rate, thus making the organism to excert.

Symptom: A perceivable physiological or psychological manifestation of a disease or disorder often taking place in a group of symptoms which constitute a syndrome.

Synapse : The point of contact between two cells, classically, this refers to the junction between an axonal terminal and another cell.

Syndrome : A group of symptoms which occur in a specific disease or disorder.

Synesthesia : The ability to perceive a stimulus of one sense as the sensation of different sense as when sound produces a sense of colour.

Syphilis : A infectious venereal disease caused by the microorganism traponema pallidum characterised by an ulcerating chancre usually on the external penitals and progressing through the lymphatic system to nearly all tissues of the body producing serious clinical manifestations.

Tachycadia : A bodily condition in which rapid heart beat and pulse rate may be occurring.

Taylor-manifest anxiety scale : It is derived from MMPl with 50 items and formed into a self-reporting questionnaire to assess anxiety of a person.

Temporal lobe : A large part of each cerebral hemisphere located below the lateral sulcus and in the front of occipital lobe which contains auditory projection area.

Testes : The reproductive glands of male, it is the place where sperm is developed and stored.

Testosterone : Male sex hormone-secreted by the testes which facilitates the development of sex characteristics like the enlargement of the testes and appearance of facial hair.

Tetrahydrocannabinol (THC): The important chemical substance in marijuana and hashish.

Thalamus : It is brain's relay point, consists of two egg-shaped lobes located in the diencephalon which receives impulses from sensory areas except olfactory and transmit them to the brain – the cerebrum.

Thanatos : Freudian psychoanalytic concept, which explains the theory of death instant. It is the Greek word personifies the death, represents the universal death instinct, opposed to Eros which personifies the life instinct.

Therapy : Generally it is a treatment for mental and emotional disorders. It is in the forms of physical (surgery), chemical (drugs) or medical treatment or psychotherapy (psychological).

Thiamine : It is one of the 'B' vitamin complex.

Thyroid gland : It is one of the endocrine lands, consists of two lobes at the base of the neck in man. It secretes hormones that control metabolism of the thyroid gland.

Trait : It is a somatic characteristic which responds in a way to one individual from another or one group from another.

Tranquilliser : The drug which reduces anxiety, tension and agitation.

Transvestic fetishism : The habit of dressing in the clothes of the opposite sex for the purpose of sexual arousal.

Trauma: A physical or psychological injury.

Treponama pallidum : The micro-organism spirochata, that causes syphilis.

Tremor : An involuntary vibration as from illness, fear, shock.

Trisomy : A condition in human body wherein there are three instead of normal (two) pair of chromosomes in the cell nucleus.

Tumour : An abnormal growth located in the brain which can be malignant and destroy the brain tissues and disrupt the functioning of the system.

Tuberculosis : It is a severe communicatable infectious disease caused by infectious Tuberal Bacillus which most frequently affects the lungs.

Type-A and Type-B : Vitamin-A : A fat-soluble yellow unsaturated alcohol occurring in green and yellow vegetables, especially in carrot, butter, egg, yolk and fish liver oil. It is essential for the prevention of night blindness and the protection of epithelial tissue.

Type-B-vitamin complex : A large group of water soluble vitamins occurring especially in liver and yeast, includes thiamine riboflavin, nicotinic acid, pyridoxine, pantheistic acid, biotin, choline, folic acid and cyhocobalamin.

Typhoid : It is an acute infectious disease caused by ingesting contaminated food or water, characterised by high fever, coloured spots in the chest or abdomen, pain in abdomen and intestinal disorders. It is caused by *Bacillus Salmonella Typhosa.*

Typhus : It is one of a group of acute infectious rickettsial diseases characterised by high fever, skin rash and severe headache which is transmitted by fleas, etc.

Ultrasound : Sound waves controlled through an instrument and used to visualize and study the internal organs without using the x-rays.

Unconditioned response (UCR) : Response or behaviour obtained by an unconditioned stimulus (UCS) is an instinctual manner.

Unconditioned stimulus (UCS) : A normal stimulus that arouses an instinctual unconditioned response. For example, a mutton piece elicits saliva in a dog's mouth.

Unconscious : A state of unawareness without any sensation. Freud had applied this concept throughout his studies. This is the major part of the mind which consists of the id, the libido and parts of the ego and super-ego. It is also the part of the personality.

Undifferentiated schizophremia : The diagnosis conducted on patients, but the psychotic symptoms do not provide any indication of classifying the schizophrenia into any category. Hence it is treated as undifferented.

Unipolar depression : According to *DSM-Ill-R* conviction, it is a disorder of a person who has experienced episodes of depression but not of mania.

Urticaria : It is a skin allergic reaction which is characterised by the formation of itchy, red or whitish raised batches usually caused by an allergy.

Vagina : Female genital organ which leads from the uterus to the external opening.

Vaginal organism : It is the sexual climax experience through the stimulation of the vagina.

Valium : A drug that reduces the anxiety, which is widely prescribed by the physicians among the available drugs.

Vertigo : The condition of dizziness.

Virilism : The abnormal development in a woman of male secondary characteristics such as appearance of beard, etc., and over-secretion of hormones from the adrenal cortex.

Viscera : The large internal organs of the body of those in the abdominal cavity.

Visceratonia : Sheldon's conception of personality type which identifies mostly with endomorph body type, which is characterised by indolence, seeking of living comforts and avoidance of difficult work or exercise.

Vitamin : Various organic substances that are very essential for making the food nutritional, acting in small quantities for the regulation of the metabolic process of the body.

Voycurism : A state of sexual deviation marked by obtaining the satisfaction by watching other people in the nude or in the activity of coitus or in the state of undress. This is also called by the terms of peeping, Tomism and scopophila.

Wernicke's disease : The B-Complex vitamin deficiency mostly is responsible for producing this chronic brain disorder marked by confusion, drowsiness, partial paralysis of the muscles.

Yellow fever : It is an acute infectious disease of tropical and semi-tropical climatic conditions characterised by fever, haemorrhages, vomiting of blood and jaundice caused by the virus transmitted by the bite of a female mosquite of the species.

Zoophilia : It is a sexual perversion in which the individual obtains sexual gratification by the use of lower animals.

Zygote : It is the fertilised ovum in which the male sperm cell fertilises the female ovum.

Bibliography

1. Aase, J.M., Leastedius, N., and Smith, D.W. LSD Dosed mothers have normal infants in Secttle, *Psychiatric News,* 1971, 6(1) 6.

2. Acbuquerque, EX, Resh, J.E., Meyer, R.F., and Setterfield, J.R. A Electrophysiological and Morphological study of the neuromuscular junction in patients with myasthenia gravis, *Experimental Neurology,* 1976, 51: 536-563.

3. Adler, A., Understanding Human Nature, *Greenwhich,* Conn: Premier Books, 192.

4. Albee, G.W., Needed a revolution in caring for the retarded, *Transaction,* 1968, 5., 67-42.

5. American psychiatric Association: Diagnostic and Statistical Manual of mental disorders: Washington, D.C.: American Psychiatric Association, 1969.

6. AMA: American medical association, Department of Mental Health. The crutch that Cripples: Drug dependence, Part-1: *Today's Health*, 1968, 46(10) 12-15, 73-75.

7. American Psychiatric Association, Diagnostic and Statistical-Manual (DSM) Washington, 1952.

8 Anant, S.S. A note on the treetment of alcoholics by verbal aversion technique, *Canedian Psychologist,* 1967, 8, 19-22.

8a. Anderson, B.E., Where is Dad? Parental deprivation and delinquency, *Archieves General Psychiatry,* 1967, 18(6) 641, 642.

9. Andry, R.G., Parental and Maternal roles and delinquency, *WHO Public health paper,* 1962, 14, 31-44.

10 . Appley, M., and Trumball, R., Psychological Stresses, New York: Appleton, *Century-Crofts,* 1967.

11. Arieti, S. Interpretation of Schizophrenia, New York: *Basic Books*, 1955.

12. Arkonae, B., and Guze, S.B.A. Family Study of Hysteria, *New England Journal of Medicine,* 1963, 768, 239-242.

13. Ballenger, J.C., Barrows, G.O., Dupout, H.C., Lesser, M., Noyes, R.E., et al. Ap7prazolam in panic disorder and Agorophobia: results from Multicentre trial, *Archieves General Psychiatry,* 1998, 45, 498.

14. Banay, R. S. Wanted an institute of criminal science, *Year book of National Publication Association,* 1945.

15. Bandura, A., Principles of behaviour modification, New York: Holt Rinehart and Winston, 1969.

16. Bandura, A., and Walters, R.H., Adolescent aggression, New York: Ronald, 1958, 2(4), 379-391.
17. Baratz, S:, and Baratz, J.C., Early Childhood intervention, The social science base of institutional racism, *Harvard Educational Review,* 1970, 40, 1, 29-50.
18. Banas, D., and Obers, S.J., The effects of extreme deprivation in infancy on psychic structure in adolescence: A study of ego development. In R.S. Eissler et al. (Eds.). *Psychoanalytic study of the child.* Vol. 5, New York: International University Press, 1950.
19. Barlow, D.H., and Weddell, M.T., Agrophobia. In D.H. Barlow (Ed.,)., *Clinical Handbook of Psychological disorders,* New York: Geinlford, 1935.
20. Beard, G.M.A., Practical treatise on nervous exhausion, (Neurosthania) its symptoms, nature, sequences, treatment (5th ed.,)., New York: E.B. *Treat,* 1905.
21. Bears, C.W., A mind that found Itself (7th ed.,) *Garden city,* New York: Double Day and Company, 1948.
22. Bellak, L. (Ed.), *Schizophrenia: A revision of the Syndrome,* New York: Lorgs Press, 1958.
23. Berger, T.W., and Thompson, R.F., Neural Pleasticity in the limbic system during. classical conditioning of the rabits, nietitating membrane response: 14 the hippocampus, Brain Research, 1978, 145, 323-346.
24. Bhatia, H.R., *Abnormal Psychology,* New Delhi: Oxford and IBH Publishing Co., 1972.
25. Bhattacharya, S., Increase in number of AIDS patients cause concern, *The Hindu,* March 4, 2003.
26. Bhurn, R., Society and drugs. Vol. 1. San Francisco; Jossey, Boss, 1969.
27. Blackburt, A.E., Mental retardation and delinquency. J. *Space,* Ed. 1968.
28. Blacker, K.H., Jones, R.T., Stones, G.C., and Pfeffecbaum, D. Chronic users of LSD: The acid heads. *American Journal of Psychiatry,* 1968, 123 (3), 97-107.
29. Blake, B. G., The application of behaviour theraphy to the treatment of alcoholism, *Behaviour Research and theraphy,* 1965, 3, 75-85.
30. Blake, B.G., Follow-up of alcoholics treatment by behaviour theraphy. *Behaviour Research and therapy,* 1969, 5, 89-94.
31. Bleuler, E., Lehrbuch der Psychiatric (4th ed.,) Berlin: Spriuger, 1923.
32. Blum, R.B., and Braunstein, L., Mind alterning drugs and dangerous behaviour: Alcohol, In U.S. President's Commission Task Force Report: Drunkenness.
33. Blum, R., Society and drugs, Vol. 1, San Francisco: Jossey Bass, 1965.
34. Boring, E.G., A history of experimental psychology, New York: *Appleton-Century-Crofts,* 1950.
35. Brecher, E., Licit and illicit drugs, Boston : Little, Brown, 1972.

36. Breuer, J., and Freud, S., Studies on hysteria, New York: *Basic Books,* 1957. The standard Edition of the Complete Psychological works of Sigmund Freud, Vol. 2, London: Hogarth, 1955, First Set in 1895.

37. Breier, A., Charney, D. S.,- and Heninger, G. R., Agrophobia, with Panic attacks, *Archieves General Psychiatry,* 1986, 43, 1028-1036.

38. Broca, P., Surla faculte du Language articute, Bulletins el. Memories de la societa 'D' Anthropologic de paris, 6, 377-393, 1865.

39. Brozek, J., and Grande, F., Abnormalities of neural functions in the presence of inadequate nutrition. In Field (Ed.), *Handbook of physiology,* Section E., Neurology; Vol. 3., Beltimores Md. Williams and Wilkins, 1960, 1891-1910.

40. Brunn, K., Significance of role and norms in the small group for individual behavioural changes while drinking, *Quarterly Journal of studies in alcohol,* 1959, 20, 53-84.

41. Burn, D.J., and Schlomo, B., Management of neurological Problems a challenge, *The Hindu,* 18.2.2002.

42. Buss, A.H., Psychopathology, New York: Wiley, 1966.

43. Busse, E.W., and Blazer, D.G., Disorders related toBiological functioning, In E.W., Busse and D. Blezer (Eds.), *Handbook of Geriatric psychiatry*, New York: Von- Nostrend-Reinhold.

44. Busse, E.W., Hypochandriesis in the elderly: A reaction to Social Stress, *Journal of American Geriatrics Society,* 1976, 24, 145-149.

45. Bynne, D., and Lamberth, J., The effect of crotic stimuli in sex arousal, evaluative responses and subsequent behaviour. The technical report of the commission on obscenity and porography, Vol. A, Washington, D.C.: U.S- Government Printing Press, 1971.

46. Cadoret, R.J., Cain, C.A., and Grave, W.M., Development of Alcoholism in adoptees raised apart from alcoholic biologic relatives. *Archieves general psychology*, 1980, 37, 561-563.

47. Caplan, C., Principles of Preventive Psychiatry, New York: *Basic Books,* 1964.

48. Cattell, R. B., and Scheler, J. H. *The meaning and measurements of neurathenism and anxiety,* New York: Megraw-Hill, 1959.

49. Centerwell, S.A., and Centerwell, W.R., Study of Children with mongolism reared in the home compared to those reared away from home, *pediatrics,* 1960; 25, 678-685.

50. Chafetz, M.E., and Demone, H.W. Jr. Alcoholism and Society, New York: Oxford University Press, 1962.

51. Changeux, J.P., Kesai, M., and Lee, C.Y. The use of a -snake venom taxin to characterize the abotinergic recepter protein. *Proceedings of the National Academy of Science,* 1970:67: 1241-1247.

52. Choi, C.W., Exicitoxic cell death, *Journal of Neurology,* 1992, 23, 1261-1276.

53. Chrismore, C.C., and Pittillo, E.S. 'I am EVE'. *Garden City: Double Day,* 1977.

54. Clark, D.M., Salkowskis, P.M., and Calkaly, A.J. Respiratory, Control is a treatment for panic attacks, *Journal of Behaviour therapy and Experimental Psychiatry,* 1985, 16, 23-30.

55. Clark, G.R., Kiritz, M.S., and Rosen, M. Program for mentally retarded, *Science News,* 1969, 96, 82

56. Cloninger, C.R., Bohman, M., and Sigvardson, S., Inheritence of alcohol abuse: Cross fostering analysis of adapted men. *Archieves of General Psychiatry,* 1981, 38, 861-868.

57. Cole, K.K., Fisher, C., and Cole, S., Women who kill, *Archieves of General Psychiatry;* 1968, 19 (1) 1-8.

58. Coleman, J.C., and Broen, W.E., Abnormal Psychology and Modern Life, Bombay: D.R. Taraporevale Sons Co., (34d., ed)., 1974.

59. Coloninger, O.R., and Gaze, S., Psychiatric illness and female criminality: The role of sociopathy and hysteria in the artisocial women. *American Journal of Psychiatry*, 1970 a, 127 (3) 303-311.

60. Conger, J.A., The effects of alcohol on conflict behaviour in the albinorats. *Quarterly Journal of studies in alcohol,* 1951, 12, 1-29.

61. Controversal theory about HIV's origin, Medical Science, *The Hindu,* June 14, 2001.

62. Cooper, A.F., Garnside, R.F. and Kay, D.W.K.A comparison of deaf and non-deaf patients with .paranoid and affective psychoses. *Britis Journal of Psychiatry,* 1976, 129, 5, 2-538.

63. Costa, P.T. Jr., Zonderman, A.B., McGrae, R.R., Cornoni-Huntley, J., Locke, B.Z., and Barbano, H.E., Longitudinal analyses of psychological well-being in a national sample: Stability of mean levels. *Journal of Gerontology,* 1987, 42, 50-55.

64. Crowe, A.K., Pauls, D.H., Slymer, D.J., and Noyas, R., Family study of anxiety neurosis : Morbidity risk in families of patients with and without mental prolapse, *Archieves of General psychiatry,* 1980, 37, 77-79.

65. Cullition, B.J., Pot facing, stringent scientific examination; *Science News,* 1970, 97, (4) 102-105.

66. Davison, G.C., and Neele, J.M., Abnormal Psychology, (5th ed.,) New York: John Wiley and Sons, 1987.

67. Diagnostic and statistical manual of Mental disorders, Second Edition (DSM=II) American Psychiatric Association, 1968.

68. Dole, V., and Nyswander, M. Methadona maintenance: A report of two years experience. In problems of drug dependence. Washington. D.C.: National Academy of Science, 1966.

69. Dybwad, G., who are the mentally retarded? children, 1968, 15, 43-48.

70. Ellinwood, B.K. Assault and homicide associated with Amphatamine abuse, *American Journal of psychiatry*, 1971, 127 (9) 90-95.

71. Ennis, P.H., Crime, Victims and the Police, *Transaction,* 1967, 4(7), 36-44.

72. Eysenck, H.J., The effects Psychotheraphy: An evaluation, *Journal of Consulting Psychology,* 1952,-16, 319-324.

73. Fagaun, J.F., and Sugar, LT., Infant recognition memory as a measure of intelligence. In L.P. Lipitt (Ed.), *Advances in infancy Research* (Vol. 2), N.J.: Ablex, 1983.

74. Fahn, New Hope for Parkinson's disease victims, *The Hindu,* 17.2.2002, P.

75. Falls, H.F. Ocular changes in Down's Syndrome help in diagnosis, Roche.*Reports,* 1970, 7. 16.

76. Federal Bureau of Investigation, 1970.

77. Feenely; D.M., and Stutten, R.L., Pharmacotheraphy for recovery of function after brain injury, *CRC critical Reviews in Neurology,* 1987, 3, 135-197.

78. Fleming, W., Brown, W., Donahue, J., and Granigin, F., National Survey of Venereal disease treated by physicians in 1948, *JAMA,* 1970.

79. Franks, C.M., Counselling and conditioned aversion Heropies in the treatment of the alcoholics. *International Journal of Addictions,* 1966, 1, 61-98.

80. Freud, S., Three contributions to the theory of sex. In A.L. Bills (Ed.), The basic writings of Sigmund Freud, New York: Modern Library 1938.

81. Gadoret, R.J., Cain, G.A., and grove, W.M. Development in adoptees raised, apart from alcoholic biological relatives. *Archieves of General Psychiatry,* 1980, 37, 561-563.

82. Gallup, G., Drug on camps, *Newsweek,* Jan. 25, 1971, P: 52.

83. Gardner, W., Behaviour modification in mental retardation, New York: Aldine, 1971.

84. Gawin, E.H., and Klaber, H.D., Abstinance Symptmology and Psychiatric diagnosis in cocaine abusers. *Archieves of General psychiatry,* 1986, 43, 107-113.

85. German, W.I. Initial symptomology in brain tumour, Canadian Medicine, 1959, 23, 636-637.

86. Gershon, E.S., and Rieder, R.O., Major disorders of mind and brain, *Scientific American,* 1992, 267 (5), 126-133.

87. Gibon, B.W., Cohen, M.B., and Eohen, R.A., On the dynamics of the manic, depressive personality, *American Journal of Psychiatry,* 1959, 115, 101-107.

88. Gibson, E.J., Principles of perception, learning and development, New York: *Appleton-century-Crofts,* 1969.

89. Glaus, A., The handling of criminal psychopaths in switzerland, Inter, Jl. Often, Thu. 1968, 12 (1), 29-36.

90. Glenn, N.D, and Weaver, C.N., Attitudes towards premartial, extramarital arid homosexual relations in the U.S. in 1970, *Journal of Sex Research,* 1979, 15, 108-118.

91. Glueck, S., and Glueck, E.T., Delinquency prediction method reported highly accurate, *Roche Report,* 1969, 6(15), 3.

92. Goldstein, A., Opiod peptide (edorphins) in pituitary and brain, *Science,* 1976, 193, 1081-1086.

93. Goldstein, S.E., and Birnborn, F., Hypochandrieasis and the elderly, *Journal of American Geriatrics Society,* 1976, 24, 150-154.

94. Gorman, J.M., Fyer, M.R., Goatz, R., Askanazi, J., Leibowritz, M.R., Fyer, A.J., Kinney, J., and Klein, D.F., Ventilatory Physiology of patients with panic disorder, *Archieves of General psychiatry,* 1983, 45, 33-60.

95. Greenaere, P., Conscience in psychopath, *American Journal of Orthopsychiatry,* 1945, 19, 495-509.

96. Greenblatt, D.J, and Shader, R.1, Mepolamate: A study of irrational Drug use, *American Journal of psychiatry,* 1971, 127 (16), 1297-1303.

97. Grinker, R.R., Spiegel, J.P., *War neuroses,* New York: Arno Press, 1945, 1979.

98. Grossman, H.J., Classification of mental retardation, Washington, D.C.: American Association of mental deficiency, 1983.

99. Grosz., H.J., and Zimmerman, J., A second detailed case study of functional blindness: Further demonstration of the contribution of objective psychological laboratory data, *Behaviour theraphy,* 1970, 1, 1185-1130.

100. Guertin, W.H., and Zilaitis, V.A., A transposed Factor Analysis of schizophranic performance on the Bender-Gestolt, *Journal of clinical psychology,* 1954, 10, 225.

101. Guilford, J.P, Personality, New York: Mcgraw-Hill, 1959.

102. Guze, S.B., The diagnosis of hysteria: What are we trying to do? *American Journal of Psychiatry,* 1967, 124, 491, 498.

103. Hank, P., Long, T.H., and Urdang, L., Collins Dictionary of the English Language, London: William Collins and Sons Co., L.D., 1979.

104. Henly, A Muggers of the mind, *Today's health,* 1971, 9 (2), 39-41.

105. Hersch, C., From mental health and Social action, Clinical Psychology in historica perspective, *American psychologists,* 1969, 24, 909-936.

106. Hershenson, D.B., Stress, induced use of alcohol by problem drinkers in a function of their sense of identify, *Quarterly journal of studies in alcohol,* 1964, 26, 13-222.

107. Herzog, E., and Lewis, H., Children in poor families: Mythes and reclities, *American Journal of Orthopsychiatry,* 1970, 40, 3, 375-387.

108. Hilgard, E.R., and Atkinson, R.C., and Atkinson, R.L., *Introduction to psychology,* (6th ed.), New York: Oxford and IBH publishing Co., 1975.

109. Hilbert, G.A., Hyperventilation as a cause of panic attacks, *British medical journal,* 1984, 288, 263, 264.

110. Hindler, C.G., Epilapsy and violence, *British journal of psychiatry*, 1989, 155, 246-249.

111. HO., D. Rota, T., Scholey, R., Kaplan, J., Allen, J., Groopman, J., Resnickal, L., Felsenstein, L., Andrews, C., and Hirsch, M., .Isolation of HTLV-111 from

cerebrospinal fluid and neural tissues of patients with neurologic symptoms related to the acquired immune deficiency syndrome. *New England Journal Medicine,* 1985, 313, 1493-1497.

112. Hobbs, N., Mental Health's Third Revolution, *American Journal of Orthopsychiatry,* 1964, 34, 822-833.

113. Hoch, P.H., and Dunaif, S.I., Pseudo Psychopathics Schizophrenia, In P.H., Hoch and Zubin (Eds.) *Psychology and Law,* New York: Gune and stratton, 1955.

114. Hope yet for children of HIV infectand women, *The Hindu,* Feb.; 27, 2002.

115. Horney, H., *Self Analysis,* New York: Norton, 1942.

116. Horney, H., *The Neurotic Personality of times,* New York: W.W. Norton and company, 1938.

117. Hover, J.E., The story of crimes in U.S., U.S., *News and World Reports,* Oct., 7, 1968, 61-68.

118. Hsu, J., Electroconditioning theraphy of alcoholics: A Preliminary Report, *Quarterly journal of studies in alcohol,* 1965, 26, 449-459.

119. Hurley, B., Poverty arid Mental retardation: *A casual relationship,* New York: Random, 1969.

120. Hutchings, B., and Medrick, S.A., Registered criminality in the adoptive and biological parents registered male adoptees, In S.A., Medinick, F., Schulsinger, J., Higgins and Bell (Eds.) Genetics, *Environment and psychopothology,* New York: Elserier, 1974.

121. Isacson, R.L., When brains are damaged? *Psychology Today,* 1970, 3, 38-42.

122. Jacobs, P.A., Bruntori, M., and Malvilli, M.M., Aggressive Behaviour, Mental Subnarmality and XYY male, *Nature,* 1965, 208, 1351, 1352.

123. Jacobs, E., Winters, P.M., Alvis, H.J., and Small, S.M. Hyperbaric Oxygen: Temporary aid for senile minds, *MAMA,* 1969, 209, 1435-1438.

124. Jaffe, J.H., Drug-addiction and drug abuse, *In Goodman and Gilman's Pharmacological basis of therapeutic behaviour,* New York: Macmillian Co., 1985.

125. James, W., Principles of Psychology, Vol. I, New York: *Holt,* 1890.

126. Jarvik, M.E., Psychopharmacological revolution, *Psychology Today,* 1967, 1, 117, 51-58.

127. Jellinek, E.M., Phases of alcoholic addiction, *Querterly Journal of studies in Alcohol,* 1952, 13, 673-678.

128. Jijo, J., and Levan, A., *The chromosome number of man meretitas,* Vol. 42, 1956.

129. Jung, C.G., *Contributions of analytical psychology,* New York Harcourt-Braco Jovanovich, 1982.

130. Kallman, F., Heredity in Health and Mental disorder, New York: W.W. Norton company, INC., 1953.

131. Kaplan, J., The New Prohibition, Los Angles, *Time,* June 21, 1970, VII, 3.

132. Kache, J.D., and Webstar, C.D., Behaviour therapy and behaviour modification, *Canadian Psychologists,* 1969, 10, 68-71.

133. Kazel, N.J., Grider, R.A., and Adams, E.H., National Servilance of colanine use and related health consequence, Morbidity and Mortality, *Weekly report,* 1982, 31, 20, 265-273.

134. Kelly, K., Females, Males and sexuality, *Albany,* New York: State University of New Vork Press, 1986.

135. Kemble, J., Idols and Invalids, New York: *Double day,* 1936. -

136. Kenyon, F.E., Hypochandriasis: A study of some historical, clinical and social aspeats, *International journal of psychiatry,* 1966, 2, 308-325.

137. Kerakhoff, A.C., and Back, K.W., The bug, *Psychology Today,* 1969, 24, 909-936.

138. Kinsey, A.C., Pomeroy, W.B., and Martin, C.E., Sexual behaviour in human male, philadelphia: Soundess, 1948.

139. Kolb, B., and Whishaw, I.Q. Performance of schizophrenia patients on tests sensitive to left or right or frontal, temporal or parietal function in neurological patients. *Journal of Nervous and mental disease,* 1983, 171, 435-443.

140. Kolb, B., and Whishaw, I.Q., *Fundamentals of human Neuro Psychology* (4th ed.), New York: N.H., Freeman and company, 1996.

141. Kowell, N.K., and Beal, M.F., Cortical somatostation, Neuropeptide NADPH diphorase neurons: Normal anatomy and alterations in Alzheimer's disease. *Annals of Neurology,* 1988, 13, 105-113.

142. Kraepelin, E., One Hundred years of psychiatry (Trans W. Beskem) New York: The citadel Press, 1962.

143. Kranz, H., Lebanschicksal Kriminaller zwillinge, Berlin: *Springer Verlag,* 1936.

144. Kretschemer, E., Physique and character, New York: *Harcourt,* 1925, 1926.

145. Kroll, P., Chamberlains, P., and Helpern, D., The diagnosis of Briquet's syndrome-in a male population, *Journal of nervous and mental disease,* 1979, 169, 171-174.

146. Lange, J., Verbraches also schikral, Leipzig: George Theme verlag, 1929.

147. Lazarus, R.S., Patterns of Adjustment (3rd ed.) Tokyo: McGraw-Hill Kogakusha Ltd., 1976.

148. Lazurus, R.S., and Davison, G.A., Clinical innovation in Research and practice, In A.E., Bergin and L.L. Gerfield (Eds.), *Handbook of psychotherapy and behavioural change: An empirical Analysis,* New York: Wilay, 1971.

149. Lazarus, R.S., *Psychological stress and the coping Processes,* New York: McGraw-Hill, 1968.

150. Leijune, J., and Turpin, R., Chromosomal Aberrations in Man., *American Journal of Human Genetics,* 1961, Vol. 13.

151. Leonard, B.E., *Fundamentals of Psychopharmacology,* New york, Wilay, 1992.

152. Lerman, P., Child convicts, *Transaction,* 1971, 8, (9-10), 35-44.

153. Lavin, S.M., Brain tumours in mental hospital patients. *American Journal of psychiatry,* 1949, 105, 897-900.

154. Levin, M., Brome Hallucinosis, *Archieves of general Psychiatry;* 1960, 2, 429-433.

155. Ley, R. Panic disorder: A hyperventilation interpretation, In L Michelson and L.M., Asher (Eds.), Anxiety and stress disorders, New York: Chilord, 1982.

156. Liften, R.J., Advocacy and corruption in the healing profession. In N.L. Goldman and D.R. Segal (Eds.), *The Social psychology of Military Service,* Beverly Hills, California: Sage, 1976..

157. Likely, off switch for epilepsy, Medical . Science, *The Hindu,* June 14, 2001.

158. Lipscomb, C.F., The cage of psychiatrically disturbed elderly patients in the community, *Amercian Journal of psychiatry,* 1971, 12-7(8), 107-114.

159. Riskov, B., Subtance induced and substance use disorders: Barbiturates and similarly acting sedative hypnotics. In J.H. Griest, J.W., Jafferson, and L. Spitzer (Eds.), *Treatment of mental disorders,* New York: Oxford University Press, 1911.

160. Lombroso-Ferrero, G. Criminal man, New York: Putnar, 1911.

161. Longston, J.W., Ballard, P., Tegrnd, J.W., and Irwin, I., chronic parkinsonism in Humans due to product of mapridine analogy sythesis, *Science,* 1983, 219, 979-980.

162. Lyle, J.C., The effect of an Institution environment upon the verbal development of Institutionalized children-I verbal intelligence, *Journal of Mental Def.* 1954, 3, 322-328.

163. Madill, M.F., Camphell, D., Laverty, S.G., Sanderson, S.F., and Vanderwater, S.L. Aversion treatment of alcoholics by Succiny1choline-induced apneic paralysis. *Quarterly Journal of studies in Alcohol,* 1966, 27, 482-509.

164. Maher, B.A., *Principles of psychopathology,* New York: McGrew-Hill, 1966.

165. Mair, W.G.P. Warrington, E.K., and Wieskrentz, L., *Memory disorder in Korse-Koffs Psychosis,* Brain, 1979, 102, 749-783.

166. Marison, T., The Industrial Organization of an Indian Provice, London: John Murray (Publishers) Ltd., 1918.

167. Mark, I.M., and Gelder, M.G., Transvestism: Clinical and psychological changes during faradic aversion, *British Journal of Psychiatry,* 1967, 113, 711-729.

168. Martin, B., The assessment of anxiety by physiological Behavioural measures. *Psychological Bulletin,* 1961, 58, 234, 235.

169. McDougall, W., *An Introduction to Social psychology,* Boston: Luce and Co., 1926.

170. McGuire, W.J., and Vallance, M., Aversion therapy by electric shock, simple technique, *British Medical Journal,* 1964, 1, 151, 152.

171. McGlothin, W.H., and Arnold, D.C., and Rowan, Marijuana use among adults, *psychitary,* 1970, 33 (4), 433-443.

172. McTaggart, N., Anderman, F., and Boss., C., A survey of cerebral tumours presented at a psychiatric Institution, canadian psychiatric association, *ANJ.*, 1961, 6, 333-338.

173. Mead, M., Coming of Age in Samone, New York: William Morrow and Company, ING., 1928.

174. Megee, R.A., What's past in prologue, *Annals of Academic political Social Science,* 1969, 381, 1-10.

175. Menninger, K., *The crime of punishment,* New York: Viking Press, 1968.

176. Meyer, A., The commonsense psychiatry of Adolf Meyer (ed.) New York: Mcgraw-Hill Book Company, 1948.

177. Meyer, V., and Chesser, F.S., *Behaviour therapy and clinical psychiatry*, Baltimore: Penguin, 1970.

178..Meyer, J.K., Weissman, M.M., Disehler, S.L., Holger, C.F., Leaf, P.J., Oxvaschel, H.A., Anthony, J.C., Boyd, Z., Burke, J.E., Kramer, M., and Stoltzman, R., Six month Prevalance of psychiatric disorders in these communities 1980-1982. *Archieves of General Psychiatry*, 1984, 41, 959-967.

179. Medniak, S.A.,-Gabrielli, U.R.,.and Hutahings, B., Genetic influences in criminal convictions: Evidence from an adoptation Cohort, *Science,* 1984, 224, 891-894.

180. Natarajan, V.A., Constipation, Helpage India, Research and development, *Journal*, 2001, Vol. 7, No. 3.

181. Nathan, P.E., and Harris, S.L., Psychopathology and society, New York: McGraw-Hill, 1975.

182. Nathan, P.E., Alcoholism in H. Leiterlerg (Ed.), Handbook of behaviour modification, New York: *Applaton-century-crofts*, 1976.

183. Navia, B.A, Cho, E., Petitio, C.K., and Price, R.W., The AIDS dementia complex-II: Neurology, *Annals of Neurology,* 1966, 19, 525-535.

184. Neitzel, M.T., Winett, R.A., Mac Donald, M.L., and Dawson, W.S., *Behavioural Approach to community psychology,* New York: Pergamon Press, 1977.

185. Nixon, R., The Sheme of the Prisons, *Time,* Jan. 18, 1971, 46-55.

186. Nonigheld, G., and Howard, A., *Psychiatric drugs: A desk reference* (2nd ed.), New York: Academic Press, 1978.

187. Nurnberg, H.C., Prudie, J., Fiori, M.; and Freedman, E., Psychopathology complicating Acquired Immune Deficiency Syndrom (AIDS). *American Journal of Psychiatry,* 1984, 141, 95, 96.

188. Ochitel, A., Conversion disorder, In H.H. Grinst, J.W. Jetterson andn R.K. Spitzen (Eds.), *Treatment of mental disorders,* New York: Oxford University Press, 1982.

189. O'Connell, D.M., Orne, M.T., and Shor, R.C., Sobb, J.C., Evenus, F.J., and Gustafson. In. A Specific motor response during sleep to sleep administered

meaningful suggestion: An exploratory investigation, *Perception and motor skills,* 1963, 20, 629-637.

190. O'Neal, B., Robins, L.M. King, L.J., and Sheefer, J., parental deviences and the genesis and sociopathic personality, *American Journal of psychiatry,* 1962, 118, 1118-1124.

191. Ostow, M., The psychology of Depression and is management, *Bulletin of the New York Academy of Medine,* 1955, Vol. 31.

192. Orme, Initial psychiatric illness in Invalutional women-II, *The Journal of Mental Science,* 1957, Vol. 103, January.

193. Parlington, M.W., The early symptoms of phenyikatonuria, *pediatrics,* 1961, 27, 465-473.

194. Parran, T., *Shadow on the land,* Raynal and Hitachock, 1937.

195. Patrick, J., and Lindstorm, J., Autoimmune Response to acctylcholine response, *Science,* 1973, 180, 871-872.

196. Perlay, M.J., and Guze, J.B., Hysteria usefulness of clinical creteria, *New England Journal of Medicine,* 1962, 266, 421-426.

197. Phillips, D.E, and Gromko, M.H., Sex differences in sexual activity-Reality or Illusion? *Journal of Sex Research,* 1985, 21, 437-448.

198. Piaget, J., Judgment and. Reasoning in the child, Little field, Paterson, N.J.: Adams and Co., 1959.

199. Pickering, D.E., and Fisher, D.A., Therapeutic concepts relation to hypothyroidism in children. *Journal of chronic diseases,* 1958, 7, 242-263.

200. Presidents commitee on mental retardation, Washington, D.C. Government publishing Office, 1970.

201. Prince, W.W., and Whatmore, P.B., Behaviour disorders and patterns of crime among xyy males identified at a maximum security hospital. *British medical journal,* 1967, -1, 533-536.

202. Pusey, W.A., The history and epidemiology of syphilis, springfield: Charles D Thomas, 1933.

203. Pushpa Khururana AIDS: Humanities Gravest challange, New Delhi: *Hind Pocket Books,* 1969.

204. Regier,. D.A., Boyd, J.H, Burke, J.D., Jr, Roe, D.S., Myers, J.K., Kramer, M., and Robin, L.S., One month prevalance of mental disorders in the United States. *Archieves general psychiatry,* 1988, 45, 1977-1986.

205. Rajamanickam, M., *Contemporary Fields of psychology and Experiments,* New Delhi: Concept Publishing company, 1999.

206. Rajamanickam, M., Psycho-Social Study of the AIDS and the Drug abuses. *Journal of community Guidance and Research,* 1992, 9, 1,.17-42.

207. Rappaport, J., Community psychology, New York: Holt Rinehart and Whinston, 1977.

208. Reymond, M., The treatment of addiction by aversion conditioning with apomorphine, *Behavioural Research and Therapy,* 1964, 1, 287-291.

209. Richter, D., (ed.) Schizophrenia: Somatic Aspects, New York: The Macmillan Company, 1957.

210. Rinnel, M., Psychodelic drugs, *American Journal of psychiatry,* 1966, 122, 14 15, 1416.

211. Robins, L.N., Helger, J.E., Weissman, M.M., Orrschel, H., Gauanberg, E., Burke, J.D., and Reiger, D.A., Lifetime prevalance of specific psychiatric disorders in three cities. *American general psychiatry,* 1984, 41, 942-949.

212. Rorvik, M., Do drugs lend Violence? *Look*, April, 7, 1970.

213. Roswelk, H.F., and Fishman, I.L. Institutionalized girl delinquents, Dis., Nerv., Sys., 1968, 29(1), 17-27.

214. Rothaschild, D., Senile psychoses and psychoses with cerebral arterioselerosis. In Kaplan (Ed.), Mental Disorders in later life (2nd (ed.)., Standford: Standford University Press, 1956.

215. Sackaim, H.A., Nordlik, J.W., and Gur, R.C., A model of historical and hypnotic blindness, cognition, motivation and awareness, *Journal of Abnormal psychology,* 1978, 88, 474-489.

216. Sanders, M.G., Alcoholic cardiomyopathy: A critical view, *Quarterly Journal of studies in Alcohol,* 1970, 31, 324-386.

217. Sarbin, T.R., and Mancuso, J.C., Failure of moral enterprise, *clinical and consulting psychology,* 1970, 35, 159-173.

218. Satter, A., Conditioned reflex theory, New York: Farrer, Streus, 1949.

219. Scherrman, M., and Clark, R.W., Delinquent adolescent girls: Resdential treatment in Municipal Hospital Setting. *Archieves General Psychiatry,* 1967, 17(4), 141-147.

220. Schewartz, B., The effect of philadelphia of pennylrania's increased penalties for rape and attesmpted rape. *Journal of criminal law,* criminal police science, 1968, 59 (4), 509-515.

221. Schilder, P., The psychogenesis, of alcoholism, *Quarterly journal of studies in Alcohol,* 1941, 2, 277-283.

222. Science Express Service, Child AIDS cases souring, *Indian Express,* Feb. 10, 1991.

223. Seigel, R.K., Cocaine Smoking, *Journal of psychoactive drugs,* 1982, 14, 277-359.

224. Sellings, L.S., Man against madness, New York: *Garden City Books*, 1943.

225. Selye, H., The physiology and pathology of exposure to stress, *Montreal: Acta*, 1950.

226. Selye, H., *The stress of life,* New York: McGraw-Hill Book Company, 1956.

227. Sergovich, F., Valentine; G.H., Chen, A.T., Kinch, R., and Smout, M., Chromosomal aberrations in 2159 consecutive new born babies, *New England Journal of Medicine*, 1969, (16), 851-854.

228. Shader, R.1., Caine, E.D., and Mayer, R.E., Treatment of dependence on barbiturate and sedative hypnoties. In R.I. Schader (ed.) *Manual of psychiatric and therapeutic practical psychopharmacology and psychiatry.* Boston: McbLobin Brown, 1975.

229. Shedel, C.A., Aversion. treatment of alcohol addiction. *Quarterly Journal of studies in Alcohol,* 1944, 5, 216-228.

230. Siegler, P.C., and Costa, P.T., Jr. Health Behaviour relationships. In J.E. Bivren and K.W. Scherie (Eds.), *Handbood of psychology of Being (2nd ed.),* New York: Vans Nostrand Reinbhold, 1985.

231. Smart, E.G., Effects of alcohol on conflict and violent behaviour. *Quarterly Journal of studies in Alcohol,* 1965, 26, 187-205.

232. Smith, J.J. Medical approach to problem of drinking, *Quarterly Journal of studies in Alcohol,* 1949, 10, 251-257.

233. Smith, D.N., Balizzard, R.M., and Wilkins, I., The mental proznsis in hyperthyroidism in infancy and childhood, *pediataics,* 1957, 19, 1011-1020.

234. Snider, V.D., Simpson, D.M., Nielsen, S., Gold; J.W.M., Metroka, C.E., and Posner, J.B.,. Neurological complications of acquired immune deficiency syndrome: Analysis of 50 patients. *Annals of Neurology,* 1983, 14, 403-418.

235. Soddy, K., *Mental Health: Contemporary thought.*

236. Strange, J.R., *Abnormal psychology,* New Delhi: TATA-Mcgrew-Hill Publishing company Ltd., 1965.

237. Suresh, N., Cheaking AIDS and Health Education, *Science Express, Indian Express,* Nov. 30th, 1980.

238. Sullivan, H., *The interpersonal theory of psychiatry,* New York: W.W. Norton and company, 1953.

239. Swartz, M., Blazer, D., George, L., and Landerman, R., Somatization disorder in community population, *American Journal of psychiatry,* 1986, 145, 1403-1408.

240. Szasz, T.S., The myth of mental illness. *The American psychologist,* 1960, 15, 2, 113-118.

241. Thanti, Thina, Oct. 2002.

242. Thigpen, C.H., and Cleaklay, H., A case of multiple personality, *Abnormal. and Social psychology,* 1954, 49, 135-151.

243. Thiman, J., Conditioned reflex treatment of alcoholism, *New England Journal of Medicine,* 1949 a, 17, 368-370.

244. Thorne, F.C., The etiology of sociopathic reactions, *American Journal of psychotheraphy,* 1959, 19, 319-330.

245. Trimble, M.R., Interictal psychoses of epilepsy, *Advances in Neurology,* 1991, 55, 143-157.

246. Tonkonegy, J.M., Violence and temporal lobe lesion: Head CT, and MR-1 data, *Journal of Neuropsychiatry and cilinical Neuroscience,* 1991, 3, 189-196.

247. Treffert, D.A., The idiot savant: A review of the syndrome, *American Journal of psychiatry,* 1988, 145, 563-572.

248. Twelve steps and twelve traditions, Alcoholism anonymous, *World Science,* INC., 1982.

249. Ullman, J., and Krasner, L., Psychological approach to abnormal behaviour (2nd ed.), Englewood Cliffs, N.J.: prentice-Hall, 1925.

250. Ultmann, M., Balman, A., Ruff, H., Novick, B., Cone-Weeson, B., Cohen,- H., and Rubinstein, A., Developmental abnormalities in children with Acquired Immune Deficiency Syndrome (ADIS) and AIDS related complex. *Developmental Medicine and Child Neurology,* 1985, 27, 563-571.

251. Uniform Crime Reports, Federal Bureau of Investigation, United States Department of Justice, 1971.

252. U.S. News and World Report, Crime Experience now up to 51 billions a year, Oct. 26, 1970, 30-34.

253. Valde, R.W, Half of. serious crimes laid to Juvenile delinquency, *Los Angles Time,* April 4, 1971, 1, 2.

254. Voetglin, W.L., Lerner, F., and Bros, W.R., Conditioned reflex therapy of alcoholic addiction-III. An evaluation of present results in- light of previous experience with this method. *Quarterly journal of studies in Alcohol,* 1940, 1, 501-515.

255. Venkoba Rao, A., AIDS and Health Education, Science Express, *Indian Express,* Nov. 30th, 1990.

256. Wainstein, K.A., Davison, D.C., Dequatte, V., and Allan, J.W., Type of behaviour and cognitions: Hostility the bad actor, paper presented, *at the 94th Annual convention of the American psychlogical Association,* Washington, D.C. 1996.

257. Weiner, S., The xyy syndrome in A Montegu, Chromosomes and crime, *psychology Today,* 1968, 2(5), 42-49.

258. Weinstein, F.A., Psychitric aspects of head injury, New York: *Journal of Medicine,* 1961, 61, 1879-1786.

259. Watson, J.B., and Reyner, R., Conditioned emotional reactions, *Journal of experimental psychology,* 1920, 3, 1-14.

260. Whybrow, P.C., and Mendals, J., Toward a biology of depression: some suggestions from neurophysiology, *American Journal psychiatry,* 1969, 125, 137 (3) 45-54.

261. Widner, H., et. al. Belateral fetal mesencephalic, grafting in two patients with parkinsonism induced by 1-methyl, 4-phenyl, 1, 2, 3, 6 tetra hydropridine (MPTP). *The New England Journal of Medicine,* 1992, 527, 1556-1563

262. Wikler, A., Opiod dependence: Mechanism and treatment, New York: Plenun, 1980.

263. Wilkinson, R., The prevention of drinking problems, New York: Oxford University Press, 1970:

264. Wilkins, W.J., The identification of character and behaviour disorders in the Military life. U.S. *Navy Medical News Neuropsychiatric Research Unit.,* San Diago 52, California, Washington, D.C.: Navy Department, Bureau of Medicine and Surgery, 1961.

265. Williams, R.J:, Biochemical individuality and cellular nutrition: Prime factors in alcoholism. *Quarterly Journal of studies in Alcohol,* 1959, 20, 452-463.

266. Wirt, R.D., Briggs, F.F., and Golden, J., Delinquency prone personalities-III, The sociopathic personality: Treatment. Minnesota Med., 1962, 45, 289-295.

267. Woetglin, W.L., Lamere, F., and Bros, W.R., Conditioned reflex theraphy of alcoholic addiation III. An evaluation of present results in light of previous experience with this method. *Quarterly journal of studies in Alcohol.* 1940, 1, 501-515.

268. Wood, H., and Duffy, E., Psychological factors in alcoholic Women, *American Journal of psychiatry,* 1966, 123 (3), 341-345.

269. Woolf, I.I., Griffiths., and Moncgrieff, A., Treatment of phenylketonuria with a low in phenylalanine, *British Medical Journal,* 1955, Vol. 1.

270. Yelon, I.D., Organic brain disease of senility marglanid St., *Medical Journal,* 1955, Vol. 1.

271. Zax, M., and Cowen, E.L., Research on early detection and prevention of emotional dysfunction in young school children. In G.D. Spilberger (Ed.), *Current topics in clinical and community psychology* Vol. 1, .New York: Academic Press, 1969.

272. Zilborz, G.R., and Hensy, G.W., *A History of medical Psychology,* New York: Norton, 1941.